CONFESSING THE FLESH

VICTORIAN LITERATURE AND CULTURE SERIES
Herbert F. Tucker, Editor
William R. McKelvy, Jill Rappoport, and Andrew M. Stauffer,
Associate Editors

CONFESSING THE FLESH

Reading Hopkins in Context

LESLEY HIGGINS

UNIVERSITY OF VIRGINIA PRESS
Charlottesville and London

The University of Virginia Press is situated on the traditional lands of the Monacan Nation, and the Commonwealth of Virginia was and is home to many other Indigenous people. We pay our respect to all of them, past and present. We also honor the enslaved African and African American people who built the University of Virginia, and we recognize their descendants. We commit to fostering voices from these communities through our publications and to deepening our collective understanding of their histories and contributions.

University of Virginia Press
© 2025 by the Rector and Visitors of the University of Virginia
All rights reserved
Printed in the United States of America on acid-free paper

First published 2025

9 8 7 6 5 4 3 2 1

LIBRARY OF CONGRESS CATALOGING-IN-PUBLICATION DATA
Names: Higgins, Lesley, author.
Title: Confessing the flesh : reading Hopkins in context / Lesley Higgins.
Description: Charlottesville : University of Virginia Press, 2025. | Series: Victorian literature and culture series | Includes bibliographical references and index.
Identifiers: LCCN 2024060914 (print) | LCCN 2024060915 (ebook) | ISBN 9780813953205 (hardback) | ISBN 9780813953212 (paperback) | ISBN 9780813953229 (ebook)
Subjects: LCSH: Hopkins, Gerard Manley, 1844–1889—Criticism and interpretation. | Hopkins, Gerard Manley, 1844–1889—Religion. | Christian poetry, English—19th century—History and criticism. | Flesh (Theology) in literature. | LCGFT: Literary criticism.
Classification: LCC PR4803.H44 z6485 2025 (print) | LCC PR4803.H44 (ebook) | DDC 821/.8—dc23/eng/20241230
LC record available at https://lccn.loc.gov/2024060914
LC ebook record available at https://lccn.loc.gov/2024060915

Cover art: The Confession, Ludwig Passini. Watercolor heightened with white on paper laid down on panel, 100.4 x 66.3 cm. (Christie's Images / Bridgeman Images)
Cover design: Cecilia Sorochin

FOR
MICHAEL F. SUAREZ, S.J.

The vault and scope and schooling
And mastery in the mind

CONTENTS

Acknowledgments | ix
List of Abbreviations | xi

Introduction: Telling a Different Story   1

1 Historical Investments   27

2 Victorian Confessional Crises   82

3 Living "in Flesh"   121

4 Professing the Flesh   172

Conclusion: Comfort?   213

Appendix | 221
Notes | 229
Bibliography | 271
Index | 293

ACKNOWLEDGMENTS

For more than three decades my research has been generously supported by the Social Sciences and Humanities Research Council of Canada, York University, and, most recently, the York University Faculty Association.

I would like to thank Angie Hogan at the University of Virginia Press for believing in the project and making it happen, and to the Victorian Literature and Culture Series editors: Herbert F. Tucker, William McKelvy, Jill Rappoport, and Andrew Stauffer. Also at the Press, I am very grateful to Wren Morgan Myers, Ellen Satrom, and Colleen Romick Clark. The anonymous readers for the Press provided excellent editorial guidance.

Two people made my Hopkins work possible initially: Norman MacKenzie, who supervised the dissertation but also mentored and vouched; and Peter Hackett, S.J., master of Campion Hall, Oxford, in the 1980s, whose welcoming kindness was crucial to all my manuscript adventures. I have also benefited enormously from the editorial expertise and friendship of Noel Barber, S.J., Jude Nixon, Catherine Phillips, and Kelsey Thornton.

The invaluable research assistants who have contributed to my Hopkins projects include Rachelle Stinson and Julianna Will. Two organizations that have provided excellent audiences (with great questions) for my presentations are the Victorian Studies Network at York (VSNY) and the Victorian Studies Association of Ontario (VSAO).

Amanda Paxton read the typescript and provided timely scholarly advice. David Latham has been an unfailingly wise and generous collaborator in my Pater work. Other collegial friends whose support has mattered most: Ken Daley, Alison Halsall, Julia Saville, and Carolyn Williams.

It is a pleasure to recognize the exceptional Graham Pugin, S.J., whose friendship has meant so much over the decades. Always splendid, always themselves: Mary Gelinas, Ruth Kinzie, and Karin MacIsaac.

Without the tutelage and insights of Marie-Christine Leps (1953–2022), a treasured friend and colleague, the Foucault work would not have been possible.

All papers of Gerard Manley Hopkins are copyrighted by the Trustees for Roman Catholic Purposes, and I am grateful for their permission to publish here.

ABBREVIATIONS

IGNATIAN TEXT

SE Ignatius Loyola, *Spiritual Exercises*

TEXTS BY MICHEL FOUCAULT

Ab *Abnormal: Lectures at the Collège de France, 1974–1975*

DP *Discipline and Punish*

FL *Foucault Live*

HS *History of Sexuality*

P/K *Power/Knowledge: Selected Interviews and Other Writings, 1972–1977*

WDTT *Wrong-Doing, Truth-Telling: The Function of Avowal in Justice*

HOPKINS'S WRITINGS

CW   *Collected Works of Gerard Manley Hopkins*

EPM   *Early Poetic Manuscripts and Notebooks*

LPM   *Later Poetic Manuscripts*

PW   *The Poetical Works of Gerard Manley Hopkins*

INTRODUCTION

TELLING A DIFFERENT STORY

A YOUNG MAN HARBORING SEXUAL SECRETS; a priest burdened with sin and spiritual aridity; poems written in exquisite, sometimes desperate anguish. That book practically writes itself. But, what if the story could be construed and told differently? Rather than attempting to ferret out or expose the "real" Gerard Manley Hopkins, what if the goal were to understand how he was habituated to think, feel, act, and imagine—how he was, simultaneously, both "counter, original"[1] and wholly predictable, a product of his historical and discursive moment? In other words, what if, instead of concentrating solely on Hopkins's exceptionality—and he was and is exceptional—one focuses on his writings to comprehend why an obsession with sinning, the flesh, and rituals of confession is one of the most typical things about him? Rather than describe why he is an "immortal diamond," I am using Hopkins prismatically to investigate how various facets of Victorian life and culture interact—new forms of knowledge clashing with entrenched principles—from religious beliefs and political machinations to scientific controversies and dramas of gender discrimination.

This is not a book about a particular faith and its inarguable truths, or a defense of Hopkins's religious certainties (or John Henry Newman's, or Duns Scotus's). In that regard, even some of the most informative Hopkins critics exercise a narrow kind of intentionality: this is what he wants to do or say; this is what the poem means in terms of various theological positions (positions that are, in fact, often contested or contradictory). Instead, this book offers an analysis of aesthetic and religious discourses in dialogue, considering how, in the second half of the nineteenth century, religion is expressed, lived, and debated, and why it matters so much. As Maureen Moran states, the "saturation" of Victorian "culture by Christianity and its denominational variants makes religion always and everywhere a presence" (*Catholic* 3). Some people were trying to separate life into "secular" and "religious" domains, but Hopkins was not one of them. His writings—prose and poetry—are exemplary for the ways in which they demonstrate that struggles with and *for* faith always enfold theology, psychology, selving.[2]

But why focus on "confessing the flesh"? This book explores the Victorian ways in which confession and the "flesh"—that is, not merely the body, but the body as the site of sin and potential degradation, both somatic and spiritual—pertain to definitions of the licit and illicit, relate to personal and textual dramas of obedience and disobedience, and inform an aesthetics that embraces the sensuous and the sensational. The discussion constantly shifts from the broadest topics and most vociferous controversies to the "small things"[3] that inform Hopkins's daily existence and textual experiences. Of course there are elements of his life, his preoccupations, in everything that he writes, but each poem and even the most intimate diary entry is also, I hope to explain, a textual and aesthetic creation; every speaker or narrator is both a projection and a fiction.[4] In his letters, the adult Hopkins has a different "voice" for each familiar correspondent: he writes to his mother with affection but also religious concern; with Robert Bridges, a poet and doctor, he is both peer and potential patient; with Alexander Mowbray Baillie, a friend from Oxford days and a well-traveled person of cultural refinement, Hopkins is worldly, curious, and well-read; with his brothers Arthur and Everard, who become accomplished illustrators, he is an uncompromising critic. Initially as an Anglican and then devoutly as a Roman Catholic and Jesuit priest, he is rearticulating what he has gleaned from classical philosophy, the Bible,[5] the Book of Common Prayer, medieval scholasticism, Ignatius's *Spiritual Exercises,* and the writings of religious heroes and antagonists alike. What he thinks about the sacrament of penance and all its attendant rituals and crises is shaped, to some degree, by Augustine of Hippo, John Cassian, Peter Lombard, Raymond of Penyafort, and the members of the Fourth Lateran Council. How and why he worries about the flesh, the literal and figurative "blight" of humanity, has been predicted by religious training, intellectual concerns, and the poetry, prose, and visual art that he finds acutely stimulating. In the most profound sense, Hopkins lives with language and *in* language—in English, Latin, Greek, and sometimes Welsh[6]—acutely perceptive yet also unaware to what extent he is conditioned by the discourses and institutions that frame or "scaffold" (*PW* 201) his life.

"Conditions" is a very Paterian term, one that highlights how individuals are shaped by their historical moment (and thus by everything from family, education, and religion to physical environment, cultural opportunities, and artistic enterprises). The argument being offered in this book does not suggest Hopkins is a victim of circumstances—he is, instead, the product of material circumstances, texts, controversies, values, and personal experience. (As Brenda Silver suggests, "Value judgments, like value itself, are not only contingent, but contextual, enmeshed in structures that confer authority" [347]. Such structures are defined by Michel Foucault as "the order of things," of power-knowledge relations that provide the "fundamental codes" by which we know, think, dread, and desire.[7]) One can correlate what Hopkins fears, what he loves, how he imagines himself and his God, to the discourses that shape then-contemporary understandings of subjectivity ("self in self steeped"[8]), identity (including gender, race, nation), science, imperialism[9] and civilization, and soteriological certainties. Hopkins the reader, for example, absorbs not only classical philosophy and Catholic theology; he appreciates poetry in several languages written over a five-thousand-year span, enjoys contemporary fiction (not just George Eliot and Thomas Hardy, but Edgar Allan Poe, Jean Ingelow, and Mark Twain), and is an avid reader of periodicals in an era in which the gradual repeal of the three "taxes on knowledge" as they are termed (duties or taxes on paper, advertisements, and print media such as newspapers and journals) encourages the proliferation of the popular press. He is a deeply religious Christian at a time when the academic and ethnographic study of world religions is emerging,[10] and a Jesuit in an era in which members of the Society of Jesus are being expelled from Spain (as of 1868)[11] and from the newly unified Germany (as of 1871, part of Otto von Bismark's

Kulturkampf), and technically occupy shaky legal and social ground in England.¹²

For Hopkins, however, the "condition" of human existence that supersedes and also envelopes all others is the existence of God. For "believers,"¹³ to live in *"the felt Presence of God,"* as Edward Pusey explains in his "Letter of Guidance," is everything (*Penitence* 61). The speaker of "The Wreck of the Deutschland" concurs: "Over again I feel thy finger and find thee" (*PW* 119). That commitment to a "transcendent Creator beyond" and yet immanent within the natural and human realms is "the highest, most real, authentic" truth and "a good which is beyond, in the sense of independent of human flourishing" (Charles Taylor 15). The implications of putting one's faith in a "higher" power will be discussed throughout this study. At this introductory stage, I want to stress what it means, for Hopkins, to acknowledge a secure, inviolable basis for his values and to know that there exists a special relationship between himself, his soul, and his God. And because, to quote Robert Browning's Bishop Blougram, "Belief or unbelief / Bears upon life, determines its whole course" (351),¹⁴ it is important to grasp the enormity of all that Hopkins thinks to be true—acknowledging that his adult faith, as a confirmed Catholic and priest, is in fact a palimpsest featuring elements of Judaism (especially the personification of God as the vengeful Almighty), New Testament narratives, ancient and medieval asceticism, early Christian teachings (particularly those of St. Augustine and John Chrysostom), medieval Roman Catholicism (Thomas Aquinas, Peter Abelard, the *Sentences* of Peter Lombard, Duns Scotus), Victorian Church of England dogma and Tractarian practices, Ignatian spirituality (exemplified by the *Spiritual Exercises*), and Jesuit theology (Francisco Suárez, Alphonsus Liguori). Today's reader should consider carefully the foundations of Hopkins's fervent beliefs in the seen and the "unseen"¹⁵ and the extent to which he knew these things to be literally true. He believed in the following:

> —metaphysical reality, which "alone gives meaning to laws and sequences and causes and developments" (*CW* 4:288).
> —God, and the holy Trinity of God the Father, God the Son (Christ), and God the Holy Ghost. As he explains to Bridges, "There are three persons, each God and each the same, the one, the only God: to some people this is a 'dogma,' a word they almost

chew, that is an equation in theology, the dull algebra of Schoolmen; to others it is news of their ~~three~~ dearest ^friend or^ friends" (*CW* 2:619). On the one hand, he knows that however vivid or dramatic the metaphors (Master, Good Shepherd, light of the world, "hero of Calvary," the comforting dove), none is sufficient to "Grásp Gód" (*PW* 121, 127). On the other hand, complementing God's active presence throughout creation is the human ability to experience the noumenal ("His mystery must be instressed, stressed" [*PW* 120]).

—the Incarnation of God as Jesus Christ; the life, crucifixion, death, and resurrection of Christ, and his ascension into heaven; and believed in the Second Coming of Christ, on Judgment Day (which Hopkins described in great detail for his parishioners on 30 November 1879; *CW* 5:233). Furthermore, like Duns Scotus, Hopkins believed that Christ "emptied himself" into human form (kenosis) voluntarily, not simply as atonement, to satisfy God's understandable anger about human sinfulness, but as the ultimate gift of love.

—the existence of the devil ("Dark-out-for-ever Lucifer" [*PW* 140]) and evil. "Beware of the devil's wiles," Abbé Gaume warns in his manual for confessors;[16] "the author of, and tempter to evil," Edward Pusey emphasizes, "is ever busy with our souls."[17] Hopkins knew this to be true from bitter personal experience: one is besieged by "pride and rebellion, on one hand, and mere cowardice and yielding, on the other, being partly active, partly passive towards both sides, neither consenting to the tempter nor yet rejecting the tempting thought" (*CW* 5:371).

—Heaven and Hell.

—sin—both the stain of Adam and Eve's "original sin" of disobedience, which blights every human soul, and the near occasion of sin in everyday life.

—the forgiveness of sins through the sacrament of penance.

—the "Real Presence" of Christ in the Eucharist (the bread and wine transubstantiated during the Eucharistic liturgy of the Mass).

—angels and also guardian angels. In "appointing us guardian angels God never meant they shd. make us proof against all the ills that flesh is heir to," he instructed parishioners in October 1880, "but he meant them, accompanying us through this world of evils and mischance, to turn all its chances[,] sometimes warding off its blows and buffets, sometimes leaving them to fall, always to be leading us to a better; which better world, my brethren, when you have reached and with your own eyes opened look back on this you will see a work of wonderful wisdom in the guidance of your guardian angel" (*CW* 5:318).[18]

—the efficacy and power of the Church's seven sacraments (baptism, penance, "first communion," confirmation of one's faith, marriage, ordination, and anointing the sick).

—all the implications of Christian eschatology: "Death, Judgment, Heaven and Hell" (Gaume 56).

—the resurrection of the body (as promised in 1 Corinthians 15:12–22).

—the exemption from sin of Mary, the mother of Christ (for Roman Catholics, the Blessed Virgin Mary),[19] and in her ascension into heaven. Marian devotion reached its apogee in the mid-nineteenth century when, in 1854, Pius IX promulgated the doctrine of Mary's "immaculate conception." The mother of God thus confounds gender norms and reaffirms them (she is a powerful intercessionary figure *and* archetypal mother overwhelmed with sorrow, the *mater dolorosa*), and is brilliantly deployed as the human "face" of a global religious institution.

—the priesthood, and its sacred mission.

—and, as of 1868, in the Society of Jesus (its mission, rules, and the sanctity of its vows of poverty, chastity, and obedience).

And he trusts in these truths: not with the assurance of a dry Scholastic pedant, but with "a passion and a conviction" (Dubois 18). He wants to believe, needs to believe, is nurtured by his beliefs, and also tormented by them. As a Jesuit, however, he also believes and lives by Ignatius's "Rules for Thinking with the Church," including Rule 13: "To make sure of being right in all things, we ought always to hold by the principle that the white that I see I would believe to be black if the Hierarchical Church were so to rule it."[20] The destabilizing potential of such a commitment will be explored throughout my analyses.

To quote Hopkins's translation of a prayer by Thomas Aquinas, "What God's son has told me take for truth I do: / Word of Truth speaks truly or there's nothing true"[21] (*PW* 111). The couplet expresses a wholehearted acceptance of Christian truths, playing effectively on the apostle John's figuration of the Messiah as the "Word" ("In the beginning was the Word, and the Word was with God, and the Word was God"), the New Testament answer to the Genesis declaration "In the beginning God created the heaven and the earth" (Gen. 1:1). The speaker's initial statement, "Godhead, I adore Thee down on bended knee" (*PW* 111), expresses both the emotional investment and the willingness to be subjugated that shape Hopkins's life of religious commitment. Hopkins readily acknowledges the limits of the human imagination in comprehending divine truths:

> We guess; we clothe Thee, unseen King,
> With attributes we deem are meet;
> Each in his own imagining
> Sets up a shadow in Thy seat[.] (*PW* 92)

What challenges the limits of Hopkins's tolerance is apostasy. One is either faithful or faithless, as defined in stanza 6 of "The Wreck"; or, in the words of "Spelt from Sibyl's Leaves," one of "twó flocks, twó folds—bláck, white; | ríght, wrong" (*PW* 191). The admirer of "Two Beautiful Young People" asks, "Where lies your landmark, seamark, or soul's star? / There's none but truth can stead you. Christ is truth" (*PW* 192). The implied rhyming of "soul's star" with "polestar" (the North Star, Polaris) demonstrates the agile metaphors with which Hopkins can express his beliefs. He can also reiterate them prosaically: "I can hardly believe," he informs Henry Liddon, his Oxford confessor, "anyone ever became a Catholic because two and two make four more fully than I have."[22]

Considering the metaphors that illuminate Hopkins's poetry to express "the glory of God" and Christ—everything from electrical charges and terrifying storms to the "juice [that] rides rich" through nature and the starry "fire-folk sitting in the air" (*PW* 191, 139)—one can appreciate how these beliefs function as the ground of his existence. In Charles Taylor's evocative summary, many "see our lives, and/or the space wherein we live our lives, as having a certain mortal/spiritual shape. Somewhere, in some activity, or condition, lies a fullness, a richness; that is, in that place (activity or condition), life is fuller, richer, deeper, more worth while, more admirable, more what it should be. This is perhaps a place of power: we often experience this as deeply moving, as inspiring" (5). Inspiration, however, can be both refreshing and harrowing for Hopkins, as this study will demonstrate. The argument being presented stresses that the most important, intimate relationships in Hopkins's adult life are with his God and/as Christ, yet also sets aside such "metaphysical fixity—fixed origin, nature, identity, development, and destiny" (Dollimore 181) and instead considers what a culture of religious absolutism looks like from outside the parameters of shared belief.

DISCLOSING ALL

The polestars of this study are confession (both sacrament and personal impulse) and considerations of the flesh. Confession "has spread its effects far and wide," Foucault suggests, "It plays a part in justice, medicine, education, family relationships, and love relations, in the most ordinary affairs of everyday life, and in the most solemn rites; one confesses one's crimes, one's sins, one's thoughts and desires, one's illnesses and troubles; one goes about telling, with the greatest precision, whatever is most difficult to tell.... One confesses—or is forced to confess."[23] Confession was not only good for the Victorian soul, it was excellent for the publishing industry: nineteenth-century British readers had more than four hundred titles to choose from promising sacred, secular, or personal revelations. Sacred titles ranged from the austere, such as *Christ and Christianity: Studies on Christology, Creeds and Confessions,* to the melodramatic, such as *The Liberty of Britain Imperilled by Confessing Priests*. Secular disclosures were equally diverse: everyone from An Actor, a Shy Bachelor, and an Atrocious Murderer to a Coquette, a Court Milliner, and a Little Man during Great Days had a story to tell. Regardless of station or occupation—Preacher, Poacher, Publisher, Medium, Princess, Anarchist, Constable, Spy—professional insights and intimate disclosures were being shared. Fiction titles dominated the list of creative works on offer,[24] but confessional poetic discourse was also available. And throughout the era, well-known nonfictional books by St. Augustine, Jean-Jacques Rousseau, and Thomas De Quincey continued to command a readership. In addition, what one could term confessional elements or disclosures certainly informed the era's major life-writing exercises, including Newman's *Apologia pro Vita Sua* (1864), John Stuart Mill's *Autobiography* (1873), Harriet Martineau's *Autobiography: With Memorials by Maria Weston Chapman* (1877), Anthony Trollope's *An Autobiography of Anthony Trollope* (1883), and John Ruskin's *Praeterita* (1885–89). "As is well known," Clinton Machann notes, "reticence and the concealment of 'private' matters, notably those related to sexuality, are conventional in Victorian literary autobiographies, but there is a persistent tension between these conventions and the impulse to 'confess' matters that would seem to be essential to the 'selfhood' that is supposed to be related to the narrative of the development of one's ideas and the production of one's published works" (14–15).

In the context of this cultural zest for disclosure—a fascinating mixture of revelation and self-display—how is one to reconsider the confessional elements of Hopkins's writings? Confession, as part of the sacrament of penance, offers the believer the gift of absolution from sin and the promise of grace; its redemptive blessings—however undeserved—are supposed to balance out the mental and possibly physical scourging involved (the examination of conscience with which one prepares for confession; the penance required afterward). To borrow a major trope from "The Wreck," confession involves both being mastered (the ode begins with a thundering acknowledgement: "Thou mastering me / God!" [*PW* 119]) and self-mastery ("a domination of oneself by oneself" [*HS* 2:61]). In the mid-nineteenth century, the practice of confessing one's sins to a priest is both a regular religious obligation for Roman Catholics (a duty, and Victorians such as Hopkins love being dutiful) and a controversial, even scandalous activity for Anglicans (one of the most "explosive religious issues, both morally and theologically" of its time, according to Nigel Yates ["Jesuits" 202]). Thus, what would seem to be a straightforward, even holy exercise intersects with and exacerbates—vexes—social and cultural fears, political and legal crises ranging from church/state bonds to obscenity (discussed in chapter 2), strife within the Church of England, and tensions between Anglicans and English Roman Catholics. Furthermore, imbricated in the storm of protests and institutional measures are medical authorities, academics, intellectuals, and major religious figures. (Hopkins reveres John

Henry Newman, admires Edward Pusey, has regular contact with Henry Liddon for two years, and meets Henry Edward Manning).

Before there is confession, however, there is the flesh, and before flesh, there is sin. The Hebrews' God tells Moses, "Speak unto the children of Israel, When a man or woman shall commit any sin that men commit, to do a trespass against the Lord, and that person be guilty, then they shall confess their sin which they have done" (Num. 5:6–7). Sins are many, thanks to human resourcefulness or perfidy, but their basic definition is straightforward: "Sin signifies a falling away or distortion of humankind's original perfection through disobedience to God's beneficent will. Since sin enters the world by human choice, it incurs objective guilt in human beings" (McFarland 473).[25] To think of sin as disorder and disruption is to understand, in part, why an awareness of it serves as catalyst, almost a trigger, for the frequent, ominous shift in tone and verbal texture in Hopkins's Petrarchan sonnets. All too regularly, the octave celebrates nature, yet the sestet is preoccupied with the implications of sin. "God's Grandeur" is one of the few poems in which a recovery from the consequences of sin is staged: an awareness of all that sears, blears, and smears human and natural existence (they are tainted with "man's smell") dislocates the octave, but the sestet is rescued by the "ah! bright wings" of "the Holy Ghost" (*PW* 139).

As for the flesh—well, one could blame Tertullian. Famous in Carthage two centuries (ca. 160–225 CE) before Augustine, Tertullian was the early polemicist now credited for being one of the founders of Christian theology and, in *De anima*, "the originator of the concept of the flesh," and the "elaborator of the idea of original sin. . . . In Tertullian's striking phrase, penitence is achieved through *publication sui*—the making public of oneself (*De paenitentia*, X. 1)" (Elden 299). The flesh includes the corporeal body, but it is always wholly, yet not irremediably, "consumed by concupiscence" (Elden 299). The latter, according to Tertullian, is associated with lusts and desires, but is not only sexual; it is that which "turns the will away from God" (McFarland 109). (As experts ranging from Chaucer's Parson to Edward Pusey warn, "the fire of concupiscence" rages within the flesh because the flesh is "the seat of our concupiscence.")[26] It is Augustine who ties concupiscence, the flesh's fundamental weakness, to original sin and stresses its sexual implications. Hopkins concurs. The "spirit and flesh started together," Hopkins observes in his 1880 retreat notes, "flesh being the name for a condition of matter" (*CW* 5:435). He draws upon many theological arguments to make that point, including St. Paul's vision of a life "in the flesh" that separates one from Christ (Phil. 1:22–24). Flesh is the material body horribly imbued by, stained with, original sin—it is, according to Hopkins, "the fatal consequence" (*CW* 5:352). Hence my use of Foucault's argument that the flesh "should be understood as a mode of experience—that is, as a mode of knowledge and transformation of oneself by oneself, depending on a certain relationship between a nullification of evil and a manifestation of truth"—to demonstrate how "the 'discovery' of the self" takes place in Hopkins's poetry and prose (*HS* 4:36).

Foucault, in his comments about Homer's *Iliad*, describes a race between Achilles and Antilochus in terms of its underlying "function, which is to be the visible ceremony of a truth that is already visible."[27] For Fr. Hopkins, the visible ceremonies of truth include the Mass that he celebrates, the rituals of Jesuit life he undergoes, and the poems he composes. His truths are immutable, "higher" than mere human knowledge and conjecture.[28] What he would most certainly reject is Foucault's insistence that one ask, But *how* is this true? This question requires interrogating "the normative standards by which claims of truth, authenticity, and legitimacy are established" (Caughie 195) and relocates truth-telling as "as a social practice." One of the aims of this book is to study Victorian truth claims as "a means of modifying relations of power among those who speak" and, sometimes, "as a weapon in relationships between individuals" (*WDTT* 28). Through discourse analysis, one can pivot from notions of congenital sinfulness and fleshly guilt to a critique of Victorian ideas of moral responsibility, guilt, and atonement.

"OTHER METHODS WILL SUGGEST THEMSELVES"

My argument is situated at the interstices of literature and aesthetics, Christianity and philosophy, body studies, and the multifarious resources of Victorian culture. Among the investigations that have helped me enormously are studies of the century's "crises" of faith by Susan Budd and A. N. Wilson; of nineteenth-century anti-Catholicism, by Susan Griffin; of personal and literary confessional practices, by Susan Bernstein and Chloë Taylor; of gender norms, sexual difference, and queer subjectivity by Eve Kosofsky Sedgwick, James Eli Adams, Oliver Buckton, Herbert Sussman, and Julia Saville; and of Catholic "sensationalism" by Maureen Moran.[29] My feminist Foucauldian approach[30] enfolds somatic, spiritual, and intellectual discourses not only to think about Hopkins's writings "aslant," to borrow Emily Dickinson's wonderful term, but to explore the power dynamics of faith, fear, and subjectivity that inform and sustain them.

Hopkins's ingenious mind is fueled by binaries. Certainly, he admires "pied beauty," that which is "original, spáre, strange" (*PW* 144); in an undergraduate essay, he suggests that the "always recurring coexistence of contraries is highly exciting to thought" (*CW* 4:216).[31] Nonetheless, continuity and sameness are his ethical and spiritual standards, not difference and discontinuity. Foucault, however, whose works are characterized by "a profound distrust of essences, natures, and other kinds of unifying, totalizing, and exclusionary thought that threaten individual freedom and creativity" (Flynn 39), privileges difference and discontinuity, exposes the ways in which institutional pressures to normalize behaviors and thinking, discipline bodies, and demonize desire have had a direct bearing on all aspects of our most intimate and most social lives.

Foucault's emphasis on power and knowledge is something Hopkins might appreciate—after all, he believes in an all-powerful and omniscient deity, the "giver of breath and bread; / Wórld's stránd, swáy of the séa" and perpetually "únder the wórld's spléndour and wónder" (*PW* 119, 120). His very Victorian cultural imaginary stresses the significance of powerful empires, powerful authorities, and powerful "great men." Foucault, however, always insists that power "is not an institution, and not a structure; neither is it a certain strength we are endowed with; it is the name that one attributes to a complex strategical situation in a particular society" (*HS* 1:93). Its omnipresence is "not because it has the privilege of consolidating everything under its invincible unity, but because it is produced from one moment to the next, at every point, or rather in every relation from one point to another." Power is everywhere, he adds, "because it comes from everywhere" (*HS* 1:93). Foucault's goal, throughout diverse and historically wide-ranging investigations, is to locate and expose forms of power at both the macro and micro levels: "the channels it takes, and the discourses it permeates in order to reach the most tenuous and individual modes of behavior" (*HS* 1:11). In "Two Lectures" (1976), he reiterates that a major concern is "the *how* of power" and how it operates through discourses of truth—the issue so close to the heart of my project.[32] "We *must* speak the truth," he explains with a ventriloquist's flourish; "we are constrained or condemned to confess or to discover the truth. Power never ceases its interrogation, its inquisition, its registration of truth: it institutionalizes, professionalizes, and rewards its pursuit" (*P/K* 93). Most emphatically, Foucault suggests that these dynamic, organized, hierarchical (*P/K* 198) but also heterogeneous relations of power are variously disposed by agents, "privileged enunciators," instruments such as buildings (churches, barracks, hospitals, asylums, schools, novitiate houses), documents, and innumerable "practices and rituals" (Rouse 106).

More specifically, my title and critical impetus come from Foucault's *Les aveux de la chair*, confessions and/or avowals of the flesh (the double nature of the noun is explored in chapter 1). His volume's complex history requires a short explanation. For decades, it was just a rumor: one of several books in the projected six-volume *History of Sexuality* that Foucault never produced.[33] But he did write it (the original title: *La chair et le corps*, the flesh and the body), as a follow-up to the first volume in the series, *La Volonté de savoir*.[34] Thus, it bridges "the chronological and conceptual gap" between volume 1 (1976) and what are now the *History*'s volume 2, *The Use of Pleasure* (1978), and volume 3, *The Care of the Self* (1983).[35] Foucault was never wholly satisfied, however. "By the early 1980s, Foucault was very close to a publishable book. By now this manuscript had the title *Les aveux de la chair*.... [He] gave the manuscript to Gallimard in October 1982, but told them it was not to be published immediately.... In early 1984, Foucault took back the manuscript . . . and began making final edits" (Elden 295, 296)[36] but died in June 1984 before completing the task. His instructions were to leave *Les aveux* in the archive, unpublished, but the estate released the volume in 2018 (first English translation, 2021).[37]

All four volumes of the *History of Sexuality* return to classical authors and early Christian teachings to tell a different story about sexuality, insisting that "[it] must not be described as a stubborn drive, by nature alien and out of necessity disobedient to a power which exhausts itself trying to subdue it and often fails to control it entirely. It appears rather as an especially dense transfer point for relations of power: between men and women, young people and old people, parents and offspring, teachers and students, priests and laity.... Sexuality is not the most intractable element in power relations, but rather one of those endowed with the greatest instrumentality" (*HS* 1:105). Sex and suspicion became inextricable, Foucault suggests: "The general and disquieting meaning that pervades our conduct and our existence, in spite of ourselves; the point of weakness where evil portents reach through to us; the fragment of darkness that we each carry within us: a general signification, a universal secret, an omnipresent cause, a fear that never ends" (*HS* 1:69).

Foucault's efforts to understand how Victorians working assiduously in several fields (education, religion, medicine, biology, psychiatry) constructed "around and apropos of sex an immense apparatus for producing truth" (*HS* 1:56)[38] clarify that nineteenth-century imperatives cannot be fully understood without tracing the tentacular, historically complex effects of Christian teachings and practices (according to which sex "constituted the soul's most secret and determinant part" [1:127]).

Two key elements emerge from Foucault's studies of early Christianity. First, in terms of teachings: the "doctrine of the flesh" ("the weakness that had marked human nature" since the "Fall" of Adam and Eve) (*HS* 2:50), all the precautions "that have to be taken in order to prevent desire from entering the soul surreptitiously, or to detect its secret traces" (2:39); and the ways in which morality, sexuality, and "self-formation" (2:28) are deliberately, relentlessly, enmeshed. The Christian's journey should be directed toward salvation,[39] but the flesh has other plans. Second, in terms of practices: there is confession. The flesh is a pervasive and unyielding threat to purity; confession provides techniques of purification. Building on classical philosophers' commitment to self-examination (the monitoring of desire), and early Christian monks' devotion to asceticism (the eradication of desire), writers such as Ambrose and Augustine extolled the virtues of confessing, and subsequent church authorities devised ways to institutionalize public forms of confession. *Confessions of the Flesh* enriches the *History of Sexuality* by concentrating on a particular mode of power—pastoral power—as defined from the second to twelfth centuries by Christian authors. Pastoral power, Foucault argues, "individualizes by granting, through an essential paradox, as much value to a single one sheep as to the entire flock. It is this type of power that was introduced into the West by Christianity and took an institutional form in the ecclesiastical pastorate: the government of souls was constituted in the Christian Church as a central, knowledge-based activity indispensable for the salvation of each and every one."[40]

According to Foucault, making confession a crucial part of the sacrament of penance (today, the sacrament of reconciliation) enabled church authorities to accomplish four basic goals: define transgressions, monitor thoughts and behaviors, regulate punishment, and manage more effectively the members of ever-growing, international congregations. Put another way: confession is formalized at the same time that the minor sect becomes a world religion, the "Christian empire" (*HS* 4:35). Taking the long view, Foucault proposes that modern, Western subjectivity continually struggles with Christian theories of concupiscence, sexual desire, and the politics of truth, in which discourses trace "the meeting line of the body and the soul, following all its meandering: beneath the surface of sins, it would lay bare the unbroken nervure of the flesh" (*HS* 1:20).

Confession involves both truth-telling and submission. Foucault wants to capture "the moment of emergence of a ritualized truth obligation, of an injunction of verbalization by the subject, of truth-telling about oneself.... [;] the Christian moment of 'pastoral governmentality': 'truth acts' (telling the truth about oneself) hinging on practices of obedience" (Gros ix).[41] In terms of my title, however, why "confessing" and not "confession"? Hopkins not only explores the interrelations of nouns and verbs, transmuting one into the other with experimental flare ("the just man justices" [*PW* 141]), he uses participles frequently (mastering, living, riding, meaning, wanting, calling, unfathering) to express the godly energy within nature and people ("His mýstery múst be instréssed, stressed" [*PW* 120]) and to encourage the reader's response (a participatory aesthetic fully at work). Moreover, participles indicate ongoing action—dynamic, ever-changing, volatile. Both the natural world and human nature are, for Hopkins, thus animated; life is a continual albeit fraught engagement with the Lord. Confession is an activity, a ritual for priest and penitent alike; confessing is a vigorous, continual awareness and the constant need to speak one's truth, however sin-soaked. As such, confessing is a keen facet of "selving," that fundamental experience and practice of Christianity subjectivity as Hopkins understands it. When and as appropriate, I will discuss how Hopkins's texts negotiate the central paradox of Christian subjectivity: that the ultimate cost of self-definition and preservation is nothing less than self-annihilation. And I will do so in relation to an allegory of selving involving mind, body, soul, and flesh, and mindful of how a "masculine ideal of bourgeois respectability" is in fact a "multiple, complex, and unstable constructio[n]."42

As Alan Sinfield suggests, "There are no selves without culture" (176). How are we to understand what was written some 150 to 170 years ago? Post-Wilde, post-Freud, post-Foucault, how are we to grasp textual gestures and nuances? "The Victorians placed emphases that we do not place, saw vices where we see trivia, allowed confusions where we would expect clarity" (Sinfield 102). Sometimes inadvertently, sometimes deliberately, Hopkins transgresses Victorian orthodoxies of gender, sex, religion, and poetry. Yet, as Frank Turner advocates, scholars should "regard religious *behaviour* as a product of social and psychological interaction among human beings rather than as a manifestation of the interactions of human beings and the divine" (11). Turner takes his lead from Foucault, who has demonstrated that sexuality is a historical construct and not "a furtive reality that is difficult to grasp" (*HS* 1:105).

Hopkins would have said that his life is governed by a "voluntary" yet essential Christian morality; Foucault would counter with the suggestion that "coercive regimentation" is predominant (*HS* 2:167). Hopkins alternately fears and loathes his body, and the pull of sexual attraction; Elizabeth Grosz argues that the body, bound up as it is "in the order of desire, signification, and power," must be understood "through a range of disparate discourses and not simply restricted to naturalistic and scientific modes of explanation" (20). What is gained from such "counterpoint[s] of dissonance" (*CW* 5:201)? Using Foucault to form "a different grid of historical decipherment" when reading Hopkins (*HS* 1:90) enables one to appreciate more fully the pressures exerted on Hopkins's writings and his life.

That grid of intelligibility is incomplete if national interests are not factored in: if the role of the nation, that "imagined community," in constituting an individual's identity is not underscored, and the political aspects of the Church *of England* are not emphasized. It was and is the *state* religion; accommodations for other faiths are a product of this past century, not Hopkins's century. Repeatedly, Hopkins proudly declares that he is "England's fame's fond lover" (*PW* 199). That phrase is featured in the third stanza of "What shall I do for the land that bred me" (1885); the speaker, perhaps a soldier, boasts with Tennysonian vigor: "Spend me or end me what God shall send me, / But under her banner I live for her honour" (*PW* 199).[43] Of course when Hopkins converts to Catholicism, he switches allegiance from one theological framework to another, one "established" church to what he now considers to be the "true" Church. The speaker of "The Half-way House" (1865) admits as much, but obliquely, using an Old Testament reference: "My national old Egyptian reed gave way" (*PW* 85). The spiritual rewards of such a move are never doubted by Hopkins, but the "costs"—in personal and sociocultural terms—should not be overlooked. The economic metaphor is apt, because in October 1866 he was, to some degree, throwing away his chances for a typical, assured English life of accomplishment and prosperity (hence the fears expressed in letters sent to him by his parents). Suddenly, he is no longer "one of us"—he is "one of them," affiliated by faith with untrustworthy "foreigners" from the Continent and, heaven forfend, Ireland. "Suspicion of Catholics as creatures of divided loyalty—to King and to Pope," Moran confirms, "was well embedded in the [English] national psyche from the late sixteenth century in ways that reinforced the Church of Rome as a dangerous religious *and* secular opponent" (*Catholic* 5).[44] How marginalizing, how alienating is Hopkins's status as a *Roman* Catholic? Newman's 1851 summary of these costs is both pointed and poignant:

> The convert to Catholicism is dismissed by his employer; the tradesman loses his custom; the practitioner his patients; the lawyer has no longer the confidence of his clients; ... business is crippled, the shop cannot be opened; ... his friends fight shy of him; gradually they drop him, if they do not disown him at once. There used to be pleasant houses open to him, and a circle of acquaintances. People were glad to see him, and he felt himself, though solitary, not lonely; ... [now] he gets no more invitations; he is not a welcome guest; ... and where his presence once was found, now it is replaced by malicious and monstrous tales about him, distorted shadows of himself, freely circulated and readily believed. What is his crime?—he is a Catholic among Protestants. (*Lectures* 183)[45]

He isn't exaggerating the animosity, or the "losses" incurred. In 1878, editors of the *Whitehall Review* felt compelled to publish the names of more than 1,900 women and men who had converted—a ritual of public shaming with the title of *Rome's Recruits: A List of Protestants Who Have Become Roman Catholics*. Today, one could think of it as a cross between a roll of dishonor (naming names, à la Joseph McCarthy) and a list of the religiously brave and independent. Prefaced by a letter of endorsement from William Gladstone, the twenty-four-page pamphlet outs Hopkins's friends and acquaintances such as William Addis, Tom Arnold, Henry Coleridge, S.J., Edward Caswall, A. W. Garrett, E. B. Harding, William Kerr and Henry Schomberg Kerr, Henry and Charles Karslake, Henry Cardinal Manning, Frederick Myers, John Henry Newman, Henry Oxenham, Coventry Patmore, Edward Purbrick, Frances Paravicini, and Henry Ryder. And on page 18: "Gerard R. [*sic*] Hopkins, B.A., Balliol College, Oxford. A Jesuit" (*Rome's Recruits* 18). Only when he relocates to Ireland, in February 1884, does Hopkins fully realize that his "Catholic" identity is both multifaceted and regarded with suspicion. Now "at a third / Remove," a stranger "Among strangers" (*PW* 181), he is an *English* Catholic, not a "cradle" or recusant Catholic but a convert, and a Newman-identified one at that (Hopkins's hero had been much admired but also polarizing since the mid-1840s). Hence his admission to his mother, Kate Hopkins, in March 1885: "The grief of mind I go through over politics, over what I read and hear and see, in Ireland about Ireland and about England, is such that I can neither express ^it^ nor bear to speak of it" (*CW* 2:715). Yet to his brother Everard, in December 1885, he writes in a wholly antithetical mood: "The Pope has written the most beautiful letter to the English bishops,[46] speaking in terms of such heartfelt affection for England that I kiss the words when I read them" (*CW* 2:755).

Despite the papal olive branch, Hopkins's second, very "catholic" religion is, for too many English Victorians, a national irritant and perhaps even an enemy, at a time of the "often desperate and deliberate work of *reimagining* nationhood in the face of growing diversity, expansion, and secularization" (Griffin, *Anti-Catholicism* 62). Small wonder that Frederick Faber, another famous convert (and founder of the Brompton Oratory), hopefully yet gingerly declares in the preface to *Growth in Holiness* (1855), "I have done no more than try to harmonize the ancient and modern spirituality of the Church, with somewhat perhaps of a propension to the first, and to put it before English Catholics in an English shape, translated into native thought and feeling, as well as language" (*Growth* viii). This is not simply a conflict over creeds, or who genuflects or not—it is nothing less than national and religious truths inextricably entwined and contested.

The rhetoric of condemnation devoted to Catholic converts is revealing. One of the favorite terms to denounce and denigrate the religious Other is *pervert*. Before the term is uniformly ascribed to sexual dissidents at the end of the nineteenth century—Hopkins's life coincides with the emergence of a psychologizing and pathologizing approach to sex[47]—it is used to rail against those foolish or demonic enough to be doctrinally insubordinate. William Thackeray, in an 1846 letter, "mimics common parlance in an off-the-cuff remark about the spread of Catholicism: 'But I think Romanism begins to be drawn rather milder; and the Poop of Room . . . is not perwhirting so many as fommly.'" Almost twenty years later, John Cumming uses the same language of deviance and irresistible sexual allure to represent the danger of Church of England Ritualists who lean toward Rome: "'Prodigious efforts are being made by the Ritualists to enlist converts, or rather I should say perverts'" (Moran, *Catholic* 188).[48] Of the plentiful examples of how, when the normative is believed to be natural, then anything or anyone different is considered to be unnatural and perverse, I will cite only two others. In Martin Tupper's 1860 sonnet "Hear the Church," the speaker demands, "who shall strike the truth / Between opposing factions, priest and lay, / The one, to Rome perverting half our youth, / The other leading liberally astray?" (65). Similarly, the preface to *Rome's Recruits* (1878) boldly and broadly boasts, "The idea of issuing such a statement of 'Perversions' or 'Conversions' was received with unanimous favour" (iii). As Jonathan Dollimore demonstrates, "Perversion is not only a culturally central phenomenon," it is "a crucial category for cultural analysis"—in this case, to understand the vehemence, even violence, of the denunciations hurled at those deemed to have deviated "from the true religion to the false" (179, 182). As chapter 2 will demonstrate, the confessional is, for virulent anti-Catholics, both the seat and the symbol of perversion; it is a convenient and scandalous point of contention for decades. Overall, this book is designed to show how, and why, Hopkins was not a *pervert*, as the cruelest among his contemporaries liked to call converts to

Catholicism and sexual dissidents, but he was *perverted*, his mind and spirit turned in directions both injurious and liberating.

CHAPTERS AND VERSES

Reading Hopkins in context is both the purpose and the method of this project. Two chapters are devoted to confessional history and practices; two, to the religious and aesthetic implications of the flesh. The conclusion is framed in terms of a concept vital to Hopkins's personal and textual life: "comfort."

Chapter 1, "Historical Investments," prepares the ground for Hopkins's confessional activities by exploring how a practice generally recommended in the Old and New Testaments was institutionalized in 1215 as a sacrament of the Catholic Church, and why a simple innovation, the confessional, is best understood as a heterotopia, defined by Foucault as a space or site that interrogates all others.[49] The keywords informing the analysis are concupiscence, conscience, guilt, shame, and scruples. Confession, I argue, sacramentalizes human failure: predicts it, tolerates it, accommodates it, relieves it. Three predominant issues in the emergence of the penitential sacrament have a direct bearing on Hopkins's life and writings: the authority of the Church and the individual priest; the degree of absolution obtained; and the validity of public or private confessional practices. Also crucial: the shift from acknowledging sin in terms of specific acts to naming each person a *sinner*, someone whose very thoughts and desires, as well as actions, must be constantly examined and monitored. Hence my underlying argument that Hopkins's rituals of "confessing the flesh" are not "individually determined but historically contingent and culturally embedded" (Buckton 10). In sixteen centuries of thinking and arguing about auricular confession, a substantial tradition of *writing* about confession has emerged. Four texts are considered to establish the discursive field to which Hopkins contributes with his poetry, diary entries, sermons, and Jesuit commentaries: the penitential Psalms of the Old Testament, Augustine's *Confessions*, St. Patrick's *Confessions*, and the medieval play *Everyman*. Also discussed: the specific genre developed to bolster the sacrament: the penitential guide or manual. Hopkins's confessional notes from 1865–66 are analyzed to demonstrate how prescriptive and prescribed his "lists of sins" are. Hopkins is definitely the product of a vehement "shame culture" (Sedgwick, *Touching* 62).

Chapter 2, "Victorian Confessional Crises," considers how and why the confessional became a convenient, scandalous point of contention in Victorian life. Drawing upon pamphlets, books, broadsides, manuals, verse satires, and two novels, the chapter explores how the confessional, such a small heterotopic space, could inspire outsized disagreements. For believers, the confessional was not just the place to speak, it was the place to say everything, tell everything about your sins and your sinful self. Yet it was also, for anti-Catholics, the place where the unspeakable was recalled, recited, and shared, both the seat and the symbol of perversion. Parliamentary and papal moves and countermoves that had the net effect of inflaming arguments and intensifying prejudices are assessed, from the Roman Catholic Relief Act (1829) and the papal bull *Universalis Ecclesiae* (1850) to the Public Worship Regulation Act (1874). The legal repositioning of Catholics in nineteenth-century Britain and the anti-Catholic and anti-Jesuit vituperation such maneuvers inspired are summarized. I consider, for example, *The Liberty of Britain Imperilled by Confessing Priests; or, The History of The Confessional Unmasked* (1873) and H. J. Brockman's *Letter to the Women of England: On the Confessional* (1867), which declares, "I know not another reptile in all animal nature so filthy, so much to be shunned and loathed, and *dreaded by females,* both married and single, as a Roman Catholic Priest ... who practices the degrading and demoralizing office of Auricular Confession." Secondly, Anglicans' internecine quarrels about auricular confession and other ritualistic practices, from the 1840s to the 1880s, are considered. (Pusey, at the forefront of these struggles, was Hopkins's Anglican confessor 1864–66.) Given these cultural clashes, Hopkins's decisions to convert to Catholicism and then become a Jesuit priest are reconsidered, and his critiques of the era's religiopolitical quarrels and of Ritualism are assessed. To demonstrate further the reach and vehemence of anti-Catholicism in the Victorian era, two sources for fomenting and circulating the scandals are discussed: *Punch,* the satirical weekly, and the poetry of Martin Tupper. Also considered: farcical poems such as "Ye Great Anglican Revival" (1871) and the hilarious 1875 Hogarthian satire *The Ritualist's Progress; A Sketch of the Reforms and Ministrations of the Rev. Septimius Alban, Member of the E.C.U., Vicar of St. Alicia, Sloperton,* by A. B. Wildered, Parishioner.

Chapter 3, "Living 'in Flesh'" considers the second crucial focus of this cultural investigation and discusses how, and to what effects, the flesh is "taken as a 'form of experience' and a 'form of subjectivity'" (*HS* 1:65). With Pauline intensity and Augustinian abhorrence, Hopkins continually engages with and is sometimes "whelmed" by "all the insinuations of the flesh: thoughts, desires, voluptuous imaginings, delectations" (*HS* 1:19). This chapter considers the disturbances of the flesh, including masturbation, which beset Hopkins and the drama of the flesh enacted in the *Spiritual Exercises*. Four examples of the ways in which Ignatius Loyola guides the Jesuit to work against the flesh are considered—"flesh being the name for a condition of matter," Hopkins notes (*CW* 5:435). In terms of somatic discipline, "wrestling" with the flesh is examined, along with the ethos of mortification Hopkins endorses. The homoerotic underpinnings of some Hopkins poems are assessed, as well as the paeans to heroic, working-class bodies that serve as antidotes to mere flesh. Hopkins's "Meditation on Death" and key sermons are analyzed in this context as well as a selection of poems from the 1860s to 1889 that probe how "Flesh fade[s], and mortal trash / Fall[s] to the residuary worm" ("Heraclitean Fire"). In the final section, the paradoxes of confessing the flesh in "The Wreck" and "Caradoc's Soliloquy" are compared. Foucault's analysis of how "docile bodies" are produced in a disciplinary society is central to the argument and is juxtaposed with the writings of Newman and Hopkins's Jesuit contemporaries. Whether Hopkins is annotating his Bible, taking notes from Rev. Henry Liddon's lectures on Corinthians, or delivering a homily on the Incarnation, he pays particular attention to what it means to be "τῇ σαρκί {in the flesh}, physically" and metaphorically (*CW* 5:91). It is the corruptibility of the human condition writ large; the flesh leads the soul astray and, most hazardously, seems to have a mind of its own. To recover the Victorians' complex relations with their "flesh filled" (*PW* 181) lives, the discussion ranges from early Christian teachings and medieval legend to headlines from the *Times* in 1875. Religious warnings, cultural prohibitions, and medical treatises, all of which contribute to the era's "robust power structures" (*WDTT* 26), are interwoven with Hopkins's poetry to tell the flesh's story.

Chapter 4, "Professing the Flesh," suggests that there are three other crucial contexts in which to consider Hopkins's poetry: the aestheticization of the flesh practiced by members of the Pre-Raphaelite "Fleshly School"; the sensationalization of the flesh produced by the Pre-Raphaelites' harshest critic; and the centrality of the flesh in the emergence of what became known as decadent discourse. The chapter's analyses are necessarily intermedial: the concentration on somatic materiality was shared equally among poets, prose writers, and visual artists such as Dante Gabriel Rossetti, John Everett Millais (both much admired by Hopkins), and Simeon Solomon (to whom Hopkins was introduced in 1868). The chapter begins with a discussion of Robert Buchanan's excoriating critique entitled "The Fleshly School of Poetry" (1871), then considers how Hopkins is variously indebted to or shares affinities with Buchanan's main targets: the works of D. G. Rossetti and A. C. Swinburne. The writings of Hopkins and Walter Pater are then compared. The Brasenose don willingly embraced the potential of decadence; the Jesuit priest no doubt thought he was doing otherwise. The two ways in which Pater anticipates Foucault, by suggesting that "nothing can be rightly known except relatively" and that numerous discourses, institutions, and historical circumstances produce the "conditions" of possibility for the constitution of the subject, are also explored.

Throughout the discussion, the function of the "strange" and grotesque, the "dangerous" aspects of aesthetic appreciation, and the frisson of the corpse resonate. I also consider how the male body in Pater's writings becomes aesthetic spectacle, object of desire, and, in James Eli Adams's phrase, a "medium of understanding." The complexities of Hopkins's textual responsiveness to masculine beauty are carefully assessed.

The conclusion is organized according to the notion of comfort. The counterpoising energy of comfort/desolation is outlined in Hopkins's major poems: how the paradigm functions as both a motive for confessing, in the broadest sense of the word, and a respite from the flesh. As Hopkins's speaker enjoins, "[L]eave comfort root-room" (*PW* 186). The appendix summarizes events and publications concerning Catholicism and Ritualism from 1796 to 1898.

"EXTREME CASES IN THEIR OWN KIND"

Given this project's subject matter, the range of theological treatises and commentaries, spiritual writings, and lectures consulted (some, at the Collège de France) will not be a surprise. But also featured are works of fiction and poetry, paintings, polemical pamphlets, and *Punch* cartoons. Throughout the discussion, analyses of Hopkins's poetry, sermons, letters, diaries, and journal entries will be included. This is not to suggest that the personal writings offer a different "proof" of the poetic discourse or provide a greater truth, but for Hopkins, textual experience is paramount, whether registering observations, testing metaphors, rehearsing ideas, measuring counterarguments. Spiritual responsiveness, however, is always more important than doctrinal qualification. Just as he discerns inscape and instress[50] *before* he learns that Duns Scotus had put a name to "this-ness" (*haecceitas*), Hopkins is always exploring, firsthand, the affective as well as intellectual dimensions of religious belief.

For all that I consider the many centripetal and centrifugal forces exerting pressure on Hopkins, I also want to explore the "counter-conduct" elements of his life and writings.[51] To some degree he is, in John Stuart Mill's sense of the word, eccentric. "In this age," Mill declares in *On Liberty* (1859), "the mere example of non-conformity, the mere refusal to bend the knee to custom, is itself a service. Precisely because the tyranny of opinion is such as to make eccentricity a reproach, it is desirable, in order to break through the tyranny, that people should be eccentric. . . . That so few now dare to be eccentric, marks the chief danger of the time" (269). Hopkins does not hesitate to challenge university instructors when an intellectual argument is at stake; to go against religious advisers, parents, friends, and the pressures of conformity when he thinks his soul is at risk; to push the limits of rhythm, syntax, and lexicon in his poetry, even when his best friend and fellow poet objects. His conversion to Rome is, at one and the same time, both the ultimate act of submission (to religious discipline, beliefs, and behaviors) and a very Victorian kind of counter-conduct. Hopkins is an experimental poet at a time when European and North American painters and poets are asserting their independence. In an era of extremes (industrialization has resulted in extreme wealth and poverty; women's campaigns for educational and legal equity are met with extreme misogyny; the expansion of the empire is met with extreme resistance, including the Indian Rebellion of 1857 [also known as the Sepoy Mutiny], and the Riel and Métis rebellions in the Canadian west, 1869–70 and 1885), he is more than uncompromising. He is inspired, equally, by the delicate curve of a petal and the whisper of an aspen but also the fiercest of storms. Christ's extreme suffering is, for Hopkins, the apotheosis of self-sacrifice; his religious heroes are martyrs tortured unto death. And therein lies the paradox: in personal commitments, aesthetic choices, and religious attachments (including the Society of Jesus), he is an extremist, but theologically he is devoted to orthodoxy. In an 1864 letter to Baillie in which he considers the differences between "Parnassian" and "Olympian" poetry, Hopkins pauses to consider the characteristics of "moderate men": "I assure you," he insists, "Dr. Newman, the extremest of the extreme, so extreme that he went beyond the extremes of that standard and took a large fraction of his side with him, is a MODERATE MAN" (*CW* 1:71). The emphatic capital letters suggest an underlying admiration for "the extremest."[52]

By restoring the body to Hopkins—a writer whose readers have sometimes *dis*embodied him, construing him as someone above or somehow removed from the full range of tensions, demands, desires, and perturbations of the flesh—I hope to provide new possibilities of reading.

This Foucauldian, feminist study of "confessing the flesh" as it animates Hopkins's writings is an intervention into the ways that the texts, and the life, have been typically discussed. No knowledge of Christian or Catholic tenets is presumed; no shared faith commitments are required. Instead, I assemble representative examples of the discourses that "mak[e] the man and what / The man within that makes" (*PW* 160) and demonstrate what truths emerge from the texts once they are no longer obliged to confirm a reader's religious investments. In that respect, the argument is not so much corrective as recuperative.

1

HISTORICAL INVESTMENTS

My soul needs this.
—HOPKINS, "To R. B."

BUT WHAT *IS* CONFESSION, EXACTLY—and what is the story about the box? The sacrament of penance, known more familiarly as confession, is a four-part process requiring the examination of one's conscience, the articulation of sins, the priest's absolution (never automatic), and a penance gauged to the severity of the sins. In the words of Karl Rahner and Herbert Vorgrimler, "The repentant sinner has the guilt of those sins... committed *after* baptism *blotted out* by the Church through the absolution which the priest pronounces by the authority of Christ" (370–71). One's sacramental ambition is nothing less than salvation; to realize that goal, one accepts a three-fold "obligation": "the obligation of regular confession, the obligation of continuity [one must express every sin committed since at least the previous confession], and the obligation of exhaustiveness."[1] Extremes of guilt and submission are involved, an ethics of self that stresses purity, control, and a commitment to eternity. One may believe, with Rahner and Vorgrimler, that by this sacrament "damnation is averted and deliverance to the power of the devil rescinded" (371). One could also acknowledge that the "operation of penance," in Foucault's terms, makes possible "the continual management of souls, conducts," and bodies (*Ab* 184). As an individual Christian, Hopkins wants to be managed; as a priest, he manages the souls and lives of "Jessy or Jack," bugler boy or dying farrier, with equally insistent fervor.

The central drama inside the confessional is a verbal exchange—part instruction, part inquisition, part revelation—between an ordained Roman Catholic priest and a penitent. For the truly contrite, it is nothing short of a mini-miracle: their sins, however grievous, are expunged. When a penitential Hopkins kneels behind the wooden door or heavy curtain, or when Fr. Hopkins slides back the panel covering the screen between himself and the parishioner, what transpires? In Hopkins's day, the ritualized conversation unfolds as follows (quoting from the dictionary coedited by a friend from his Oxford days and a Dublin colleague[2]):

> The penitent, kneeling[,] ... says, "Pray, Father, bless me, for I have sinned." The priest gives the blessing prescribed in the Roman Ritual. "The Lord be in thy heart and on thy lips, that thou mayest truly and humbly confess thy sins, in the Name of the Father, and of the Son, and of the Holy Ghost." The penitent then recites the first part of the Confiteor,[3] enumerates the sins of which he has been guilty since his last confession, and then adds, "For these and all my other sins which I cannot now remember I am heartily sorry; I purpose amendment for the future, and most humbly ask pardon of God, and penance and absolution from you, my spiritual Father." (Addis and Arnold 207)[4]

All Catholics must go to confession at least once a year, before Easter, and whenever needed before taking Holy Communion. For someone who confesses frequently, the list of sins might be reasonably short. If necessary, however, "the Confessor will teach the penitent how to examine his conscience, so as to recall all his sins and their circumstances, going through his whole life, first dividing it by age, childhood, youth &c. then by his various conditions, before and since marriage &c. then by circumstances, such as prosperity, adversity, health or sickness, employments, society, places, &c. examining under each head wherein he sinned, in thought, word or deed. He should also teach the necessary conditions which are involved in a good Confession, putting them as briefly and simply as possible" (Gaume

150–51). These instructions are taken from the famous *Manual for Confessors* produced by Abbé Jean-Joseph Gaume (1854) and edited and translated by Hopkins's Anglican confessor, Edward Pusey. According to Gaume, the emotions one should experience during the process of "reconciliation" are fear (the very condition of one's soul is at stake) and sorrow (for having offended God); humility is the bass note of the experience (149). Yes, it is very formulaic—but there can be comfort in repetition (as a performance) and one's membership in a faith community is reaffirmed.[5]

This chapter prepares the ground for Hopkins's own confessional activities by exploring how a practice generally recommended in the Old and New Testaments was institutionalized as a sacrament of the Catholic Church and why a seventeenth-century innovation, the confessional, is best understood as a Foucauldian heterotopia, a property of language or an actual site that can detach cultural codes from their relations of power by making visible the contingency and variability of accepted truths. Whereas utopias provide "consolation" through idealizing fabula, heterotopias unsettle the grounds of such myths, "desiccate speech, stop words in their tracks" (Foucault, *Order* xviii, 10); they are the spaces or sites that interrogate all others (*EWF* 2:179). Metaphors most closely associated with confession—drawn from scientific, judicial, and economic discourses—will be examined, and their impact on Hopkins's texts assessed. Catholic confessions are auricular, yet sketching the textual genealogy of confessing the flesh will be my focus, from the tradition of penitential Psalms to priests' manuals, from Augustine's fusion of life-writing and theodicy to Hopkins's lists of "sins" while an undergraduate and his Jesuit sermons (the recommendations of Ignatius's *Spiritual Exercises* will also be examined). This is not, however, a totalizing history, one that "confirm[s] our present sentiments and strivings"; universalizing claims will be contextualized, not affirmed (Chloë Taylor 6). There will be no suggestion that moral authority and exemplarism have "a *natural* connection to narratives and representations of human persons, both real and fictional."[6] Instead, I will explore the power-knowledge relations that produce Hopkins's most intimate fears and "the roll, the rise, the carol" of his texts.

Throughout the chapter, I will highlight the ways in which confession has always been a polyvalent term in Latin and French (confirmed by St. Augustine, who establishes a rhetorical dexterity that is emulated for seventeen centuries). There is the confession of sins, *confessio peccatorum*, the predominant usage by the Victorian era, but also the confession/profession of faith, *confessio fidei* (typically translated as "avowal" in English), and the confession of praise, *confessio laudis*, such as one finds in the Jesuit motto *Ad majorem Dei gloriam* (*AMDG*), "for the greater glory of God." Hopkins captures all three meanings in the unfinished lyric "Margaret Clitheroe," when the English martyr (1556–86), who is about to be pressed to death for not disclosing priests' whereabouts, salutes "The Immortals of the eternal ring, / The Utterer, Utterèd, and Uttering" (*PW* 137).

Truth claims are at the heart of all three types of utterance. As Foucault suggests, the "duty of truth, as belief and as a confession, is at the center of Christianity" (*HS* 4:320). Also central is the "cost of enunciation" (*WDTT* 15), because through the "verbal act ... the subject affirms who he is, binds himself to this truth, ... and modifies at the same time his relationship to himself" (17). Power relations not only operate externally, but also internally. The speaker of "The Wreck," for example, accepts the necessity and the pleasure of submitting to God's will, but without considering that acceptance and duty are also elements of subjugation. The "truth" of the Christian self is only possible "insofar as one is capable of sacrificing oneself" (*WDTT* 112), a commitment some find blessed and others deem repugnant.

"WORDING IT HOW"?

Of the five keywords informing this chapter—concupiscence, conscience, guilt, shame, and scruples—the first was defined in the introduction ("coveting carnal things," *OED*), and the last two will be discussed, in relation to obedience and its punitive implications, in the chapter's final segment. All five terms contribute to what Maureen Moran defines as "Catholic pessimism about human nature, particularly in its bodily and material manifestations ... rooted in a preoccupation with Original Sin and the resulting propensity in humanity to evil" ("Lovely" 70). Newman and Hopkins certainly share such a pessimism. Hopkins's is intensified by his exposure to the spirituality defined by Jan Roothaan, S.J., "who was superior general of the Jesuits for twenty-one years (1832–53) and had an enormous influence on all aspects of Jesuit life," including the men's "understanding and practice of the *Spiritual Exercises*" (*CW* 5:24), because they used Roothaan's Latin translation of the Spanish text, and also his guidebook, *The Study and Use of the Spiritual Exercises*. As Noel Barber, S.J., summarizes, Roothaan's "stultifying literalism" as a commentator combined with his "austere asceticism" produced a daunting legacy: a "pessimistic theology of the human person" that also "failed to reflect Jesuit spirituality in its full richness" (*CW* 5:25). In Roothaan's writings, Barber concludes, there is "a perceived clash between [human] nature and grace that could well be termed puritanical" (*CW* 5:25). Hopkins's poetry is often animated by such clashes.

As the speaker of "The Candle Indoors" insists, any discussion of self-scrutiny or sacramental dispensation should focus on conscience. That profound *syneidesis*, or "knowing-with," which "originated in [ancient] Greek philosophy's identification of the experience of self-awareness in the forming of moral judgments," mandates that people "evaluate the moral worth of their behaviour in the light of their beliefs" (Mahoney, S.J. 184–85). In Pauline usage, *syneidesis* is understood both collectively and in a very "personal sense, that of the will or the moral personality, the centre of the soul where choices are worked out and responsibilities are undertaken" (Mahoney, S.J. 185–86). Several kinds of judgment are involved, according to Thomas Aquinas, "'for conscience is said to witness, to bind, or to incite, and also to accuse, torment, or rebuke.'"[7] Thus the fear and the *necessity* of being, in the words of Hopkins's speaker, "cast by conscience out" (*PW* 158). The fact that this penultimate, abject phrase appears in question form in "The Candle Indoors" (1879)—"Are you that liar / And, cast by conscience out, spendsavour salt?"—only highlights the risks involved in alienating the self from the self in order to "mend" the "close heart's vault" (*PW* 158).

Six years before "The Candle Indoors," Hopkins was immersed in Newman's *An Essay in Aid of a Grammar of Assent* (1870), in which conscience plays a crucial but not unexpected role.[8] Conscience is Newman's "first principle," a "connecting principle between the creature and his Creator," he explains, "and the first hold of theological truths is gained by habits of personal religion. When men begin all their works with the thought of God, acting for His sake, and to fulfill His will . . . they will find everything that happens tends to confirm them in the truths about Him which live in their imagination, varied and unearthly as those truths may be" (Newman, *Grammar* 105, 117). More succinctly, the conscience is where, and how, one finds God: "He who has once detected in his conscience the outline of a Lawgiver and Judge, needs no definition of Him" (315). It is thus a "means of knowledge" and a reason for remaining vigilantly fearful ("where conscience is, fear must be" [390, 426]). Assent, appropriately, produces the "self-approving glow of conscience," the light by which one checks thoughts, desires, and behaviors (204). Conscience "teaches us, not only that God is, but what He is; it provides for the mind a real image of Him, as a medium of worship; it gives us a rule of right and wrong, as being His rule, and a code of moral duties. Moreover, it is so constituted that, if obeyed, it becomes clearer in its injunctions, and wider in their range, and corrects and completes the accidental feebleness of its initial teachings. Conscience, then, considered as our guide, is fully furnished for its office" (390). Newman sometimes uses the Wordsworthian term "intimations" to convey the operations of one's conscience, but the metaphor of the voice—"that conscience is the voice of God has almost grown into a proverb" (122)—is more imaginatively resourceful. According to Newman, conscience "does not repose on itself, but . . . reaches forward to something beyond self, and dimly discerns a sanction higher than self for its decisions. . . . And hence it is that we are accustomed to speak of conscience as a voice, . . . and moreover a voice, *or the echo of a voice,* imperative and constraining, like no other dictate in the whole of our experience" (107; my emphasis). According to Hopkins's "The Leaden Echo and the Golden Echo," conscience is an ongoing dialogue in which the sinful self, always too close to "Despair, despair, despair, despair," is counseled by a golden, imperative voice ("Spáre!") that reorients the subject "yonder," "back to God beauty's self and beauty's giver" (*PW* 170).

The conscience teaches one to fear because of guilt, which is aptly defined by Ambrose St. John as one of two "bitter fruits . . . produced in the soul by sin: first, *Guilt,* which deprives us of grace and the friendship of God; and second, *Its Penalty,* which forbids us the enjoyment of God in Paradise. . . . Guilt, together with the eternal penalty of sin, is entirely remitted to us by means of the infinite merits of Jesus Christ in the Sacrament of Penance."[9] St. John, Newman's foremost companion and Hopkins's colleague,

1867–68, at the Birmingham Oratory, is using guilt to underscore the need for prayers and other "indulgences" for the souls of those in Purgatory. Here on earth, guilt—an unflinching Old English word—entails delinquency, offense, failure of duty (to God, theologically), and culpability. Hopkins absorbs an obsession with sin and guilt from Liddon's lectures, which he attended; the Tractarian pamphlets he read; and, as a Jesuit in training, from sources such as Thomas à Kempis's *The Imitation of Christ* and Alphonsus Rodriguez, S.J.'s *The Practice and Perfection of Christian Virtues*, "which were part of the daily reading during his novitiate (1868–70)" (*CW* 5:26). "We are all guilty" of ingratitude to God, Hopkins stresses in his sermons (5:189)—all humans except the "Bd. Virgin," because of the grace of her immaculate conception (5:239).[10] In Hopkins's August 1880 retreat notes, guilt is experienced as an integral part of his "pitch":

> I find myself both as man and as myself something ~~to me~~ most determined and distinctive, at pitch, more distinctive and higher pitched than anything else I see; I find myself with my pleasures and pains, my ~~faculties~~ ^powers^ and ^my^ experiences, my deserts and guilt, my shame and sense of ~~honour~~ ^beauty^, my dangers, hopes, fears, and all my fate, more important to myself than anything I see.... Nothing else in nature comes near this unspeakable stress of pitch, distinctiveness, and selving, this selfbeing of my own: nothing explains it or resembles it, except so far as this, that other men to themselves have the same feeling. (5:348–49)

When one stresses the place of guilt in the "development, refinement, condensation" (5:349) of Hopkins's self-formulation, its toxicity is all the more vivid. Later in the same meditation he refines the definition of "my self": "[A]bove all my shame, my guilt, my fate are the very things in feeling, in tasting, which I most taste that selftaste which nothing in the world can match. The universal cannot taste this taste of self as I taste it, for it is not to it, let us say / to him, that the guilt or shame, the fatal consequence, the fate, comes home" (5:352).[11] Small wonder that the speaker of "No worst" is "pitched past pitch of grief" (*PW* 182). As Hopkins's "Meditation on Hell" emphasizes, "All will be punished according to their guilt, according to their knowledge and their power; there are light pains and heavy pains, many stripes and few" (*CW* 5:530). (Those stripes of corporeal punishment—mortification, literally and figuratively—will be discussed at length in chapter 3.)

For the Church, guilt and confession occupy a kind of Möbius strip (an 1858 discovery): seemingly two different sides of human existence but actually only one. In Peter Brooks's assessment, "The more you confess, the more guilt is produced. The more the guilt produced, the more the confessional machine functions.... As a speech act, 'I confess' implies and necessitates guilt, and if the guilt is not there in the referent, as an object of cognition, it is in the speech-act itself, which simultaneously exonerates and inculpates" (22). Hopkins's texts reveal the burdens of excessive inculpation only occasionally relieved by divine or personal exoneration.

"MYSELF UNHOLY": EXTREMES OF SIN

Repentance involves contrite thoughts—the ability to distinguish among "ignorance, inadvertence, carelessness,... contempt" (Mahoney, S.J. 8)—and contrite actions. Centuries-old theories of human agency and freedom are implicated, as well as cultural and religious practices of shaming and retribution. Repentance and confession have complex private and public "characters," as I shall suggest; both are concerned with the "interplay of licit and illicit" (*HS* 1:85), that "traditional preoccupation" (Mahoney, S.J. viii) with evil and transgression known familiarly as sin. One of the Hebrew words used most frequently in the Septuagint to designate sin "literally means 'twisted'" (*HS* 1:137), a term with manifold metaphorical possibilities. The common English translation, *iniquity*, just doesn't have the same figurative charisma. Put another way, sin poises the believer at the harrowing interstices of subjugation and punishment; its immorality obtains to that which is thought, committed, or omitted.[12] Historians of moral theology explain that a "radical relocation of sin within" humankind was effected in the Middle Ages; Peter Abelard, to name just one famous theorist, overturned "earlier conceptions in which a more external definition of guilt was the norm," emphasizing instead mental and emotional "agreeing-to-sin"—the intentions *prior to* actions (Hahn 30). Perhaps Abelard had turned to the New Testament for written sanction—to Mark, for example, who features Christ rebuking the Pharisees as follows: "That which cometh out of the man, that defileth the man. For from within, out of the heart of men, proceed *evil thoughts,* adulteries, fornications, murders, thefts, covetousness, wickedness, deceit, lasciviousness, an evil eye, blasphemy, pride, foolishness: All these evil things come from within, and defile the man" (Mark 7:20–23; my emphasis). Mark's gospel, like so many Christian writings, not only anatomizes sin but provides a primer for its rhetorical elaboration. Throughout his Oxford diaries (1863–67), Hopkins notes his "evil thoughts" and repeatedly faults himself for every "foolishness" and occasion of pride as well as the "wickedness" resulting from concupiscence.

For the faithful, sin is both burden and threat—the threat of damnation: "There is a Righteous GOD Who sends the good to Paradise, and the evil to Hell" (Gaume 148). Death, in these circumstances, is not the worst thing imaginable: it is merely a prelude to eternal suffering. The Catholic Church teaches that there are two kinds of sin, "mortal" (seven "deadly" sins in all, the three greatest of which are "murder, idolatry, and adultery"[13]) and "venial" or minor infractions. Mortal sins, if unconfessed at the time of death, result in an infernal perpetuity; venial sins would mean a season in Purgatory, where one's soul is eventually freed from sin. Confession, one could argue, sacramentalizes human failure: predicts it, tolerates it, accommodates it, relieves it. As Julia Saville observes, a number of Hopkins's undergraduate lyrics, such as "My prayers must meet a brazen heaven" and *"Nondum,"* stage "a confrontation with failure that seems irremediable. They function to keep at bay the moment when the speaker relinquishes his desire in the silence that is death" (*Queer* 51). The "long success of sin" (*PW* 83) is imagined as "Battling with God" (twenty years before another Hopkins speaker wrestles "with [my God!] my God") (*PW* 83, 183). Rather than thriving, the speakers "move along life's tombdecked way," starving on "sin's wages" (*PW* 93, 26). Morris, S.J.'s guide for Jesuit novices recommends an ethos of everyday extremism because of sin, a "confession and communion made as though they were our last," and an "admirable plan" whereby you "set aside one day in each month for special recollection and preparation for death" (Morris, S.J. 64). Gaume concurs; his manual includes a telling anecdote about St. Philip Neri (for whom the Oratorian confederation, including Newman's community, was named), who "once cured a dissolute youth by gently requiring him to say a prayer seven times a day, kissing the ground, and saying, 'To-morrow I may be a dead man'" (Gaume 320). Hopkins endorses such sentiments in his notes regarding "the comforts of death": knowing that our "need is sorest" when dying, God provides in the "last sacraments" of penance, "Extreme Unction, and the Holy Communion" to give "the grace of contrition, and holy hope" (*CW* 5:535). And of these sacraments, penance is "the most necessary" (*CW* 5:535).

Vigilance about sin is vital because, after all, the devil is always waiting, ready to misdirect one's thoughts. Pusey makes this point when promoting regular confession: it is necessary because sinning becomes customary—too often, one is dealing with "the case of an inured or habitual or besetting sin" (Gaume cliii)—and Satan never tires in his quest: "The devil may 'depart from' those who have been his slaves 'for a season,' to renew his attack, if they should become self-confident. Our Lord tells us, that he is watching his opportunity to return" (cliv).

Both Augustine and Aquinas return to the "classical concept of *ordo*, or the divine order of all things" to distinguish between the mere *matter* of the sin and the "moral disorder of these acts which gives them the character of sin" (Mahoney, S.J., *Making* 67). St. Thomas calls this order "the *form* of the sin" (Dailey, S.J. 141). Chaos as signifier is prevalent throughout Hopkins's writings, from the intimations of a disordered psyche in "A soliloquy of one of the spies left in the wilderness" to the unruly Dublin notebook into which he tumbled verse, academic work, scholarly notes, and quotidian memoranda. In Ireland poems such as "Spelt from Sibyl's Leaves" and "That Nature is a Heraclitean Fire" both the *matter* of the text and the *form* become more and more "unbound" as the speaker succumbs to sinful, "dragonish" thoughts (*PW* 191). Only in "Heraclitean Fire" are the ties that bind restored.

Two further comments about sin and penitential rites help to contextualize Hopkins's abiding concerns—and fears. Sin is not only extreme, it is temporal, in that past sins overshadow the present and threaten one's ultimate future, but atemporal in that the sacrament of penance resets the clock, promises a new beginning. The sacrament has "two principal results," according to Gaume: "sanctifying grace which effaces past sin and justifies the sinner; and sacramental grace which acts as a preservative for the future, giving powerful helps against further falls" (Gaume 286). What

Gaume does not consider fully is the second point: because of confession, the individual "has the duty to explore who he is, what is happening within himself[,] ... and to tell these things to other people, and thus to bear witness against himself" (*EWF* 1:178).[14] Some are appalled by such an idea; Hopkins would retort, "[M]y soul needs this" (*PW* 204).

"IF YOU SEE THE FORCE OF THE METAPHOR"

Complementing the order/disorder antinomy that defines the power of confession are the plethora of suggestive metaphors promulgated by biblical writers and patristic commentators and revisited by Hopkins time and again.[15] The goal is to make the noumenal and its mysterious operations seem concrete, imaginable. Isaiah, for example, establishes the use of natural metaphors: "I have blotted out, as a thick cloud, thy transgressions, and, as a cloud, thy sins: return unto me; for I have redeemed thee" (44:22); "though your sins be as scarlet, they shall be as white as snow; though they be red like crimson, they shall be as wool" (1:18). Revelation is both more dramatic and personal, preferring the binding/unloosening trope: Christ "loosed us from our sins by His blood" (1:5). For the purposes of this project, four major metaphorical clusters will be mentioned, emerging from pastoral, legal, economic, and medical-scientific discourses. In each, penitential justification is suggestively proffered. Metaphor, one should remember, not only illuminates through imaginative comparison, it classifies, imposes or reinscribes hierarchies, and articulates historically embedded and specific ideologies of gender, class, nation, and race.

The New Testament is replete with "good shepherd" analogies for Christ; Catholic iconography celebrates the Lamb of God, who takes away the sins of the world.[16] Therefore references to a "godless flock" and its "bitterness of sin" do not surprise us in an 1864 Hopkins poem (*PW* 31), nor the severe division of sinner and saved into "two flocks, two folds" in a text first drafted in 1884. Priest and laity alike are schooled in such pastoral images. Patristic writers, however, tended to eschew such homely figures, preferring instead the more imposing register of judicial discourse. As Mahoney, S.J., observes, biblical "court-of-law imagery" was "developed further and systematized theologically to become enshrined in due course in the 'sacred tribunal' teaching of the Council of Trent on confession" (14).[17] Gaume provides two examples of this usage: "If disinterestedness is necessary to a secular judge, how much more to the Confessor who is a judge of consciences" (Gaume 95); while serving as confessor, "the priest is not merely the minister of Christ as in all the other Sacraments, but a real judge appointed by the Saviour with power to bind and loose" (Gaume 359–60). Interestingly, it is in the undergraduate poem "*Summa*" that Hopkins baldly refers to sin as the "sordidness of care and crime" (*PW* 94). "In the Valley of the Elwy" features a reference to God as the "lover of souls, swáying considerate scales" (*PW* 143); the unfinished lyric "The times are nightfall" concludes with the speaker's self-admonishment to work in "your world within. / There rid the dragons, root out there the sin. / Your will is law in that small commonweal" (*PW* 176). Yet these are hardly the dominant phrases or poems within the Hopkins canon. Similarly, despite the beauty of Christ's "unchancelling poising palms ... weighing the worth" of souls in "The Wreck of the Deutschland," economic references are infrequently deployed. In "*Angelus ad Virginem*" Gabriel informs the "gentle maiden" Mary, "Lost mánkind shall be bought / By thy sweet childbearing" (*PW* 168), but Hopkins underplays the dire Pauline lesson that "the wages of sin is death" (Rom. 6:23).

Medical discourse, on the other hand, energizes numerous texts, a function of three factors at least: the example of Christ's ministry; the extent to which the "traditional theme of healing" is characteristic of penitential literature (Mahoney, S.J. 13); and the cultural predominance of medical discourse in mid-Victorian England. The widely read Penitential of Columban, for example, stresses the need to be "cleansed" from the "interior vices and sickness of an ailing soul before the union of true peace and the bond of eternal salvation" (Mahoney, S.J. 13). Apparently even Martin Luther, no longer a Roman Catholic, spoke favorably about confession in those terms: "'I would not wish it to cease; rather, I rejoice that it exists ... for it is a singular medicine for afflicted consciences'" (Bossy 26). Gaume often refers to "foul sins" as "impurities" or "spiritual sores": just as those "whose duty takes them among infectious illnesses, are wont to carry some disinfectant about them, so should confessors have holy thoughts at hand to disperse the painful impressions caused by what they are constrained to hear" (Gaume 307, 386).[18] Typically, however, Hopkins stresses the disabling effects of sin-as-disease. Consider the speaker of "The Alchemist in the City," who laments, "Yet it is now too late to heal / The incapable and cumbrous shame / Which makes me when with men I deal / More powerless than the blind or lame" (*PW* 76).[19] Minds and bodies are too often "havoc-pocked" by the "corruption" of sin that was and is "the world's first woe" (*PW* 192). Why is patience such a "hard thing," according to Hopkins? Because, paradoxically, it "wants wounds"—both in the sense of needing to overcome them, as manifestations of the "rebellious wills" that "bruise" our hearts, and by virtue of being without such afflictions (*PW* 185). Such a medicinal approach avidly yet negatively reifies the Victorian code of *mens sana in corpore sano* (a healthy mind in a healthy body). Fixing the textual gaze on what St. Paul terms the "infirmity of [one's] flesh" (Rom. 6:19) has the effect, in Hopkins's writing, of turning any poem, letter, or journal entry into a textual infirmary.

In an era of widespread industrialization, the "Great Stink" of London (summer 1858), and miasma theories of contagion, it is not surprising that metaphors of pollution are common. Gaume, for example, defines sin in terms of "polluting vices" (Gaume 304). Hopkins frequently links a physical world in which "rack or wrong" are creating havoc ("Ribblesdale") to the state of human souls, increasingly "treacherous the tainting" of them. Post-Freud, some commentators discuss confession in terms of therapy, consolation, and cure; Foucault posits instead that such a view encouraged people, in the later nineteenth century, to categorize sexual "sins" as a kind of "sexual morbidity," a new classification in which "instincts, tendencies, . . . pleasure, and conduct" were inscribed within an "unstable pathological field" (*HS* 1:67). And if a person is "susceptible to pathological processes," the response is "therapeutic or normalizing interventions" (1:68). Whether one argues that confession normalizes or transforms ("it exonerates, redeems, and purifies," unburdens, liberates, and promises salvation [1:62]), one is better placed to judge if familiar with how, and when, the sacrament of penance was fully institutionalized.

HISTORY LESSONS

"Reading history is very laborious to me," Hopkins confided to Dixon in June 1883; "I can only digest ~~and~~ ^or^ remember a little at a time" (*CW* 2:581). This chapter's history lesson is delivered as succinctly as possible. Three predominant issues in the emergence of the penitential sacrament have a direct bearing on Hopkins's life and writings: the authority of the Church and the individual priest; the degree of absolution obtained; and the validity of public or private confessional practices. Also crucial: the shift from acknowledging sin (specific acts) to naming each person a *sinner,* someone whose very thoughts and desires, as well as actions, must be constantly examined and monitored (*WDTT* 148). "I believe that this moment," this paradigmatic shift, Foucault states, "marked the birth of what we might call a hermeneutics of the self in the Western world. A hermeneutics of the self whose primary object... was the *cogitatio, ira qualitas,* and its *origo:* thought, [its] quality, and its origin" (*WDTT* 148–49). Newman's sermons certainly substantiate this claim. In the homily entitled "Secret Faults," for example, Newman stresses the need "to obtain a correct knowledge" of oneself:

> Self-knowledge is at the root of all real religious knowledge; and it is in vain,—worse than vain,—it is a deceit and a mischief, to think to understand the Christian doctrines as a matter of course, merely by being taught by books, or by attending sermons, or by any outward means, however excellent, taken by themselves. For it is in proportion as we search our hearts and understand our own nature, that we understand what is meant by an Infinite Governor and Judge; in proportion as we comprehend the nature of disobedience and our actual sinfulness, that we feel what is the blessing of the removal of sin, redemption, pardon, sanctification, which otherwise are mere words. God speaks to us primarily in our hearts. (*Parochial* 1:42–43)

Yet, what Newman terms "our own nature," one could also understand as the hegemonic truths one has naturalized.

The earliest Christian intellectuals, dedicated to interpreting holy writ, establishing dogma, codifying sacraments, and theorizing the individual's relationship to the divine, had as crucial points of reference classical authors' treatises on codes of conduct and the "veridiction of the self" (*WDTT* 103). Augustine quotes and paraphrases Plato, Cicero, and especially Plotinus; John Chrysostom—whose masterful sermons were a staple of Hopkins's homiletic training[20]—cites Pythagoras (*HS* 4:70). As Chloë Taylor summarizes, self-examination in ancient Greece and Rome relied upon "relatively simple techniques based on an un-complex conception of the self. They involved discipline but in the form of rationally chosen and cultivated self-discipline, however culturally circumscribed the notion of the good life (and who had access to it) entailed may have been" (16). Seneca, for example, in book 3 of *De ira,* "offers the example of another type of examination: the one that he conducts every evening, before going to sleep. . . . Here the judicial model is present (and no longer the medical one). . . . But it should be noted that this inquiry doesn't lead to condemnation or punishment or remorse" (*HS* 4:83).[21] Epicureans "had a very strict and hierarchical organization in which those . . . who were directors for the youngest among them . . . carried the name of *hēgemones:* they were the ones who guided" (*WDTT* 130).

The authority of penitential rites in Christianity developed slowly, however, and not without controversy. In the early church, there were "three forms of voluntary confession in more or less frequent use—confession to God, to the congregation gathered in the church, and to a priest or some other holy man. St. Ambrose supplies us with evidence of them all" (Lea 178). When Christianity was "confined to zealous and selective communities," there was "little need for ritualized penance. As the community grew, however, a method was required for 'restoring sinners' who strayed" (Chloë Taylor 18). Two quite different mechanisms emerged. The first was what the Greek writers termed *exagoreusis:* based on contemplation and obedience, one underwent a permanent or constant verbalization of one's thoughts and sins to a spiritual director (a major feature of monastic life). The second practice, *exomologesis,* championed by Tertullian in chapters 9 and 10 of *De paenitentia,* was a "radical departure from the ancient self-examination" because in *exomologesis* the self "whose truth is made manifest is thus simultaneously destroyed, and a new, purified self is in the process of being born" (Chloë Taylor 19). ("Destroyed" sounds almost melodramatic, but the insistence that one must die, metaphorically, in order to be reborn as God's truly deserving servant is a recurring theme in the New Testament—Romans 6:4–8, for example, or John 3:3–7). *Exomologesis* also instilled, in Foucault's view, an acute sense of fear, something that Tertullian stresses: this "need for 'fear'... in the very life of the Christian," not just the fear of God's wrath but "the fear of oneself," the self always susceptible to sinning anew and thus committed to self-surveillance (*HS* 4:44).[22]

Intense debates among notable Christians focused on the relationship between confession and baptism, a foundational sacrament of purification based on Christ's life (and the actions of John the Baptist as reported by Matthew, Mark, and Luke; see also Acts 19:4). Baptism is at one and the same time a "mechanism of forgiveness," a seal of "commitment and belonging," and a promise of regeneration and illumination ("it dispels the darknesses which are both of evil and of ignorance") (*HS* 4:38). From enclaves in the second century CE to Victorian Anglican pulpits, however, people questioned whether the promises of baptism are compromised or nullified by a formal discipline of penitence. At the same time, the human propensity for sin was acknowledged; wholesale rejection of the sinner by the ecclesiastical community was neither humane nor practical (*WDTT* 104).

As Rahner and Vorgrimler summarize, in "Christian antiquity, from the 2nd to the 6th century, the sacrament of penance could be received only once.... Against the heresies of Montanism and Novatianism the ancient Church firmly maintained the principle that she is able to absolve *all* sinners" (373–74). Tertullian, one of the first to refer to a holy Trinity, and the person who introduced a distinctly masculinist emphasis into Christian discourse—the "spiritual combat" against Satan and one's own predilections (*HS* 4:56)—contributes to the "growing place occupied, in the economy of every soul's salvation, by the manifestation of one's own truth" (4:53). Specifically, in *De resurrectione carnis* (the resurrection of the body), he borrows from Paul's epistle to the Romans the analogy of Christ's torment and penance: "the killing of the old self" is repeatedly required; one must "'crucify it so that the body of sin is destroyed'" (4:54)—a paradigm of destruction/rebirth Hopkins utilizes frequently. Most importantly, in *De paenitentia*, Tertullian stresses the need for penitential practices, actions or labors of moral purification (4:45). John Cassian (ca. 360–after 430), author of the *Conferences*, was chief among those who integrated monastic practices of self-examination and ascetic penitential rituals into mainstream Christianity. "Cassian is especially concerned that his monks confess," Karmen MacKendrick explains, "with an eye to minimizing or even eliminating their erotic dreams and 'nocturnal pollutions,' the most hidden, most evidently unwilled, pleasures of the flesh" (43).[23] Like Basil, Cassian stresses that "the purity of the body is a direct consequence of the purity of the soul" (Lorenzini 459).

Celtic missionaries of the sixth century endorsed the practicality of confession, rather than mere contrition: regular penitential rites intensified the moral suasion of their ministries and enabled local priests to control more effectively the administration of God's forgiveness. Often, however, these activities consisted of public confessions to the community.[24] Members of the Council of Châlons, 813, equivocated: they acknowledged the differences between those who advocated that one confess to God alone, and those who believe in confessing to priests. "'Confession made to God purges sin, but that made to the priest teaches how they are to be purged'" (Addis and Arnold 647, citing the Council's canon 33).

Auricular confession was finally institutionalized in 1215, when the Fourth Lateran Council, guided by Pope Innocent III, "imposed on the whole Church the obligation of what is popularly known today as 'Easter duties'" (canon 21) (Mahoney, S.J. 17),[25] the need to "make a valid confession once a year if one is consciously guilty of any serious sin" (Rahner and Vorgrimler 372). The "seal" of the confessional to protect penitent and priest alike was also asserted. The proper age of the penitent, however, was not specified by the Lateran Council; local or regional variations resulted in children of twelve, ten, and even seven years being introduced to the sacrament. Charles Borromeo, whose special contribution to penitential rites is discussed below, thought that the age of five was not too young to become indoctrinated (Lea 402). (Augustine had expressed similar thoughts in the *Confessions:* "so tiny a child, so great a sinner."[26]) Also subject to debate: whether "sacramental confession is a divine law or merely a precept of the Church" (Lea 168). Abelard and Bonaventure held the latter position; Aquinas (*Summa Theologica,* Supplement Q 6. Art. 2) and Scotus insisted upon the former, strongly recommending the "intervention" of priests (Chloë Taylor 51). It was left to the Council of Trent (1545–46), the signature event of the Counter-Reformation, to settle the matter: the

Council declared that sacramental confession is, in fact, of divine law (Lea 170). Thus, in Foucault's words, "The sacramental armature of penance is explicitly maintained and renewed, and then, within and around penance in the strictest sense, an immense apparatus of discourse and examination, of analysis and control, spreads out. . . . Hence the formidable development of the pastoral, that is to say, of the technique offered to the priest for the government of souls" (*Ab* 177). Absolution is now one of the priest's crucial powers; obedience to the Church is inextricably connected.

The "massive proliferation" (Mahoney, S.J. 27) and "institutionalization of regular church confession" during the Middle Ages not only systematized a means of salvation, it produced for the Roman Catholic Church a powerful "instrument of discipline" (Hahn 34, 32).[27] As Mahoney, S.J., admits, auricular confession generated "a preoccupation with sin; a concentration on the individual; and an obsession with law" (27). The Church was also inspired to classify, quantify, and summarize "all possible data" on sin, to the point where the Council of Trent could acknowledge fully "'the species of sin'" and protect the "integrity" of the sacrament by demanding that the penitent search exhaustively all the "'nooks and shadows'" of the conscience (Mahoney, S.J. 19, 31). Put another way, the Church consolidated its ability to define transgressions more rigorously, to probe individual minds more stringently, and to control behaviors with uncompromising strictness. An emphasis on sexual sins, needless to suggest—thoughts *and* actions—was paramount. Thus in 1865, when Liddon insists that Hopkins keep a daily record of his "sins," he is indoctrinating Hopkins into the Council's formidable exercise of pastoral power and redefining how Hopkins "knows" himself.

The sacrament of penance even had its own putative patron saint, Raimundo de Peñafort (Raymond of Penyafort, ca. 1180–1275; beatified, 1542; canonized, 1601), a Dominican canon lawyer whose casebook (1224–26), the *Summa de casibus poenitentiae* (Summary concerning the cases of penance), became *the* authoritative work in which sins and appropriate penances, doctrinal issues, and Church law were synthesized. According to St. Raymond (as summarized by Foucault),

> The confession had to be prompt; it had to be frequent; it had to be bitter, that is, accompanied by tears; it had to be integral; it had to

be voluntary; it had to be faithful, that is, rooted in the faith; it had to be pure, in the sense that it could not be mixed with vanity (one could not be proud of the sins one had committed); it had to be *nuda,* naked, that is, it had to be done face to face; it had to be *morose,* that is, done slowly (one must not ... list one's sins like an accountant would count sums); it had to be accusatory, that is, one had to show how one was guilty; it had to be *propria,* that is, concerned with the self and not with one's neighbor; it had to be true; it had to be discrete, that is, each sin had to be isolated one from the other. (*WDTT* 188–89)[28]

Small wonder that Jesuit theologian John Mahoney, S.J., suggests the Church's teachings target "man in his moral vulnerability; by which is meant not just man in his weakness, but more in his awareness of weakness, his helplessness" (28). Consequently, he argues, the Church was itself "heavily responsible for *increasing* [people's] weakness and moral apprehension, with the strong sense of sin and guilt which it so thoroughly strove to inculcate or reinforce, and the humiliations and punishments with which it drove its message home. The pessimistic anthropology from which it started, and which served inevitably to confirm and reinforce itself[,] ... drove moral theology increasingly to concern itself almost exclusively with the ... insubordinate side of human existence" (Mahoney, S.J. 28).

What are the consequences of this institutional "commitment to spiritual pathology"? The murk of sin "which emanates from the penitential literature and from the vast majority of moral theology manuals is ... profoundly disquieting" (Mahoney, S.J. 28). Certainly, the fact that confession "took for its object" or its primary focus, *sexual* sins, "what was unmentionable but admitted to nonetheless," goes a long way in explaining how the pessimism flourished and the pathology intensified. Hence my underlying argument that Hopkins's rituals of "confessing the flesh" are not "individually determined but historically contingent and culturally embedded" (Buckton 10). Commentators who have framed Hopkins's life and writings in terms of a personal neuroticism have overlooked—refused to contextualize—his beliefs and practices.

"LET ME CONFESS WHAT I KNOW OF MYSELF"

In sixteen centuries of thinking and arguing about auricular confession, a substantial tradition of *writing* about confession has emerged. Four texts will be considered in this section to establish the discursive field to which Hopkins contributes with his poetry, diary entries, sermons, and Jesuit commentaries: the penitential Psalms of the Old Testament, Augustine's *Confessions*, St. Patrick's *Confessions*, and the medieval play *Everyman*. In the subsequent section, I will consider the specific genre developed to bolster the sacrament: the penitential guide or manual.

Of the one hundred and fifty Psalms (traditionally ascribed to King David, but probably written by several people), many are tributes to God ("Sing unto the Lord a new song"); many are lamentations for Israel or the speaker who cries out for remediation ("leave not my soul destitute"). Major themes include the Creator and his creation, the future of Israel, the necessity and burden of the law, and prayers for mercy. "Supplicant" is the speaker's typical subject position. Seven texts, known as the "penitential Psalms," dwell on the tensions between human iniquity and heavenly redemption, despondency and hope, justice and mercy, diseased flesh and godly deliverance, and human vanity and profound contrition. As Hopkins observes in "Pagan and Christian Virtues," an essay written for Walter Pater in 1866–67, "The character and process of humility is exactly explained by a verse in the Penitential Psalms, chosen for use in the acquirement of this and other virtues—For lo, thou requirest truth in the inward parts and shalt make me to understand wisdom secretly" (*CW* 4:226). The language of these Psalms is alternately very direct—"from the voice of my groaning"—and figuratively arresting—"My days have declined as a shadow: and I am withered as grass" (Ps. 101:6, 12). In the Douay-Rheims translation, these special Psalms are numbered 6, 31, 37, 50, 101, 129, 142; in the King James version of the Protestant Bible, they are numbered 6, 32, 38, 51, 102, 130, 143. Having been raised in the music of the latter,[29] Hopkins was probably surprised by the harsher and more vivid tone and imagery of the Douay-Rheims texts. In Psalm 6, KJV, the speaker enjoins, "In the grave who shall give thee thanks?" but the D-R speaker asks, "And in hell who shall confess to thee?" [in inferno autem quis confitebitur tibi?]. In KJV 32, one learns, "Many sorrows shall be to the wicked," but the D-R version, Psalm 31, baldly states, "Many are the scourges of a sinner" [multa flagella peccatoris]. Of course the Vulgate, a late fourteenth-century reworking of St. Jerome's fourth-century translation (confirmed as the official Latin Bible by the Council of Trent), stresses the themes and attitudes then being enshrined in Church teachings. In terms of rhetorical register, the Douay-Rheims penitential Psalms are starker, more punitive. Common to both versions, however, is evocative bird imagery, a sacred symbolic geography ("from the depths," "my life in the earth," and the heaven of salvation), and an overwhelming sense of sorrow. Also contributing to the texts' sense of urgency: a clear distinction between the mere body ("my bones grew old," D-R Ps. 31:3 [inveteraverunt ossa mea]) and the corruptible flesh ("there is no health in my flesh," D-R Ps. 37:8 [non est sanitas in carne mea]), a distinction to which I will return in chapter 3. Also shared: a speaker eager to "flee" to his Lord for deliverance, which Hopkins transfigures in "The Wreck," stanza 3: "And fled with a fling of the heart to the heart of the Host" (*PW* 119).[30]

Augustine of Carthage (354–430) draws upon the wisdom and penitential spirit of the Psalms throughout his writings. The bishop of Hippo is famous for many things, but three stand out for the purposes of this project: his reluctance to become a Christian ("Grant me chastity and continence, but not yet" [*Confs* 145]), his innovative *Confessions* (ca. 398–400), and his gift of metaphor.[31] Hopkins is very aware of all three. In "The Wreck," the speaker contrasts the conversion of St. Paul ("at a crash") and that of "Áustin, a língering-óut swéet skíll" (*PW* 121). Hopkins first records his familiarity with Augustine (*Tractates on the Gospel of John*) while at Oxford (*CW* 5:105). According to the Porter's Log that Hopkins helps to maintain during his novitiate, readings during mealtime in December 1869 include chapters from the *Confessions* (*CW* 5:126); he also learns that Ignatius Loyola "urged that Augustine provided the model for the Society's homiletic conventions" (*CW* 5:43). In a letter to Baillie, late 1879, he states, "I think Boswell [the biographer of Samuel Johnson] is with the exception of St. Austin's Confessions, and some other spiritual ~~books~~ ^works^ the most interesting book I ever read" (*CW* 1:379). References to a range of Augustine's texts inform his 1873–74 lecture notes on poetry (*CW* 6-pt1:320), sermons delivered in December 1879 and May 1881 (*CW* 5:239, 329), a letter to Patmore in December 1883 (*CW* 2:643), and retreat notes made on 5 January 1889 (*CW* 5:567).³² Augustine brilliantly demonstrates how to repurpose biblical figures, such as the eunuchs "who have made themselves eunuchs for the kingdom of heaven" (Matt. 19:12, D-R; *Confs* 25). Augustine admits, "Had I paid careful attention to these sayings and 'become a eunuch for the sake of the kingdom of heaven' (Matt. 19:12), I would have been happier finding fulfilment in your [God's] embraces" (*Confs* 26).³³ Hopkins's speaker ridicules himself as "Time's eunuch" in "Thou art indeed just, Lord" (*PW* 201); he laments, in the January 1889 retreat notes, "I am like a straining eunuch" (*CW* 5:565). Harnessing the force of metaphors is another Augustinian trait. God is wholeness, Augustine states: "You raise us upright. You are not scattered but reassemble us" (*Confs* 4). Hopkins answers with "Spelt from Sibyl's Leaves," in which the scattering seems beyond amelioration. In book 2 of the *Confessions*, Augustine acknowledges, "For you were always with me, mercifully punishing me, touching with a bitter taste all of my illicit pleasures" (*Confs* 25). "I am gall, I am heartburn," Hopkins replies in "I wake and feel": "God's most deep decree / Bitter would have me taste: my taste was me" (*PW* 181). The dialogue with Augustine's texts is ongoing and enriching.

In the *Confessions*, Augustine does what had previously been almost unthinkable, especially for a major religious figure: he uses his own life and intimate thoughts to explore, at length, all three confessional modes: confession of sins, profession of faith, and confession of praise.³⁴ The performance of candor is key: after all, he is the bishop of Hippo at the time that he broadcasts his immorality and recounts his life in self-lacerating terms. Henry Chadwick suggests that the impetus for writing was a "wish to answer critics both inside and outside the Catholic community" and to "come to terms with a past in which numerous enemies and critics showed an unhealthy interest" (xii, xiii). So prompted, Augustine established the possibilities of life-writing for sixteen centuries. He "helped to change the axis of Western thinking about human life," Walter Woods states: "directed its attention to an internal forum, and encouraged further exploration into the nature and effects of personal knowledge, freedom, and love" (184). The layers of self-reflexivity achieved in the text are fascinating: Augustine's narrator creates a personal deity to whom he reports—the most important interlocutor imaginable—but is always mindful of his fourth-century readers[35] and answerable to his own soul (*Confs* 62). Nine of the thirteen chapters are memoir,[36] interlaced with biblical citations, but the sense of immediacy he achieves when narrating how he steals the pears as a boy, how he feels when his son dies, when he converts in Milan,[37] and when his mother, Monica, perishes is outstanding. The *Confessionals* is not just "influential"—it is, for many Christians, determinant, and for those who do not share the bishop's religious commitments, a literary milestone. "Initiated by Augustine," Anne Hartman observes, "assimilated by Protestant journals, secularized by Rousseau, and adapted into contemporary autobiographical narrative—this genre came to produce not only notions of privacy and selfhood but also ideas of publics and communities" (538). Augustine's desires, qualms, and spiritual certainties help to shape Hopkins's, directly and indirectly. What Augustine fears, Hopkins fears; what Augustine tries to formulate about the efficacy of confession—and he does so, long before it is institutionalized in the Church—Hopkins takes for granted.

What impresses, still, is the capaciousness of Augustine's religious imagination. One must remember that he has sources—Plato, Plotinus, Virgil, and, unlike his anti-Semitic peers, the Old and New Testaments—but few complementary doctrinal tracts and tomes to provide guidance. He synthesizes sources effectively and moves with supple purpose from the interactions of mind, body, and soul to, for example, the most recent rebuttals of the Manichees (*Confs* 89). The *Confessions* is quite the assemblage: not only spiritual autobiography, but theological debate, biblical exegesis, polemic, a tribute to his mother, Monica, and a social history. The final four books are more general, faith-based commentaries on memory, time and eternity, Platonic and Christian theories of creation, and the significance of Genesis. God is both beyond the scope of human comprehension yet a felt presence in the narrator's life (the same productive tension between an all-powerful yet tender Being informs "The Wreck," although for Hopkins's speaker, God is the rod of wrath and majesty, and Christ is the suffering Sacrificed lamb). Augustine's God is both personalized ("Your intention was," *Confs* 25) and personified, in terms of his heart, eyes, ears, and his smile (also featured in Hopkins's "My own heart"). Even in Hopkins's inventive "Heraclitean Fire," when "In a flash, at a trumpet clash," the speaker is "all at once what Christ is," he is echoing tropes that Augustine helped to confirm for Christian discourse. If "the images of earth, water, and air are quiescent," Augustine observes, one could still "hear" God's word, and "at that moment we exten[d] our reach and in a flash of mental energy attai[n] the eternal wisdom which abides beyond all things" (*Confs* 172).

It is almost unsettling to recognize the confessional similarities between Augustine and Hopkins. Augustine reminds God, "Here I am climbing up through my mind towards you who are constant above me" (*Confs* 194). Hopkins imagines something more terrifying:

> O the mind, mind has mountains; cliffs of fall
> Frightful, sheer, no-man-fathomed.[38] Hold them cheap
> May who ne'er hung there. (*PW* 182)

They enter into this "innermost citadel" (*Confs* 123) riven with self-loathing in order to create a litany of "sins," including admissions of evil deeds and words (155), shame (19, 29), and consternation because of the deliberate "waste" of time on "follies" (19). They know themselves to be unclean, metaphorically, by their sweat (193; "their sweating selves," *PW* 182). Unlike Hopkins, however, Augustine relishes the "wickedness": "I had no motive for my wickedness except wickedness itself. It was foul, and I loved it. I loved the self-destruction, I loved my fall.... My depraved soul leaped down from your [God's] firmament to ruin. I was seeking not to gain anything by shameful means, but shame for its own sake" (*Confs* 29). Such an admission gives heft to the project one could call the invention of the Christian self, an identity that has a religious dimension (developed in comparison with his deity) but is also the product of disobedience, discipline, sin, shame, and sexual desire. Concupiscence tarnishes everything imagined, everything experienced, everything confessed. Most importantly, however, the narrator who is enthralled to his Almighty insists on "the free choice of the will" (113). As he succinctly states, "The nub of the problem was to reject my own will and to desire yours" (155).[39] Without that self-annihilation—that ultimate conversion (154)—deliverance is impossible. Such is the Christian subjectivity Hopkins endorses, a combination of the exceptionalist selfhood of liberal humanist individualism and the identity formation regulated by Christian moralizing.

Augustine acknowledges his sexual desires and pleasures,[40] but the *Confessions* produces toxic equations whereby sex equals sin and sin equals remorse. He never identifies the "concubine" with whom he lives for many years, the mother of his son (who is named)—as if naming her would make her a person rather than a lustful opportunity. But he does pause to congratulate himself for being faithful to her (53). At the same time that he teaches readers how to confess, he teaches them how to devalue women and demand their subjugation (302). His mother is the exception, but she can only be represented in misogynistic terms: "My mother stayed close by in the clothing of a woman but with a virile faith, an older woman's serenity, a mother's love, and a Christian devotion" (160). Marriage for the purposes of procreation is permissible, even necessary in his society (25), but women are otherwise positioned as threats to the male penitent's "recovery" (251). Intriguingly, Augustine does not hesitate to appropriate a gestation metaphor for himself: his mother "suffered greater pains in my spiritual pregnancy than when she bore me in the flesh" (83). Hopkins follows suit in "To R. B.," in which the "fine delight that fathers thought" impregnates the mind, "a mother of immortal song. / Nine months she then . . . Within her wears, bears, cares" for the progeny (*PW* 204). For all readers, Augustine establishes an attitude of contempt for the life of the body ("I do not know whence I came to be in this mortal life, or, as I may call it, this living death" [*Confs* 227]), but promises that the "tears of confession" will enable him to enjoy the "consolations" of God's "mercies" (*Confs* 6).

A "WORTHY" IRISH EXEMPLUM

On 4 August 1883 Hopkins sent Bridges a textual gift and a promise: "I enclose something very beautiful and almost unique ["St. Patrick's Hymn" or "Breastplate"]. I am hoping myself to publish a new and critical edition of St. Patrick's 'Confession,' a work worthy to rank (except for length) with St. Austin's Confessions and the Imitation and more like St. Paul's and the Catholic Epistles than anything else I know, unless perhaps St. Clement of Rome" (*CW* 2:678). Bridges's response to the gift is unknown. The critical edition—like so many of Hopkins's projects—was launched with great fanfare but fizzled out like a Roman candle in a thunderstorm. Yet, his enthusiasm for another story of deliverance from sin and hard-won sanctity (but this time with pirates), a combined exercise in life-writing and

Christian subject formation that is both exploration and exposé, deserves further attention.

Church historians disagree whether the "apostle of the Irish" died ca. 460 or ca. 490. His *Confession* was written and distributed approximately fifty years after Augustine's. Patrick is also intensely intertextual—his narrative voice develops in conjunction with allusions to and direct quotations from the Old and New Testaments, including the Psalms—but not learned like Augustine. Original insights and formulaic statements are skillfully combined. Both Augustine and Patrick have stories of separation to impart, but the Carthage man leaves home willingly, in pursuit of ambition and pleasure; the British man is taken into captivity and forced to live in Ireland. Only later does he voluntarily return to that country as a missionary.

Retrospection and introspection are the keys to both texts; the narrators are the objects of scrutiny as well as the subjects of the confession. "But why make excuses close to the truth," Patrick observes, "especially when now I am presuming to grasp in my old age what I did not gain in my youth because my sins prevented me from making what I had read my own?"[41] A humility topos is featured throughout: he is "evidently unlearned," "a fool," and altogether "not worthy." "I am imperfect in many things," he stresses, "nevertheless I want my brethren and kinsfolk to know my nature so that they may be able to perceive my soul's desire" (¶ 6). Although "for some time I have thought of writing," he explains, "I have hesitated until now, for truly, I feared to expose myself to the criticism of men, because I have not studied like others, who have assimilated both Law and the Holy Scriptures equally and have never changed their idiom since their infancy . . . while my idiom and language have been translated into a foreign tongue" (¶ 9). At the heart of this history of his "inner" life he finds his Lord: "And on a second occasion I saw Him praying within me, and I was as it were, inside my own body, and I heard Him above me—that is, above my inner self. He was praying powerfully with sighs" (¶ 25). Small wonder that Hopkins responds with such enthusiasm to Patrick's text.

Structurally, the *Confession* starts and ends with a textual "act of contrition": "I, Patrick, a sinner" is the simple beginning; the conclusion eloquently avows,

> Behold over and over again I would briefly set out the words of my confession. I testify in truthfulness and gladness of heart before God and

his holy angels that I never had any reason, except the Gospel and his promises, ever to have returned to that nation from which I had previously escaped with difficulty. But I entreat those who believe in and fear God... that nobody shall ever ascribe to my ignorance any trivial thing that I achieved or may have expounded that was pleasing to God, but accept and truly believe that it would have been the gift of God. And this is my confession before I die. (¶ 61, 62)

The pirates are certainly the most thrilling part of Patrick's story, but his struggles with Satan are presented more emphatically: "The very same night while I was sleeping Satan attacked me violently, as I will remember as long as I shall be in this body; and there fell on top of me as it were, a huge rock, and not one of my members had any force" (¶ 20). Throughout his life, he is privileged to receive prophetic warnings. His return to Ireland as a missionary, after the years of "slavery" and "trials" (¶ 35), is the great mark of his devotion to "the living God" (¶ 27).

Patrick is a self-described "convert"; Hopkins surely enjoys that aspect of the narrative, as well as the insistence that the saint's inner strength is derived from Christ, which "vindicated my faith before God and man" (¶ 30). Two other resonant themes should be mentioned: the virtue of toiling in obscurity (¶ 56)[42] and the much more dramatic possibilities of being a virgin martyr. (A third theme, his lifelong struggle with "the hostile flesh," is discussed in chapter 3). Patrick tells the story of "a most beautiful, blessed, native-born noble Irish [Scotta] woman of adult age whom I baptized": within two weeks of that event, "opportunely and most eagerly, she took the course that all virgins of God take, not with their fathers' consent but enduring the persecutions and deceitful hindrances of their parents" (¶ 42). What Hopkins does not know, in August 1883, is that in six months he, like Patrick, will be toiling among the Irish. Patrick's missionary work was voluntary, however; Hopkins, ever "Fortunate's football" in terms of his Jesuit assignments,[43] goes there obediently but with myriad misgivings.

One other vital aspect of St. Patrick's legacy is relevant to this brief history of confession. In the sixth century, Irish priests shared the penitential practices of the monasteries with laypeople. To aid this ministry, they developed "manuals which listed and classified sins as well as punishments to be imposed for each specific sin, and which also advised priests on how to go about receiving confessions" (Chloë Taylor 47). This theological initiative had a rippling effect throughout Christendom: in "the seventh century, private penance reached the continent and was spread by Anglo-Saxon missionary monks" (Chloë Taylor 48). Thus, by inspiring generations of confessional endeavors, Patrick had an impact on the Fourth Lateran Council, according to which all Christians were obliged to confess.

DRAMATIZING THE "VOIDER OF ADVERSITY"

Just as the "tears of confession" refresh Augustine (*Confs* 6), the soul's tears are announced at the beginning of *The Summoning of Everyman* by the Messenger, who warns, "Ye think sin in the beginning full sweet, / Which in the end causeth the soul to weep, / When the body lieth in clay."[44] I am mentioning this medieval play (late fifteenth century) rather than Dante's *Divine Comedy* or the "Parson's Tale" in Chaucer's *Canterbury Tales* for two reasons: because it demonstrates the legacy of public, vernacular instruction endorsed by the Church to disseminate the teachings promulgated by various Councils, and because it employs so vividly the allegorical techniques Hopkins uses to great effect in "The Wreck" and in Ireland poems such as "Carrion Comfort." Part the First of "The Wreck" begins with a paean to the "Lord of living and dead" (*PW* 119); Part the Second, with Death personified:

> "Some fínd me a swórd; sóme
> The flánge and the ráil; fláme,
> Fang, or flood" goes Death on drum,
> And stórms búgle his fáme. (*PW* 121)

At the outset of *Everyman*, Death is commanded by God to teach Everyman a vital lesson: his "sure reckoning" is upon him. Unlike Hopkins's histrionic figure, however, the medieval Death speaks directly, plainly, rather than melodramatically (although the performer could certainly ham up the delivery).

Everyman pleads for more time to order his affairs; Death agrees. When Everyman implores his friends for help, he is serially forsaken by Fellowship, Kindred and Cousin, and Goods (and Riches). Only Good Deeds provides timely advice, and introduces him to Knowledge, who promises, "Everyman, I will go with thee, and be thy guide / In thy most need to go by thy side" (*Everyman* 214). Knowledge wastes no time in beginning their pilgrimage: "Now go we together lovingly / To Confession, that cleansing river" (214). When Everyman meets Confession in "the house of salvation," he is immediately contrite: "Wash from me the spots of vice unclean, / That on me no sin may be seen. / I come with Knowledge for my redemption, / Redempt with heart and full contrition" (214). Confession is both gracious and generous in response:

> I know your sorrow well, Everyman.
> Because with Knowledge ye come to me,
> *I will you comfort as well as I can,*
> And a precious jewel I will give thee,
> Called penance, voider of adversity;
> Therewith shall your body chastised be,
> With abstinence and perseverance in God's service.
> Here shall you receive that scourge of me,
> Which is penance strong that ye must endure,
> To remember thy Saviour was scourged for thee
> With sharp scourges, and suffered it patiently;
> So must thou, ere thou scape that painful pilgrimage....
> Ask God mercy, and he will grant truly.
> When with the scourge of penance man doth him bind,
> The oil of forgiveness then shall he find. (215)[45]

This is Confession's only speech in the allegorical drama, but it is pivotal. Everyman accepts Confession's advice willingly; he turns to his adviser and says, "Knowledge, give me the scourge of penance; / My flesh therewith shall give acquittance: / I will now begin, if God give me grace." Immediately, he begins to flog himself, declaring, "Take this, body, for the sin of the flesh!" (216). Confession, penance, redemption; the play's lessons are succinct and vivid. Interestingly, the play dramatizes the major theories concerning the sacrament circulating from the sixth to the fifteenth centuries: "that penance was medicinal and that it was punitive."[46] It also captures a time when public confessions and penitential acts, "public humiliation before the congregation"—rituals of shaming—co-existed with individual confessions to the priest (Oakley 44).⁴⁷

After Everyman is scourged, neither Discretion, Strength, Five Wits, nor Beauty can help him: only the priest dispensing the sacraments can do that, as Five Wits reminds him (and in this way reaffirms the play's didactic message):

> Here in this transitory life, for thee and me,
> The blessed sacraments seven there be:
> Baptism, confirmation, with priesthood good,
> And the sacrament of God's precious flesh and blood,
> Marriage, the holy extreme unction, and penance;
> These seven be good to have in remembrance,
> Gracious sacraments of high divinity. (*Everyman* 219)

Everyman dies in the final scene, but this is supposed to count as a happy ending; the Angel symbolizes providential grace and the Doctor, in his final summation, concurs. Everyman will live "body and soul together" hereafter (225), with God, because he is shriven. Thus, *Everyman* confirms the three-fold function of confession—witnessing/professing, confessing, praising—with dramatic flair and economy. As Foucault suggests five centuries later, avowal is "of the order of drama or dramaturgy. If one understands the 'dramatic' not as a mere ornamental addition, but as every element in a scene that brings forth the foundation of legitimacy and the meaning of what is taking place, then I would say that avowal is part of the judicial and penal drama" (*WDTT* 210).

COUNTER-REFORMATION STRATEGIES AND INVENTIONS

Between "the age of Chaucer and the age of... Pascal," John Bossy observes, "an economy of sin organized around the idea of hatred was converted to a different economy dominated by sexuality" (35), and there emerged a "strong tendency to psychologize the sacrament" of penance because sin, it was argued, occurs in the mind before, during, and after any action is committed (27). The Jesuit Francis de Sales (1567–1622) was one of the major proponents of this psychologizing approach; it informs his extensive guides for spiritual formation and direction. In the *Introduction to the Devout Life* (1609) de Sales includes a chapter entitled "How to Make a General Confession," another "On Confession," and suggestions for "The Practice of Bodily Mortification." De Sales's gentle, consoling tone and ready use of natural imagery make the *Devout Life* enjoyable as well as salutary. (The text is frequently cited by Gaume and Pusey.) His chapter on confession has special interest for a Hopkins reader because of the animal imagery:

> Our Saviour has bequeathed the Sacrament of Penitence and Confession to His Church, in order that therein we may be cleansed from all our sins, however and whenever we may have been soiled thereby.... If the lioness has been in the neighbourhood of other beasts she hastens to wash away their scent, lest it should be displeasing to her lord; and so the soul which has ever so little consented to sin, ought to abhor itself and make haste to seek purification, out of respect to His Divine Gaze Who beholds it always. (de Sales 112)

Perhaps it is de Sales's motif informing stanza 17 of "The Wreck," in which the "tall nun" is represented as a "lioness [that] arose breasting the babble, / A prophetess towered in the tumult" (lines 135–36).

One could think of de Sales as the friendlier face of the Counter-Reformation, which most historians date from the inception of the Council of Trent, in 1545, to the European wars of religion in the 1660s. His antithesis was the Catholic official who did the most to enforce the reforms relevant to confession: the archbishop of Milan, Charles Borromeo (1538–84; archbishop as of 1564). I have already outlined the Council of Trent's strategic refurbishing of the sacrament of penance—it is divine law, the Council declared. Borromeo, who was made cardinal in 1560, "tried to revive public penance, to make the confessional period conform more exactly to the ancient penitential season, to institute, by the systematic practice of delayed absolution, something akin to the ancient practice whereby satisfaction preceded rather than followed absolution. He added to his instructions a fearsome compilation of penitential canons from the Dark Ages" (Bossy 29). Borromeo was also responsible for the general implementation of what is now the signature symbol of penance:

the confessional. In 1565 Borromeo prescribed "the use of a rudimentary form of the confessional—a seat with a partition (*tabella*) to separate the priest from the penitent. Eleven years afterwards, in 1576, he order[ed] confessionals placed in all the churches of the province of Milan" (Lea 395). In 1614 the invention was recognized in the *Rituale Romanum*, the "official service book" (Livingstone 484) of Roman Catholicism; its use was common in the Netherlands by 1607, and in France, by the 1650s (Bossy 30, 32).

The confessional was always much more than a convenient guarantor of privacy: one can think of it as the perfect setting for this "transformation in the understanding of confession which was itself symptomatic of a transformation in human self-understanding. Sin was becoming less a matter of submission to God's laws and more a question of the sinner's relation to his or her own conscience.... The confessional box corresponds at an architectural level to that change" (Chloë Taylor 50). But it does more. The confessional is a space of alteration and thus, in Foucault's term, it is a heterotopia (*EWF* 2:178). Typically, a heterotopia works to destabilize the grounds of established order but does so by juxtaposing several spaces and times in a single location; it is "a place that affects a return to my position and forces me to reflect on its conditions" (*EWF* 2:179). The confessional is the exclusive space in which penitent and priest stage the allegory of deliverance from sin. One enters the confessional a sinner, soul-sick and psychologically burdened; one exits imbued with the grace of absolution (assuming one's penance is expeditiously performed).

This religious heterotopia was, for Borromeo, not only a means of organizing bodies and protecting privacy, it was also a device for regulating activities by gender. Ideally, Bossy states, "he seems to have wanted each parish to possess two confessionals, one for women and one for men, so that men and women would not come to confession 'confusedly mixed up and squeezed together'; but in his legislation the confessional was only compulsory for women, and this remained the case when the *Rituale Romanum* generalized the invention in 1614" (32). Chapter 2 returns to the confessional to analyze why it became the quintessential emblem for Victorian anti-Catholicism. This chapter now shifts from the architectural to the textual invention that was crucial in sacramental history: the penitential guide. The discussion culminates in an analysis of Hopkins as penitent *and* confessor.

MANAGING "THE PROBLEM OF PENANCE"

If the confessional is the stage, then what constitutes the sacramental script? The penitent's lines, with ample room for fresh sinful summaries, were quoted at the outset of this chapter; the sacramental rite features prompts for individual statements. The confessor's responses were also scripted, by many hands, over centuries. Accompanying the growth of auricular confessions "from the first, and despite the disapproval of higher ecclesiastics," was the explosive development of penitential literature. "There were produced, in abundance, summas for confessors, summas of moral cases, summas of moral theology" (Mahoney, S.J. 15, 20) and guidelines for the administration of penance. In Mahoney, S.J.'s wry assessment,

> the problem of penance still remained, or indeed increased, with the introduction of repeated confession of sins. And as a guide to the growing numbers of individual confessors there developed the fascinating and repelling literature which we know as the Penitential Books, which may have originated in the Welsh synods held under the influence of St. David in the sixth century, before proliferating in Ireland and spreading thence with the Celtic missionary movement to the Frankish lands, England, Italy, Spain, stimulating other native products as they went.... Although there is much positive material to be found in the Penitentials taken as a whole, the overall impression gained from them is coloured more by vice than by virtue. (5, 7)

Sources for these manuals included canonical letters by Greek religious leaders such as Basil the Great and his brother, Gregory of Nyssa. Basil, for example, concentrated on appropriate penances for "violation of virginity, second marriage, magic, violation of graves, homicide of various kinds, adultery, incest, theft, perjury, abortion, idolatry, infanticide, and other offences" (Oakley 25). The first extant penitential was *Paenitentiale Ambrosianum;* other well-known examples in England were produced by the Venerable Bede and David of Menevia; the collection known as *Canones Hibernenses* "exerted a very strong influence upon the English penitentials as well as upon the administration of penance in Ireland" (Oakley 38). After 1215, as Jacques Le Goff states, priests "were embarrassed and in some cases even frightened by their new responsibilities, particularly if they were not well educated" (139). "How to confess and how to hear confession, what to confess and what to ask, and, for the priest, what penance to impose for those avowals of sin that were neither enormous nor extraordinary but generally modest and routine—all these were questions that needed to be answered" (Le Goff 138).

Among those most willing to provide solutions was John Mirk (or Myrk, fl. ca. 1382–ca. 1414), whose collection of sermons entitled *Festial* was "the most widely read English sermon cycle in the fifteenth century" and then "the most frequently printed English text before the Reformation" (Powell). Mirk composed two penitentials: *Instructions for Parish Priests*, a basic handbook written in rhyming couplets, and the *Manuele sacerdotis*, a spiritual guide in Latin prose. Both are "loosely based on William Pagula's *Oculus sacerdotis* of the 1320s" (Powell), demonstrating again the degree to which these manuals became a palimpsest of cumulative wisdom and practical experience. In his role as "shrift-father," Mirk is charming in his analogy for the Trinity—think of water, which can appear in the forms of snow and ice but is always water (lines 472–74)—and only too typical in his dismissive, patronizing attitude toward female parishioners and their "shrewish" speech (lines 57–60).

Without question, the drafting, copying, circulation, and eventual printing of penitentials in the British Isles and continental Europe contributed significantly to the standardization of practices and penances, and contributed to the wholesale cultural investment in the sacrament. They were canonical both in the sense of being the most recognized and important examples of the genre and as they interpret canon law and translate its ideals and prohibitions into rules for administering spiritual justice. When Hopkins judges himself for daily indiscretions in 1865, or judges parishioners for their sins thirteen years later, he is doing so entirely on book.

A historian of the sacrament suggests that "the duties of the conscientious confessor are the most arduous and exacting, the most intricate and complex, that can be imposed on the fallibility of human nature" (Lea 172). In this spirit, a rationale for penitentials is easily provided. As Gaume admits, "Out of a hundred confessions scarcely two or three will require any unusual science, but all will require great love in receiving, bearing with, and helping the penitent" (Gaume 77). His recourse to scientific discourse is intriguing: assigning the appropriate penance is no longer guesswork, or even the consequence of experience; it is a matter of measurement, consultation, sacramental equations. "Mere moral science," he further suggests, "only aims at a right absolution of the sinner; ascetic science leads him on to perfection" (78). Some would argue that an economic register is more appropriate than the scientific: confessing is transactional (so many sins, of specific degrees of vilification, equal so many penitential practices).

Of the many penitentials available for study, I have selected Gaume's *Manuel des confesseurs* (1854) for three reasons.[48] One, for the synthesis of previous texts he provides, an amalgamation best summarized in the most famous English translation of the book, *Advice for Those Who Exercise the Ministry of Reconciliation through Confession and Absolution, Being the Abbé Gaume's Manual for Confessors or His Extracts from the Works of S. Francis de Sales, Charles Borromeo, S. Philip de Neri, S. Francis Xavier, and Other Spiritual Writers*. (Gaume is partial to de Sales because his "marvellous sympathy opened the most reluctant hearts, extracted the evil hidden within, and confirmed them in good dispositions and resolutions" [27].) Two, because it was published during Hopkins's lifetime—when he was ten, in fact. And three, because it was translated and edited in 1878 by Edward Pusey, Hopkins's occasional confessor, 1864–66, to help the Tractarian cause. Gaume's work is an adaptation of Alphonsus Liguori's *Moral Theology* (1753–55). In addition to quoting from his three core "Masters of the spiritual life," Borromeo, de Sales, and Philip Neri, Gaume occasionally cites Teresa of Àvila,[49] Augustine, and (infrequently) Aquinas. Francis of Assisi's manner in dealing with the sick and dying is recommended (Gaume 350–53); the insights of Popes Benedict XIV and Innocent XI are also quoted, a special kind of imprimatur for Gaume's own project. For confessor and parishioners alike, he recommends Thomas à Kempis's *Imitation of Christ*, Ignatius's *Spiritual Exercises*, as well as the *Lives of the Saints* (Gaume 23), texts with which Hopkins was very familiar.

Gaume marshals precepts of moral theology, advice from his favorite experts, case studies, and his own kind of common sense to address seven major topics: the duties and qualities of a successful confessor (as father, healer, and teacher); precautions before hearing confessions; the confessor's precautions; interrogations; treating different kinds of penitents, especially "difficult" cases; how to deal with bad habits and relapses; and the challenges of absolution. The sacramental "seal" of the confessional is also defended. Paraphrasing de Sales, Gaume explains that "there is no office so important or so difficult as the Confessor's. The most important, since final salvation is the aim and end of all wisdom; the most difficult, for the Confessor's work requires a knowledge of almost all subjects, and a great power of combining and adapting that knowledge" (75). Yet, as Hopkins learned, there are "many perils" in the office of consoler.[50] "Fear them," Gaume advises confessors, "and let your holy fear be life-long. 'Blessed is the man that feareth always.'"[51] But keep that fear within due limits, so that you do not become discouraged, and forsake your work; "let it rather move you to renewed hope, and more earnest watchfulness, self-mistrust, and confidence in God" (390).[52]

In terms of extracting knowledge of sinning from the penitent, how extensive should the questions be? Gaume distills advice from the Church's "doctors" (including Raymond of Penyafort) and reasserts, for the Victorian era,

> Sit simplex, humilis Confessio, pura, fidelis
> Atque frequens, nuda et discreta, libens, verecunda,
> Integra, secreta et lacrymabilis, accelerata,
> Fortis et accusans, et sit parere parata. (1511)

> [Let the confession be simple, humble, pure, faithful and frequent, naked and discreet, willing, modest, entire, secret and lamentable, rendered useless, brave and accusing, and ready to obey.]

Adroitness is crucial for the best "clear-sighted" physician-judge-father confessor, "adroitness in discovering where the evil lies" (Gaume 35), because it resides, waiting to harm, in thoughts, desires, actions, and the burden of past sins. The proximity of sin is dangerous because the "devil is wont to redouble his efforts to ensnare the faithful" at any time, and especially "on the days of their Communion" (44). For the confessor, knowing how to anticipate doctrinal problems, sinful scenarios, and various types of penitents is crucial. Gaume is also sensitive to the fact that children[53] are to be treated differently than young adults, and the latter differently from "an older formed" and mature woman or man (290). Interestingly, "cautious indulgence" of venial sins is recommended: rather than threaten, one should encourage righteousness (290). Overall, and always, "avoid extremes of indulgence or severity"; the good confessor "must warn and rebuke them according to their need" (291, 48). This message is repeated several times throughout the guide: the "severe Confessor (*rigoriste*)" helps neither the sinner nor the Church (10). A "rigid ascetic" or a theological pedant will not suit the role of good shepherd; as a consequence, the "wandering sheep" may "hate both fold and shepherd, and fly both for ever" (13).

In terms of demeanor—and this would be a matter of voice, especially, in a confessional—never "shew any signs of surprise, even should their language be coarse" (55). Promoting fear is anathema to Gaume: "A Confessor who frightens his unlucky penitents by harshness and untimely reproof is greatly to blame. He ought on the contrary to maintain a calm mind, a gentle expression, and a kindly manner which may attract penitents, and induce them to feel that everything he does is for their good. Teach them so that they may listen and submit willingly to you" (15). (In other words, this skillful strategy for subjugation results in what Foucault would term the ultimate type of discipline: self-discipline.) Nonetheless, the confessor should "also urge upon the heads of families the duty of training their children in God's holy fear, causing them to be duly instructed in Christian doctrine" (22). It is an intriguing strategy: the paterfamilias uses the verbal rod, but the Father of the church exudes verbal charity. Similarly, Gaume argues that the effective confessor "should move the penitent to accuse himself of all the sins which he remembers" (151). Two pages are devoted to this key psychological strategy: the sinner must not only acknowledge the sins but denounce herself as sinner—dread her own innermost propensities. Sinning is a clash of wills, according to Gaume. Nothing less than complete surrender will suffice, and done not only voluntarily but gladly, "rooting out [one's] own will, and transform[ing] it in God, by simply willing that which He wills" (220).

Reluctance or any show of weariness on the confessor's part are frowned upon (20). Zeal also has no place in the confessional, Gaume suggests; it should be mistrusted unless "accompanied with patience and the love of toil" (10). Nonetheless, his definition of "suitable" penances, "proportioned to the faults committed" (365, 360), begins with an emphasis on that which is and "should be *penal;* penance should not only be medicinal and protective to the new life, but also vindicative in expiation of past sins. These penal works are divided under the heads of fasting[,] alms and prayer. Under fasting, we include every kind of bodily mortification: under prayer, confession and Communion, and all interior acts of charity, contrition, and of the Presence of God: and it is generally taught that all these acts may be given as penance" (364). Habitual sinners and those who frequently relapse also require special measures, so that the person may "conceive greater horror at his sin" and be inspired to achieve true amendment (298). Delays in absolution are recommended, as just one means of a "prolonged and arduous course of treatment: for the passions, which seemed to be conquered to-day, spring forth afresh to-morrow" (279).

Passions, not surprisingly, test the responsible confessor the most. Gaume is particularly reticent about sins of a sexual nature, but at the same time persistent; he writes gingerly "with respect to purity" and advises special care when hearing the confessions of children. It is "of greater importance not to teach evil to one who is ignorant of it," he insists. "Thus, if you are hearing the confessions of children, speak so as to be understood only by those who are guilty" (11). When in doubt, prevaricate. In terms of sexual sins, Gaume relies upon innuendo: "bad thoughts," "vicious habits" (in the full sense of the word *vice*), "evil habits," and "impurity" (categories that will be discussed, below, in relation to Hopkins's lists of his "sins").

As for women, Gaume sets aside several pages for the "treatment of women" that are based on the teachings of de Sales, and utters precautions throughout his guide (a young man can be addressed as "my dear son," but "prudence dictates that you should not call a young woman 'my dear daughter'" [106]). One should be "affable" with men but always "severe" with women (107). (When in doubt, treat them as you would children.) Beware of those who are overly pious, he states (205–6). "Young" women is code for those who could be sexually inspired or motivated—or at least a distraction to the priest. "Teach them to be very obedient," Gaume insists, "and to do whatever is wanted at home" (207). There is also a suspicion, one that irrupts into the text several times, that female parishioners who are too devoted to a young priest may be wasting his time in the confessional. "Confessors should not give themselves so wholly to confessing women as to refuse men who may seek them," Gaume warns. "It is a sad sight to see confessors giving their whole morning to young women-devotees, while they dismiss men or married women" who have genuine spiritual needs

(108). Overall, the confessor's watchwords should "be 'brevis et austerus' on all subjects with women. Do not omit any thing that is necessary for their soul's health, but carefully avoid long discourses, even upon spiritual matters" (104; see also 408). Victorian gender norms are thus confirmed and reinscribed by Gaume, another example of how women are punished, prior to any act, for the sin of being female.

"TO TRY HIS FAITH"

Foucault suggests that confession is "a formidable tool of control and power. As always, it uses what people say, feel and hope for" (*FL* 216). Three concerns emerge from Gaume's manual that provide a framework for considering Hopkins's roles as penitent and confessor: obedience, shame, and scruples.[54] All are important to the exercise of pastoral power (*HS* 4:310), which is "productive, not repressive," as Bernauer, S.J., asserts: "Paramount in the exercise of this pastoral power is a virtue of obedience in the subject, a virtue which, unfortunately, all too often becomes an end in itself" ("Confessions" 559–60). All three concepts are inflected by issues of control: papal, institutional, priestly, and the penitent's control of mind and body. Religious regulation is explicit; social regulation is implicit. Doctrinal issues are also relevant, as Moran states: "Whereas private judgement and personal conscience provided sufficient basis for the Protestant control of the self, Catholic authority came from without, from the teaching of the Church. Catholic views of the Incarnation provide a main doctrinal principle for such submission to Rome" ("Lovely" 70).

As a dutiful Victorian child and young adult, Hopkins practices obedience sedulously—until he refuses to do so, an aspect of the "counter-conduct" mentioned earlier. He counters the tyranny of his Highgate schoolmaster, Dr. Dyne; he counters his parents' entreaties that he not convert, and social pressures not to become a Jesuit. Within the Society of Jesus, however, obedience is vital to his identity and his vows: "paupertatem, castitatem, et obedientiam perpetuam in Societate Jesu," perpetual poverty, chastity, and obedience in the Society of Jesus (*CW* 5:140). Absolute humility is required; submission is all-inclusive. As MacKendrick suggests, "Dogmatically, obedience is not mere incidental accord of will, ... but an active submission of one will to another.... [It is the] will's willful sacrifice of willing" (35–36) (or the mortification of the will that is complemented by the mortification of the body, discussed in chapter 3). Foucault concurs about "he who obeys": "All the modes of domination, submission and subjugation are ultimately reduced to an effect of obedience" (*HS* 1:85; see also *STP* 176–77). Yet, to "achieve this perfect and exhaustive obedience ... exercise is essential: constant examination of oneself and perpetual confession" (*HS* 4:90).[55] The title of a sermon by Newman delivered while still an Anglican neatly sums up the position he and Hopkins held true: "Obedience the Remedy for Religious Perplexity." When in doubt, Newman advises, obey: "To all those who are perplexed in any way soever, who wish for light but cannot find it, one precept must be given,—*obey*. It is obedience which brings a man to the right path; it is obedience keeps him there and strengthens him in it. Under all circumstances, whatever be the cause of his distress,—obey" (*Parochial* 1:230).[56]

And what happens when one does not obey, or one sins in some other way, whether grievously or expediently? Hopkins has a phrase for that condition, of course: the "incapable and cumbrous shame / Which makes me when with men I deal / More powerless than the blind or lame" (*PW* 76). Lessons in shame's disabling power are readily and variously available in the mid-nineteenth century. In his classical studies, for example, Hopkins finds Plato's attempt to locate shame in the θυμός or soul, the argument of *Gorgias* and *Phaedrus* (in which Phaedrus learns to feel shame at what is disgraceful, and ambition for that which is noble).[57] For Plato, shame has a special role to play in regulating sexual desires and activities.[58] Aristotle's *Rhetoric* teaches one how to use *aischron* or shame effectively in speeches. The Bible stresses the close association of shame and dishonor, yet uses shame to punctuate key events or teachable moments, from Genesis, Isaiah, Psalms, Proverbs, and Jeremiah to Paul's epistles and Revelation (in which the shame of one's metaphorical nakedness, or sinfulness, both harkens back to Eve and Adam and promises a final, irrevocable judgment). Augustine blends stories of biblical warnings and personal misdeeds throughout his narrative: "I did not see the whirlpool of shame into which 'I was cast out of your sight' (Ps. 30:23)," he declares. In book 8, it is the example of the court official Ponticianus, who is "filled with holy love and sobering shame" (*Confs* 143), that helps Augustine to realize why becoming a Christian is necessary. His depravity is best summed up with the admission, "I was seeking not to gain anything by shameful means, but shame for its own sake" (*Confs* 29).[59]

What Shakespeare describes as "all-eating shame" (sonnet 2) is never far from Ignatius Loyola's mind. In the *Spiritual Exercises,* shame is featured in the First Week, so that from the outset one learns "to ask for shame and confusion at myself" (*SE* 24). In terms of imaginative role-playing, the exercitant is asked to dwell on "those many sins of mine . . . as if some knight were being arraigned before his King and his full assembled Court, stricken with shame and confusion" (*SE* 45). Hopkins responds fully, abjectly to Ignatius's verbal thrusts in the 1882 retreat notes (previously quoted, in relation to "pitch"): "I find myself with my pleasures and pains . . . my shame and sense of ~~honour~~ ^beauty^, my dangers, hopes. . . . [But] above all my shame, my guilt, my fate. . . . the guilt or shame, the fatal consequence, the fate, comes home" (*CW* 5:348–49, 352). The emphatic centrality of shame in this meditation on "selving" is very telling.

Among Hopkins's associates and peers, shame circulates in public discourse both plangently and stridently. Shame and sorrow, according to Addis and Arnold, linger long after the confession of one's offences (649). Gaume lists the "inducements to hearty repentance" in this order: "shame, fear, trust, and love" (41). Pusey, in his preface to Gaume's manual, quotes Jeremy Taylor's advice that shame is a "good instrument of repentance" but cautions that one should not be "swallowed up by too much sorrow and shame" (cviii, cxix). In his guide for *Penitence,* Pusey repeatedly acknowledges the necessary "pain and shame of confession" (5–6, 15). In Coventry Patmore's poem "Reprobate," the "relapsing" man's soul, "cast down by shame and grief, / [is] Too weak to call for Christ's relief," yet any good religious person would reply that the Savior is always prepared to release someone from sin (201).[60] In the pamphlet and periodical "wars" concerning the efficacy of confession, opponents on all sides invoke shame to strengthen their arguments. John Laidlaw, for example, who held the chair in systematic theology at New College, Edinburgh, dwells on "the shame, the stain, the exposure which belongs to sin" and praises the moment when Christ "opens our eyes to the awful depth of shame that separates us from Him" (9, 15). Rev. John Ross, writing against Roman Catholicism, nonetheless concurs that crimes are prevented because of the "fear of shame"

(60). And Frances Power Cobbe, one of the rare female voices in this very public debate—also a vehement critic of auricular confession—notes "the kind of shame which consists in the pain of exposure" (380).

For those wanting to argue against shame's salutary qualities—to break the "self-regard/shame circuit"—Eve Kosofsky Sedgwick demonstrates how to tackle its historically embedded role as a "permanent, structuring fact of identity" because it is "both peculiarly contagious and peculiarly individuating" ("Queer" 14, 5). She does so first in an essay about Henry James's fiction, and then in *Touching Feeling: Affect, Pedagogy, Performativity*. Asking "good questions about shame and shame/performativity," she insists, "could get us somewhere with a lot of the recalcitrant knots that tie themselves into the guts of identity politics" ("Queer" 14).[61] Those who "treasure" shame and guilt, she observes, ardently enforce "proper" behavior; the "conventional way of distinguishing shame from guilt is that shame attaches to and sharpens the sense of what one is, whereas guilt attaches to what one does" (*Touching* 37). Sedgwick's analyses are based on the work of psychologist Silvan Tomkins, a theorist of affect from the 1960s to the 1990s. Shame, together with interest, surprise, joy, anger, distress, disgust, and contempt, constitutes what Tomkins calls the "basic set of affects"; he "places shame, in fact, at one end of the affect polarity *shame-interest*" (Sedgwick, "Queer" 7). Shaming oneself is transformational; shaming someone else is stigmatizing. It is, Sedgwick notes, "a kind of free radical that . . . attaches to and permanently intensifies or alters the meaning of—of almost anything" (*Touching* 62). (As a cue for interpreting scenes in novels and poems, or even retreat notes: Sedgwick points out that shame lives in the face: "Blazons of shame, the 'fallen face' with eyes down and head averted—and, to a lesser extent, the blush—are semaphores of trouble" [*Touching* 36]). Sinners' revelatory blushes (*erubescentia*) have been noted since the days of Origen of Alexandria (184–253) and Alcuin of York (735–804).[62] It is not an exaggeration to think of Hopkins's era as a "shame culture";[63] he is both product and victim of its tentacular reach. Hence, when in "Brothers," the speaker watches Henry watching his younger brother perform in a school play, "His tear-tricked cheeks of flame / For fond love and for shame" are duly noted (*PW* 166).

Interestingly, the same people who endorse the instrumentality of shame warn against a tendency to be too "scrupulous." This is the final term to be considered in order to read Hopkins's confessional notes effectively.

Today, someone might use "scruple" as a synonym for moral efficacy, "as if it were something respectable," like conscientiousness (Faber, *Growth* 241)—but that usage is inconsistent with the term's history in English. A scruple is a "thought or circumstance that troubles the mind or conscience; a doubt, uncertainty or hesitation in regard to right and wrong, duty, propriety[,] ... especially one which is regarded as over-refined" (*OED*). In Latin, a *scrupus* is a hard or rough stone; a *scrupulus* is the irritating pebble in one's shoe—figuratively, any cause of uneasiness or discomfort, which is how Cicero uses the metaphor (*OED*). Among religious advisers, Gaume warns against the scrupulous, who "torment themselves about their past confessions, fearing that they did not fully explain all their sins or the attending circumstances"; the Church "doctors," he adds, "teach, that even if through inadvertence they have omitted some mortal sin, scrupulous persons are not obliged to return to the subject.... Be resolute in enforcing obedience on this point" (179). Gaume's inflexibility on the subject may be surprising, but he worries about harmful zeal: "Scrupulous people ought to be treated with great severity," he insists, "for if they lose the anchor of obedience they are lost; they will either go mad, or plunge into sin" (180). It behooves him to recommend de Sales's advice: "'Do not let yourself be tormented with scruples, or too many wishes; go on gently and bravely'" (183). Philip Neri is also quoted: Neri taught people "to despise scruples. He would accordingly forbid scrupulous penitents to come so frequently to confession" (321). Equating scruples with "morbid sensitiveness" is also the strategy of Frederick Faber, who suggests that their "causes" are three: "God, the devil, and ourselves, or the human spirit, and to these last the body contributes as well as the soul" (*Growth* 242). For Faber, scruples are a kind of sickness, the product of a "melancholy temperament," which the alert priest should try to cure. "Scruples have nothing to do with God for his own sake," Faber insists; "there is no devotional spirit about them, not even a mistaken one" (*Growth* 244). So concerned is he about the matter, which he denounces as a kind of false holiness (and "a vain fear of sin"), that he devotes an entire chapter of *Growth in Holiness* to the topic (241). His bracing conclusion: "A scrupulous man teases God, irritates his neighbour, torments himself, and oppresses his director" (240).

Benjamin Jowett, Hopkins's principal tutor at Balliol College, tried to warn students against the excesses of Roman Catholicism, Ritualism, and scrupulosity of any denomination. In a late 1860s college sermon he stresses that a devout person can be the "victim of sorrow and sadness; he may be full of doubts and scruples, waging an unequal warfare against his own passions" and, consequently, "has no comfort or certainty in religion" (*College* 305). Hopkins's Jesuit colleague John Morris makes a similar point in his instructions for novices: in terms of past sins, "adhere strictly to what you have been told and put away the thought that it is necessary or wise to accuse yourself of such sins. By so acting you will defend yourself against scrupulosity, which is an unreasonable fear, causing often great pain, though resting on no sure ground" (42). Hopkins, alas, either missed these lessons or could not help but ignore them. Posthumously, the first person to accuse him of being overly scrupulous is Bridges—who does so, very publicly, in *Testament of Beauty*:

> And so,
> when the young poet my companion in study
> and friend of my heart refused a peach at my hands,
> he being then a housecarl in Loyola's menie,
> 'twas that he fear'd the savour of it, and when he waived
> his scruple to my banter, 'twas to avoid offence. (iv: lines 433–38)[64]

Critics from Bischoff (1957) and Bergonzi (1977) to Beasley (2020) have continued the tradition of referring to Hopkins's "extreme" or "morbid scrupulosity." Only a fresh assessment of his confessional notes will confirm or challenge such a conclusion, that he was "swallowed up by too much" scrupulosity—but he certainly thought so.

BEWARE THE "SELFTORMENTER"

Hopkins's private confessional notes extend from winter 1865 until spring 1866. A brief summary of his life in those tumultuous months will help to contextualize what he wrote, why, and for whom. He arrives in Oxford on 17 April 1863, and matriculates (becomes a full member of the university) the next day. That term, he meets Henry Liddon, Pusey's staunchest ally, and starts attending Liddon's Sunday evening Bible lectures. Many

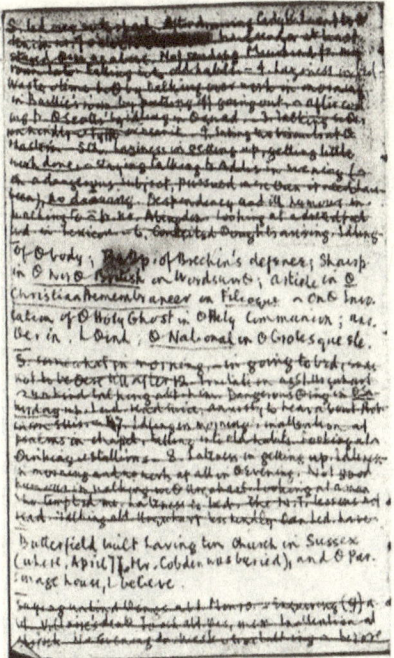

FIG 1 A representative page from Hopkins's diary, April 1865. *Diaries, Journals, and Notebooks,* edited by Lesley Higgins (Oxford: Oxford University Press), 289, 637. (© British Province, Society of Jesus)

people describe Liddon as a "saintly" and "charismatic" man; Mary Arnold Ward declares him "the arch wire-puller and ecclesiastical intriguer in University forces," with "perfect rhetoric" (*Writer's* 1:180). In winter term 1864, Hopkins is very busy with classes, writing weekly essays for Jowett and other tutors. Liddon becomes his confessor on 2 February,[65] just weeks before Lent begins, but the extant list of "sins" commences thirteen months later, on 25 March 1865: "**S**. Dawdling in going to bed (not very much), March 25. Inattentions at morning chapel, 26" (*CW* 3:285).[66] Hopkins also confesses to Liddon on 11 March 1864 (just before Easter) and 26 November (before Advent); on 16 December, to Pusey (*CW* 3:339). In February 1865, he meets Bridges's cousin Digby Dolben and develops an intense crush—feelings that exacerbate an already acute sense of sinfulness (thus demonstrating, *avant la lettre,* Sedgwick's argument about the toxic imbrications of shame, sexual desire, and identity formation). The following year, 1866, is truly momentous. He confesses to Liddon on 6 February and 17 May. By mid-July, he is convinced that he should convert to Catholicism. Initially, he plans to delay until after he graduates. But by late August he can wait no longer; he writes to Newman 28 August to announce that he is "anxious to become a Catholic" (*CW* 1:93); is "received" into the Church by Newman on 21 October; and on 4 November is confirmed by Archbishop Manning (also a convert).[67] Throughout late 1866 and 1867, he considers his religious and vocational future, as he completes his Oxford studies (in July 1867), but makes no decisions until May 1868.

The *Diaries* represent Hopkins as a young man of extremes. There are mundane memoranda about neckties to purchase or letters to write, and exacting revisions of poems. There are entries of quiet rapture, his attention caught by the unexpected sight of a bluebell or "some delicate flying shafted ashes—there was one especially of single sonnet-like inscape—between which the sun sent straight bright slenderish panes of silver sunlight beams down the slant towards the eye" (*CW* 3:603). Paintings, sculptures, and works of literature are carefully assessed, his aesthetic principles freely exercised. There are also nightmares relived; undergraduate "sins" unsparingly recorded; "signs" of heavenly mercy happily noted; small acts of "kindness" from others, both unexpected and restorative, gratefully acknowledged. Like most diarists, Hopkins is committed to life-writing practices not simply to itemize daily activities, but to explore the possibilities of textual selving. The space of the page is the incitement for reporting what has been seen, what has been felt, what has been feared, in order to memorialize the experiences and to make possible subsequent rereadings. Thus, the diary is a summary of the present and an investment in—even a prediction of—future responses. Entries pertinent to this project exist in two small, pocket-size journals (catalogued in Campion Hall, Oxford, as C.I and C.II). Initially, he makes notes eclectically: philological inquiries, sketches of architectural or natural elements, serial "to-do" lists, drafts of poems, animadversions on things he has read, discussed, puzzled about. Then C.II becomes almost entirely internalized, self-scrutinizing, as Hopkins "[y]ields to the sultry siege of melancholy" (*CW* 3:308). C.I, the earliest extant diary, begins in September 1863, just before Hopkins's second term in Oxford commences. C.II is a direct continuation—but the entries cease in winter 1866. A new journal is started in May 1866, and maintained while he decides to convert, but there is no extant diary for autumn 1866, when he becomes a Roman Catholic (letters written and received, however, are humming with people's emotional reactions). Thus he becomes his own Cumaean Sibyl, with tantalizing fragments scattered variously; thus one interprets what has been gathered and preserved duly chastened by thoughts of what has been lost.

As a diarist Hopkins changes his tone often and his method several times. One discerns, in fact, at least three different discursive modes: frank immediacy, chaotic variety, and studied composure. Prior to Lent 1864, he is an eager and discerning observer, keen to note his fascination with words, Oxford, nature, and new intellectual challenges. After working with Liddon, however, he becomes an ever-more-vigilant morality monitor, dutifully and zealously recording every fault, every "sin," every transgression of mind and body.[68] Instead of purchasing and using another "[l]ittle bk. for sins" (*CW* 3:291), Hopkins converts C.II into a confessional repository. Who eventually advises him to abandon such excoriating textual rituals? A letter to Newman on 15 October 1866 provides the answer: "Monsignor Eyre seemed to say that I ought not to make my confession by means of a paper as I have been used to do. Will you kindly say whether you wd. prefer it so or not?" (*CW* 1:113). Newman's answer has not survived, but Hopkins certainly changed his mode of writing—or at least, the venue—by May 1866. By the time he begins writing in a new, large-format notebook (A.I) he has become a different kind of journal writer: impersonal and documentary rather than personal and self-punishing. No longer is he obsessively analyzing his own behavior; as he states on 9 May 1871, he focuses instead on the "behaviour of the cloudscape" (*CW* 3:509) and other natural phenomena. Writing is a mode of experience for Hopkins, and an aesthetic performance; language is his instrument while he works "[t]o match and more than match" words to the play of ideas and feelings. To paraphrase a poem from 1879, "Who shaped this page has shewn / The music of his mind" (*PW* 159).

One could imagine all of Hopkins's writings as a kind of textual fugue, but only if prepared for significant degrees of dissonance. The self-lacerating inventories of the Oxford diaries, for example, are in many ways contradicted by the contents of his undergraduate essays (similarly, the excruciatingly dull reports in the Birmingham-era journals in winter 1868 are gainsaid by notes inspired by pre-Socratic philosophers and the first textual explorations of "inscape" and "instress"). One example of the disconnection will have to suffice: the last day of March 1865. According to the diary, the day was marred by the following "sins": "Inatt. at chapel in morn. Wasting morning. Intemperance in food—biscuits. Wine twice a day. Relapsing into old impurities. Irreverence at a prayer. Altogether self-indulgence" (*CW* 3:288).[69] According to the evidence of his undergraduate essays, however, he is studying Plato's *Republic* with Jowett, Greek history and Herodotus with William Newman, Aristotle's *Nicomachean Ethics* with Henry Wall; writing several essays a week on various topics; attending Robert Scott's lectures on Paul's epistles to the Romans, Jowett's lectures on Thucydides, and Max Müller's lectures on German prose writers of the seventeenth and eighteenth centuries, beginning with Leibniz. According to the "log" kept by the master of Balliol, Robert Scott, Hopkins's performance throughout that Lent term is "very steady & creditable" (*CW* 4:19).

Initially, in March 1865, the lists of transgressions occupy two or three lines of the small diary. Within months, however, the near and actual occasion for "sins" is consuming both the page and the young man's life; the *aide de memoire* becomes monstrous, and in the spirit of the Anglo-Saxon notion "agenbite of inwit," devours page after page. (As he later observes of his friend Martin Geldart, Hopkins is "a selftormenter."[70]) Few aspects of daily existence are not jeopardizing, whether dining with friends, eating biscuits, staying in bed too long in the mornings, not going to bed early enough at night, gossiping, mocking his father's mannerisms,[71] being impatient with siblings. Frequently, he also chastises himself for "forecasting" a desire to convert (especially in autumn 1865). But even during this intimate self-scrutiny he is playing a role, or, more precisely, following a script. The basic plot is outlined in the Tractarian writings of Newman and Pusey: to embrace fasting and self-mortification, to focus excessively on the "flesh," yet simultaneously fear the consequences of its sensual thrall. Particulars are supplied by Liddon: by the ascetic standards he broadcasts; his insinuating presence in targeted undergraduates' lives; and the confessional obsessions he promotes with publications such as *Questions for Self-Examination: For Common Use* (1861), a pamphlet I found among Liddon papers in Oxford's Keble College Library.[72] If Hopkins is not following this specific publication's strictures, he is reading something remarkably similar (as is Liddon, whose meticulous diaries are equally self-lacerating and programmatic). The twelve-page pamphlet skillfully combines expectations and prohibitions, advice and admonitions. The interrogation is so thorough yet seemingly benign—here is a path to mercy and righteousness reclaimed—that a submissive, attentive reader would necessarily be persuaded of his or her "impurity" (*Questions* 2). Almost every "besetting sin" documented by Hopkins in his diary is predicted by the pamphlet: waking up too late; "evil thoughts"; not being "temperate in all things"; "dangerous" thoughts, reading, companions; lack of obedience to one's parents; anger; "worldly activities"; "idling" and other types of "slothful" indolence; and looking at anything "dangerous" ("have I looked at immodest pictures or other objects of the kind?" [*Questions* 10]). The feelings expressly targeted by the publication, pride and conceit, simmer in Hopkins's self-examinations. There are also keen prohibitions against knowledge of other faiths: "Have I gone to any worship other than that of the Church of England? or in any way encouraged such schismatical worship?" (*Questions* 7). Of course, it is possible to read, or even to use, the *Questions for Self-Examination* with appreciative curiosity. But the cost of doing so, for Hopkins, was great.

By the time that Hopkins undertakes the great religious schism of his life, from July to October 1866, he is no longer reliving his "basenesses" (*CW* 2:570) in his main journal; the mode of self-reporting changes dramatically. Sadly, however, the "selftormenter" returns while living in Ireland. The worn and smudged appearance of some diary pages' corners implies numerous rereadings. Various intertextual resonances suggest that Hopkins revisits the diaries, as well as old letters, while living "at a third remove" in Dublin, and they contribute to a "sadness . . . much like madness" that overtakes him (*CW* 3:734, 731).[73] Morris, S.J.'s handbook for Jesuit novices predicts as much. One should be satisfied that sins are "laid at rest forever" after a sound confession, he advises, but—but—this "does not mean that you are to lay aside sorrow for your past sins. . . . And in order to move yourself to more sorrow for them, include them in every act of contrition you make, and accuse yourself of them in general terms . . . every time you go to confession" (40, 41). Encouragement for "more sorrow" is never what Hopkins needs.

The 1865–66 lists of sins serve multiple functions. Most immediately, they summarize indulgences and transgressions—actual or imagined—in what becomes a daily ceremony of self-castigation. Every few months, they provide evidence of "sinfulness" to be offered up during auricular confession, thus enabling Hopkins to participate in rituals of admission, penance, and expiation. The entries are written in pencil, in an increasingly small hand, then canceled—but canceled carefully, with a thin ruled line: thick enough to indicate which sins have been confessed, but thin enough so that he can revisit his transgressions and indulge in further self-loathing. As the entry for 1 September 1865 succinctly states, his is a noxious seesawing state between "Scrupulosity. Temptations." The particular temptation of that day is not a young man but "[w]eakly reading a stupid story" (*CW* 3:326). For someone who regards the natural world with such sensitive delight and ingenuity, whether looking closely at a crystal formation or absorbing a panoramic view, Hopkins's perspective on his own life is wholly skewed.

Even as he is castigating himself for "evil thoughts" and "temptations," Hopkins is gathering indictments of homoerotic desire.[74] Yet the diaries also make clear that his sexual experiences are limited to watching, fantasizing, writing, and masturbating. The daily verbal scourges in C.II may be regarded as textual evidence—but what do they prove, exactly? Hopkins is twenty and twenty-one during that "self-wrung, selfstrung" year between Lent 1865 and Lent 1866, yet many of the "sins" seem strikingly adolescent: looking up provocative words in the dictionary; noticing keenly the bodies of other people; fixating on genitalia (in a statue, a painting, a dog); mooning over one's first major unrequited crush. If C.II constitutes a sexual record of Hopkins's life during a year of emotional crisis, then it must be read with Sedgwick's advice in mind: "The sexual histories of English gentlemen, unlike those of men above and below them socially, are so marked by a resourceful, makeshift, sui generis quality, in their denials, their rationalizations, their fears and guilts, their sublimations, and their quite various genital outlets alike" (*Between Men* 173). More than anything else, Hopkins is too aware of his body as something charged with responsiveness—always unbidden, alarming, but to be carefully documented in his diary. On 4 December 1865, for example, he feels "[p]hysical danger while having my arm in Baillie's and speaking affectionately" (*CW* 3:338). The intense homosociality of his Oxford life is also rife with moral and sexual "danger" engendered, in part, by the homophobia he has internalized.

Hopkins does not record the meeting with Dolben; there is only an oblique note, sometime afterward, regarding "Dolben's carte" or photograph, his *carte-de-visite* (*CW* 3:275; the cancellation implies that Hopkins wishes to request a copy or has received a copy). Subsequently, Hopkins enshrines Dolben's address on a page of the diary (*CW* 3:294) and discusses him with their mutual friend Vincent Coles (who had known Dolben at Eton) and perhaps others. 23 April 1865: "Dangerous talking abt. Dolben, no reading what ever" (*CW* 3:295). 5 May 1865: "Desire to hear things connected with forbidden subj., as questions abt. Dolben" (*CW* 3:299). 22 October 1865: "Running on in thought last night unseasonably against warning onto subject of Dolben, and today and some temptation" (*CW* 3:333). The entries for 6 and 8 November 1865 confirm that Dolben's religious interests are as much an issue as Hopkins's physical and emotional attraction to him: "6. Inatt. O.H. Temptation. Going on into a letter to Dolben at night agst. warning. Lateness. No L[essons]. (On this day by God's grace I resolved to give up all beauty until I had His leave for it; and also Dolben's letter came for wh. Glory to God.)" (*CW* 3:335); "8. No L. Spiritual pride abt. Dolben" (*CW* 3:335). One month later, writing to Dolben is again a source of pleasure and self-concern: "14. O.H. Waste of time in evening. Conceit over letter to Dolben" (*CW* 3:339). Clearly Hopkins is involved in textual affairs that both attract and dismay. Two weeks later, at home for the Christmas vacation: "Dangerous scrupulosity abt. finishing a stanza of Beyond the Cloister for Dolben" (*CW* 3:340). That same entry, for 22 December 1865, also states: "Discontent and idleness. Foolishness at Grandmamma's with talk abt. Catholicism" (*CW* 3:340). Like Dolben, Hopkins cannot help but flaunt his "dangerous" religious views. But after that oblique reference, absolute silence, in the extant journals, concerning his feelings for Dolben. He is not mentioned again in C.II, nor in A.I, the journal kept from May to July 1866. News of Dolben's death by drowning, June 1867, is recorded when Hopkins returns from Europe one month later.

One cannot "blame" Liddon and Pusey for Hopkins's "scrupulosity," but one can certainly hold them accountable for encouraging their young charge. As Rev. Thomas Carter observes in an 1877 public epistle to the archbishop of Canterbury, "Confession increases spiritual sickness, by fostering an over-scrupulous introspective habit of mind. If such be the case, it can only be through the fault of the confessor."[75] MacKendrick makes a similar observation: "Confession requires a confessor, a superior, not only as the complicitous force in the breaking of the will but as a witness" (40). Hopkins's inventories of sins indicate stinging self-condemnation but few balms of remediation or cure.[76] He lives in a state of permanent vigilance and permanent suspicion.

Since the days of Pythagoras and Seneca the Elder, self-examination is supposed to be "purifying" (*WDTT* 96), not eviscerating. Seldom does Hopkins articulate the same generosity of spirit that his colleague Rickaby, S.J., advises: "A good examination of conscience is as much a review of God's bounties as a review of our sins, the former making an excellent motive of contrition for the latter" (66). As an Anglican, Hopkins learns the lesson that his Catholic and Jesuitical training will only intensify: that to speak "the truth about one's sin" (*HS* 4:74) is to speak the truth about one's self. Catholic confessors may grant him absolution—forgiveness—but he is slow to forgive himself. As the speaker of "Kingfishers" observes of all human conduct, "*What I do is me*" (*PW* 141).

LICENSED TO HEAL

Self-examination is singular, solitary; confession is a two-person ritual of admission and penitence. As a priest, Hopkins is partly responsible for the salvation of others, a responsibility that sometimes oppresses him, but often produces joy and satisfaction. This final section of the chapter completes my historical survey of penitential rites from Augustine to the Fourth Lateran Council to Victorian England by considering how Rev. Fr. Hopkins functions in this particular sacramental role.

"How is the Confessor," Gaume asks, "worthily to exercise his triple office of judge, physician, and doctor, without true prudence guided by supernatural light?" (145). Crucially, the priest must be ready to serve in the confessional at any time, which requires him to "maintain an habitual state of grace, never to be lost by any mortal sin" (97). The challenges are many, but "many a good confessor has experienced a great gift of devotion, which does not arise within himself, but which comes direct from our Dear Lord" (84). Nonetheless, Gaume fully acknowledges that this "office" is "at once wearisome to the body and full of anxiety both as to your own soul and to those of your penitents. The demand upon you for patience and charity in receiving, assisting, bearing with those who come to you, is great" (84). The rituals of listening to people confess, guiding them, assigning penances, constitute a special kind of "constant mortification" for the priest, but it is also a "sanctification" (84). Several times the "fatigue or weariness" that are the result of hearing confessions (86) are stressed in the manual, and Hopkins's brief comments about the physical and mental depletion he feels, the somatic suffering he experiences, attest to Gaume's observations. A letter to Bridges begun 5 September 1880 is very candid: "Dearest Bridges,—I take up a languid pen to write to you, being down with diarrhoea and vomiting, brought on by yesterday's heat and the long hours in the confession. Yesterday was in Liverpool the hottest day of the year" (*CW* 1:400). By that time, he had been licensed *ad audiendas confessiones* (to hear confessions) for three and a half years. In October 1878, he mentions to Dixon that he has no time for extracurricular reading: "I hear confessions, preach, and so forth; when these are done I have still a good deal of time to myself, but I find I can do very little with it" (*CW* 1:318). Should one be surprised that he sometimes attends to correspondence in the confessional? He begins an extended letter to Baillie on 22 May 1880 with the admission, "I do not know how it is, when your letters give me so much pleasure to get, I am so slow in answering them. At least I can see say my Liverpool work is very harassing and makes it hard to write. Tonight I am sitting in my confessional, but the faithful are fewer than usual and I am unexpectedly delivered from a sermon which otherwise I should have ^had^ to be delivered of. Here comes someone" (*CW* 1:395). A year later, wry humor does not disguise his lack of enthusiasm. Writing to Bridges on 30 April 1881, he states, "Today in lieu of tomorrow, May day, is fixed for the Liverpool yearly procession of horses, which I am in a few minutes going out to see something of. But the procession should begin properly at 2, at which hour I must be in my own loose box; I mean my confessional" (*CW* 1:400). A year later, he expresses great pleasure in participating in a "mission" at Maryport,[77] where he had to "speak very plainly and strongly (I enjoyed that, for I dearly like calling a spade a spade)," then adds, in a very different tone, "On my way back I was detained here [in Preston] to hear confessions again" (*CW* 1:522).

"Of all pastoral ministrations," Addis and Arnold suggest, "we firmly believe there is none which involves a more self-denying devotion to a monotonous duty" than hearing confessions, "none where the good effects are so plain and visible, and very few which are more seldom marred by human weakness and sin" (649). Hopkins's candid remarks certainly stress the monotony of his duties and the challenge of presenting a fresh mind and demeanor, a soulful seriousness, when yet another person confesses a too-familiar infraction. And yet—as Gaume warns, the consequences of "careless" confessors are nothing less than "murdered souls!" (315). Consequently, he advises that confession-weary priests need a "re-kindling of fervour" (111). For Hopkins, hour after hour of conscientiously witnessing the "sweating selves" (*PW* 182) of parishioners and trying to assign appropriate and meaningful penances "lapped strength, stole joy" (*PW* 183).

Clearly Hopkins's hours in the confessional are long, and scheduled variously (evening sessions to accommodate workers, for example). To imagine him there, one learns again from Gaume, who reminds priests that hearing confessions is a performance, for which there is, or should be, a dress code and stylized actions: "There is no sacrament in which it more behooves us to maintain due gravity and solemnity, than that of Penance, in which we sit as God's appointed judges. You should wear cassock and surplice, stole and biretta; your countenance should be friendly but grave, and you should guard against allowing any expression of weariness or annoyance to rest on it, for fear of leading others to imagine that your penitent is telling you dreadful things" (116). And there he is.

In a May 1883 tribute to the Virgin Mary, Hopkins's speaker asks for her support regarding his threefold commitment to "patience, penance, prayer" (*PW* 176). Penance, as this chapter has demonstrated, is a crucial facet of the rites that evolved over sixteen centuries, from personal self-scrutiny and public admission of sin to codified sacramental obligations. Shame, I have suggested, is a primary emotion for the penitent, but so too is fear—fear of God (quintessence of righteousness and might), fear of the self, of facing death not having been relieved of one's sins, of final judgment and possible damnation. "I fear mortal sin," Hopkins confides to his diary on 19 November 1865 (*CW* 3:336). He had been trained to think that way, and he believed it to be an essential aspect of his existence—in this world, and the next.

The focus of chapter 1 has been doctrinal matters. The focus of chapter 2 is political matters—or, more accurately, the heated politicization of religious doctrine and practices in the Victorian era. Confession is again the subject matter, for two reasons: to understand the Anglican practices Hopkins rejected while an impressionable undergraduate, and to consider the vehement anti-Catholic and anti-Jesuit sentiments to which he was exposed after he converted in October 1866. It is a story of intolerance that is hydra-headed in its menace and bite.

2

VICTORIAN CONFESSIONAL CRISES

It is difficult to throw ourselves back into the force of
documents of a past age; but we may try to picture it.
—EDWARD PUSEY, "Preface"

ACCORDING TO THE *OXFORD ENGLISH DICTIONARY*, the word "sectarian*ism*" entered the English language in the nineteenth century, in Coleridge's *Biographia Literaria* (1817), and then was taken up by the likes of John Stuart Mill, Charles Kingsley, and critics for the *Athenaeum* and the *Spectator*. In all of the examples cited, religious factionalism is being noted: religion and politics are embroiled, antipathies abound, and bigotry is either implied or lamented. Some people, like Henry Liddon, actually embrace the conflict: "I am not at all frightened by the word 'sectarian,'" he stated in 1884; "Christianity *is* sectarian as against the non-Christian world" (qtd. Johnston 331). Yet the crises and controversies analyzed in this chapter, either directly or indirectly concerned with auricular confession, do not involve non-Christians. Instead, the antagonists are composed of Protestants and Roman Catholics, or Anglicans and those other Anglicans known as Tractarians or Ritualists. In all cases, the stakes of the debates and legal actions are presumed to be high, and the positions taken are often intractable. Drawing upon pamphlets, books, broadsides, cartoons from *Punch*, verse satires, and two novels—one virulently anti-Catholic and anti-Jesuit, with Gothic flourishes; the other, somber and poignant—this chapter explores how the confessional, such a small heterotopic space, could inspire outsized controversies from the 1820s to the 1890s. For believers, the confessional is not just the place to speak, it is the place to say everything, tell everything about your sins and your sinful self. Yet it is also, for anti-Catholics, the place where the unspeakable is recalled, recited, and shared. Some of the people caught up in the disputes seem to be spoiling for a fight, whatever the particular issue; many others are vehement because they believe that this life and the next are in jeopardy. Like Edward Pusey, they can imagine their "tender" souls covered "over and over with sores" and seek the means of alleviating that suffering (*Penitence* 37, 21).

As an Anglican, confessing to Liddon and Edward Pusey certainly contributed to Hopkins's theological redirection—a shift with profound religious and cultural consequences. What he never anticipated, I would wager, was the vehemence of the anti-Catholic, anti-convert, and anti-confessional campaigns of his day. This chapter considers both the legal repositioning of English Catholics in the nineteenth century and the anti-Catholic and anti-Jesuit vituperation such maneuvers inspired, as well as the Anglicans' internecine quarrels about auricular confession and other ritualistic practices.

LAWS, BULLS, AND SOCIOCULTURAL BULLYING

The word "complicated" inadequately describes the parliamentary and papal moves and countermoves that had the net effect of inflaming arguments and intensifying prejudices from the 1790s to the 1870s. Even when legislation or a decree was supposed to be beneficial, the opposition it garnered was acute. Often, the greater the official tolerance of Catholics, the more vociferous the anti-Catholic attacks. Three statutes, three papal initiatives, and a publication that occasioned a rebuke in the House of Lords must be surveyed in order to understand why confession gained so much notoriety.[1] One must also understand that the persistence of Catholicism-related public debates avers to Anglican nation-making. As Peschier states, "The No-Popery climate of 1850–51 was characterised by a strong Evangelical impulse and the extravagant imagery employed in the agitation revealed something like hysteria. There are also numerous invasion scares, Catholic Europe invading Protestant England" (284).² As I suggested in the introduction, Hopkins was an ardent nationalist—perhaps overly keen to attest to his patriotic and imperialist loyalties in poems such as "The Bugler's First Communion" and "What shall I do for the land that bred me" because of the people who questioned a Catholic's true or primary allegiance. In John Ross's incendiary anti-Catholic blast *On Penance and the Confessional, as Unscriptural and Immoral* (1851), confession is denounced as an intrusive form of domination at the micro level that mirrors Rome's macro-tyrannous aspirations: "This is the chain that is now forging in this land, and that Rome is busily endeavouring to rivet round us. This is the tyranny that priestly despotism is struggling to obtain over the enlightened minds of Englishmen of the nineteenth century" and trying to "extend... over the nations of Europe" (13, 15). Through auricular confession, Ross insists, the Church makes "her subjects slaves; and she throws around it the mantle of antiquity" (44–45). The pope, a dubious "foreign prelate," uses any means possible because of his "insatiable grasping after temporal power, for dethroning kings, absolving subjects from the oaths of their allegiance[,] . . . establishing wherever he rules his odious confessional, and by every nefarious means seeking to form a kingdom of this world" (38). (In chapter 4, I will discuss how A. C. Swinburne's poetry reaffirms such sentiments.)

Post-Reformation, the legal status of Catholics in England and Great Britain was complex and, in some ways, precarious. Officially, they could not purchase land, for example, nor join the army. As the unapologetic long title of the Roman Catholic Relief Act (1791) suggests, there were numerous and "certain penalties and disabilities to which papists, or persons professing the popish religion, are by law subject" (31 George III. c. 32).³ Some "disabilities," such as not having steeples or bells for chapels, seem symbolic and also petty; some, such as the need to "register" with authorities, or swear an oath to support the Protestant Succession, had substantial consequences (as did the inability to endow schools or colleges). George III was unwilling to accede to any further reforms. In April 1829 his son, now George IV, reluctantly agreed to endorse the new Roman Catholic Relief Act (10 Geo. IV c. 7),⁴ according to which the "sacrifice of the Mass" was no longer forbidden; Roman Catholics who took the oath of allegiance could sit and vote in Parliament (but not priests), vote at elections, hold many civil and military offices, and serve as members of business corporations. Attending universities or colleges, however, was still forbidden. Roman Catholic ecclesiastics were confined to their "usual places of worship." And Jesuits—well, if already residing in Britain, they could stay on British soil but had to register with the local clerk of the peace; they were not allowed to "come into this Realm" from abroad (§ 29).⁵ Philanthropists could now "endow Roman Catholic charities, but any bequest that allocated funds for 'superstitious' purposes such as Masses or candles for the dead were void. Roman Catholics were excluded from the government's education grants until 1847"; "thereafter they could qualify for aid only under conditions that they deemed insulting" (Paz 6).

Twenty-one years after these legislative "reliefs," Pope Pius IX decided to restore or reestablish the Roman Catholic hierarchy in Britain (territorial offices for twelve bishoprics). People who assumed it was merely an administrative move must have been shocked that the September 1850 papal bull *Universalis Ecclesiae* was denounced, by many, as "an act of 'Papal Aggression' [and] unleashed anxious, even paranoid responses from the contemporary press and other quarters" (Casteras 162). The day after the bull was pronounced, Nicholas Wiseman, "vicar apostolic of the Central District, and the most prominent member of the English Roman Church," was named the first cardinal archbishop of Westminster (Paz 8). Wiseman (1802–65), born in Spain but Irish in nationality, was in his era the chief, sometimes the most combative, promoter of Catholicism in Britain. As Griffin points out, Wiseman's "confrontational manner" informed the first pastoral he published, "Out of the Flaminian Gate," which "injudiciously" proclaimed how "'we govern, and shall continue to govern, the counties'" of England (*Anti-Catholicism* 116).⁶

At least three times in the ensuing decades, the pope and his cardinals exercised their doctrinal authority in ways that had direct and indirect impacts on anti-Catholic campaigns, and on Catholics such as Hopkins. On 8 December 1854, Pius IX declared as dogma of the Church the "immaculate conception" of Mary, the mother of Christ (papal bull *Ineffabilis Deus*).⁷ The Mariolatry it inspired (expressed, for example, in the final stanzas of "The Wreck" and Hopkins's suite of Blessed Virgin poems) also played into Victorian gender politics.⁸ One decade later, on 8 December 1864, the *Syllabus of Errors* (*Syllabus Errorum*) was published, an annotated list concerning the eighty "errors" or heresies that were not and would not be countenanced, including those relating to pantheism, latitudinarianism, socialism, communism, Bible societies, and liberalism in any and every political form. Of course its issue "aroused a storm of protest" (Livingstone 544).[9]

In 1870 the first Vatican Council concluded, after a year of deliberations, with the declaration *Pastor aeternus,* proclaiming the infallibility of the pope when pronouncing on doctrine (speaking ex cathedra). William Gladstone, for one, was slow to react to these papal salvos, but in November 1874 the once and future prime minister published a riposte, *The Vatican Decrees in Their Bearing on Civil Allegiance,* insisting that "no Englishman could now convert to Roman Catholicism 'without renouncing his moral and mental freedom, and placing his civil loyalty and duty at the mercy of another'" (Griffin, *Anti-Catholicism* 160). More than 145,000 copies of the pamphlet were printed in less than two months (MacKenzie, *Excursions* 308). On 6 December 1874, Hopkins's team for the St. Beuno's Debating Club argued for the "following formula[:] 'The position of Catholics has been in no wise changed by the decrees of the Vatican Council' being liable to misrepresentation [and] cannot safely be adopted in the present contest between Gladstone and Rome"; the motion carried (Thomas, S.J., *Hopkins* 247). Hopkins's intense dislike of Gladstone—whom he believed guilty of "surrender[ing] the empire" (*CW* 2:718)—peppers his letters in the 1870s and 1880s.

ASSAILING THE "HOUSE OF ROME"

There were so many anti-Catholic monikers to choose from: papist, filet-o-fish, left-footer, Lent trap, creeping Jesus, mick, and mackerel snapper (an American favorite). The preface to an 1869 pamphlet, *Confession, a Help to Heaven,* provided even more collective insults: traitors, apples of discord, slaves of conscience, polluters of souls, and purveyors of immorality (iii). An 1873 publication, *The Liberty of Britain Imperilled by Confessing Priests; or, The History of The Confessional Unmasked,* itself an edited reprint of an Irish text with a wonderfully inflammatory title—*The Confessional*

Unmasked: Showing the Depravity of the Priesthood, the Immorality of the Confessional, and the Questions Put to Females in Confession, Etc., Etc., Being Extracts from the Theological Works Used in Maynooth College[10] and *Sanctioned by the "Sacred Congregation of Rites." With Notes*—not only recycles appellations such as Romanists and "Romish idolators" but adds to the mix "popish priestcraft" and, quoting Revelation 17:5, "the mother of harlots and abominations of the earth."[11]

It is an exaggeration to suggest that, if you have read one nineteenth-century anti-Catholic tract, you have read them all, yet the main arguments remain consistent. Only the levels of vituperation vary. *The Confessional Unmasked* is particularly revealing—perhaps entertaining, today, but one can imagine the indignation and indignities it inspired. Exposed to its figurative vehemence, one must put aside all clichés about Victorian reticence and "good form" in public discourse. The anonymous author declares, "One can easily conceive how such *Skunks* and *Cobras* as Confessing Priests would be annoyed by the exposure of their foul and venomous doings.... Every means therefore at their disposal was used to 'bend and break' those who thus dared to expose their diabolical doctrines, practices, and designs" (*Confessional* 13). Apparently the confessional, best considered the "Tribunal of Iniquity," is "the true base upon which the whole politico-Pagan edifice stands" (*Confessional* 19, 16). And the House of Rome flourishes because priests "use the Confessional: (1) To obtain the secrets of the *individual*, the *household*, or the *State*. (2) They use it to *corrupt, pervert,* and *enslave* their victims. (3) They use it to satiate their own *lust, avarice, ambition,* and *malice*. It is the Church's closet for prying, intrigue, and ambiguous familiarity" (*Confessional* 19). Among the testimonials and expert opinions the author cites, there is an excerpt from Canon Hugh Stowell's *Lecture at Leeds:* "'You can tell at a glance the Papist who has gone willingly to the CONFESSIONAL, for the practices of the dark den of the Confessional have left him a broken, crushed, degraded being. I cannot feel myself free to think that any Englishman will ever go himself, or allow his wife or daughter to go to that slaughter-house of freedom and purity. And the Clergyman who dares to drag that loathsome Auricular Confession into the Church of England, ought to be booted out of society'" (*Confessional* 22).[12] Known as a "firebrand" type of preacher, Stowell (1799–1865) was "an untiring opponent of Roman Catholicism" who inspired parishioners, thousands of readers (of his sermons, essays, lectures, pamphlets, polemical works), and members of the Protestant Association. His parish was in Salford, near Manchester; Stowell helped to foment anti-Catholic protests in Lancashire from the 1830s to the 1860s.[13] Hopkins lived and taught in Lancashire, at Stonyhurst, for several years: as a Scholastic, 1870–73, and as a teacher, spring 1878 and August 1882 to February 1884.

The rhetorical edifice of Victorian anti-Catholicism had its foundations in "the hoary myths of Bloody Mary, the Armada, the Gunpowder Plot, and the Glorious Revolution, but the developments of the first half of the nineteenth century," as Paz suggests, "created a distinct climate especially conducive to anti-Catholicism. These developments included the creation of an urban public thirsting for entertainment; the organization of self-improving and voluntary societies; the simultaneous emergence of a new, harder variety of Evangelicalism and a new, romantic Catholicism; the growth of militant denominational identities; the economic, social, and political aspirations of the landed gentry, the middling classes, and workers; and the emergence of mass communications and mass culture" (299). Among the unfounded, sensational rumors circulating about Catholics (a stew of political plots, convents fronting for brothels, and scheming Jesuits) was the ever-popular suspicion that Irish Catholic "servants sprinkled holy water on unsuspecting Protestant families" and secretly taught their children papist ideas (Paz 301).[14] The "legitimization of the Catholic hierarchy that spawned... the 'antipapist excitement' of the 1850s" also offered "a rationale for the English discrimination against Irish Catholic immigration, heightened by the potato famine of the 1840s" (Bernstein 45). In the late 1870s and early 1880s, Hopkins would be serving in the parishes of large, "repulsive" English and Scottish industrial cities where the "poor Irish, among whom [his] duties lay" congregated (*CW* 2:524).

So heated were the public debates by the 1860s, and so vicious the pamphlets circulating, that the bishop of Birmingham, Dr. Ullathorne,[15] gave an "Address on the Confession" in St. Mary's Catholic Church on 17 March 1867, and the following Sunday, 24 March, at St. Patrick's. Three months later, William Murphy, a well-known "no-popery demagogue" who had had great success lecturing and inspiring violence in Plymouth (June 1866) and Wolverhampton (February 1867), as well as London, Bristol, Bath, and Cardiff (Paz 256), incited a large crowd in Birmingham's Carr's

Lane, near St. Mary's (5.1 kilometers or 3.2 miles from the Birmingham Oratory,[16] where Hopkins would reside from September 1867 until April 1868). As Bernstein reports, Murphy's "widely advertised lecture on the evils of the confessional booth was billed as the most spectacular event in a given program. Often this performance behaved as the ultimate showstopper," after which "members of the audience could purchase their own copy of his oration, 'The Confessional Unmasked,' for private delectation" (Bernstein 50). So persuasive was Murphy in Birmingham that two days of sectarian rioting ensued after his presentation.

Reissuing or recycling anti-Catholic publications was a particularly successful strategy. So Jeremy Taylor's *A Dissuasive from Popery to the People of England and Ireland* (2 parts, 1664 and 1667), which includes two chapters railing against confession, found new generations of readers when it appeared in Rivington's 1828 edition of his "whole works." (Hopkins was very familiar with Taylor's *Rule and Exercises of Holy Living*, 1650.[17]) The 1859 exposé *A Peep behind the Curtain; or, An Exposure of the Popish Confessional, Furnished by Popish Writers* borrows liberally from a 1610 pamphlet by Rev. John White (directly inspired by the Gunpowder Plot) in order to expose schemes designed to reconcile people to the Church of Rome and to utter dire warnings about "roving confessors [who] were to perambulate the land, for the purpose of shriving, *i.e.* confessing the people, and culling all the information they could in respect of the civil, as well as religious, affairs of the nation."[18] Similarly, Anthony Gavin's *The Great Red Dragon; or, The Master-Key to Popery* (1724) enjoyed "numerous printings in England and in the United States" in the nineteenth century, including an 1854 edition (Bernstein 51). Thus, anti-Catholicism seemed to be both timeless—and thereby necessary—and a phenomenon of what Wai Chee Dimock terms "deep time."[19] Among the influential French authors of the era who promoted anti-Ultramontanism and anti-Catholicism were Edgar Quinet and Jules Michelet. Quinet (1803–75), a respected, cosmopolitan historian and poet, published *Génie des religions* [The Genius of Religions] in 1842, an early contribution to world religion studies, but his verbal and published attacks on the Roman Catholic Church led to his dismissal from the Collège de France in 1846. His friend Michelet (1798–1874) was a prolific historian and anticlerical republican (and chair of history at the Collège de France) who documented French confessional practices in *Du Prêtre, de la femme, de la famille* (1845),[20] an English translation of which, *Priests, Women, and Families,* was also available in 1845, and extracts from which were published in a volume by Seeleys, in 1850, part of its "Hints to Romanizers" series.[21] For those who preferred novelistic critiques of confession and Catholicism, there was George Sand's *Mademoiselle la Quintinie* in 1863.

One of the most inventive English anti-Catholic publications was the anonymous *The Oxford and Roman Railway: The Chief Ministers in Church and State and Their Ladies Are Directors and Managers* (1871). With a disrespectful nod to the "underground" railway or network of abolitionists that smuggled American Blacks to freedom in Canada in the nineteenth century, *The Oxford and Roman Railway* suggests that a local, nefarious system delivers people into papal bondage. The author imagines "a Railway direct from Oxford to 'The City of the Seven Hills' with Branches in all parts of the Country" (Anon., *Oxford* 2). Newman, not surprisingly, "was for some time considered the Chief Engineer, and went to Rome to consult *the Oracle of the Jesuits* as to the best route" (Anon., *Oxford* 2; my emphasis). Oxford is named for its particular associations with Tractarianism, but also for the general insinuation that the English educational system is threatened at its historic core. In addition to the (usual) denunciation of Roman Catholic clergy, who "exercise as much tyranny, malice, and blasphemy as if they were the ambassadors of Satan," the author suggests that Romanism "defiles its victims before it destroys them" and does so, with "indecent" efficiency, with the confessional (Anon., *Oxford* 19). There is nothing ambiguous, nothing subtle, about this verbal attack. The pope is the "Vicar of Satan upon earth" and the confessional is both "Jezebel's Reception Room" and the secret "Council Chamber wherein they concoct their dark schemes" (Anon., *Oxford* 5).

The reference to Jezebel is another reminder that the threat or promise of sexual sins or "symbolic transgressions against the family" (Traver 128) always hover in the background of anti-Catholic critiques (whether discussing priests' "unnatural" vow of celibacy or the prurient content of coerced confessions). Jezebel, a Phoenician princess from Tyre and consort of Ahab of Samaria (1 Kings 16), promoted the pagan worship of Baal. Many of the anti-Catholic and anti-confessional texts promote the idea that women and girls are especially threatened by "the filthy Confessional"

(John Armstrong 6). In his 1845 review of Michelet, George Henry Lewes observes, "The priest, as confessor, possesses the secret of a woman's soul, he knows every half-formed hope, every dim desire, every thwarted feeling. The priest ... animates that woman with his own ideas, moves her with his own will, fashions her" ("Michelet" 192). As John Armstrong decries in *The Confessional: Its Wickedness* (1856), the "position in which the Priests stand with regard to females is the great evil of the Confessional," great because when women divulge their sins, or listen to the priests' insinuations, both are at risk of "losing their souls" (7). Similarly, those enlightened by the *Church Association Lectures* of 1867 learned that "the sanctity of our homes is at stake!" ([Church Association] 16)—"our" referring to the patriarchs whose wives, daughters, and sisters were at risk of being spiritually polluted or, worse yet, of exercising their own judgment by converting and/or confiding in a priest. As Griffin points out, many male Victorian commentators articulated a "more subtle suspicion" when they attacked Catholicism: "The fear that the confessional gives another man access to the married woman, to that inner self who should be known only by the husband *to whom it belongs*.... What confession to a priest, like female control of property, implies is that the wife exists not within ... but beside her husband. Like the arguments for married women's property, confession to another man asserts the wife's separateness and autonomy (albeit a false autonomy, as the priest's ability to dominate her demonstrates)" (*Anti-Catholicism* 167–68). A scene from E. Lynn Linton's anti-Catholic novel *Under Which Lord?* (1879) aptly summarizes these unsettling, even scandalous possibilities. Richard Spence is almost overwhelmed by the idea that his wife, Hermione, would seek out the confessional: "'Confession—absolute obedience—suffering another man to come between husband and wife—to rob the parents of their child—giving to another man, call him priest or what you will, the most sacred feelings of your heart, the deepest and strongest of your love—you, a wife, submitting to the indelicacy of inquisitorial questions, to the indignity of regulations'" (Linton 3:60–61).[22] Few situations in life would apparently be more ignominious—for both spouses. Of course, one could also suggest that all Richard Spences resent any person, or any institution, usurping their privilege to regulate and discipline.

"FASCINATED BY THY SERPENT SMILE"

Vitriol and condemnation were not confined to pamphlets or the podium. The "folklore of anti-Romanism" (Reed 221) became pseudo-fact in market-specific journals such as *The Armoury: A Magazine of Weapons for Christian Warfare, Christian's Penny Magazine, Bulwark, Evangelical Christendom,* the *Christian Observer, English Presbyterian Messenger, Baptist Magazine, Penny Protestant Operative, Protestant Witness,* and *The Guardian.* In the *Bulwark* for 1 January 1852, for example, readers learned, "There are two classes of Romish priest. There is your sleek, oily, rollicking, leering, capon-lined emissary of Babylon, whose priestcraft is a mere trade; and there is your lean, intellectual, intense, credulous devotee."[23] Working-class and middle-class periodicals such as *Family Herald, Lloyd's Penny Weekly,* and the *Illustrated London News* contributed further to the accumulation of exposé and exposure. As Paz and Griffin have demonstrated, "One of the reasons for the popularity of anti-Catholic narratives is that they come to serve not merely as a means of attacking Rome, but as a flexible medium of cultural critique" (Griffin, *Anti-Catholicism* 17). To demonstrate further the reach and cultural capital of anti-Catholicism in Hopkins's era, two unlikely partners in circulation will be discussed: *Punch,* the satirical weekly, and Martin Tupper, an ardent poet.

Henry Mayhew and Ebenezer Landells established *Punch, or The London Charivari* in 1841: too late to capitalize on the Roman Catholic Relief Act of 1829 but perfectly primed to take advantage of—and intensify—the furor surrounding "Papal Aggression" in the early 1850s. The controversy and the periodical were made for each other. *Punch,* one could say, took an administrative issue and helped to transform it into a divisive, national cause célèbre.[24] Mockery, exaggeration, and sensationalism are always key to a successful *Punch* cartoon. Also crucial: the ability to link a current event or crisis to a well-known narrative, so that readers are given implicit emotional and historical cues with which to absorb the editorial message. The illustration for the 9 November 1850 article "Expectations from Rome," a satirical piece in which Mr. Bull issues verbal challenges to the "the Roman Pontiff," is one of the simplest and most eloquent: the initial letter of the article, *T* ("The gentleman whose probity and magnanimity...."), becomes an elongated confessional barrier between the foxy, sitting priest and the

FIG 2 "Expectations from Rome," *Punch, or The London Charivari* 19 (9 Nov. 1850): 193.

goosey, kneeling young woman about to unburden her conscience. This simple juxtaposition of predator and prey vividly encapsulates the argument about papal control and the "mortification and ascetism" that Catholicism demands.[25] Similarly, a cartoon of 5 April 1851, "Little Red Riding Hood,"[26] depicts a Roman clerical wolf preying upon a vulnerable young woman. Literally, the cartoon promotes the histrionic idea, then circulating in popular and always salacious "nunnery" tales, that priests were kidnapping young women and confining them in convents. Figuratively, the cartoon implies that papal aggression lurks everywhere.

Just as fears concerning papal aggression were waning in the late 1850s and 1860s, Pusey, the Tractarian leader committed to auricular confession, and the Ritualists (see below) became the gifts that keep on giving for *Punch*'s writers and cartoonists. "Religion à la Mode," published 26 June 1858, shows an indignant and whip-wielding John Bull, protective father, lambasting a smug Anglican priest, "'No, no, Mr. Jack Priest! After all I have gone through, I'm not such a fool as to stand any of this disgusting nonsense!'"[27] The priest is ensconced on the parlor sofa; Bull's daughter is perched on a chaise lounge, turned to the priest as if in a confessional. The scene's editorial "key" is the name on the spine of the book that the priest is holding: *Peter Dens,* the Flemish Catholic theologian. There is nothing subtle and everything comical about the 7 January 1865 cartoon in which a papal "Bull" charges a wall bearing word-signs such as "Science," "Common Sense," and "Toleration."[28] (In the visual personification allegory, animal imagery subtly dehumanizes the non-normative figures in the various outrages.) In June 1877, when the scandal regarding the confessional manual *The Priest in Absolution* reached the House of Lords, *Punch* had an apposite cartoon ready: "A Wolf in Sheep's Clothing" features an impressive, powerful John Bull taking a cowering, slightly sinister ritualistic priest (cassock, beard, large hat, large crucifix hanging around his neck, a rolled-up paper with the name "Holy Cross" sticking out of a pocket, and a copy of "The Priest in Absolution" in one hand) by the ear, as one would an errant child. Bull addresses the scornful figure of Britannia reassuringly: "Mr. Bull (*to Britannia*). 'Whenever you see any of these sneaking scoundrels about, Ma'am, just send for me. *I'll* deal with 'em, never fear!!'" In many cartoons, some detail of the home—a doorway, a drawing room—reminds readers of the religious controversies' domestic implications.

Like so many of his contemporaries, Hopkins read *Punch* whenever it was available.[29] He had ample time to do so when he was an undergraduate, 1863 to 1867, but was especially interested in the 1870s, when his brother Arthur, an illustrator, began contributing to its pages.[30] One of the best overviews of *Punch*'s profitable commitment to fomenting anti-Catholicism is found in F. C. Burnand's essay "'PUNCH' and Pontiffs," written for the *Dublin Review* in 1901.[31] Given the venue, and Burnand's stature at the time—*Punch* editor since 1880, popular columnist, lauded

FIG 3 "Religion à la Mode," *Punch, or The London Charivari* 34 (26 June 1858): 257.

FIG 4 "A Wolf in Sheep's Clothing," *Punch, or The London Charivari* 72 (30 June 1877): 295.

and inexhaustible comic playwright[32]—it is not surprising that he fluctuates between defensiveness (when he joined the *Punch* staff in 1863, he was "the youngest member and the only Catholic" [Burnand 313]) and placating criticism. Typically, Burnand suggests, Mr. Punch has been "a cynical, yet genial, English gentleman and man of the world," but also "fairly entitled himself to be described as Protestant England's 'Licensed Jester'" (307). Succinctly put, the journal's editorial position (prior to Burnand's tenure) was anti-Catholic, anti-Wiseman, anti-papacy, and anti-Irish; its motto could have been, "'When hard up for a subject jeer at the Pope'" (Burnand 312). Looking back fifty years, Burnand ruefully acknowledges that "the scare of 'The Papal Aggression' sent England absolutely off its head. *Punch*, represented by Thackeray, Jerrold, Leech, Leigh, and its editor, Mark Lemon, with the proprietors, Messrs Bradbury and Evans at their back, suffered from a most virulent attack of 'Anti-Roman fever.' They had it violently" (308).

In the 1850s, the poet whose name was synonymous with anti-Catholicism was Martin Tupper (1810–89). Educated at Oxford, where his classmates included William Gladstone, Tupper published prolifically, including the volume *Three Hundred Sonnets* (1860). No one would confuse the latter with sonnets by Elizabeth Barrett Browning, Christina Rossetti, or Hopkins. The most disparaging have unsubtle titles such as "Protesting Truth," "Unholy Alliance," and "The Papal Aggression." The speaker of "Hear the Church" wants to "love and honour and obey" the Church of England, "But where—where is She?," he laments, "who shall strike the truth / Between opposing factions, priest and lay, / The one, to *Rome perverting half our youth,* / The other leading liberally astray?" (Tupper 65; my emphasis). There are excellent reasons why Hopkins's sonnets have only gained admirers since 1889 and Tupper's have become more than obscure. Yet it is Tupper's success in the 1850s and the 1860s that reveals the extent to which the need to vilify Catholics saturated English culture, and the ways in which both *Punch* cartoons and literature were discursively energized by the controversies. In 1851, five thousand copies of this sonnet, "Romish Priestcraft.—1851.," were distributed on the streets of Manchester (Paz 65) to incite and inspire citizens:

> What! after all our charitable pains,
>   And long conciliation's liberal hope,
>   Can we endure to see this subtle Pope
> Scheming to bind our freedom in his chains?
>   Ungrateful, feeble, and perfidious knave!
> Never again through Britain's fair domains
>   Shall tyrannous old priestcraft make us grope
>   In thy dark deep of Intellect's own grave,—
>   Never again shall thou the Mind enslave.
> And yet, who knoweth? haply for awhile,
>   The penalty for gifts and grace abused,
> Some weaklings may be cozened by thy guile,
>   Trick'd at thy boldness, with thy pomps amused,
> And fascinated by thy serpent smile! (Tupper 274)

The poet is too liberal with pseudo-Shakespearean diction (perfidious, knoweth, haply, cozened) and too willing to recycle motifs that already, in 1851, seem tired (papal "chains" threatening to imprison honorable Britons; the Satanic smile hiding the prelate's evil intentions). But the speaker's urgent sense of cultural mission should register: Tupper is anticipating readers who understand that poetry's remit includes anti-Catholic propaganda. Hence the address to "England!" in the sonnet "Church-Dividings," which damns the "pestilent miasma bred at Rome / This inward cancer to the Church and State" that, if not checked, will destroy the country's "vitals" (Tupper 275).

THE "TERRIBLE JESUITS CREEP AND CRAWL"

Given the widespread, often rabid anti-Catholicism that I have been documenting, small wonder that Kate Hopkins, when informed by her son that he was converting, responded in these anguished terms: "All we ask of you is for your own sake to take so momentous a step with caution & hesitation; ~~you~~ ^have^ we not a right to do this? Might not our love & sorrow entitle us to ask it? & you answer by saying that as we might be Romanists if we pleased the estrangement is not of your doing. O Gerard my darling boy are you indeed gone from me?"[33] What must her reaction have been when she learned, in spring 1868, that he was going to join the Society of Jesus? Hopkins alludes to her feelings in a letter to Baillie, 12 February 1868: "But if I am a priest it will cause my mother, or she says it will, great grief and this preys on my mind very much and makes the near prospect quite black" (*CW* 1:176). As this section and the next demonstrate, Mrs. Hopkins's "grief" was not unwarranted: despising Jesuits was not just a facet of the more general Catholic antipathy, it was its own cultural and discursive enterprise. To quote the author of *The Oxford and Roman Railway*, the Jesuits' "calumny" outdoes the "abominations" of Romanism writ large (94).

As mentioned earlier, anti-Jesuit suspicion and fearmongering had been enshrined in several British statutes, including the Catholic Emancipation Act (1829). (Attempts by various popes to suppress, dissolve, or otherwise expel the Order must have been inspiring.) Throughout the century, lecturers and pamphleteers never hesitate to win their audience's endorsement by taking a swipe at "Jesuit Conspirators" (Anon., *Confessional Unmasked* 13). Despite the Society's Spanish founder, its members' behaviors and schemes are deemed Machiavellian in the mainstream Protestant imagination. What is the worst gossip one can spread about John Henry Newman in the

1830s? That he is "a secret Jesuit"—such a well-known "fact" that the London *Times* "report[s] the allegation" (Griffin, *Anti-Catholicism* 82). Dreadful suspicions that "Jesuitry" could "again prevail in this country" ([Church Association] 9) seep into sermons, essays, cartoons, and novels. Of the many characteristics Jesuits are purported to have, a craving for power (ambition and political maneuvering), cruelty, secrecy, avariciousness, and blind obedience are deemed the most noxious. The Society is especially dangerous because, according to an 1846 "history" of the order, "chameleon like, it assumes different shades and colours according to the different parties it has to conciliate" (Overbury 258). Also frequently mentioned: the Jesuits' history of worldwide missionary work is considered proof of its empire-building aspirations and dedication to "extinguishing the light of the Reformation" everywhere (Overbury 167). "Their real design," according to Richard Overbury's 1846 assessment, "was not to make sincere and enlightened converts to the religion of Jesus, but to make proselytes to the Roman Catholic see; and to bring these nations, by means either fair or foul, to wear at least, the outward badge of the Antichrist" (127). As Maureen Moran observes, "The Jesuit has a global reach, disrupting social structures throughout the world with impunity because he is a master of disguise. In historical scholarship and polemical writing of the period, Jesuit viciousness is tackled—though only at second hand—through rumours and a trail of disasters. Past outrages laid at the door of the Society, such as the Gunpowder and Titus Oates Plots and the Great Fire of London, are replaced by contemporary events to update the Jesuit challenge to civil authority" (*Catholic Sensationalism* 34). And last but not least: Jesuits move strangely, preternaturally. In the first chapter of Helen Dhu's *Stanhope Burleigh: The Jesuits in Our Homes* (1855), the narrator guides the reader to the Church of Sant' Ambrogio in Genoa: "How many sleek Jesuits have glided noiselessly under those shadowy arches," he queries (18). Another version of the "danger within and without" narrative, Andrew Steinmetz's novel *The Jesuit in the Family* (1847), features a conversation in which Mr. Bainbridge warns Mrs. Malcolm that "'popery displays her seducing arts, enticing from the bosom of the church the guideless, the unstable, the infirm of our Protestant homes.... Yes; the emissaries of Rome are abroad—the terrible Jesuits creep and crawl, meditating destruction'" (Steinmetz 23).

Fears about "new Jesuits" are expressed in the opening sentences of *A Peep behind the Curtain; or, An Exposure of the Popish Confessional* (1859), which denounces "the sycophant, the traitor, the deluder, the betrayer, the poisoner" who is "playing a game" and ever ready to "giv[e] the Judas kiss" (vi–vii). John Ross pauses long enough in *Penance and the Confessional* to condemn Jesuits' "evil designs" and unquestioning obedience (a menacing form of solidarity) (19, 30). Frances Trollope concurs: at one point in *Father Eustace,* Fr. Ambrose travels to Rome to meet with his Jesuit Superior General, Fr. Scaviotoli, "the man before whom he gloried to prostrate himself, both body and soul" (153). Also suspect: Jesuits' special reverence for the figure of the Virgin Mary, the kind of devotion expressed in such Hopkins poems as "Ad Matrem Virginem" and "The Blessed Virgin Compared to the Air We Breathe." The English "were well aware that the dreaded Society of Jesus had, from its inception, actively promulgated belief in the Immaculate Conception as a means of directly challenging the Reformation" (Griffin, *Anti-Catholicism* 117). Fundamentally, Jesuits could play any role that the anti-Catholic author deemed appropriate: "dangerous alien," the enemy within, or countercultural menace. "As cultural metaphor," Moran suggests, "the figure of the invisible but ever-present Jesuit is a shadowy reminder of the hidden inconsistencies concealed by the idealized British character—upright, resilient and selfless, tolerant and committed to individual freedoms" (*Catholic Sensationalism* 29).[34]

Intolerance, nonetheless, contributes to familiar, even cliché representations of Jesuits as being almost "a different species—cold, calculating and reptilian" (Peschier 290). As the narrator of Trollope's *Father Eustace* sneeringly suggests, the Jesuits "have, each and every one of them, more eyes than are fabled in the head of a spider.... No race, or rather no society, congregated on the surface of the earth, understand their own concerns better than do the inheritors of the power of Ignatius Loyola; and those who, under any circumstances, presume to suspect them of doing less for the advancement of their power than they can do, are altogether blunderers and ignorami" (71–72). The Society's emphasis on educating its members only intensifies their apparent fearsomeness and reputation for being "the very figure[s] of the disguised Satanic rhetorician[s]" (Wilt 3). As Judith Wilt observes, "Spiritually and psychologically, the Jesuit is both the excess and the default form of every attribute of priesthood—its knowledge, its authority, and above all, its intellectual and sexual 'reserve'" (3).

Almost as inventive as the many anti-Jesuit novels that proliferate in the nineteenth century are the purported "histories" or studies of the Society that flourish. Four titles should be mentioned because each contributes particularly lurid insights and displays tactics designed to discredit.³⁵ Overbury's history *The Jesuits* (1846), which I have already cited, bolsters its argument by quoting seventeenth- and eighteenth-century critics and contemporary authorities such as Michelet and Quinet. In order to solidify the argument about the order's "perversity," Overbury also quotes from the Jesuit Constitutions. Criminality is the underthought of his chronicle. Among the crimes committed by Jesuits are regicide, murder, assassination, *"perjury, lying, and false-witness"*; the "morality of the Jesuits is truly the devil's last great masterpiece" (Overbury 75, 85, 86). Further examples of their blasphemy, cruelty, "cunning craft and sophistry," and "boundless ambition" are supplied throughout the book (121, 125). Toxicity is another motif informing the "history": first, the head Jesuit, or Superior General, whose power is "of the most absolute and unlimited kind" (47), helps to ensure that the minds of individual Jesuits are poisoned; second, members of the Society poison the minds of all whom they encounter. The confessional is the site where they dissemble most effectively (56, 66). And, in an era in which St. Francis of Assisi had many admirers among Anglican readers, and "secular saints" were popular, Overbury takes great pains to besmudge the reputation of Ignatius Loyola, the "dupe of Satan and of his own deceitful, depraved, self-righteous, vain, and ambitious heart" who converted from "the character of a profligate soldier to that of a blind votary of a blind and groveling superstition, and of a more complete child of the devil than he was before" (16). Hopkins, of course, believed the opposite: Ignatius, a humble and saintly person, was "one of the most extraordinary men that ever lived" (*CW* 1:504).

According to Overbury, Jesuits' secrecy and mystery inform "the spirit of the cloister, the cell, and the confessional." Claiming to be quoting from "secret" Jesuit documents, he warns of their plans to inveigle money and endowments from rich widows (101–2), monopolize intelligent male students, and generally "catch" souls to carry out their nefarious plans. In 1854 Giovanni Nicolini also asserts that the Jesuits have "designs" on the English populace and the world (global domination of souls is never far from their plots); he manipulates the historical record to expose their "disgraceful celebrity": "If they hated England and Queen Elizabeth in the sixteenth century, they bear no less hate to England and Queen Victoria in the nineteenth. Let an opportunity present itself, and you shall see them again heading the rebellion, and preaching murder as the most meritorious of all actions" (iii, 169). Like Overbury, Nicolini pauses to remind people that the Jesuit confessional is used by and "for those who wish to sin in all surety," yet another example of the Society's "diabolical dexterity" (463). But Nicolini, at least, demonstrates some wit in his character assassinations:

> Every monastic order is distinguished by a peculiar character. Plots and machinations against Protestants, and against all civil and religious freedom, are the characteristics of the Jesuits. A Benedictine monk will sit calmly in his very comfortable room, sip his chocolate, take a hand at whist, and not even dream of converting any one. A Franciscan, of any denomination, will sit jocosely before a succulent dinner, which he has provided by going door to door, distributing, in return for provisions, snuff and images, without uttering a word about his or your religion, and only relating some pleasing anecdotes of the holy founder of his order, St. Francis. A Dominican will assuredly report your conduct to Rome, and will try to convert your daughter to—his principles, but will care very little about the conversion.... The Jesuit, on the contrary, has ... no other occupation or desire than to make converts; and this we need not take the trouble to prove, since they themselves confess it. (466)

Not surprisingly, Nicolini acknowledges the works of Quinet and Michelet as historical inspiration, especially their coauthored book, *Jesuits and Jesuitism*.[36]

The fourth example of anti-Jesuit disclosure is Isaac Taylor's *Loyola: and Jesuitism in Its Rudiments* (1857), which takes Thomas Carlyle's "heroes and hero-worship" strategy and inverts it. Part 1 is a two-hundred-page "personal history" of Ignatius that suggests how and why he "might have been matched with Machiavelli in subtle command of the springs of human action—with Richelieu in the practice and art of governing mankind—with Hobbes in daring paradoxical consistency" (16). Ignatius was "neither the mystic nor the completist," Taylor insists; his goal was nothing less than "an absolute domination over the spirits of men, and of a centralization of all powers on earth" (20, 16). Part 2 provides an assessment of the Society's malevolent cohesiveness, achieved through the

Spiritual Exercises, the Jesuit Constitutions, and thoroughly disciplined lives. Rounding out the discussion is a summary of Blaise Pascal's critique of the Society.

Kate and Manley Hopkins's responses when told that their son was joining the Society of Jesus have not survived. Newman, however, had only praise and encouragement: "Don't call 'the Jesuit discipline ^hard^,' it will bring you to heaven. The Benedictines would not have suited you" (*CW* 1:178).[37]

THE "MUFFLED THUMP OF FANATIC WORSHIPPERS"

In *Mornings among the Jesuits at Rome* (1849), a journalistic exposé, M. Hobart Seymour suggests that the Jesuits are masters of dissembling and disguise, whether assuming the roles of "private tutor in some family of influence, or as a footman to act as a spy in some important family—whether as a learned and subtle controversialist, or as a meek and gentle and courtly friend to insinuate his opinions" (21). His summary of nefarious possibilities could double as the casting guide for countless anti-Catholic, anti-Jesuit novels. Of the many one could consider—whether now-canonized texts such as Charlotte Brontë's *Villette* (1853)[38] or the long-forgotten *Beatrice; or, The Unknown Relatives* (1852) by Catherine Sinclair, in which a "venerable" Anglican bishop refers to Jesuits as the "Thugs of Christendom" (126)[39]—I have selected Wilkie Collins's *The Black Robe* (1881)[40] and Mary Arnold Ward's *Helbeck of Bannisdale* (1898) for a brief comparison. *Helbeck* is subtle where *The Black Robe* is coarse; psychologically insightful, where *The Black Robe* is mundane and replete with caricatures.[41] Ward explores gender roles insightfully; Collins relies upon casual misogyny throughout.[42] Ward eschews sensationalism, which is Collins's modus operandi. Ward's narrator assumes the reader is prepared to think about issues, and allows Roman Catholic dogma to speak for itself, as it were: "Sin and its Divine Victim, penance, regulation of life, death, judgement—Catholic thought moves perpetually from one of these ideas to another" (*Helbeck* 305). Collins's narrators, on the other hand, pander to an audience delighted by intrigue and extreme revelations. Ward's critique of Catholicism is actually sharper because it depends upon close observation. Collins rushes through conventional plot elements (spying servants, devious Jesuits, an inheritance crisis) and a few Gothic or melodramatic ones (a duel, a man tormented by a past mistake, a woman whose chastity is compromised) to arrive at a satisfactorily appalling ending. Nonetheless, the aesthetic differences between the novels only heighten one's awareness of their shared goal: to interrogate Catholicism, and especially Jesuits, and to expose their "fatal influence" (Wilkie Collins 1:24). Both certainly explain Kate Hopkins's "sorrow."

In *The Black Robe,* set in the late 1850s and early 1860s, Fr. Benwell, S.J., is the living embodiment of "papal aggression"[43] and Jesuit scheming. Before the "dissolution" of the monasteries, Vange Abbey, now the ancestral home of Lewis Romayne, had belonged to the Church. Benwell, who is Falstaffian in appearance and demeanor but Machiavellian in his conniving, does everything possible—including hiring a private detective to ferret out information; bribing servants for gossip; "planting" a Jesuit in Romayne's household—to secure the rights to the property. Benwell is mercenary and mendacious, and unapologetically so. He is not even respectful about the Society. When Romayne eventually joins the Order, Benwell interrupts the sanctity of the *Spiritual Exercises* and makes slighting remarks about "the wise monotony of discipline at The Retreat" (Wilkie Collins 2:151). Benwell also preens about his schemes when recounting his machinations for his "superiors" in Rome: "'I make no attempt to excuse myself. You know our motto:—THE END JUSTIFIES THE MEANS'" (2:50).

Lewis Romayne is the perfect convert: an extremist in personality and psychologically damaged. Romayne's beautiful wife, Stella, who conspires to conceal an almost bigamous marriage to Bernard Winterfield, is vehemently anti-Catholic. Arthur Penrose, the young Jesuit whose homoerotic sensibility is archly presented, becomes her rival for Romayne's attention. When Lewis and Stella are irrevocably estranged, he joins the Society and quickly becomes a prominent preacher in Rome. His sermon on hell, a zealous tour de force, traces "the downward progress of the lost man, from his impenitent death-bed to his doom in hell. The dreadful superstition of everlasting torment became doubly dreadful in the priest's fervent words" (2:229).[44] A final jab at Jesuits comes in the form of Winterfield's observations while visiting the Society's main church in Rome: within its forebodingly dark interior, he hears the "wailing notes of the organ, accompanied at intervals by the muffled thump of fanatic worshippers penitentially beating their breasts" (2:228).

In *The Black Robe* Penrose, a "gentle, self-distrustful, melancholy man," is "innocent of suspicion and self-seeking" and therefore too easily "perverted to dangerous uses in unscrupulous hands" (Wilkie Collins 1:88). *Helbeck of Bannisdale* also features a "gentle" young Jesuit, Teddy Williams, once a gifted painter of Pre-Raphaelite sensibilities who was forced by the Society to "give up his art." Helbeck explains to Laura Fountain, "'Of course it has been his great renunciation. His superiors thought it necessary to cut him off from it entirely. And no doubt during the novitiate he suffered a great deal. It has been like any other starved faculty'" (Ward, *Helbeck* 258–59).[45] Williams, "in some ways, singularly handsome," is described in detail: "the features delicate without weakness, the high brow narrowed by the thick and curling hair that overhung it, the small chin and curving mouth, kept still something of the look and bloom of the child—a look that was only intensified by the strange force of expression that was added to the face whenever the lids so constantly dropped over the eyes were raised.... Such a look one may often see in the eyes of a poetic and morbid child" (263).[46] According to editor Brian Worthington, this is Ward's portrait of Hopkins, her father Tom Arnold's colleague in Dublin (17).[47] Hopkins and Arnold (whose religious doubts and serial conversions devastated the lives of his wife and children[48]) almost crossed paths in Birmingham; both taught at Newman's Oratory school in the late 1860s.[49] When the Jesuits assumed control of the Catholic University in Dublin (rechristened University College), Arnold and Hopkins became colleagues in February 1884. And it was for Arnold's *Lives of the Poets* series that Hopkins composed the short biography of Pre-Raphaelite poet Richard Watson Dixon.[50] The plot of *Helbeck* is not designed to flatter Teddy Williams, who eventually leaves the Society. His function is to demonstrate one of three ways of being a priest. The genial rather than intelligent Fr. Bowles is the second ("He disliked Jesuits, and religious generally, if the truth were known" [Ward, *Helbeck* 77]); Fr. Leadham, S.J., who preys upon Helbeck, is the third.

Collins's male protagonist, Lewis Romayne, is emotionally volatile, a melodramatic religious zealot. He falls in and out of love with Stella Eyrecourt precipitously. Ward's female protagonist, Laura Fountain, is devoted to the memory of her father, an agnostic, and so conditioned by his hatred of organized religion that falling in love with Helbeck, an ardent recusant Catholic, is actually torment. Collins exploits his readers' anti-Catholic sentiments to thrill and titillate. Ward argues against the "spiritual intrusiveness of Catholicism, its perpetual uncovering of the soul—its disrespect for the secrets of personality—its humiliation of the will—that made it most odious in the eyes of this daughter of a modern world" (*Helbeck* 278). Eventually, the ending of *Helbeck* is more shocking than anything Collins or another sensation novelist could imagine: in the spirit of Ibsen's Rebecca West (*Rosmersholm,* 1886), Fountain drowns herself.[51] Neither living without Helbeck, nor succumbing to his religious example (these "Catholic figures were to her so many disagreeable automata, moved by springs she could not possibly conceive" [*Helbeck* 277]), is tenable.[52] Helbeck, for his part, is almost undone by the notion of marrying "an unbelieving wife"; he is "racked with desire for this little pagan creature, this girl without a single Christian sentiment or tradition, the child of an infidel father, herself steeped in denial and cradled in doubt, with nothing meekly feminine about her" (228, 229). And so the reader is caught, as Ward's uncle Matthew Arnold had predicted in "Stanzas from the Grand Chartreuse," "between two worlds, one dead, / The other powerless to be born."[53]

The Black Robe is a conversion novel dressed up as a sensation story; *Helbeck of Bannisdale* is a refusal-to-convert New Woman novel. Both narratives are calculated to engender a robust response: *Robe* is designed to shock; *Helbeck,* to appall. In both, mendacious priests prey upon a wealthy man; Jesuits especially are scheming mercenaries. For Collins, the dangers of religion are only external, and sectarian: Catholics, especially Jesuits, represent coercive forces that a "good" English Protestant can ultimately defeat. For Ward, however, the dangers of religion—of any denomination—are internal, psychological, and omnipresent. In *The Black Robe,* all the trappings of Romanism, including the confessional, are props to intensify the narrative frisson. In *Helbeck of Bannisdale,* such elements intensify Laura Fountain's anguish and "passionate repulsion": "What a gross, what an intolerable superstition!—how was she to live with it, beside it?" (74). Ultimately, she can't, and she won't.

Dr. Friedland, the wise Cambridge don who has befriended Fountain all her life, ruefully observes, "'There again, how little the Protestant understands what he reviles!'" (Ward, *Helbeck* 332). The following two sections consider the Anglican revulsion occasioned by Tractarian and Ritualist "scandals" within the Church of England, 1840s to 1880s, and detail why auricular confession—which Hopkins was enjoined to practice as an undergraduate—was at the eye of the critical storms.

"THE PUSSEY CATS ARE COMING"

Of all the Victorian anti-confessional propaganda one can read, the 1850s broadside ballad "The Flare Up in the Confessional. The Pussey Cats Are Coming" is one of the most entertaining. Three excerpts (from the beginning, middle, and end) will suffice:

> COME cheer up old England, don't be in the lurch,
> With the broom beat the pussey cats out of the church;
> Never mind the confessional, let us have hope
> We don't care for pussy cat, priestcraft, or Pope[.]
> . . . .
> Oh! ladies, young ladies, of pussies beware!
> If you go to confession, you'll be caught in a snare,
> You must tell all you do; and the length of your nose,
> How many nails you have got on your fingers and toes;
> How many times you have washed yourself under the pump,
> And how many times you have fell on your rump;
> . . . .
> There will soon be a stop to such doings we hope,
> Away with the pussey cats, laugh at the Pope[.]
> Be courageous old England, of thorns clear the way,
> Hurrah for brave Westerton,[54] jolly and gay,
> He will turn the confessionals all inside out,
> And then all the pussey cats, put to the rout. ("The Flare-Up")

The "pussey cats" are the followers of Edward Pusey, another polarizing Victorian religious figure: revered by so many for his asceticism, devotion, and intellectual breadth; reviled, in equal numbers—as the broadside attests—for encouraging people to respect Roman Catholicism, and for promoting, or so it would seem, an unholy interest in the confessional. It is Pusey's impact on Hopkins's life and writings that shapes this segment of the "confessing the flesh" argument.

In the 1830s, Oxford-based Anglicans such as Pusey, John Keble,[55] Newman, R. W. Church, and Hurrell Froude began reexamining the principles of the "early" Church—theological and academic investigations that also identified common ground between Anglicanism and Roman Catholicism. (As Nigel Yates observes, the Tractarians "had, in several respects . . . pushed the Church of England well beyond the confines of traditional High-Church theology" [*Anglican* 47–48].) They published their findings and religious speculations in a series of "tracts," launched by a reprint of Keble's 1833 sermon entitled "National Apostasy." The pamphlets and books most important to Hopkins included Newman's "The Catholic Church" (Tract 2, 1833), "The Present Obligation of Primitive Practice. A Sin of the Church" (Tract 6, 1833), and "The Mortification of the Flesh" (Tract 21, 1834); Keble's "The Annunciation of the Blessed Virgin Mary" (Tract 54, 1835); Froude's "The Position of the Church of Christ in England, Relatively to the State and the Nation" (Tract 59, 1835); and Pusey's "On the Benefits of the System of Fasting Prescribed by Our Church" (Tract 66, 1835).[56] Newman's heterodox "Remarks on Certain Passages in the Thirty-Nine Articles" (Tract 90, 1841) was the final publication (the bishop of Oxford intervened)—and, in retrospect, it symbolically marked the end of the Oxford Movement's first wave. Newman's conversion in 1845 was one of many; suspicions that "Oxford undergraduates were being converted to Romanism" multiplied, and a campaign was waged in what an 1869 publication termed "all those crushing volumes, pamphlets, articles, and speeches, whose name is legion" (Anon., *Confessional Unmasked* iv).

These religious debates were a catalyst for national crises. Both Westminster and the palace were on high alert by 1850; the prime minister, Lord John Russell, advised the Queen that the "growth" of Roman Catholic proclivities in the "bosom" of the Anglican Church should be a source of "national alarm": "Dr. Arnold says very truly, 'I look upon a Roman Catholic as an enemy in his uniform; I look upon a Tractarian as an enemy disguised as a spy'" (qtd. Sturrock 92). Similarly, the worst thing Richard

Overbury could suggest about Keble, Pusey, and Newman is that they are doing now, in the nineteenth century, "the work of the Jesuits in the sixteenth, by impeding the progress of the truth and of the Reformation, and by subjecting us once more to all the miseries of ecclesiastical despotism" (41). Critics of Tractarianism were quick to blame its instigators for "treachery": for creating "the schism in our ranks" by succumbing to "the embraces of Popery" (Ross 65, 64). Private, auricular confession was the issue that generated the most controversy and invective. The "tone of the debates" was "nearly hysterical," as Anne Hartman suggests; the "very mention of the word 'confession' could provoke a range of responses: anti-Irish and anti-Catholic fervor; intense nationalism; anxiety over the production of sexual knowledge; and fear for the stability of the domestic sphere" (536). Yet, "confession was at times misidentified as the cause of these anxieties when in fact it worked to secure a location where these anxieties could be articulated and maintained" (536).

So the question remains: of all the Tractarian theological issues presented for public debate, why were the form, function, and sacral status of confession among the most contentious? Confession is neither a fundamental Christian rite, like baptism, nor as imaginatively demanding as transubstantiation, which requires one to believe that Christ's body and blood exist in the communion wafer and wine. As Hopkins explains to a friend in 1864, "The great aid to belief and object of belief is the doctrine of the Real Presence in the Blessed Sacrament of the Altar. Religion without that is sombre, dangerous, illogical, with that it is—not to speak of ^its^ grand consistency and certainty—*loveable*. Hold that and you will gain all Catholic truth."[57] There is nothing "loveable" about confession; instead, it is supposed to be *instructive,* in terms of the self-examination required in preparation for the event, and *constructive,* in terms of the relief experienced after divulging one's transgressions. What Pusey and his followers understand, however, and what their critics intuit if not fully grasp, is that confession is *productive:* it produces relations of power, knowledge, and subjectivity. Complete with striking props and heterotopic energy, it dramatizes how authority is invested, wielded, and accepted. When Pusey acknowledges that "controversialists" have "spoken against" confessions as something "injurious to the soul, and interfering between it and its Redeemer" ("Preface" clii), he is only partially correct. Confession is controversial because pastoral power is fully on display, and many are made uncomfortable by such frankness. As Frank Turner observes, "The sphere of religion during [those] years and after touched upon more and more personal and public concerns" (14).

Pusey's ideas are anchored in the writings of John Keble (1792–1866), whom Hopkins cites variously as one of the "Oxford poets" (*CW* 3:293) and a member of the "Lake School," which "expires in Keble and Faber and Cardinal Newman" (*CW* 1:610). In his esteemed poetry and sermons, Keble embraces the spirit of auricular confession but will not insist upon it. Throughout *The Christian Year* (1827), an anthology of poems "for each Sunday, saint's day, and service of the Book of Common Prayer" (Gilley, "Keble") that was "probably the widest selling book of poetry in the nineteenth century" (Butler),[58] Keble stresses the role of one's conscience to keep "self-commanding hearts" pure ("All Saints' Day") but mentions confession reservedly. "True confessors in faith" are saluted in "Advent Sunday," but only in "Ash-Wednesday" is "Confession's smart" acknowledged (Keble, *Christian* 10, 95). The speaker for the "First Sunday after Easter" admits that "Wild Fancy" tempted him, but his "better soul confess'd" and accepted Christ's "whisper'd warnings, kind and soft" (Keble, *Christian* 158).[59] In his sermons, however (ten volumes when published), the "Necessity of Confession" is addressed directly (*Sermons* 3:139–50). The sinner, Keble insists, must "come out of his hiding-place, leave all his vain excuses, force himself to confess his sins and forsake them" (*Sermons* 3:148).[60] Operations of force, however, should be individual rather than institutional. Keble suggests that those who are "unconfessed and unrepented of" their sins risk "eternal incurable punishment" but is equivocal as to whether the Church of England should mandate confession (*Sermons* 3:195, 193).

Certainly, he reiterates concern for those "who have never told before God on their knees the sad story of their own particular sins" (Keble, *Sermons* 3:193). An obligation to confess is mentioned in "National Apostasy" (1:30) and recommended in "Conscience, an Earnest of the Last Judgement" (1:135); multiple sermons on "The Christian Priesthood" cite, among the clergy's major responsibilities, the need to "listen" to parishioners, "to pray with them, to confess their sins and their faith, and to praise God" (1:352). In "The Duty of Public Worship," he imagines the typical ritual of confession: one's duty is to "render Him homage in the sight of men and Angels: to confess with lip and knee as well as with heart" (2:295). Theoretically and theologically, Keble was committed to *confessing*, but only gradually would he endorse regular, ritualized, and authorized *confession*. Only in various *Letters of Spiritual Counsel and Guidance*, collected and edited after his death, could the general public see Keble admitting, "Whoever can discreetly and effectually bring in Confession, will do, I should think, one of the best things for this poor Church as she is at present" (42). On the one hand, he continues to sit on the doctrinal fence when he comments, "For a penance, I scarcely know what to recommend; the only thing which occurs to me is, whether it might be well (if not too sharp) to confess it . . . and make a rule to do so if it recurred: but this should not be done in a hurry. I only *mention*, I do not *recommend*" (Keble, *Letters* 198). He mentions, positively, some Roman Catholic practices, but prefers Church of England rules and strictures, despite the fact that

> [o]ne sees, of course, that there is the greatest room for abuse and self-deceit in these things, as there is, no doubt, in the permission to dispense with Auricular Confession altogether, which yet I believe you allow to be granted by our Church. We may wish it otherwise, but we must take things as we find them; and although it would greatly simplify matters and make the task of a clergyman, in a certain sense, much easier, to tie ourselves to the foreign rules, I feel that, in spite of ourselves, the line which our Church has taken compels us to modify them in very charity to the many souls which would, I fear, otherwise be repelled from their best hope of recovery. (*Letters* 72)

When John Taylor Coleridge published *A Memoir of the Rev. John Keble* in 1870, he included a letter penned by his friend in 1844: "'We go on working in the dark, and in the dark it will be, until the rule of systematic confession is received in our Church. . . . We are in our parishes like people whose lantern has blown out,[61] and who are feeling their way, and continually stepping in puddles and splotches of mud, which they think are dry stones'" (J. T. Coleridge 298). The year before Keble died, according to Coleridge, he continued to support those who preferred "the auricular and secret confession to the Priest" (545).

Pusey, Keble's staunchest advocate, is adamant rather than evasive about recommending confession. From the 1840s onwards, Pusey knows he is traversing treacherous religious and public territory, but he persists, because confession provides "consolation, counsel, and absolution," even if it is not officially a Church of England sacrament ("Preface" xxxv). It is partly a preventative measure and partly a remedy. Among his riskier rhetorical strategies: in his introduction to Gaume's *Manual,* a document central to Pusey's campaign to reinstate confession (or at least have it be tolerated), he singles out the "Oxford Martyrs"—Thomas Cranmer, Nicholas Ridley, and Hugh Latimer, burned at the stake for their defense of Protestantism during Queen Mary's persecutions—and turns Latimer's words into a ringing endorsement of his own position: "'But to speak of right and true Confession, *I would to God it were kept in England; for it is a good thing*'" (Pusey, "Preface" xxxvi). (The pyres for all three men were arranged on what is now Broad Street, Oxford: an "X" marks the spot on the pavement just beyond the front gate of Hopkins's Balliol College. One year, his rooms provided an excellent view of the so-called Martyrs' Memorial, a statue of Cranmer, Ridley, and Latimer by George Gilbert Scott that was installed on St. Giles Street, on Balliol's western flank, in 1843.[62]) In that same contentious document, Pusey tries to repatriate confession, or at least expunge its forbidding foreign otherness. In one paragraph, for example, Englishness is featured four times: "Great injustice has been done not to us only, but to our English families. But for our habitual English reserve and modesty, and the nature of the subject, in which people cannot even repudiate calumny without a sense of defilement, there would have been one burst of indignation at these implications, that our English Clergy would have asked such questions of our English wives or daughters, *or that they would have borne such questions*" (Pusey, "Preface" xviii). Pusey's other consistent strategy is marshalling quotations of support from post-Reformation Anglican authorities, everyone from Bishop Berkeley, Richard Hooker, Lancelot Andrewes, and John Donne to Archbishop Laud and Puritan writers such as William Turner, dean of Wells.[63] The more incongruous and eclectic the list, the better, so that the historical record seems to endorse his position.

Pusey's own confessional and ascetic practices help one to identify, if not understand, Hopkins's self-abasing strictures. In 1846, when Pusey persuaded Keble to serve as his confessor, he "gave Keble in tabulated form a list of the austerities he had set before himself. They included 'Never to look at the beauty of nature without inward confession of unworthiness'... 'not to smile (if I can help it) except with children; to drink water at dinner'... and from time to time in winter to do without a fire, avoiding it as a 'type of hell.' He even complained that the hair shirt he wore was not sufficiently uncomfortable" (MacKenzie, *Excursions* 52–53).[64] That hair shirt ethos informs his *Hints for a First Confession* (1851), both a brisk how-to manual and a prediction of "the dark catalogue of sins" each person carries within (31). Childhood is "a very sacred age," according to Pusey, but also the "starting-point in some sin" (21, 22). More practically, he encourages penitents to keep a list of sins as a daily inventory and an *aide-memoire* for confession: "You had better mark them down for yourself by some abbreviations which others cannot understand, else you might forget them" (4).[65] (Hopkins's abbreviations include "E.T." for "evil thoughts" and "O.H." for "old habits." Pusey stresses the fact that "the will is good but weak, and evil habits strong"; "some enduring evil habit" will always threaten [14, 6].) For "sins of the senses," Pusey recommends that one discern "what different senses were engaging in it—as the sight, hearing, touch; whether it were resisted, or whether... committed almost as often as the temptation occurred" (6). Hopkins's most Tractarian poems of the mid-1860s, such as "Barnfloor and Winepress" and especially "The Habit of Perfection"[66] stress "the bitterness of sin" (*PW* 31) by conducting an inventory of sensory transgressions.

Pusey also recommends a "composition of place" technique not unlike Ignatius's in the *Spiritual Exercises*: "Try to bring everything before you: each separate scene in every place—the fields, or streets, or houses around your home or abode, your walks, rides, society, loneliness and lonely thoughts, the rooms you lived in, their very furniture—everything helps to recover the memory of your past life, and so bring back (alas!) the memory of sin" (*Hints* 4). Hopkins defines "composition of place" plainly: "how strongly [Ignatius] means us to realise the scene" (*CW* 5:447). Put another way, no place is safe from associations of sinfulness—not the natural world, the neighborhood, nor one's innermost thoughts. The octave of Hopkins's "Myself unholy" (June 1865) reveals what such a presumption of "fault" produces:

> Myself unholy, from myself unholy
> To the sweet living of my friends I look—
> Eye-greeting doves bright-counter to the rook,
> Fresh brooks to salt sand-teasing waters shoaly:—
> And they are purer, but alas! not solely
> The unquestion'd readings of a blotless book.
> And so my trust confusèd, struck, and shook...
> Yields to the sultry siege of melancholy. (*PW* 76–77)

The speaker's inability to trust himself is both genuine and acquired. (As Foucault suggests, in terms of pastoral tactics, "the man who undergoes the procedure of redemption must never be completely sure of himself" [*HS* 4:44].) Yet the "siege of melancholy" is more than a medievalizing allegorical gesture; the "unholy" speaker wishes to rout sin and regain purity, be more like Christ and his friends, but instead his equilibrium is destabilized. As the speaker of "A Voice from the World" (1864–65) also concludes, the burden of one's "unworthiness" can crush one's heart and mind (*PW* 51).

Hopkins first hopes to hear Pusey preach in June 1863 and defends him as a "moderate" man to Baillie three months later (*CW* 1:39, 71). Because Hopkins recorded his activities sporadically in his Oxford diaries, there are only persistent traces of Pusey. In February 1864, for example, he plans to attend "Dr. Pusey's lectures on Thursdays 8 o'clock" (*CW* 3:139), and the following year, his lectures on the Old Testament book of Daniel (*CW* 3:279); in 1865, he wants to read a book recommended (prefaced) by Pusey, Lorenzo Scupoli's *The Spiritual Combat* (*CW* 3:277) as well as Pusey's own "sermon[s] on Everlasting Punishment, and on The Remedy for Sin of the body" (*CW* 3:279). And in Advent 1865: "I confessed to Dr. Pusey Dec. 15 16, 1865" (*CW* 3:339).[67] In May 1866, just before deciding to convert, Hopkins hears Pusey preach in Oxford, one of the afternoon "University Sermons" at St. Mary-the-Virgin (*CW* 3:361). When he informs his parents of his plans to convert, he agrees to their request that he consult with Pusey, but Pusey refuses to see him just "to satisfy relations" (*CW* 1:118).

How profoundly Pusey's person and writings affected Hopkins is suggested in two tropes from *Hints for a First Confession, Penitence, and Eirenicon* that continue to echo in Hopkins's poetry in the 1870s.

Sifting—literally, in the sense of winnowing, and figuratively, in terms of examining closely—is a favorite metaphor for Pusey: in *Hints,* he acknowledges that people "will often complain that they are sifting themselves just as if they were the sins of some other they were looking into. The very process makes them feel cold and dead" (57). In *Penitence,* he warns about the dangers of an "unexamined, unsifted, conscience" and recommends "not judging himself only, but sifting himself through and through; acts, motives, and circumstances; the aggravations of his sins, and their endurance" (17, 25). In "The Wreck," a poem in which the speaker judges himself continually, finding himself wanting (in both senses of the word) in relation to the "tall Nun," he evocatively acknowledges, "I am sóft síft / In an hourglass—at the wall / Fast, but mined with a motion, a drift" (*PW* 120). It is one of the most brilliant metaphors in the ode. In *Eirenicon,* Pusey explains that union with Christ is "organic," but more than just a question "of will, or of mind, or of love": it is a "union through His indwelling spirit. . . . As Thou, Father, art in Me, and I in Thee, that they also may be one in Us" (46). These remarks could be a prose précis of "As kingfishers catch fire," which insists that "Each mortal thing does one thing and the same: / Deals out that being indoors each one dwells; / Selves—goes its self, *myself* it speaks and spells, / Crying *What I do is me: for that I came.*" The final flourish, however, is pure Hopkins: "For Christ plays in ten thousand places, / Lovely in limbs, and lovely in eyes not his / To the Father through the features of men's faces" (*PW* 141).

Of Pusey's many Tractarian disciples, none was keener or more sedulous in guiding the minds and souls of Oxford students than Henry Liddon. Many called him a saintly man, but it is also possible to think of him as a spiritual predator. Benjamin Jowett, exasperated, called "Mr Liddon" an Anglican "perverter" who encourages the "'worship'" of his followers (*Dear Miss* 51). In July 1865 Jowett explained in detail his sense of betrayal when "some" pupils

> get wafted off to the Confessional & then no amount of personal kindness or obligation weighs a feather against their fanaticism. They lose all sense of loyalty or regard. This is one of the unpleasantnesses of Oxford at present. I think the best way is to ignore it & treat them as if I did not know that they do & repeat what I say to Pusey & Liddon.[68] When they

have thoroughly taken the disorder, they really are such fanatics that they know not what spirit they are of. Some of them will become Romanists & then, perhaps, they will become liberal. Any Catholic direction would be far better than they get in Oxford. (*Dear Miss* 64)

With the exception of the later "liberal" tendencies, Jowett had unwittingly predicted the "direction" of Hopkins's Oxford life. In relation to people like Hopkins, whose confessions he heard for more than a year, Liddon certainly did not follow Philip Neri's advice, quoted and endorsed by Gaume: "Confessors, who are drawn to certain pious exercises or meditations, ruin the healthiness of their penitents" (322).[69]

SMELLS, BELLS, AND "DEATH IN THE POT"

Blaming Pusey for anything and everything even remotely tied to Tractarianism, or for the excesses of the Ritualism that flourished from the 1850s to the 1880s (perhaps a "logical extension" of the Oxford Movement [O'Malley 8], but not part of its reforming mandate), became a public and publishing sport. The author of the *Oxford and Roman Railway* insists that "Puseyism perverts and destroys" (Anon. 22). An 1871 pamphlet produced by the Evangelical Mission and Electoral Union is even blunter: *Dr. Pusey's Insane Project Considered*. A commitment to Ritualism was expressed in two ways: in terms of personal behavior and material culture. The former was encouraged by Pusey's life and writings; the latter was actually antithetical to Pusey's asceticism. As Yates explains, habitual confession was only one of many ritualistic practices "linked to the performance of austerities by the penitent: self-flagellation, rigorous fasting or eating unpleasant food, cold baths, wearing hair shirts and frequent almsgiving were all penances" deemed acceptable and desirable (*Anglican* 213). Ritualism's other major aspect, the aesthetic pleasures borrowed from Roman Catholicism—a kind of Catholic baroque/rococo that only an English imagination could invoke—appealed to "theatricalized and theatricalizing selves" (Griffin, *Anti-Catholicism* 82): church decorations such as crucifixes, candles, stained glass, flowers; music and chanting; elaborate vestments; and incense.

Two lampooning poems vividly summarize popular scorn about such affectations. *The Oxford and Roman Railway* quotes "Ye Great Anglican Revival," three stanzas of which advise,

> Crosses behind and Crosses before,
> Crosses as soon as you enter the door;
> Candles and incense, lights by the score,
> Copes and Stoles and a jolly lot more
>   In "Ye Anglican Church."
>
> . . . .
>
> Convents and Brotherhoods: Sisters and Co.,
> Altars and Sacraments—All that they know,
> Do these wolves in sheep's clothing bring up from below,
> To make the old follies of Rome "all the go"
>   In "Ye Anglican Church."
>
> Confessional boxes, and I don't know what,
> Beware! English Ladies—"There's death in the pot."[70]
> Let Altars and Sacraments all go to rot,
> Ere you let yourselves down to this foul Popish blot
>   In "Ye Anglican Church." (22)

The conversion of an Anglican church into a "rank Popish den" seems like nothing more than religious dandyism—until the suggestion that this stew of artificiality could actually kill souls. In 1875, a sustained satire—103 pages of light verse in a Hogarthian spirit—appeared: *The Ritualist's Progress; A Sketch of the Reforms and Ministrations of the Rev. Septimius Alban, Member of the E.C.U., Vicar of St. Alicia, Sloperton*, by A. B. Wildered, Parishioner. The problems began, the speaker explains, when "Some months ago, our parish, / Which holds quiescent 'views,' / Was wondrously excited / By a piece of startling news": "Mr. Alban, / In a hideous Popish dress, / *Was actually forcing* / *The people to 'Confess!'*" (Wildered 49, 50). Confession becomes one of many Ritualist ploys. All seems frivolous and good fun until one parishioner, from the "horrid 'Low-Church' crew," reminds everyone that:

"The Confessional's a power
  So serpent-like and great,
As seriously to hamper
  The business of a state;
For whilst man tells his secrets
  (As usual, since the Fall.)
To the female of his species
  The 'priest' will know them all!" (Wildered 58)

Fortunately for the people of Sloperton, their vicar does not "go over" to Rome, but certain "weaker sisters" cannot resist papist blandishments. And thus, comically, A. B. Wildered demonstrates how adroitly he can use all the anti-Pusey, anti-Ritualist arguments then circulating.

Ritualists were, to some degree, innovative, challenging conformity and welcoming a more cosmopolitan sensibility (Yates, *Anglican* 2–3). Ironically, Pusey "remained uncomfortable, at least in his public pronouncements, in his grudging support for ritualists. He declined to join most of the ritualist societies" (Yates, *Anglican* 55). Hopkins, for his part, refused to join the Liddon-sanctioned Brotherhood of the Holy Trinity in February 1864 (friends Samuel Brooke, Henry Challis, Alfred Garrett, Frederick Gurney, and Edward Urquhart belonged).[71] Distrust of Ritualism intensified after his conversion. In January 1877 he commented to Baillie that his eldest sister, "Milicent, is given to Puseyism: she is what is called an out-sister of the Margaret Street Home, which is a mummery nunn nunnery. Consequently, she will be directed by some Ritualist, which is ^are^ the worst hands she could fall into: these men are imperious, uncommissioned, without common sense, and without knowledge of moral theology" (*CW* 1:257).

How worried were Anglican and state authorities about Ritualism? Their determination to quash such practices—which some deemed popish, some considered effeminate, and many simply abhorred—was carried out in a two-part, wholly governmentalized process. First, there was an official inquiry, the Royal Commission on Ritual, that was "created in 1867 to inquire into the differences in ceremonial practice in the Church of England." Four reports ensued: on "Eucharistic vestments (1867), incense and lights (1868), the lectionary (1869), and Prayer Book revision and other subjects (1870)" (Livingstone 484).[72] All four were inconclusive. Dissatisfied with these results, in May 1873 more than sixty thousand people signed a "memorial" or petition presented to the archbishops of Canterbury and York "demanding 'the entire suppression of ceremonies and practices adjudged to be illegal'" (Yates, *Anglican* 235). Gladstone was reluctant to act—but he lost the 1874 election to Disraeli, and the new prime minister backed the Public Worship Regulation Act, which was drafted in March and received royal assent in August 1874 (Yates, *Anglican* 236). Hansard's reports of the debates inadvertently inspire risible thoughts. Imagine it is 20 April 1874. The archbishop of Canterbury, Archibald Tait, stands in Pugin's Westminster Palace, London, in order to address the House of Lords. His purpose is to introduce a private member's bill concerning an "unseemly" threat to the sanctity and dignity of Church of England services and churches. And he denounces—candles. More specifically, he attacks the use of candles, incense, ostentatious vestments, "invocations to the Virgin Mary," and other "arrangements of the Church unbecoming a place devoted to the worship of God."[73] Taken together, he asserts, such elements are a "desecration" that "all Churchmen ought to unite in condemning"; Ritualism is "some great unsettlement of the arrangements made at the Reformation," and as such needs to be quashed.[74] "Danger" is a word that infiltrates Tait's presentation; condemnation of "a spurious Romanism" is his subtext.[75] And what particularly offends him? In "certain churches it is thought extremely desirable that confessional boxes should be erected. Your Lordships will know that these are boxes used in Roman Catholic churches for the purpose of auricular confession."[76] Those who agreed with Tait during the debate included Earl Nelson, who decried the "state of lawlessness" that existed in some parishes, with their "very extreme practices." Lord Selborne concurred, urging "obedience to laws" and the end of "innovations dangerous in their tendencies."[77] Of course the legislation passed.

The forty-year shift from somber Tractarian pamphlets to outlawing confessionals, candlesticks, and incense might seem Monty Pythonish, but the title of the legislation should be considered more carefully. Public worship—how one enacts one's beliefs, how a faith community behaves—was subject to state "regulation," the ultimate kind of disciplinary power. Thus the force of the British state was brought to bear against practices that were initially deemed the outward expression of an oppressive, foreign religious regime; thus the patriarchal establishment asserted its right to clamp down on yet another challenge to its authority. And it had one more arrow in its quiver.

In 1855 six like-minded, "Puseyite" Anglican priests founded the Society of the Holy Cross. Their goals included personal support, working with and for the poor, and promoting Tractarian and Ritualist ideas and practices. In the 1860s one of the members, J. C. Chambers, produced a confessor's manual based on Gaume's *Manual* and Johannes Reuter, S.J.'s *Neo-Confessarius*. Part 1 was published and circulated privately in 1866 (the second edition, 1869, was later withdrawn). Seven years later, however, Chambers delivered part 2 of *The Priest in Absolution: A Manual for Such as Are Called unto the Higher Ministries in the English Church*, and copies made it into public hands. On 9 May 1873, members of the Society asked the Church of England's Convocation to "alter" the Book of Common Prayer so that "duly qualified confessors" could practice auricular confession (Yates, "Jesuits" 203). The request was denied—and public scrutiny of the Society's activities and publications became intense. Controversy regarding *The Priest in Absolution* was such that, by the mid-1870s, "145,000 copies had been printed, 120,000 of them in a popular edition" (Griffin, *Anti-Catholicism* 167).[78] Another round of pamphlets, denunciating speeches, and angry letters exchanged in the *Times* ensued. On 14 June 1877, the Earl of Redesdale shocked the House of Lords by reading into the record passages from the Holy Cross manual. His outrage was echoed by the archbishop of Canterbury, once again in the House to condemn a disgraceful attempt by rogue priests to destabilize the established Church.[79] The Earl of Harrowby also lambasted this "dangerous and widely-spreading disease of the encouragement and practice of auricular confession in the Church of England," a very "pestilence, which threatened to invade the sanctity of our homes and to destroy the character of our people."[80] One month later, the very public censure of these private religious rites continued.[81]

The events of 1874 and 1877 bookend the three exceptional years when Hopkins, "[a]way in the loveable west, / On a pastoral forehead of Wales" (*PW* 125), at St. Beuno's, was studying theology and preparing for ordination. Deliberately cut off from quotidian events, much less newspapers, one doubts he knew about the Royal Commission, the Public Worship

Regulation Act, or the *Priest in Absolution* scandal.[82] But as an impressionable undergraduate, he had been subjected to the pressures of Tractarian beliefs and practices on a regular, sometimes daily basis; in various letters announcing his conversion, October 1866, he expressed gratitude that Tractarianism had brought him to Catholicism.[83] As a Jesuit, he was studying moral theology and learning about his sacerdotal commitments, including the sacrament of confession and the power of absolution. He was also absorbing even more reasons to dread the flesh—the subject of the next chapter.

3

LIVING "IN FLESH"

Thou hast clothed me with skin and flesh, and hast fenced me with bones and sinews.
—JOB 10:11

As the body may be tended, cherished, and exercised with a simple view to its general health, so may the intellect.... [Yet] bodily health is not the only end of man, and the medical science is not the highest science of which he is the subject. Man has a moral and a religious nature, as well as a physical. He has a mind and a soul; and the mind and soul have a legitimate sovereignty over the body.
—JOHN HENRY NEWMAN, *The Idea of a University*

IN THE OPENING CHAPTER OF his *Confessions*, St. Augustine acknowledges the "sin and the vanity of life" by citing Psalms: "I was 'mere flesh, and wind going on its way and not returning'" (*Confs* 15).[1] It is a matter of cupidity, he laments to God: "Beside the lust of the flesh which inheres in the delight given by all pleasures of the senses (those who are enslaved to it perish by putting themselves far from you), there exists in the soul, through the medium of the same bodily senses, a cupidity which does not take delight in carnal pleasure but in perceptions acquired through the flesh" (*Confs* 210–11). Hopkins shared this obsession with fleshly failings: his writings certainly produce a "cartography of the sinful body" (*Ab* 187) from its "scaffold" of "brittle bones... whose breath is our *memento mori*" (*PW* 201) to the "sweating" and "groaning" of our "mortal trash" (*PW* 198).

What Augustine helps to define and Hopkins hopes to instantiate is the "art of living in the Christian manner," which, from Foucault's perspective, not only depends upon restraint, temperance, and "the prudence of bodies," but obsesses about "the sins of 'the flesh'" that result from temptation and concupiscence (*HS* 4:5, 27, 29, 35). Through the twin models (and engines) of penitential discipline and monastic asceticism, "the problem of 'the flesh'" gradually took central place in the Christian experience (*HS* 4:36). This chapter expands Foucault's argument that the flesh "should be understood as a mode of experience—that is, as a mode of knowledge and transformation of oneself by oneself, depending on a certain relationship between a nullification of evil and a manifestation of truth" to demonstrate how "the 'discovery' of the self" in Hopkins's poetry and prose is inseparable from the perturbations of the flesh (*HS* 4:36).

The wide-ranging discussion unfolds by considering the intersections of body, flesh, and subjectivity; the promise of "mansex fine" (*PW* 161); the trials of the flesh, including masturbation; and the drama of the flesh enacted in the *Spiritual Exercises*. The special privileges of the virginal body will also be discussed. In terms of somatic discipline, "wrestling" with the flesh will be considered, along with the ethos of mortification Hopkins endorses. In the final section, the paradoxes of confessing the flesh in "The Wreck" and "Caradoc's Soliloquy" will be explored. Throughout the chapter, one must remember that even if the word "body" can be used abstractly, generically, to suggest a transhistorical materiality, it—like flesh—is always temporal, always inching toward death. Since the time of Chaucer, poets in English have used *body* (from the Latin *corpus* and its French cognate *corps*) knowing that the corpse awaits. As Hopkins describes the "palsied" men, "their body is their corpse, and yet they live" (*CW* 5:208).

When a Hopkins speaker wants to identify beautiful human or artistic forms, the term "mould" is used, which amply suggests God's handiwork *and* expresses aesthetic appreciation. Thus, "Men go by" the speaker of "The Lantern out of doors" whom "either beauty bright / In mould or mind ... makes rare" (*PW* 140). In "The Loss of the Eurydice," the stark contrast between life and death is noted by those who "saw one seacorpse cold / He was all of lovely manly mould" (*PW* 151). Felix Randal is celebrated for "his mould of man, big-bóned and hardy-handsome" (*PW* 165). Hopkins explains his theory of a "moulding force" to Patmore in 1883: "~~Beauty~~ ^Fineness^, proportion, of feature comes from a moulding force which succeeds in asserting itself over the resistance of cumbersome or ... [restraining] matter; the bloom of health comes from the ~~vitali~~ abundance of life, the great vitality within. The moulding force, the life, is the form in the philosophic sense" (*CW* 2:605). This force, in effect, is the ethical counterpart to instress.

As this chapter will explain, *body* is a general or aggregate signifier for Hopkins, explored variously as beautiful, sacrificial (especially virginal), and eschatological. Given that "bodies are our common destiny," as Bruno Latour suggests (209), it is not surprising that the ones figured in Hopkins's writings are several: not just a religious body, but a Christian body, a Victorian body, a scientific and medicalized body, and an aestheticized body. Physiological as well as phenomenological, the Western body image Hopkins inherits is "dominated by a deep-rooted ideal of 'the natural.' This may be traced back to the Greco-Roman body-aesthetics on the one hand, and the Judeo-Christian tradition on the other. The Greco-Roman cult of natural, bodily beauty of both men and women, so richly expressed in the pictorial art of antiquity, was part of a whole 'aesthetic of existence'"; the "Christian body-image," however, of "the earthly dust, is only the temporary habitation of the soul and therefore something secondary or, as flesh, something downright evil" (Falk 100).[2] With Pauline intensity[3] and Augustinian abhorrence, Hopkins continually engages with, is sometimes "whelmed" by, "all the insinuations of the flesh: thoughts, desires, voluptuous imaginings, delectations" (*HS* 1:19). "The Escorial" (1860), for example, begins vividly, in macabre detail, by noting that the "staunch saint" Laurence "still prais'd his Master's name / While his crack'd flesh lay hissing on the grate; / Then fail'd the tongue; the poor collapsing frame, / Hung like a wreck that flames not billows beat—" (*PW* 1). One could dismiss these excessive details as a young Anglican's response to Tractarian and Continental religiosity, but this early text articulates a cluster of concerns regarding torment, witnessing, and mastery that will animate "The Wreck of the Deutschland" and some of the Ireland poems. As James Bernauer, S.J., suggests, "The Pauline flesh was not a body but rather an entire way of existing, an embrace of the carceral and slavish in contrast to that freedom of spirit discovered in living as children of God" ("Foreword" xv). When Hopkins confesses the flesh, it is always, in part, the Lenten flesh imagined in his young adulthood, abject and despised yet redeemable. After all, he has the chivalric example of Christ to emulate, "God-made-flesh" (*PW* 184), "the heaven's light" who is "True God, true man, in flesh and bone" (*PW* 168, 169). For that reason, "Man's spirit will be flesh-bound" yet potentially free (*PW* 148). As Augustine would desperately have it, *Tu Deo, tibi caro:* "'you subject to God, and the flesh subject to you'" (Mahoney, S.J. 46).

FLESHING OUT THE DEEPEST "TRUTHS"

Three questions derived from Foucault's studies of "the theme of the flesh" in ancient, Christian, and modern texts inform this study of Hopkins's fleshly obsessions (*HS* 1:33). One, what is the ethical "self" in relation to the body, the flesh, and sexual desires and practices, and how can one best understand their cultural and historical roles in defining the human subject? Two, how did the power to interpret the flesh and discipline the body become a secular as well as a sacred responsibility, one that expanded "along three axes": pedagogy, medicine, and demography (*HS* 1:116)? And three, how is it "that sexuality has been considered the privileged place where our deepest 'truth' is read and expressed?" (*FL* 214).

Insisting on the interconnections of discipline, power relations, and sexuality, Foucault argues that the body

> is directly involved in a political field; power relations have an immediate hold upon it: they invest it, train it, torture it, force it to carry out tasks, to perform ceremonies and to emit signs. The political investment of the body is bound up, in accordance with complex, reciprocal relations, with its economic use; it is largely as a force of production that the body is invested with power and domination; but, on the other hand, its constitution as a labour power is possible only if it is caught up in a system of

subjection.... The body becomes a useful force only if it is both a productive body and a subjugated body.[4]

If one grasps the myriad ways in which bodies have been socialized and mythologized, one accepts how they have been encrusted by layers of custom and cultural meaning, and bear the imprint of gender, class, and race. They have also been caught up in dualistic modes of thinking (mind/body, reason/passion, psychology/biology, form/matter,[5] self/other, culture/nature, centre/margin) that "necessarily hierarchizes and ranks the two polarized terms" (Grosz 3). The body is, in Latour's words, "an interface that becomes more and more describable as it learns to be affected by more and more elements" (206).

As Laqueur demonstrates in his studies of the "battles over gender and power" that are masked by the pseudo-objectivity of scientific writing on biology and sex, the body is "so hopelessly bound to its cultural meanings as to elude unmediated access" (*Making Sex* 11, 12). "Ideologies of masculinity and femininity," as R. McGrath suggests, "cannot simply be peeled back like a mask to reveal the 'naked truth' of the body" (58). And yet, as Grosz astutely observes, the body cannot "itself be regarded as *purely* a social, cultural, and signifying effect lacking its own weighty materiality" (21).[6] The world is charged with the grandeur of God, Hopkins promises—and the body is charged with social, theological, and personal meanings. One's *experience* of the body and with the body constitutes the bases of life.

More precisely, the body is a historically specific framework upon which diverse social, economic, religious, political, and aesthetic imperatives have been constructed and represented. Hellenic conventions of the aestheticized male body revived in the Victorian era (most especially in Oxonian intellectual circles)[7] put into discourse new manifestations of idealized phallic beauty and power. A poem such as "Harry Ploughman" demonstrates how Hopkins's texts actively participate in this densely intertextual tradition that simultaneously cloaks and reveals homoerotic encodings.[8] But looking again at "Harry Ploughman"—

> Hard as hurdle arms, with a broth of goldish flue
> Breathed round; the rack of ribs, the scooped flank; lank
>   {knee-nave;
> Rope-over thigh; {kneebank; and barrelled shank—

> Héad and fóot, shouldér and shánk—
> By a grey eye's heed steered well, one crew, fall to;
> {barrowy brawn, his thew
> Stand at stress. Each limb's {barrowy-brawnèd thew
> That onewhere curded, onewhere sucked or sank—
> Soared ór sánk—,
> Though as a beechbole firm, finds his, as at a rollcall, rank
> And features, ín flesh, whát deed he each must do—
> His sínew-sérvice whére dó.
> He leans to it, Harry bends, look. Back, elbow, and liquid waist
> In him, all quail to the wallowing o' the plough (*PW* 193)

—one finds a body, head to foot, expressing its beauty through purposeful action. Enthralled with signs of masculine potency, Hopkins's textual gaze produces word-lavish and energized, positive portraits. What is admired, what offsets the "dangerous"[9] appreciation of bodies for their own sake? Bodies that are dedicated to what Ruskin would term "significant toil," what Ignatius Loyola and "Harry Ploughman" call "service" ("Harry Ploughman" was written two years after "To what serves Mortal Beauty?"). The nature-focused poems in Hopkins's canon ("The Windhover" is an excellent example) most often involve textual acts of identification; poems that focus on the bodies of other people perform ritualized acts of aestheticized (and hence somewhat distanced) recognition. As the somatic object of scrutiny becomes a textual representation, it is evaluated for the way in which it enfleshes, makes apparent and legible, *haecceitas*.

"Harry Ploughman" also brings to mind two fundamental questions: What does writing the body tell us about bodies, and what does it tell us about writing? In this particular poem, the resources of alliteration, "chiming," metrical inversion, and caesura produce an anatomy of language's potential and limitations. The poet's undecidedness regarding key phrases reminds the reader that metaphor can "translate" brilliantly—the body is a natural site or architectural monument (kneebank/knee-nave); a ship (with its "crew" of muscles and limbs); strong ("Amansstrength") yet graceful and pure in its beauty of movement ("Wind-lílylócks-láced")—but it is always an approximation. Hopkins described "Harry Ploughman" as a sonnet with "interpolated burden-lines; sprung rhythm."[10] The choric burden-lines and the "heavily loaded" rhythms of the text (*CW* 1:477) exemplify how each Hopkins poem enacts the materiality of language, "draws attention to its physical features" (Aviram 223). Reading attentively—performing the poem by following Hopkins's stresses and slurs—one can almost hear the plough carving up the earth.[11] Thus the graphic life of the text (a visual/cognitive experience) is complemented by a sensuous oral and aural life.[12]

The ploughman's active, dutiful frame is one of several heroic working-class bodies in Hopkins's canon that serve as antidotes to mere flesh. Bodies at work, to quote Moran, "evidence a natural grace and utility which ensure that admiration of them is healthy and desexualized" ("Lovely" 76). (Not surprisingly, Hopkins admired Ford Madox Brown's 1852–65 painting *Work,* and the sonnet written to complement the canvas.[13]) Whether the figure is that of a farmer, sailor, soldier, bugler, or blacksmith, the speaker admires how he "features, ín flesh, whát deed he each must do" (*PW* 193); the flesh is the context, certainly, but "Head, heart, hand, heel, and shoulder . . . beat and breathe in power" (*PW* 163) if disciplined appropriately. It is a "muscular" Christian aesthetic absent Charles Kingsley's particular prejudices[14] and answering to Newman's call for a "Christian manhood."[15] The young bugler is just one of the figures embodying such an ideal, for Hopkins: "Breathing bloom of a chastity in mansex fine" (*PW* 161). Masculinity, for Hopkins, is neither fretted nor fractured.[16] Like Thomas Carlyle,[17] he believes that "manliness comprised a set of core values" best realized in terms of personal demeanor, social responsibility (Tosh 87), and respectability—a middle-class fantasy of gender norms glazed over with a chivalric idealism masking a paterfamilias's and imperialist's ruthlessness.[18]

Body-focused and articulate, Hopkins's poems participate in—that is, reproduce, reinforce, and reiterate—various Victorian discourses of gender and morality, revealing the ways in which masculine and feminine bodies are themselves social scripts. As Laurence Goldstein remarks, it was an era "obsessed with masculine vigor of a specific kind, and terrified by effeminacy" (viii). The thrice-reworked poem "In honour of St. Alphonsus Rodriguez" exemplifies these concerns:

> Honour is flashed off exploit, so we say;
> And those strokes once that gashed flesh or galled shield
> Should tongue that time now, trumpet now that field,

And, on the fighter, forge his glorious day.
On Christ they do and on the martyr may;
But be the war within, the brand we wield
Unseen, the heroic breast not outward-steeled,
Earth hears no hurtle then from fiercest fray.
Yet God (that hews mountain and continent,
Earth, all, out; who, with trickling increment,
Veins violets and tall trees makes more and more)
Could crowd career with conquest while there went
Those years and years by of world without event
That in Majorca Alfonso watched the door. (*PW* 200–201)

Although it has as its subject a sixteenth-century "laybrother of the Society of Jesus," the poem reiterates—almost anguishes over—Victorian gender paradigms. Chief among them is the issue of how to distinguish properly "Amansstrength" (*PW* 194). If masculine accomplishments (in this poem's terms, *exploit, strokes, fray, career, conquest, event*) can be experienced only in the public domain, both fierce and enfleshed, then how should one characterize those interiorized heroics framed entirely within a domestic setting? The "honour" to be discerned in the saintly man's passivity is neither easily grasped nor articulated by the poem,[19] which is burdened by gendered "social dichotomizing" (Merleau-Ponty's phrase).

For every observation of "favoured make and mind and health and youth" (*PW* 192) in Hopkins's canon, there seems to be a counterpointed preoccupation with disease and physical infirmity. Early poems remark casually "all the feeble knees" (*PW* 70) or the "blind or lame" (*PW* 76). Only the poems composed after Hopkins begins to live, teach, and serve in environments less cloistered than Hampstead, Oxford, or the Birmingham Oratory reveal a fixation with the ways in which bodies "are breaking, down" (*PW* 143). In the following passage from "St. Winefred's Well," St. Beuno anticipates "what sights shall be" when pilgrims congregate at the well site of his niece's miraculous restoration:

While sick men shall cast sighs, | of sweet health all despairing,
While blind men's eyes shall thirst after | daylight, draughts of daylight,

> Or deaf ears shall desire that | lipmusic that's lŏst upon them,
> While cripples are, while lepers, | dancers in dismal limb-dance,
> Fallers in dreadful frothpits, | waterfearers wild,
> Stone, palsy, cancer, cough, | lung-wasting, womb-not-bearing,
> Rupture, running sores, | what more? (*PW* 180)

The catalogue of afflictions almost overwhelms acknowledgments of God's mercy ("Those dearer, more divine | boons") and the holy well's intercessional powers. The question becomes, "what more" can the reader be expected to assimilate? In these physiological fixations, Hopkins is decidedly a creature of his times.

"O.H." AND "MY WORST SIN"

In concert or antagonistically, Christian prohibitions against the flesh and the *scientia sexualis* that have emerged since the late eighteenth century have bundled together "sex, truth, and law" according to "ties that our culture has tended to draw closer rather than loosen" (*HS* 4:285). The flesh is "taken as a 'form of experience' and a 'form of subjectivity,'" Foucault argues; the guardians of flesh and sex—including theologians, doctors, scientists, lawyers, "alienists," and eventually psychiatrists[20]—"endowed sex with an inexhaustible and polymorphous causal power.... There was scarcely a malady or physical disturbance to which the nineteenth century did not impute at least some degree of sexual etiology" (*HS* 1:65). Consequently, specialists in many fields, working in multiple discourses, concerned themselves primarily with sexual "aberrations, perversions, exceptional oddities, pathological abatements, and morbid aggravations" (1:53). *Scientia sexualis* was "subordinated in the main to the imperatives of a morality whose divisions it reiterated under the guise of the medical norm. Claiming to speak the truth, it stirred up people's fears; to the least oscillations of sexuality, it ascribed an imaginary dynasty of evils destined to be passed on for generations" (1:53). Furthermore, on the basis "of the Christian notion of the flesh," there developed the "four great strategies that were deployed in the nineteenth century: the sexualization of children, the hysterization of women, the specification of the perverted, and the regulation of the population" (1:114). Paradoxically, while these strategies were proliferating, significant control was exercised over the privilege of "enunciation" (as debates about auricular confession attest)—a "policing of statements" to the effect that "where and when it was not possible to talk about such things became more strictly defined; in which circumstances, among which speakers, and within which social relationships" (1:18). The "mechanisms of power," Foucault concludes, were and "are addressed to the body, to life, to what causes it to proliferate, to what reinforces the species, its stamina, its ability to dominate, or its capacity for being used. Through the themes of health, progeny, race, the future of the species, the vitality of the social body, power spoke *of* sexuality and *to* sexuality; the latter was not a mark or a symbol, it was an object and a target" (1:147).

Encouraged by Liddon, Hopkins's fixation on his flesh and its waywardness in 1865–66 focused on the operations of the gaze ("have I looked at immodest pictures or other objects of the kind?"[21]) and bodily sensations. Sins of "looking" were acutely felt, whether the object was a work of art or a "chorister at Magdalen" College (*CW* 3:337). The preoccupation with "bodily life"[22] in guides and manuals that came out of the archive trailing intertextual debts going back to Jeremy Taylor, Augustine, or even Aretaeus[23] demanded a ventriloquism to which Hopkins readily acceded. A case in point is these diary entries detailing "evil" temptations and actions:

> Was far too forward & familiar at my Wine/ Party. Wasted a whole HR at least.
> My exceeding wickedness and Waste of Time.... My daily trespasses and double mindedness.
> Never to touch tea again for 3 weeks:—except out at breakf[ast]. & then no sugar.
> Before this I wasted much time from my sluggishness & have rather neglected again my dev[otio]ns: and I was very inattentive in Chapel. Besides awaking in an over-indulgent State wh[ich] made me lie in bed til ½ p. 8 & led to evil dreams.... I have been careless all to-day: & not tried at all to overcome my temptation.... I have lost much time & opportunity, I have been unclean, selfish, cowardly, conceited, and still am so, I have done much harm & committed great & crying sins.... [I]nattentive & foolish [at Chapel].

Is this Hopkins? It might as well be, given the "sins" elaborated and the phrasing used, but it is not. These entries are taken from the Oxford diaries of poet Arthur Hugh Clough (1819–61), written twenty-five years before Hopkins arrived in the "towery" city.[24] The prose is more deliberately shaped than Hopkins's, but the litany of self-recriminations is consistent (unsettlingly so). To and for themselves, neither Clough nor Hopkins presents the "unquestion'd readings of a blotless book" (*PW* 77). Instead, they experience what Oliver Buckton terms the "irreducible complicity of individual desire and textuality, sexuality, and self-representation" (8).

The two young men also shared the need to record genital experiences, what Hopkins referred to as the "old habit"[25] and Clough, as "that wretched habit," "my worst sin" and "darling pleasure." For Hopkins, the phrase "old habit" or the initials "O.H." in his diaries identified masturbatory activity;[26] Clough preferred to draw a large nonverbal star to mark the occasions.[27] Both also distinguished carefully between masturbation and seminal emissions that occurred before they were fully conscious. The need to qualify and quantify such activities was clearly part of a protracted process of establishing the degree of sinfulness that defined their lives and innermost beings.

What would be the scholarly justification for prying into such matters? One must consider Hopkins's masturbatory "habits" to discern another, more disturbing way in which, having been trained "to discover what is hidden inside the self,"[28] he deciphered a fleshly "secret" both sinful and sexual. In other words, this is further evidence of how, and why, at the interstices of concealment and disclosure, he learned to pathologize himself.[29] (Small wonder that, while living in Dublin, when he reread the Oxford diaries along with letters and other papers, the textual experiences of that earlier self prompted a "state" that was "much like madness" [*CW* 2:731].)

One can contextualize Hopkins's onanistic obsessions by correlating Foucault's 1975 lecture series *Abnormal* with studies by Thomas Laqueur, Roy Porter, and Lesley Hall.[30] In the West, prohibitions against masturbation are based upon the notion of the "preciousness of the sperm," believed to be the "most potent part" of all bodily fluids; fears of degeneracy are pervasive.[31] A crusade against masturbation began in the 1720s and flourished, almost rabidly, in the nineteenth century, one that "essentially concern[ed] children and adolescents from a bourgeois milieu" (*Ab* 237). As such it was a wholly modern phenomenon, directed at a seemingly uncontrollable and antisocial activity at a time when the "realm of the private" as the "basis for civil society" was being redefined (Laqueur, *Solitary* 226, 231).[32] To quote Laqueur, "An explanation of why [masturbation] became so exigent depends on understanding why its core elements—imagination, excess, solitude, and privacy—became so problematic" (*Solitary* 21). Interestingly, given the many Victorian shibboleths regarding women and sex, masturbation was always presumed to be the "secret vice" of females *and* males, a kind of self-pollution to be treated with an equally horrific combination of potions, devices, and surgeries.[33]

The first significant book on the subject was published between 1708 and 1716, John Marten's *Onania; or The Heinous Sin of Self Pollution, and all its Frightful Consequences, in both SEXES Considered, with Spiritual and Physical Advice to those who have already injured themselves by this abominable practice. And seasonable Admonition to the Youth of the Nation of Both SEXES*. Marten was not a doctor; he was a moralizing quack hoping to sell the remedies so helpfully enumerated at the end of his treatise. Medical sanction was swift to follow, however, most notably in Samuel Tissot's *L'Onanisme: ou, Dissertation physique sur les malades produites par la masturbation* (1759), which became "an instant literary sensation throughout Europe" (Laqueur, *Solitary* 37–38). A century later, all the major European encyclopedias detailed the disease; an English man like Hopkins could take down from the shelf James Copland's *A Dictionary of Practical Medicine* (1844–58), William Acton's *The Functions and Disorders of the Reproductive Organs* (1857), or any number of "books, pamphlets, religious tracts, medical articles, newspaper advertisements, [and] self-help literature" to learn more about the perils of what one tract so succinctly defined as "'the Vice of Boyhood, the Blight of Youth, the Curse of Men, the Wreck of Manhood, and the Bane of Posterity.'"[34] In both Copland's *Dictionary* and Maudsley's *Pathology of the Mind* (1879), the discussion of masturbation is to be found under "I" for "Insanity of self-abuse."[35]

This moral and medical "physiology of the flesh" (*Ab* 193) was identified as the cause of everything from "spinal tuberculosis, epilepsy, pimples, madness, and other mental infirmities" to "general wasting, and hundreds of other diseases" (Laqueur, *Solitary* 185).[36] The following list of symptoms—and there were so many to choose from—is cited from John Law Milton's 1881 study: "'Mental wanderings, incoherence of ideas, peculiar grazing sensations occasioned by the passage of the urine, . . . shivering, palpitations, sinking sensations, gastric and intestinal symptoms, diarrhoea, anaesthesia, frightful sensations like those occasioned by electricity, . . . impairment of hearing, . . . pains in the head and vertigo[,] . . . brutish stupidity . . . insanity, and locomotor ataxy.'"[37] Shortened life expectancy was also predicted, and "greater morbidity of those who remained unmarried" (Hall 295). Furthermore, the physiological consequences of adolescent "self-pollution" or "self-abuse" would be told upon the ravaged body of the desiccated adult and his descendants.[38] Latency was the particular reason why Dr. David Skae, in the 1860s president of the British Association of Medical Officers of Asylums and Hospitals for the Insane, emphasized the "insanity of masturbation," as did Henry Maudsley, the famous late-Victorian psychologist.[39] Time and again one notes that "the mental and moral consequences of autoerotic behaviour" were always inextricably connected, causing a "transformation in the characterization of effects of 'self-abuse' from one that sought to attribute a set of consequences to specific *acts* to one that defined the signs of particular type of *actor*," the execrable "masturbator" (Ed Cohen 54). Such a figure was almost always imagined and diagnosed within the confines of normative heterosexuality. "Masturbation," as Alan Sinfield notes, "was not generally linked with same-sex passion. The danger was said to be physical exhaustion and psychological self-absorption" (102).[40] Fittingly, appallingly, only the range of remedies outdid the etiological largesse. In the pages of the *Lancet*, no less, one reads how male sexual debilitation was to be treated by "keeping up [a] slight soreness of the [penis] sufficient to render erection painful." How? Cauterization was recommended, or circumcision. The so-called "American remedy" consisted of "a ring of common metal, with a screw passing through one of its sides, and projecting into the centre, where it had a button extremity . . . to be applied to the 'part affected' at bed-time" (Lesley Hall 296). The "extensive commercial-medical network" that profited from the "disease" also made available "erection alarms, penis cases, sleeping mitts, . . . [and] hobbles to keep girls from spreading their legs" (Laqueur, *Solitary* 46). Other remedies included the application of camphor, potassium bromide, and an operation known as the "infibulation"

(Hare 10). One can only be grateful that Hopkins relied upon prayer and confession rather than "Pulvermacher's World-Famed Galvanic Belt" or the "Electric Life Invigorator" (Lesley Hall 297) for medico-sexual relief and restoration. The definitive cure for males was "inserting a permanent probe in the urethra" (*Ab* 252); for females, a clitorectomy.

Men's masturbation was to be feared, Dr. Tissot insisted, because a significant "loss of semen" not only had "disastrous effects on the corporeal economy," it had "its most deleterious effects on the brain, which could literally shrivel up in the skull... [due to] loss of seminal life force" (Laqueur, *Solitary* 196). It was only fitting, therefore, that Tissot and other experts divined several other related diseases in the "seminal 'expenditure'" family (Ed Cohen 67). Under the general rubric *spermatorrhea,* they identified a "nebulous and indistinct set of symptoms all related to forms of nonprocreative spermatic loss" (Ed Cohen 67). Although these emissions could be deemed an offshoot of masturbatory excess, they were involuntary. Such fleshy spontaneity, however, was itself extremely "threatening, a kind of 'automatism'" whereby the victim was unable to "achieve conscious control" of body and mind (Lesley Hall 303). Hence Hopkins's preoccupation with enumerating, annually (in 1864 and 1865), any incidents of "nocturnal emissions."[41] The exaggerated judiciousness with which he distinguishes between genital activities that are and are "not without sin" (*CW* 3:287) has everything to do with the pseudo-medical wisdom of his day. He prepares for confession knowing himself, his flesh, to be the near occasion of sin; he could not help but fear that the damage was somatic as well as spiritual, and long-lasting.

VICTORIANS' "MORTAL TRASH"

My goal is to situate the work of answering the flesh and writing the body in Hopkins's texts within several overlapping linguistic and cultural environments: the Victorian preoccupation with "total health" (masturbation was presumed to threaten the *mens sana in corpore sano* equilibrium); the Ignatian disposition of the body in the *Spiritual Exercises* (an imaginative intensification of Christian possibilities and apprehensions); and a Ruskin-inflected,[42] classically based aesthetic discourse which emphasizes the particularity of physical representations and capitalizes on the representation of pain. In other words, I am exploring how bodies are deployed and dramatized in his writings, complicated always by the insinuations of the flesh. The body is never simply one thing in Hopkins's texts: alternatively and sometimes concurrently it is a "bone-house" *and* a "lovescape," sometimes "bellbright" and "froliclavish" (*PW* 196–97) but just as commonly "sweating" and "groaning" "mortal trash" (*PW* 198).

Hopkins's own body—a life of medicalized flesh—is interesting insofar as it teaches one how a Victorian could suffer and be treated, and how the body became "a subject of endless fascination and an instrument of great importance" (Rice 214).[43] He certainly lived up to George Henry Lewes's somber prediction, "Few of us, after thirty, can boast of robust health" ("Training" 220). Hopkins was prone to gastrointestinal and colon problems (including diarrhea); his hemorrhoids were treated surgically; penile problems were resolved with a circumcision when he was thirty-three.[44] His blue eyes became so strained while living in Dublin, marking hundreds of examinations per term, that he imagined them "almost bleeding" (*CW* 2:915) and consulted an oculist. He believed in experts and therapeutic treatments at a time when "orthodox medicine was still based largely on what have been called 'heroic therapies': purging, bloodletting, blistering, and other invasive and immoderate ways of dealing with illness. Toxic medicines such as opium or mercury were standard prescriptions, which meant that the side effects of the treatment could be as hazardous as the disease itself" (Durbach 209). Homeopathic remedies were also welcome, as he explained to his mother 24 January 1885:

> I have spoken before this of ~~old~~ Fr. Mallac, a delightful old gentleman hailing originally from the Mauritius but since then from most parts of Europe, who is a very learned man and a believer in a wonderful system of medicine discovered by a certain Italian nobleman, Duke or Count or something Mattei, and made up into tiny ~~globules~~ ^pills, globules,^ drops, beads, like the homoeopathic ones just, and taken in water; I take ~~it~~ [them] for any ailment and am none the worse, but I must own that this cold does seem to be rather too many for Mattei. (Robert Curtis had a fit the very night after he took his first globule.) (*CW* 2:708)

Hopkins was taught to be suspicious of "fits" and other illnesses that affect the brain: his Jesuit friend and colleague Robert Curtis, by all accounts a brilliant mathematician, could not be ordained because of his epilepsy, a very misunderstood condition.[45]

Hopkins was neither tall nor robust, but he could walk for miles—with pleasure in the Oxford countryside, as a young student; resiliently, curiously, in Switzerland; and with mixed feelings in Ireland (St. Stephen's Green was not salubrious in the 1880s; Phoenix Park was a pleasant respite; the cliffs of Moher were intimidating). Jesuits in training were encouraged to go for long walks, skate in the winter, and were allowed to swim in the summer (with certain strictures[46]) because "bathing" was part of the athletics/hygiene regimen for men that Victorians eagerly embraced.[47] At a time when neurasthenia was becoming recognized as a body-mind problem, he was treated by concerned Jesuit authorities like a middle-class neurasthenic woman, someone who needed frequent rests.

For his own part, Hopkins was very aware of how the degrading material conditions of Victorian life were affecting working-class bodies, and his responses were (typically) racialized.[48] In spring 1881 he explained to Bridges in a very Malthusian way, "While I admire the handsome horses [in a pre–May Day celebration], I remarked for the thousandth time with sorrow and loathing the base and besotted figures and features of the Liverpool crowd. When I see the fine and manly Norwegians that flock hither to embark for America walk our streets and look about them it fills me with shame and wretchedness. I am told Sheffield is worse though" (*CW* 1:438).[49] Seven years later, he remarked to Baillie (in terms that anticipate those of Georg Simmel), "What I most dislike in towns and in London in particular is the misery of the poor; the dirt, squalor, and the illshapen degraded physical . . . type of so many of the people, with the deeply dejecting unbearable thought that by degrees almost all of our population will become a town population and a puny unhealthy and cowardly one" (*CW* 2:928). It is the final adjective, "cowardly," that betrays how physiology is read within a moralizing register in Hopkins's era. Not only "cheer and charm" are lost in the "shallow and frǎil tówn" (*PW* 143). "Tom's Garland" suggests that the "commonweal" is in danger of losing its humanity, "bred Hangdog dull; by Rage, / Manwolf, worse; and their packs infest the age" (*PW* 195).

"No topic more occupied the Victorian mind than Health," Bruce Haley asserts, "—not religion, or politics, or Improvement, or Darwinism.

In the name of Health, Victorians flocked to the seaside, tramped about the Alps or Cotswolds, dieted, took pills, sweated themselves in Turkish baths, adopted 'this system' of medicine or that. Partly for the sake of Health they invented, revived, or imported from abroad a multitude of athletic recreations" (3).[50] Constant "threat[s] of illness in the Victorian home made people conscious of their bodies, anxious to know how their bodies worked, and prepared to see a moral significance in the laws of life" (Haley 5–6). In this regard, they were also very European; as Ruth Waterhouse explains, "Nineteenth-century Europe witnessed the rise of numerous disciplines which gave much time to thinking, talking, and, of course, writing about bodies.... They included such diverse pursuits as Phrenology, Anthropometry, Demography, Forensic Science, Criminology, and Sexology.... Concomitant with these new disciplines was the equally innovatory technique of photography.... Thus bodies were increasingly subjected to measurement and to categorization, and checked for pathologies" (107). An insistence on imbuing scientific or pseudoscientific discourses with religious undertones was optional for many—but not for Hopkins. "Felix Randal" makes explicit Hopkins's vocational interest in illness as a means toward greater spiritual well-being—dying as a prelude to a new life with God:

> Félix Rándal the fárrier, O is he déad then? my dúty all énded,
> Who have watched his mould of man, big-bóned and hardy-
>   handsome
> Pining, píning, till time when reason rámbled in it and some
> Fatal four disorders, fléshed there, all contended?
>
> Síckness bróke him. Impatient, he cursed at first, but mended
> Being anointed and all; though a heavenlier heart began some
> Mónths éarlier, since Í had our swéet repríeve and ránsom
> Téndered to him. (*PW* 165)

The octave "endears" the farrier because his final months instantiate a paradox of Christian existence: during his "boisterous years," "powerful amidst peers," the health of his soul is a secondary consideration; only once his body is "broken" does his soul assert its needs and anticipate the "sweet reprieve" of a heavenly afterlife. By rhyming "handsome" and "ransom," the text underscores the contrast between fleshly and godly bounty it is attempting to assert. Like "The Wreck," "St. Winefred's Well," and several other poems,[51] "Felix Randal" is occasioned by a dead body. Against the fact of death, the text measures and also resurrects the meaning of human life, a significance made possible by a "heavenlier heart" (*PW* 165) and divine providence.

MUNDUS, CARO, ET DIABOLUS

Of the three "enemies" of the soul—the typological antithesis of the holy Trinity—the world and the devil are monumental, but the flesh is imagined to be both intimate and relentless. With final sibilants primed for exaggeration, the English word *flesh*, a Germanic term (quite unlike σάρξ or *caro* or *chair*), seems tailor-made for a concept that is perpetually overshadowed by Satan. It is not an exaggeration to suggest that every theological expert and text cited in chapters 1 and 2 has recourse to the flesh at various and emphatic points. From the penitential Psalms and Paul's epistles[52] to Peter Abelard's *Expositiones,* from Augustine to Patrick ("the hostile flesh is always dragging one down to death, that is, to unlawful attractions" [44]) to Pusey, flesh is both the "raw, formless, . . . mythical 'primary material'" and "a point of departure and a locus of incision, a point of 'reality' or 'nature' understood (fictionally) as prior to, and as the raw materials of, social practices" (Grosz 118). When annotating his Bible or taking notes from Liddon's lectures on Corinthians, Hopkins pays particular attention to what it means to be "τῇ σαρκί {in the flesh}, physically" and metaphorically (*CW* 5:91). It is the corruptibility of the human condition writ large, literally and figuratively; it leads the soul astray and, most hazardously, has a mind of its own.[53] And of "the thousand natural shocks / That flesh is heir to,"[54] its symbiotic relationship with mortality, carnality, and sin is the most troubling. According to "The Wreck," Christ is "under the world's splendour and wonder"; the flesh, however, is under the disgrace of the world and its persons.

Curtailing and controlling the flesh are among the principal benefits of undertaking and living according to Ignatius's *Spiritual Exercises.* On the one hand, the exercises activate the imagination. In his guide for novices, Morris, S.J., recommends that creative thinking should not be confined to the *Exercises* per se: "If you are at work in the grounds, you can think of Adam tilling the earth in the sweat of his brow, his heart full of contrition for sin.... When sweeping or cleaning the house, you may think of the Holy House of Nazareth, where the domestic work was done by Jesus and Mary" (9–10). On the other hand, the exercitant is trained to use all of his senses during religious meditation in order to experience more fully the pangs of the flesh and the providence of God. "[Imagine] yourself stretched on a bed of pain," Ignatius advises,

> losing by degrees your senses and the free use of your faculties, struggling violently against death, which comes to tear your soul from the body and drag it before the tribunal of God.... Contemplate the sad state of your body [after death]; see how the worms devour the remains of putrid flesh; how all the limbs are separating; how the bones are eaten away by the corruption of the tomb! See what remains of the body you have loved so much!—a something which has no name in any tongue, and on which we cannot think without disgust. (*SE* 96, 99)

The rebellious, undisciplined body, the all-too-wayward flesh, are the particular targets of Ignatius's rule. One is reminded, constantly, of Christ as the Word become flesh;[55] of Mary, whose flesh is spared typical human burdens (original sin, the commission of sins[56]); and of the exercitant's most unworthy flesh. As Rickaby, S.J., notes, the exercitant desires "more to know the Eternal Word made flesh (*el Verbo eterno encarnado*), that [he] may the better serve Him and follow Him" (*SE* 96); the "reality of our Saviour's Humanity, *carne carnem redimens*, 'by flesh redeeming flesh'" is gradually revealed during the four "weeks" or phases of the *Exercises*.

Four examples of the ways in which Ignatius guides the person to work against the flesh will be considered. In the First Week, both the first and second exercises ask the exercitant to "consider my soul imprisoned in this corruptible body, and my whole compound self in this vale of tears as in banishment among brute animals[;] . . . to see all my corruption and foulness of body (*corpórea*); . . . to look upon myself as a sort of ulcer and abscess, whence have sprung so many sins, and so many wickednesses" (*SE* 23, 34).

The battle between Christ and Satan is imagined as a medieval contest in "The Two Standards." During his 1881 retreat, Hopkins observes that Lucifer, "ravished" by his own beauty, "spiritual luxury, and vainglory," is the consummate example of the "sin of pride"; Christ, in his "Eucharistic sacrifice," is the antithetical and voluntary "victim of earthly and nature and of flesh" (*CW* 5:452).[57] Revisiting the "Rules for the Discernment of Spirits," Hopkins quotes Cassian to understand more thoroughly "the struggle or wrestling of the flesh with the spirit" (*CW* 5:521), the same metaphor that vividly concludes "Carrion Comfort": "That níght, that yéar / Of now done darkness I wretch lay wrestling with (my God!) my God" (*PW* 183). Fourth, there are the harrowing scenes of Christ's suffering body during the Passion, which are contemplated to appreciate the agony endured, to understand afresh the depth of human culpability for that sacrifice, and to marvel at the divinity within that spectacle:

> *What He suffers in His body.* Represent to yourself the cruel scenes of the scourging, the crowning with thorns, the crucifixion. Contemplate the sacred body of our Lord torn by the scourgers, and presenting to the eye one bleeding wound: "There is no beauty in Him, or comeliness; and we have seen Him, and there was no sightliness, that we should be desirous of Him...."[58] His head pierced by sharp thorns, which the soldiers make more painful every moment by striking Him; His shoulders bruised by the overpowering weight of the cross, which He carries to Calvary; and lastly, His feet and hands nailed to the cross, with horrible torture to the nerves, and all His body suspended and, as it were, sustained by His wounds. Then ask yourself why were all these sufferings of your God, and say with lively contrition: "He was wounded for our iniquities, He was bruised for our sins; the chastisement of our peace was upon Him, and by His bruises we are healed" (Is.liii.5). (*SE* 209)

As previously discussed, guilt and shame are encouraged by Ignatius to inspire humility and receptivity. In Ignatian terms, one casts off the sins of the flesh to find a new kind of freedom of will with the divine. It is "the holiest that shews his freedom the most," Hopkins notes during his Long Retreat of December 1881, "the wickedest that is the most slave of sin and carried with the motion of the flesh and of the world" (*CW* 5:390).

Hopkins's "Meditation on Death" is one of three sets of "Instructions" delivered to a public mission in Maryport, an industrial seaside hub in northwest England, in 1882 (the other two subjects are the "Principle or Foundation" of creation and hell). The talk begins with the obvious—"Death is certain and uncertain, certain to come, uncertain when and where"—and rises to a crescendo of deliberate "terror":

> I do not mean that the pain of dying is always great; I know well and have seen that often it is not so, so far as from outside we can judge; but often it is; and ^great^ pain or little or none, it is ~~bad~~ ^terror^ enough that life is ebbing away. And even for those who seem to die peacefully, if they have their senses to the last, one cannot without shrinking think of that very last moment when ~~body~~ ^flesh^ and ~~soul~~ ^spirit^ are rent asunder and ~~life~~ ^the soul^ goes out into the cold, leaving the body its companion dear a corpse behind. This will be to every one of you; I see your corpses here before me. (*CW* 5:533–34)

Following that stark threat and promise, he presents a peroration on the "Last Sacraments" and their "comforts," each of which "is meant to strengthen you for your ^death^ agony" (*CW* 5:536). Confession is first and the "most necessary" (*CW* 5:535).

A host of somatic possibilities emerges from Hopkins's texts: the life, times, and afterlife of the beautiful but also sin-racked body. Each foregrounds a different aspect of what Herbert Blau terms "the phenomenology and instrumentality of the body, that clinical object with a fantasy life: house of pleasure or prison house; interpellated subject or subject of entropic decay" (226). The consistency of approach expressed in the poems, from the early 1860s to 1889, demonstrates that Hopkins's Jesuit training only intensifies attitudes toward the flesh already entrenched, "smitten by death and dominated by the principle of evil" (*HS* 4:268). Overall, it is a challenge for him to think about the human condition in incarnational terms, especially when he compares "the incredible condescension of the Incarnation" amid "the mean and trivial accidents of humanity" (*CW* 1:86–87). So Pilate is imagined, after Christ's crucifixion, his flesh and life all "nerve and vein," hands "now clammy with strange blood"; the enormity of his guilty complicity is transposed onto the unforgiving, exilic landscape where he hides and experiences "stinging snow," "fierce skies," and "winds impenitent" (*PW* 19, 20, 21). So one of the spies in an Old Testament, Egyptian wilderness longs for immersion in the Nile, which "[s]hall cool our shoulders and unbake our flesh" (*PW* 23), always aware that the temptations of the Other are available in "the flesh-pots" of nearby encampments and cities (*PW* 24). "Il Mystico," a Miltonic exercise in censorious couplets, begins by lambasting the flesh's "sensual gross desires" then frets because the "soul is subtle and flesh weak / And pride is nerveless and hearts meek" (*PW* 6, 7). Because the speaker of "My prayers must meet a brazen heaven" is "[u]nclean and seeming unforgiven," he can only "feel the long success of sin" in his life, rendering his body "this clay uncouth" (*PW* 83). Although "The May Magnificat" is celebratory, for Mary's sake, the structural and thematic centre of the poem acknowledges creation's burden: "Flesh and fleece, fur and feather, / Grass and greenworld all together" and altogether endangered (*PW* 153). The poem's underthought, Isaiah's striking metaphor that "all flesh is grass" (Is. 40:6),[59] only heightens the contrast between the Virgin mother and the people desperately in need of "salvation," the poem's final word (*PW* 154). Even when a natural scene and its elements—kestrel, kingfisher, bluebell, harvest—are praised in wholly rapturous tones, "These things, these things were here and but the beholder / Wánting" (*PW* 149). Typically for Hopkins, the key participle, "Wanting," invites a double reading: wanting as in desired, and wanting as in lacking. What "Hurrahing in Harvest" expresses in muted tones "The Caged Skylark," an allegory of "Man's mounting spirit" and all that ensnares it, presents emphatically. Yes, the promise of "his bónes rísen" concludes the sonnet, but the struggle of the spirit within the all-too-human "bone-house, mean-house" is stressed, because "Man's spirit will be flesh-bound when found at best" (*PW* 148). Small wonder that, in an April 1885 letter to Bridges, Hopkins laments "that coffin of weakness and defection in which I live" (*CW* 2:722).

From sources as diverse as the *Spiritual Exercises* and Christina Rossetti's "Convent Threshold," Hopkins learns the flesh's burdens and vulnerabilities in terms of all five senses. Taste, however—the intimacy of gustatory imagery—always registers the most vividly in his texts. Flesh and the acrid taste of sin are tropes Hopkins deploys throughout his canon. An 1864 draft of a poem beginning "Glimmer'd along the square-cut steep" references a "godless flock" with disturbing appetites: "The lawless honey eaten of old / Has lost its savour and is roll'd / Into the bitterness of sin" (*PW* 31).

In 1877, even in the midst of Welsh celebrations of nature, human nature is "sour with sinning" (*PW* 142) and the flesh associated with heartburn and bitterness ("sloe," for example, is the sharp, sour fruit of the blackthorn[60]).

Ignatius refers to taste in the preface to the *Exercises,* to praise "the inward sense and taste of things" (*SE* 4), and more fully in the First Week, Fifth Exercise, a meditation on hell that advises the exercitant to "taste with the taste bitter things, as tears, sadness, and the worm of conscience" (*SE* 41). It is not surprising, therefore, that Hopkins revisits the motif in his retreat notes of August 1880:

> When I consider my selfbeing, my ~~feeling~~ consciousness and feeling of myself, ~~so mo~~ that taste of myself, of I and me above and in all things ^which is^ more distinctive than the taste of ale or alum, more distinctive than the smell of walnutleaf or camphor, and ^is^ incommunicable by any means to another man.... Nothing else in nature comes near this unspeakable stress of pitch, distinctiveness, and selving, this selfbeing of my own: nothing explains it or resembles it, except so far as this, that other men to themselves have the same feeling. But this only multiplies the phenonem~~on~~^a^ to be explained so far as the cases are like and do resemble. But to me there is no resemblance: searching nature I ~~find~~ taste self but at one tankard, that of my own being. The development, refinement, condensation of... nothing shews ~~of~~ any sign of being able to match this to me or give me another taste of it, a taste even resembling it. (*CW* 5:349)

It is in the poems of 1884 to 1888 that Hopkins revisits the metaphor and finds other, more distressing uses for it.

Of the many bitter tastes to be experienced, "gall" is the most complex in Hopkins's canon. As a noun, physiologically, it is the yellow bile produced by the liver. In the Ireland sonnets, it symbolizes the disparaged, debased, and self-tormenting flesh:

> I am gall, I am heartburn. God's most deep decree
> Bitter would have me taste: my taste was me;
> Bones built in me, flesh filled, blood brimmed the curse. (*PW* 181)[61]

So intensely does the speaker focus on the dis-functioning of his body that ontological certainty is temporarily ruptured. This is also a deliberately crude parody of Christ's suffering before his crucifixion, when "they gave him vinegar to drink mingled with gall: and when he had tasted thereof, he would not drink" (Matt. 27:34).⁶² As a verb, gall means to make sore by chafing or rubbing. So the image of embers that "Fall, gáll themsélves, / and gásh góld-vermílion," the penultimate metaphor of "The Windhover," slightly undercuts the speaker's effusive tribute to the bird and his Lord (*PW* 144). In the first version of "St. Alphonsus Rodriguez," the "scar that galls the limb" (*PW* 199) is an unsettling description of heroic action. In the poem's second iteration, "In honour of St. Alphonsus Rodriguez," the description of the warrior's body echoes the devastation of "Binsey Poplars": "those fell strokes that once scarred flesh, scored shield" (*PW* 200). The third version replaces "Glory" with "Honour," which is "flashed off exploit, so we say; / And those strokes once that gashed flesh or galled shield / Should tongue that time now" (*PW* 200). And there is at least one other intertextual impulse behind the use of "gall": a pun on oak gall, the substance (an excrescence on the tree) used in the manufacture of ink. Shakespeare's Sir Toby Belch is punning when he urges Maria to write the gulling letter to ensnare Malvolio: "Let there be gall enough in thy ink."⁶³ Hopkins, for his part, tends to have too much gall in his ink, yet the bitterness inspires him.

The First Principle and Foundation of the *Exercises*, the Preparatory Exercise, demands no less than five times, "*Who are you?*" (*SE* 16–17). Hopkins's response in his 1880 retreat notes has been preserved:

> Whatever can with truth be called a self—not merely in logic or grammar, as if one said nothingness itself—, such as individuals and persons must be, it is not a mere centre point of reference for ~~thought~~ consciousness or action attributed to it, everything else, all that it is conscious of or acts ~~if~~ ^on^ being its object only and outside it. Part of this world of objects, this object world, is ^also^ part of the very self in question, as in man's case his own body, which each man not only feels ~~with~~ in and acts with but also feels and acts on. (*CW* 5:354)

As material object, the fleshly body hopelessly undermines a subjectivity that seeks its most profound relation with God. Ignatian spirituality, among other discursive pressures, convinces Hopkins that the self fashioned "in the experience of the flesh" (Laqueur, *Making* 13) is "strained" and vulnerable. Three poems present this dilemma most starkly. "Binsey Poplars" is an elegiac lyric in which an ecological disaster prefigures the human. Because of industrialized greed (poplars were used for, among other things, the brake "shoes" of railway trains), "[s]trókes of havoc únsélve / The sweet especial scene" (*PW* 157).⁶⁴ "The Sea and the Skylark" conflates Parmenides and Genesis in a Darwinian devolutionary nightmare: "We, life's pride and cared-for crown, / Have lost that cheer and charm of earth's past prime: / Our make and making break, are breaking, down / To man's last dust, drain fast towards man's first slime" (*PW* 143). The pre-Socratic suggestion that people "had sprung from the slime" (*CW* 4:317) is seconded by the Douay-Rheims translation of Genesis 2:7, regarding "the slime of the earth" (*PW* 375). "Spelt from Sibyl's Leaves," the Dublin poem that began as a response to William Collins's "Ode to Evening,"⁶⁵ takes the possibilities of "breaking, down" a terrible step further. The "[e]arnest" and "stupendous" near-chaos of "Sibyl's Leaves" almost "whélms" the speaker with a "dragonish," somatically grounded subjectivity: "self ín self stéepèd and páshed—quite / Disremembering, dísmémbering | áll now" (*PW* 190–91). Body betrays mind to produce a lived experience akin to "a ráck / Where, selfwrung, selfstrung, sheathe- and shelterless, | thóughts agaínst thoughts ín groans grínd" (*PW* 191). The means by which Hopkins could write himself out of that tortuous drama of selving and into a triumphalist "Manshape" depended upon a belief in the theophanous body.

Daniel Harris reads the Dublin sonnets in terms of an "experience of dis-Incarnation" (55). I would suggest that they enact a nightmarish confrontation with the complete and harrowing significance *of* the Incarnation—including the "forepangs," the "gall" of wavering faith, physical humiliation and torment, and temporary oblivion—for Christ and for humanity. As well, they represent the culmination of Hopkins's commitment (as poet and priest) to an "aesthetics of pain."⁶⁶ From the time of his preliminary undergraduate poems, Hopkins experiments with the exemplification of "a sweet undoing pain" (*PW* 62); the Dublin sonnets do so searingly because the speaker no longer occupies a comfortably distanced third-person singular position—instead, these are dramas of self-loathing in the first-person singular.⁶⁷ Pain exposes; pain reveals. Years of devoted adherence to the *Spiritual Exercises* teach Hopkins the imaginative "instrumentality of pain" and the efficacy of representing "agony" (Richter 33).⁶⁸ He is also familiar with the lessons of Lessing's *Laocoon*, which states of Sophocles, "How wonderfully the poet has known how to strengthen and deepen the idea of bodily pain! And he chose a wound . . . he chose, I say, a wound and not an internal malady, because he was able to make a more vivid representation of the latter than of the former, however painful it may be" (76, 77).

"In the Victorian period," as Moran notes, "conventional social and cultural expectations—concerning gender, class and even denominational difference—are encoded in representations of the body in pain. Such images emphasize orthodox values at a time of cultural transition. . . . The Victorian 'cult' of suffering offers consolation and reassurance for those who are excluded from roles of power and from positive achievement and success" ("Hopkins and Victorian").⁶⁹ Alphonsus Rodriguez is one such figure, for Hopkins; as I discuss below, virginal religious martyrs willing to experience torture are also important.⁷⁰ Their pain is a form of witnessing—confessing the faith—and a "source of testimony" (Fitfield 123). Hopkins is also influenced by the myriad Old and New Testament examples of pain and punishment. As Elaine Scarry notes in her groundbreaking study *The Body in Pain: The Making and Unmaking of the World,* wounding in the Old Testament is typically "a scene of doubt, for it is a failure of belief that continually occasions the infliction of hurt. Unable to apprehend God with conviction, they will . . . apprehend him in the intensity of their pain in their own bodies, or in the visible alteration in the bodies of their fellows or in the bodies . . . of their enemies." Thus, she concludes, bodies are used "to make experienceable the metaphysical abstraction whose remoteness has occasioned disbelief" (Scarry 201).⁷¹ How words are deployed to overcome the difficulty of expressing physical pain is, for Scarry, both a human and imaginative dilemma—perhaps the most perplexing aspect of creativity (3). And yet, "What is remembered in the body is well remembered" (Scarry 110), as Hopkins's poetry and prose vividly demonstrate.

Read individually, several of the "terrible" sonnets offer no "root room" for comfort, physical or spiritual; the reader, like the speaker, can become lost within their "pangs." "Christian flesh," as Foucault observes, is "a perpetual source within subjectivity, within individuals, of temptation which risk[s] leading the individual beyond the limits posed by . . . common morality" (*Religion* 126). Often in the Ireland poems, the fleshly limit to which the speaker confesses is "Despair." The reader is witnessing "a self-consciousness perpetually alert to its own weakness, to its own temptations, to its own flesh" (Foucault, *Religion* 126). Only if one reads the Dublin poems as a suite, with "That Nature is a Heraclitean Fire and of the comfort of the Resurrection" as their apotheosis, can one answer the flesh's importune harassments and recover, as did their creator, an affirmative relationship between body and spirit. In doing so, one encounters the horrors and wonders of the eschatological body. The latter, within a Roman Catholic dispensation, is everyone's fate: at one and the same time death, physical corruption beyond the grave ("Flesh fade, and mortal trash / Fáll to the resíduary worm"), and an eternity that can only be imagined, "In a flash, at a trumpet crash" (*PW* 198).[72]

As Hopkins understands it, the flesh is inescapable, to be experienced (whether positively or negatively) in this life and in the next. Some poems confidently assume the example and promise of Christ's "bónes rísen" (*PW* 148), endorsing Job's steadfast belief, "For I know that my redeemer liveth, and that he shall stand at the latter day upon the earth: And though after my skin worms destroy this body, yet in my flesh shall I see God" (19:25–26). Other poems insist upon it with disruptive awkwardness. All speak in response to the "horror and the havoc and the glory / Of it" (*PW* 201). Only "Heraclitean Fire" achieves the verbal redemption of the flesh in a brilliant etymological exercise: "Thís Jack, jóke, poor pótsherd, | patch, matchwood, immortal diamond, / Is immortal diamond" (*PW* 198).

FROM THE PULPIT

Imagine, for a moment, that it is 1879, a hot summer's morning in Oxford. The poorly ventilated church is crowded; you and your family are seated, as usual, in one of the back pews, because the kids tend to get rambunctious, and the baby might cry (colic). Way at the front, behind the pulpit, the short priest—with an aggravatingly posh London-Oxford accent—is telling you, again, to fear the flesh, to "tame" its sinful desires. You've never met a Pharisee but would be happy to leave St. Clement's and spend time with a publican in the local alehouse. This is an exaggeration, of course, but no one was in attendance then to tell the faithful that Fr. Hopkins's sermons would be read, admired, and discussed one hundred and fifty years hence. Back then, in an era of excellent, compelling preachers, Hopkins's homilies were not always a resounding success.[73] As texts, however, and in the context of my argument about confessing the flesh, the sermons provide further examples of how Hopkins negotiates between two master narratives: the paradox of Christ's kenotic yet triumphant assumption of flesh, and the perils of human flesh. The former is discussed below, in the segment focusing on Christ's body. The latter I will address now, to demonstrate how the poetry and the sermons share thematic and rhetorical strategies.

The August 1879 sermon on the parable of the Pharisee and Publican[74] provides a taxonomy of sin: "sins under the 3 heads of pride of life, ~~p~~ desire of the eyes, desire of the flesh" (*CW* 5:182). The choices one has are stark (another example of Hopkins's dichotomous thinking): "commit sins of the flesh" or "tam[e]" the flesh (*CW* 5:182). And yet, as the homily concludes, the Church offers the "Goodness of contrition—Greatest sins forgiven in a moment. . . . Promise of confession, because . . . appointed by God" (*CW* 5:184). Six months later, to answer the question "In what does love consist?" Hopkins again provides two possible options: self-love, the negative choice, "consenting to and gratifying the wishes of our lower, our worst, selves, . . . ^our selves of^ flesh," or the positive choice, loving God by keeping his commandments and living in the spirit of *caritas* and duty ("Duty is love") (*CW* 5:258, 260).

"The Fall of God's First Kingdom," the subject of his 25 January 1880 sermon,[75] necessarily involves the flesh. Interestingly—but not surprisingly—Eve's "fallen flesh" is the focus as Hopkins retells the Eden story. Several times, the preacher stresses that she is the "mother of all flesh" (*CW* 5:276, 278)—Adam's paternity in that regard is never mentioned. Presented with the forbidden fruit, Eve succumbs to the "desire of the eyes; <u>and that it was delightful to behold</u>, that is / sweet and enjoyable in imagination even, and forecast, how much more in the eating and the reality! ~~she~~ and here was the desire of the flesh; she freely yielded herself to the three concupiscences; <u>she took and eat</u> ~~of the devil's sacrament~~ ^of this devil's-sacrament^; she ~~fell~~ rebelled, she sinned, she fell" (*CW* 5:278). Following the example of Milton's *Paradise Lost* (9:954–60), Hopkins suggests that Adam's uxorious choice—solidarity with Eve rather than with

God—is the second and more fateful rebellion: "God, who gave back to Abraham for his obedience his all but sacrificed son, wd. have given ^back^ to Adam ~~his fallen wife~~ for his obedience his fallen wife," but Adam "left his heavenly father and clave to his wife and they two were in one fallen flesh" (*CW* 5:278). As in other sermons, however, Hopkins does not end on a note of desolation. Instead, he suggests that the "sanctifying grace" sacrificed by Eve and Adam for their fleshly desires can be recovered, today, because God's actions, and human beings', take place within a system of "personal and political justice" (*CW* 5:280).

The long-term consequences of the Fall are stressed in the 25 April 1880 sermon that revisits Christ's agony in the garden of Gethsemane (the night before the crucifixion) to make a key point. The apostle Peter had the best intentions—to follow Christ "to prison and to death"—but he betrayed his Lord instead, because "the flesh was weak" (*CW* 5:285). Hopkins uses the example of Peter's failure to emphasize that the divine Paraclete, the Holy Ghost,[76] is the opposite of selfish human flesh: "For now, after the Fall, good in this world is hard, it is surrounded by difficulties, the way to it lies through thorns, the flesh is against it, the world is against it, the Devil is against it: therefore if a Paraclete cheers men on to good it will be ~~in the~~ ^to^ good that is hard" (*CW* 5:286). Other flesh-focused comparisons that flourish in the sermons include the difference between angels ("blissful spirits") and "fallen men ... so full of the miseries of ^the^ flesh" (*CW* 5:317), and Christ's life as "flesh and blood" and that of human beings' (*CW* 5:324, 325). At all times, and for all congregations, Hopkins stresses that people are "wretched" because they inhabit "this body of death" (*CW* 5:279), too fixated on "^our selves of^ flesh and not of spirit, our selves of this world and of time" (*CW* 5:258).

DISCIPLINE AND PUNISH: "DIRECT LIGHTS AND INSPIRATIONS"

Intransigence, however, is not the only story of the flesh that can be told, as Hopkins tries to explain to Dixon in December 1881: "When a man has given himself to God's service, when he has denied himself and followed Christ, he has fitted himself to receive and does receive ^from God^ a ~~more~~

special guidance, a more particular providence. This guidance is conveyed partly by the action of other men ... and partly by direct lights and inspirations" (*CW* 1:502). Opportunities and "inspirations" to overcome the flesh, as Hopkins understands them, are several. They are best understood in a discipline-focused cluster that includes virginity (and virgin martyrs) and mortification.

As Foucault famously demonstrates, the modern, carceral society that emerges in the eighteenth century and flourishes in subsequent eras of capitalism, industrialization, and imperialism depends upon disciplinary power relations: "The human body was entering a machinery of power that explores it, breaks it down and rearranges it. . . . It defined how one may have a hold over others' bodies, not only so that they may do what one wishes, but so that they may operate as one wishes, with the techniques, the speed, and the efficiency that one determines. Thus discipline produces subjected and practiced bodies, 'docile' bodies" (*DP* 138). Systems of authority and their institutionalized forms of knowledge, Foucault suggests, produce notions of "norms" and "deviance" that govern behavior in every context (schools, factories, prisons, barracks, hospitals, churches). Surveillance, the disciplinary mode's best tactic, is ultimately translated into self-surveillance and self-discipline, whereby docility is but one aspect of what Hopkins would term "selving."

What Foucault critiques, John Henry Newman endorses. His 1842 sermon "Dangers to the Penitent" affirms the lessons that Hopkins readily absorbs in the 1860s and 1870s:

> They cannot manage themselves; they must be guided by others; the neglect of this simple and *natural rule* leads to very evil consequences. We should all of us be saved a great deal of suffering of various kinds, if we could but persuade ourselves, that we are not the best judges, whether of our own condition, or of God's will towards us. What sensible person undertakes to be his own physician? yet are the diseases of the mind less numerous, less intricate, less subtle than those of the body? is experience of no avail in things spiritual as well as in things material? ... How can a person show himself the way, when by the very hypothesis he has lost it? how can he at once guide and be guided? (*Sermons* 48–49; my emphasis)

In this way Newman guides young men into accepting "the duty of bodily," spiritual, and emotional discipline, pronounces it "natural," and teaches his audience to admire St. Paul's admonition, "I keep under my body, and bring it into subjection" (1 Cor. 9:27).[77]

Beginning in September 1868, Jesuit life, for Hopkins, means immersion in a religious disciplinary society. Daily duties as summarized by Morris, S.J., begin and conclude with the surrender of the will and sedulous attention to detail. "Everything should have on it the impress of Religion," he insists; "you should not be satisfied till you have taught yourself to do everything as a Religious should do it. This must be true, not only of your spiritual duties, properly so called, but all of your duties without exception. They must all be duties spiritually done, even recreation, even a game" (1). At nighttime, preparing the meditation notes for the next day is crucial: "The day may be said to depend on the Meditation, and the Meditation largely depends on the way in which you have passed the time since your preparation was made. Go to bed as if you were going to die before morning. Lay your clothes aside as if you were never going to put them on again. Part with the world, with your life, as if you knew that your life was at an end and were to see the world no more" (3). Unlike Newman, who uses "nature" to advance his argument, Morris positions "nature" as the enemy: "natural impulse" and "natural tastes" are to be curtailed, even eliminated if possible. Learning to "practise holy indifference" to all tasks—and even to oneself—is the goal; in terms of manual work and duties, for example, "prefer those things that are most disagreeable" (7, 8). And in terms of the flesh? Morris only mentions the eyes, but the implications for all sensory experience are clear: "No mistake could be greater than to think of keeping custody of the eyes" (20).[78] Hopkins would be reminded, again and again, that the "Will of God" and the rules of the Society are wholly complementary. "Lend yourself to this formation of your will," Morris observes, and the rewards are inestimable. Discipline is supposed to triumph over what one wants "naturally"; "breaking in" the will, however, seems very similar to breaking the will. And yet—Hopkins willingly reconciles the two.

Selving, for Hopkins, is "arch-especial" if virginity protects one from fleshly harm. Chastity indicates a welcome degree of continence, according to the Church, but only virginity provides the most profound kind of renunciative pleasure. In terms of eschewing the "seditious flesh" (Bernaeur, S.J., "Fascinating" 42), virginity is a "glorification of self-restraint" (*HS* 2:15), but it is more than mere abstinence. As Foucault suggests, based on his readings of Cassian, Tertullian, Gregory of Nyssa, Augustine, and Saint Cyprian's *De habitu virginum*, virginity is also an art of living, an ascetic praxis: it too is part of selving because of the work that the soul "must do to itself" and to the "rebellions of the flesh" (*HS* 4:162, 149).[79] "After and through the Incarnation, virginity became possible as the restitution of angelic life within this world, despite the constraints of the flesh" (*HS* 4:149). The "productivity of virginity," as Harcourt observes, involves forming a special, albeit difficult "relation to the body—one that involves infinite labor" (63).[80]

As many critics have noted, "this mystique of virginity" (*HS* 4:155) is clearly marked in Hopkins's canon, a valorization that focuses on female virgins whose "counter-conduct" is "sweet virtue's glory" (*PW* 69). "St. Thecla," an 1864–65 poem, captures the moment when the young woman, enthralled, hears St. Paul preach:

> He praised the lovely lot of continence:
> All over, some such words as these, though dark,
> *The world was saved by virgins*, made the mark. (*PW* 70)

Rare among the exemplary virginal figures whom Hopkins salutes, Thecla does not suffer a gruesome death (the female animals who are supposed to devour her miraculously refuse to do so). Hopkins revisits Thecla in the Latin poem "*In Theclam Virginem*," ca. 1876. By that time, he has also devoted himself to four different poetic versions of St. Dorothea's story (executed),[81] imagined the "Christ-ed beauty" of Margaret Clitheroe's "mind" (*PW* 137) and the brutality she endured ("*Pressed to death*" [*PW* 136]), narrated the storm-shocks that kill the five Franciscan nuns in "The Wreck," and written two poems in honor of St. Winefred (beheaded, then restored to life by her uncle, St. Beuno). As a cultural ideal, the virginal body represents "the value and propriety of sociosexual codes" (Lloyd Davis 3). (As the First Exercise on the Incarnation advises, "Admire the privilege of virginity" (*SE* 137).) Hopkins's texts fully "participate in the 'web of discourses' which articulated ambivalent Victorian conceptions of the body 'as either valuable or problematic'" (Lloyd Davis 4). Yet, unlike the traditional "virgin's tale"—a "mythos of draconian oppression, virginal distress, and heroic rescue" (Tucker 69) that relishes, in a wholly sexist way, the crises of women poised on the brink of sexual violation—Hopkins's narratives focus upon deeds rather than threats. Thus gender specificity enables the texts to reinscribe, "for the purposes of spectacle and discipline," conventions of female martyrdom in which "female bodies . . . are displayed in both a sadistic and sexualized fashion" (Castelli 43).

Endurance is key to every martyr's success, whether virgin or not. In the name of the "Life that died" (*PW* 125), one's "search for the truth," as Foucault suggests, "must constitute a certain way of dying to oneself" (*HS* 4:110), a special kind of mortification-as-subjectivity. Throughout his poetry Hopkins privileges what one could call the enduring, traumatized, sacrificial body, whether that of sailor, saint, or young woman. The "spirit of sacrifice" and its practical consequences are well-rehearsed in the *Spiritual Exercises:* "There are some things to which we must submit," Ignatius counsels, "though nature shrinks from them,—for instance, sickness, poverty, humiliation, mortification, &c. What opportunities of practicing patience, humility, charity!" (*SE* 36–37). More specifically, the second exercise on Christ's Passion advises, "Contemplate him in Jerusalem, making also the sacrifice of all *exterior* things, which consist in these five things,—His liberty, His friends, His reputation, His happiness, His own body. In each of these sacrifices consider the Saviour as a victim and as a model; meditate on what He suffers and how He suffers" (*SE* 206).

Endurance and suffering combine in the theory and practices of penance, for which chastising the flesh has been de rigueur. Historically, types of penance have ranged from solitary prayer to exile. Given the miseries of Hopkins's five long years "at a third / Remove" in Ireland (*PW* 181), one can almost feel the irony that it was Irish monks, busy "re-Christianiz[ing] Europe" in the sixth century, who insisted upon "that early ecclesiastical penal system which condemned delinquents to a period, or even a lifetime, of 'foreignness' or *peregrinatio*" (Mahoney, S.J. 12, 11).—Most memorable, however, are the penitential experiences involving mortification. As Mahoney, S.J., summarizes, "The usual forms of self-mortification enjoined were fasts of varying intensity and duration, deprivation of sleep, multiple genuflections and recitations of psalms, long periods of standing or of silence, different degrees of discomfort at night, beatings, and, of course, sexual abstinence" (10). Thoroughly, painfully, the connections among knowledge of oneself, confession to someone else, and total obedience are vividly demonstrated in the willingness to endure, or even embrace, such deprivations. As Foucault observes, these Christian techniques have a specific aim: "to get individuals to work at their own 'mortification' in this world. Mortification is not death, of course, but it is a renunciation of this world and of oneself: a kind of everyday death. A death which is supposed to provide life in another world."[82] Saville astutely extends the argument in relation to Hopkins: "The mortified flesh of the ascetic becomes his medium of self-expression and an index to the world of his spiritual worth. Paradoxically, then, a practice seemingly aimed at self-denigration, effacing the body, can readily translate into public spectacle, with the body as the focus of attention" (*Queer* 12).

"Easter Communion" (Lent 1865) provides the most vivid account of a "sergèd fellowshi[p]" dedicated to the "ever-fretting shirt of punishment": "Pure fasted faces draw unto this feast: / God comes all sweetness to your Lenten lips. / You striped in secret with breath-taking whips" (*PW* 70). Whether the poem fascinates or repulses (or both), one has to agree that it is among the most significant works of the 1860s. Structurally, aesthetically, the sonnet *is* accomplished: end-rhymes and alliterations are supple; the trochees launching several lines demonstrate fledgling efforts to find a new, more expressive rhythm. Without the apprentice work of "Easter Communion" and "Barnfloor and Winepress" (in which Christ's Eucharistic "heavenly Bread" is made possible by his "bruised" body "Scourged upon the threshing floor" [*PW* 26]), would "The Wreck" be so extremely accomplished? To paraphrase "*Nondum*," Hopkins's imagination is definitely chastened and "chastening."

Yet, how is one to define or measure Hopkins's ascetic excesses when the examples available to him were equally or even more drastically severe? He was spared, at least, the publication of Charles Kingsley's sadomasochistic drawings of his wife, Fanny Grenfell, naked and nailed to a cross (among other positions) (Chitty 74–75). But John Henry Newman's 1833 essay entitled *Mortification of the Flesh a Scripture Duty*, number 21 in the ninety *Tracts for the Times*, was readily available in Oxford in the 1860s and amply praised by those who believed that the most effective way to reprove the flesh, to cleanse it, was, in Newman's words, to experience "bodily privation and chastisement" (1).[83] Such "bodily discipline" should be considered a "duty," Newman argues, not an indulgence (3). Among the mortifying practices endorsed by Tract 21 is fasting, a necessary means of "humiliation."

What Newman treats in a handful of paragraphs, however, Pusey devotes twenty-eight pages to defending in Tract 18, *Thoughts on the Benefits of the System of Fasting, Enjoined by Our Church* (1833). For Pusey, fasting is both a "voluntary discipline" and "an especial privilege" (*Thoughts* 24). Hopkins undoubtedly read the tract (*CW* 3:277); he might also have heard a Pusey sermon on the subject of "God's Presence in Loneliness." As Pusey admonishes his Lenten audience, "Fasting is a spiritual exercise, acting on the soul through the body for good, as the body so often acts on the soul for evil. Yet, therefore, must we the more take heed, that we stop not short in the body, and the soul lose not its refreshment through the body's privations. While we bring the body low, or 'into subjection,' by fasting, the soul must be cleansed by humiliation, fed by contemplation" (*Sermons* 197). Hopkins did not need to attend a public service, however, to appreciate Pusey's particular antidotes for what the Tractarian called "periods of ease, of temptation, . . . of growing corruption" (*Thoughts* 7). As I have mentioned, Pusey was Hopkins's confessor on several occasions in 1864 and 1865, and the spiritual director of Hopkins's primary Anglican mentor, Henry Liddon.[84] To put Hopkins's immoderate mortifications in perspective: he may have enjoyed, imaginatively, that "ever-fretting shirt of punishment," but Pusey actually wore one, from 1846 until the end of his life. "In daily prayer he was to ask for trouble and for sharp bodily pain" (Geoffrey Faber 400). Pusey was known for being a sober and holy man, but his writings are animated by a distinctly Gothic sensibility. "I know not which to the sinner is the most overwhelming," he observed in a Lenten sermon, "those outstanding sins, the memory of which ever haunts him, or that entangled impenetrable mass of sins, negligences and ignorances, which he cannot recall, which seems the thicker, because he cannot distinguish them, the daily, hourly, unceasing sins of a life passed in forgetfulness of God" (*Sermons* 228). Small wonder that Hopkins could describe so acutely what it meant to be "[u]nclean and seeming unforgiven," overly exposed to the "long success of sin" (*PW* 83). As Foucault suggests, to believe in the efficacy of mortifying the flesh is to commit to "a deliberate, diligent, and continuous elimination of everything in the body and soul that might be attached to sin" (*HS* 4:55).[85]

It is in the context of fasting and other rituals of mortification that Hopkins's untitled[86] Ireland sonnet articulates its truly shocking admissions:

> Not, I'll not, carrion comfort, Despair, not feast on thee;
> Not untwist—slack they may be—these last strands of man
> In me ór, most weary, cry *I can no more*. I can;
> Can something, hope, wish day come, not choose not to be.
> But ah, but O thou terrible, why wouldst thou rude on me
> Thy wring-world[87] right foot rock? lay a lionlimb against me? scan
> With darksome devouring eyes my bruisèd bones? and fan,
> O in turns of tempest, me heaped there; me frantic to avoïd thee and
>   flee? (*PW* 183)

The initial "Not" announces the "dialectic of negation" (Hurley 932) animating the poem; the lines that follow constitute a kind of anti-credo or summary of what the speaker does not or will not believe, do, say, embrace, endorse, or demonstrate. In this particular religious allegory, the Everyman/speaker personifies the deadliest sin, despair—deadly because the despairing person puts herself, or assumes himself to be, beyond God's forgiveness.[88] The poem, a tissue of biblical and Shakespearean allusions (one hears Job, Revelation, and Hamlet declaring "to be or not to be"), is challenging in part because the strategy of address shifts precipitously: despair is clearly identified in the initial line, but "O thou terrible" seems to indicate that God is now invoked in the drama of near-unselving. The sestet focuses on the speaker, he of "bruisèd bones" and wretched spirit, perhaps assaulted by Christ (the "héro whose héaven-handling flúng me, fóot tród / Me?" for his own good [*PW* 183]); some version of my / I / me appears on every line, to maximize self-loathing. In the context of this poem, "kiss[ing] the rod" hardly seems beneficial; the Lord's "darksome devouring eyes" see everything and too much. The only relief achieved in the text is found in the final line, when the speaker shifts from future and present tense to the past: "now done darkness" suggests that the wretched conditions dramatized in the sonnet have ebbed, if not ended. Thus, the poem immerses the speaker and reader in the rituals of mortification then offers a measure of recovery. Yet the damage, however metaphorically expressed—"That my chaff might fly; my grain lie, sheer and clear" (*PW* 183)—and however imagined to be necessary, is also clear. Hopkins once remarked approvingly, in the context of St. Teresa of Ávila's comments about the "lost spirit" in hell that "dashes itself like a caged beast and is in prison," that "[t]he keener the consciousness the greater the pain" (*CW* 5:415).

Interestingly, Abbé Gaume does not agree with those spiritual directors who "seem to think that the progress of a soul depends upon subjecting it to the severest bodily mortifications" nor with those who find such practices "useless" (231). Instead, he teaches that the body "is guilty of dragging us into evil through pursuit of its own pleasures," and advises, "Let us then be brave, and carry on a courageous mortification of self; let us mortify the body, eyes, tongue, taste, all the senses, and we shall win a reward of great peace" (114). More specifically he recommends "the discipline for about a quarter of an hour a day. Forbid hair-cloth for it much injures health" (242–43). According to Joseph Becker, S.J., "The traditional novitiate had a number of penitential practices that were dropped in the 1960s. The discipline (a whip of small cords to be used on the back) and the chain (a metal circlet with dull points to be worn around the waist or thigh) were formerly given to each novice during the thirty-day retreat. Thereafter, all the novices used these instruments on prescribed days. After the novitiate the use of the instruments was to continue but at times determined by the individual in consultation with his spiritual director" (246).[89] The flagellant, as Bill Burgwinkle observes, "is active and passive: judge, victim, and the mass of flesh to which he is tied" (15).

Discounting the phrase "flesh and blood," in reference to Christ, Ignatius uses the word "flesh" sparingly in the *Exercises*, but always effectively. The tenth "addition" of the First Week explains that "exterior penance" involves three kinds of "chastisement for sins committed" (*SE* 47): "The third way is to chastise the flesh (*las carnes*), to wit, by putting it to sensible pain, which is inflicted by wearing hair shirts, or iron chains on the bare flesh, by scourging oneself, or wounding oneself, and by other modes of austerities. What seems the more suitable and safer thing in penance is for the pain to be sensible in the flesh, without penetrating the bones, so as to cause pain and infirmity" (48). Among the examples provided: "scourge oneself with minute cords, which cause pain externally, rather than in any other way which might cause serious internal injury" (48). Rickaby, S.J.'s annotation is equally jarring: Ignatius "does not forbid disciplines to blood. But we should not practice such penance without advice.... It is a good rule that no bodily penance profits unless it humbles you.... When you take the discipline, say 'I deserve to be whipped like a dog'" (52).

Thinking and writing in another register, Gaume suggests that the most "useful and least dangerous mortifications are negative; ... e.g. depriving oneself of seeing or hearing curious things; talking little; ... willingly going without something one wants" (232). For Hopkins, in 1868, that "something" was poetry; not being creative was another kind of mortification, believed to be a sacrifice for a grateful deity. In a letter to Patmore, September 1885, he admits to another kind of emotional self-chastisement: "I can scarcely believe that ... anything of mine will ever see the light—of publicity nor even of day. For it is widely true, the fine pleasure is not to do a thing but to feel that you ~~can~~ ^could^ and the mortification that goes to the heart is to feel ~~that~~ it is the power that fails you.... So with me, if I could but get on, if I could but produce work I should not mind its being buried, ^silenced,^ and going no further; but it kills me to be time's eunuch and never to beget" (*CW* 2:744).⁹⁰

Of course, mortification practices of any kind are anathema to the anti-Catholic and anti-Tractarian critics—yet a wonderful opportunity to sensationalize or even demonize papists. The author of *The Oxford and Roman Railway,* for example, is suitably scandalized to report that ecclesiastical warehouses in London catering to Romanists actually stock hair shirts, disciplines (both the seven-tail and nine-tail versions), "massive waist chain[s], armlets," and other items used for scourging the flesh (38). "Instruments of Torture," the commentator protests, would be a more apt title than "Articles of Piety" (*Oxford and Roman* 39). Certainly, the collection displayed in *The Oxford and Roman Railway* resembles a medieval torture trove, but Hopkins would have recognized at least some of the devices and would have used at least two of them (variations of nos. 5 and 6, and 16, the discipline and the chain). To "change our hearts," Newman once recommended, to embrace self-denial, is "to unlearn the love of this world" (*Parochial* 7:50). To unlearn the ways of the flesh,

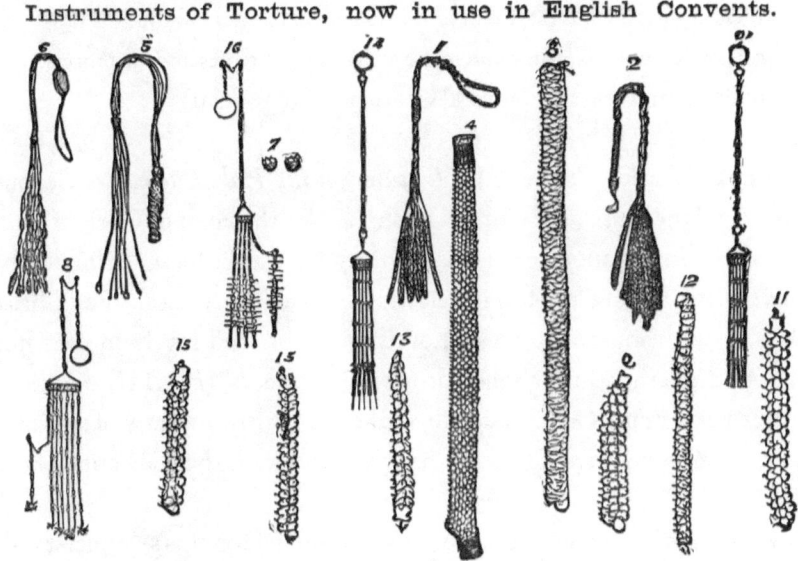

FIG 5 "The Tender Mercies of Romanism: Instruments of Torture, Now in Use in English Convents," from *The Oxford and Roman Railway* (1871), 39.

Hopkins was willing to accept a "chastening wand" (*PW* 93) both literally and figuratively.

CORPUS CHRISTI

Virgin, martyr, and voluntary victim of tortuous mortification, Jesus is the ultimate hope of redeeming the flesh. Not surprisingly, of all the feasts in the Church calendar, it was Corpus Christi that elicited the most, and most fervent, comments from Hopkins. As he tried to explain to Bridges in 1882,

> Corpus Xti differs from all other feasts in this, that its reason and occasion is a present. The first Christmas Day, the first Palm Sunday, ... Easter[,] ... and so on were to those who took part in them festivities <u>de praesenti</u>, but now, to us, they are anniversaries and commemorations only. But Corpus Christi is the feast of the Real Presence~~s~~; ~~and~~ therefore ^it is^ the most purely joyous of solemnities. Naturally the

Blessed Sacrament is carried in procession ^at it^, as you saw. But the procession has more meaning and mystery than this: it represents the process of the Incarnation and the world's redemption. (*CW* 2:531)

To quote Charles Coupe, S.J.'s *Lectures on the Holy Eucharist,* Corpus Christi is "the Festival of Christ's Flesh.... Not the Feast of Christ's Soul, nor of His Personality, nor of His Divinity, but of His Flesh" (202). Hopkins's writings avow the full implications of the Incarnation: "For Christ plays in ten thousand places, / Lovely in limbs, and lovely in eyes not his / To the Father through the features of men's faces" (*PW* 141). As priest, he both experiences and presides over the Eucharistic mystery of transubstantiation; as penitent Christian, he anxiously awaits the realization of the Beatific Vision.[91]

As Joseph Bizup suggests, we must consider Hopkins's "understanding of the Incarnation as two separate events, the *Ensarkosis* or 'taking of flesh' by which the world was created, and the *Enanthropesis* or 'becoming man' by which Christ entered the world as a specific historical person" (141). The clarity, intimacy, and resourcefulness with which Hopkins writes the body of Christ also suggest, to quote Daniel Harris, that "Hopkins' view of the Incarnation permits no comparison of terms, no transformation of one term into the other; it insists that both terms—God and man—are absolutely and simultaneously real, and that the copula between them is a literal metaphysical truth" (44). Without doubt, the body of Christ and its sacrificial example occasion some of the most exquisite and the most harrowing textual gestures in Hopkins's canon. He is inspired, like his hero Newman, to focus on Christ "as He was in the days of His Flesh" (*Parochial* 1:241).

Time after time, text after text, Hopkins's speaker is empowered by the opportunity to re-member Christ's incarnate form, "to take" and remake "His lovely likeness more and more" (*PW* 138). As one of Hopkins's most unusual coinages expresses, Christ's body is a "[l]ovescape" (*PW* 125) fusing or synthesizing divine love with the ultimate inscape or form, a fleshly symbolic landscape to be mapped and revisited. The complete phrase from "The Wreck" addresses Christ's "Lovescape crucified," a prominent fixation of the poetic writings to which I will return. First, however, there is the November 1879 sermon famous for its positive evocation of the "beautiful" body of Christ:

> There met in J. C. all things that can make man lovely and loveable. In his body he was most beautiful. This is known first by the tradition in the Church that it was so ~~and~~ // and by holy writers agreeing to suit those words to him / Thou art beautiful in mould above the sons of men: \\ we have even accounts of him written in early times. They tell us that he was moderately tall, well built and slender in frame, his features straight and beautiful, his hair inclining to auburn, parted in the midst, curling and clustering about the ears and neck as the leaves of a filbert, so they speak, upon the nut. ~~This hair, was never touched as well as a forked beard~~ He wore also a forked beard and this as well as the hair locks upon his head were never touched by razor or shears; neither, his health being perfect, could a hair ever fall to the ground. The account I have been quoting... we do not indeed for certain know to be correct, but it has been current in the Church and many generations have ~~pictured~~ ^drawn^ our Lord accordingly / either in their own minds or in ~~works of art~~ his images. (*CW* 5:225)

On one level, we can admire Hopkins's sustained attempt to express Christ's humanity, to make the deity seem accessible because physically familiar (yet, exceptional). Aesthetically, it is Christ's perfection that is stressed:

> Another proof of his beauty may be drawn from the words <u>proficiebat sapientia et aetate et gratia apud Deum et homines</u> (Luc. i ii 52)[92] / he went forward in wisdom and bodily frame and favour with God and men; that is / he pleased both God and men ^daily^ more and more by his growth of mind and body. ~~b~~But he could not have pleased by growth of body unless the body were strong, healthy, and beautiful that grew. But the best proof of all is this, that his body was the special work of the Holy Ghost. He was not born in nature's course, no man was his father; had he been born as others are he ~~wd.~~ must have inherited some defect of figure or of constitution, from which no ~~fallen man or is wholly free~~ man born as fallen men are born is wholly free unless God interfere to ~~prevent it~~ ^keep him so^. But his body was framed ~~by~~ directly from heaven by the power of the Holy Ghost, of whom it wd. be unworthy to leave any the least botch or failing in his work. So the first Adam was moulded by God himself and Eve built up by God too out of Adam's rib and they cd. not but be

perfect works of perfect ^two pieces, both,^ of faultless workmanship: so ^the same^ then and much more must Christ have been. His constitution too was tempered perfectly, he had no neither disease nor the seeds of any: weariness he felt when he was weary^ied^, and fasting ^hunger^ when he fasted, thirst when he had long⸺ gone without drink, but to the touch of sickness he was a stranger. I leave it to you, brethren, then to picture him, in whom the fulness of the godhead dwelt bodily, in his bearing how majestic, how strong and yet how lovely and lissome in his limbs, in his look how earnest, grave but kind. In his Passion all this strength was spent, this lissomness crippled, this beauty wrecked, this majesty beaten down. But now it is ^more than^ all restored, and for myself I make no secret I look forward with eager desire to seeing the ^matchless^ beauty of Christ's body in the heavenly light. (*CW* 5:225–26)

The Christ represented in the sermon is a product of Victorian pieties, sentimentalism, and xenophobia, a function of the same visual rhetoric at work in William Holman Hunt's *The Light of the World* (in both, Christ's features are remarkably Anglo-Saxon rather than Semitic). The medical discourse that is enunciated to intensify Christ's perfection is also revealing ("to the touch of sickness he was a stranger").

What consternates if not divides readers today, however, is the issue of how one should interpret the speaker's gaze, how to read Christ's body as the object of Hopkins's desire. "This confusion of the legitimately homosocial with the dangerously homoerotic," Moran suggests, "was a problem faced by various writers of the period who sought to reconcile Christianity with the explicitly masculine rather than the unmanly.... Hero-worship was one solution" ("Lovely" 78). At the very least, one is struck by the sermon's energized need to put Christ's body into discourse (*HS* 1:11), to produce an enfleshed deity that would empower speaker and auditors alike. Knowledge of Christ's physique is a part of a greater "will to knowledge" (*HS* 1:12) that both anticipates and promises a final reckoning with God. The instrumentality of Christ's body is suggested in the ecstatic conclusion of the sermon, which composes a new, somatically charged *Gloria:* "Glory be to Christ's body; Glory to the body of the Word made flesh; Glory to the body suckled at the Virgin Blessed Virgin's breasts; Glory to Christ's body in its beauty; Glory to Xt'^s body^ in its weariness; Glory to it ^Xt's body^ in its Passion, death, and burial; Glory to Xt's body risen; Glory to Xt's body in the Bd. Sacrament; Glory to Christ's soul; Glory to ~~this~~ his wisdom and genius; Glory to his unsearchable thoughts; Glory to his saving words; Glory to his ^sacred^ heart; Glory to ~~his~~ ^its^ courage and manliness; Glory to ~~his~~ ^its^ meekness and mercy; Glory to its every heartbeat, to its joys and sorrows, wishes; fears; Glory in all things to J. C. God and man" (*CW* 5:228).[93]

In June 1881, Hopkins is again inspired to explore the meanings of "Christ's whole flesh," this time focusing on the "sacred heart," a symbol to which Jesuits were and are particularly attached (*CW* 5:332). As Nixon and Barber, S.J., explain, "Devotions to the 'heart' of Christ, first popularized in the seventeenth century by Gertrude of Gelfta and Jean Eudes" feature a "pierced or flaming heart" to represent "the desire of Christ, aflame with the love of the Father, to be endlessly solicitous for the care of his people." Although spiritually sound, the emblem was "often mawkishly presented—the symbol becoming a substitute for the substance" (*CW* 5:302). Hopkins acknowledges that for some "it is repulsive" to have one "piece of Christ's flesh ^thus^ nakedly thrust upon their mind's eye" (*CW* 5:332) but proceeds to explain why and how the heart is "one of the noble or honourable members of the body"; there is no need to consider the topic "revolting" (*CW* 5:332). The sermon is instructive in terms of how hard Hopkins is willing to work to justify metonymic thinking and how often he stresses that one's response to Christ's holiness—"True God, true man, in flesh and bone" (*PW* 169)—should be unalloyed "worship": "Want of reverence then there cannot be in the worship of the Sacred Heart" (*CW* 5:333).

As stated earlier, the 1879 Bedford Leigh sermon on Christ "our hero" is typical of Hopkins in its remarkable religious ardor, but atypical in that its imaginative energies are almost entirely positive.[94] Consistent in Hopkins's poetry—from early, derivative undergraduate texts to "The Wreck" and "In honour of St. Alphonsus Rodriguez"—is an emphasis on Christ's suffering body, what an incomplete lyric starkly hails as "Jesus Christ sacrificed / On the cross" (*PW* 185). Two unfinished versions of "New Readings" (1864), for example, attempt to combine the sowing / grain / grapes motif of "Barnfloor and Winepress" with an evocation of the indignities suffered by "CHRIST'S Head" (*PW* 28) when the soldiers "plaited thistles round" it (*PW* 27). "*O Deus, ego amo te*" (ca. 1872–74) revisits the crucifixion as a means of comprehending the depth of Christ's love: "Thou, thou, my Jesus, . . . / . . . For my sake sufferedst nails and lance,[95] / Mocked and marrèd countenance, / Sorrows passing number" (*PW* 106–7). As I discuss in a subsequent section, "The Wreck" represents a new command of poetic discourse, but its Christological interests are unchanged.

Scarry succinctly summarizes the cultural significance of Christ's body: "Throughout the Old Testament, God's power and authority are in part extreme and continually amplified elaborations of the fact that people have bodies and He has no body. It is primarily this that is changed in the Christian revision, for though the difference between man and God continues to be as immense as it was in the Hebraic scriptures, the basis of the difference is no longer the fact that one has a body and the Other has not. The change that occurs is a change less in the object of belief than in the very structure of belief, a change in the nature of the religious imagination" (210). Throughout his poetry, sermons, and spiritual writings, Hopkins strives to respect the Otherness of the deity and at the same time cherish the concrete, embodied truth of Christ. He "mingled Himself with our nature," as Pusey observes in *Eirenicon*, and in that way his "true flesh" redeemed humanity's fallen flesh (48, 53). In Augustine's words, Christ's sacrificial body, his voluntary[96] degradation as the Word made flesh, healed the "blindness of the flesh" to which all people are condemned, so that "mortal flesh should not for ever be mortal" (*Confs* 294, 64). As Morris, S.J., advises Jesuit novices, "Never fail to 'discern the Lord's Body'" (59).

READING THE WRECKS

To conclude this analysis of Hopkins's "flesh-bound" writings, and to demonstrate how closely they are intertwined with modes of confessing, I present a final exercise in counterpoint with "The Wreck of the Deutschland" and Caradoc's soliloquy from *St. Winefred's Well*. Superficially, the exceptionally polished ode and the unfinished scene[97] have little in common. The valiant Tall Nun who commands so much attention in "The Wreck" is the antithesis of the unremorseful murderer (who some suggest is Hopkins's answer to Milton's Lucifer or Stevenson's Mr. Hyde[98]).

Yet both texts explore the three meanings of confession I have been elaborating—confession of sins, profession of faith (avowal), articulation of praise—and they do so in the context of horrific deaths lavishly described. Both are corpse poems; both feature male speakers obsessing about the demise of a sacrificial female virgin; both are riddled with questions that the speaker only partially answers. And both are catalyzed by the anguished queries that initiate Caradoc's speech: "My heart, where have we been? | What have we seen, my mind?" (*PW* 177).

Avowal predominates in "The Wreck," a poem that revels in divine mastery and asserts its significance for the speaker and the Nun. Literally and figuratively, the poem circles back to that central, abiding truth. The first stanza begins, "Thou mastering me / God! giver of breath and bread" and concludes, "Óver agáin I féel thy finger and fínd thée" (lines 1–2, 8[99]). This recursive pattern also marks stanza 10, which concludes Part the First: "Make mercy in all of us, out of us all / Mástery, bút be adóred, bút be adóred Kíng" (79–80). The final stanza, in Part the Second, exchanges the brute force of God with the heroic love of Christ, "Oür héart's charity's héarth's fíre, oür thóughts' chivalry's thróng's Lórd" (279–80), but the desire to be dominated is reaffirmed. The Nun's professions of faith are unwavering, despite the "searomp over the wreck" (132); they constitute, for Hopkins's speaker, her greatest attraction. Her "vírginal tóngue tóld" (136) and tolls twice—indirectly in stanza 17, as imagined by the speaker, who is summarizing newspaper accounts of the shipwreck, and directly in stanza 24: "She to the black-about air, to the breaker, . . . / Was cálling 'O Chríst, Chríst, come quíckly': / The cross to her she calls Christ to her, christens her wild-worst Best" (189–92).[100] Her dramatic protestations, however, occasion the speaker's temporary doubt in his own ability to comprehend and to do justice to her witness (stanza 28):

>But how shall I . . . Make me room there;
>Reach me a . . . Fancy, come faster—
>Strike you the sight of it? look at it loom there,
>Thing that she . . . There then! the Master,
>*Ipse*, the ónly one, Chríst, Kíng, Héad:
>He was to cure the extremity where he had cast her;
>Do, deal, lord it with living and dead;

Let him ride, her pride, in his triumph, despatch and have done
with his doom there. (217–24)[101]

It is the genius of the poem to interweave a previous personal crisis and a recent, newsworthy spectacle and at the same time test, dramatically, the limits of poetic discourse. (Three voices are heard in the text: that of the speaker, the Nun, and Death.) For the speaker and the Nun, emotions range from grief to ecstatic joy; for the reader, to be caught up in the "violent immediacy" (Muller 43) of the text is to be pitched from wonder, dread, terror (I am summarizing the key emotive verbs), fear and relief to delight, stress, bliss, fright, pleasure, woe, cringing fear, pride, terror, hopelessness, heartbreak, calm, self-loathing, agony, sorrow, anguish, horror, pride, shock, pity, compassion, *and* hope. Such emotional "extremity" is enhanced by Hopkins's newfound, unsettling,[102] and "kinesthetic" style (Vendler 94),[103] which is intensified, made truly performative, by "features" (*CW* 1:295) including the strongly felt stresses of sprung rhythm; dense alliteration, assonance, and internal rhyme (after the Welsh *cynghanedd*, the complex "chiming" of consonants and vowels); original portmanteau words and phrases; interrogatives; exclamation marks; dashes; excessive commas; the rhetorical flourishes of aposiopesis; and the fracturing possibilities of anacoluthon. Some techniques are connective; they enhance the dynamic, sensuous flow of words. Others, as in stanza 28, restrain or arrest signification; they heighten (or threaten) disconnection.

Confessing the flesh and praising his Lord are the two poles of the speaker's harrowing, eminently productive experience. After the exhausting efforts of stanza 28, the speaker's tone changes and his perspective shifts—from reporting the wreck with dramatic fervor to ruminating on its significance for the present and future ("is the shípwrack then a hárvest, / does témpest carry the gráin for thee?" he asks of Christ [247–48]). He worries for those who do not heed the wreck's providential lesson: "Heart, go and bleed at the *bitterer* vein for the / Comfortless unconfessed of them" (243–44; my emphasis). This admission offsets the declaration in stanza 2: "I did say yes / O at líghtning and láshed ród; / Thou heardst me, truer than tongue, confess / Thy terror, O Christ, O God" (9–12). Framing that stanza with the rhyming words *yes, confess,* and *stress* accentuates the challenges of combining penitential desires and adulation. Certainly the shipwreck—the suffering, the lives lost, the families ruined by the deaths—is a challenge to anyone's faith, as the speaker admits by referring to "the dark side of the bay of [Christ's] blessing" (95). Nonetheless, the final stanza salutes the Nun as another beneficent, female intercessionary figure (Mary is the focus of the penultimate stanza) who exemplifies "the heaven-háven of the rewárd" (274–75) awaiting the devout.

Caradoc's soliloquy (on its own, another superb Victorian dramatic monologue) is both a defiant self-defense and an unwitting confession. To amplify the textual experience, Caradoc's speech features "two voices": the intimacy of first-person expostulation, and impersonal and hence unsettling declarations in third-person statements such as "In a wide world of defiance / Caradoc lives alone, | Lóyal to his ówn soul, láying his / ówn law dówn" (*PW* 178–79). His bifurcated mind and psychic distress are the consequence of the "havoc" he has created[104] and now tries desperately to rationalize. In terms of the saint's drama, Caradoc is at this time a murderer: Winefred's uncle, Beuno, has yet to restore her head and her life. It is Caradoc's vehement unrepentance that fascinates. "And I do nót repent" he insists, "I do not and I will not | repent, not repent" (178). And the consequence of that refusal to own his sin and confess? "In a wide world of defiance | Caradoc lives alone" (178). Despite his claims that he is "unwavering," that "no flinching" marks his insolence, Caradoc almost immediately frets: "And in this darksome world | what comfort can I find" (179), a question that echoes in both "The Wreck" and "Carrion Comfort." The speech marks the prince's pivotal moment: he can confess and ask for God's mercy, or choose, as he does, to "brazen despair out, / Brave all, and take what comes" (179).[105]

In both the soliloquy and the ode, the flesh's peculiar "fiery strain" (*PW* 179) is apparent. Devastated *and* blessed bodies populate "The Wreck," the first stanza of which addresses the "Lord of living and dead":

> Thou hast bóund bónes and véins in me, fástened me flésh,
> And áfter it álmost únmade, what with dréad,
>   Thy doing: and dost thou touch me afresh?
> Óver agáin I féel thy fínger and fínd thée. (lines 5–8)

As with "confess," Hopkins emphasizes the importance of "flesh" by positioning it last on the line, making it a key end-rhyme (in this stanza, *flesh* and *afresh,* with the additional assonantal chime of *bread, dead,* and *dread*). Several stanzas linger on Christ's body. Stanza 7 introduces the subject of the "dense and the driven Passion, and frightful sweat" (line 53); the next stanza identifies Christ as the "hero of Calvary" and directs the reader's attention to his feet and their wounds (63).[106] A fully embodied representation of the crucifixion is deferred, however, until Part the Second, after the presence of the "coifèd sisterhood" of five nuns is established (154). Then, the symbolic resonances between their number and Christ's wounds (and the stigmata of St. Francis of Assisi) can be fully told:

> Five! the finding and sake
> And cipher of suffering Christ.
> Márk, the márk is of mán's máke
> And the word of it Sacrificed,
> But he scores it in scarlet himself on his own bespoken,
> Before-time-taken, dearest prizèd and priced—
> Stigma, signal, cinquefoil token
> For léttering of the lámb's fléece, rúddying of the róse-fláke. (169–76)

It is Christ's volunteerism that especially strikes the speaker: the crucifixion wounds and torments are "bespoken," self-scored, long before the Word was made flesh.

"The Wreck" is structurally sophisticated and densely patterned; it demonstrates, one could argue, the coherence of poetic creation and God's creation. Just as Part the First begins by acknowledging the flesh and its burdens, so Part the Second, stanza 11, commences with a reminder that people are, essentially, "Dúst! / Flesh falls within sight of us: we, though our flower the same, / Wave with the meadow, forget that there must / The sóur scýthe crínge, and the bléar sháre cóme" (85–88). All flesh is grass, indeed. The eleventh stanza is also proleptic: its general statement about humanity's flesh-death introduces the shipwreck narrative.

With an intriguing textual discretion, however, Hopkins refrains from representing the nuns' dreadful death-throes or their dead bodies.[107] Instead, stanza 16 redirects the reader's gaze to the heroic sailor who becomes a public spectacle of mortification:[108]

> One stirred from the rigging to save
> The wild woman-kind below,

> With a rope's end round the man, handy and brave—
>   He was pitched to his death at a blow,
> For all his dreadnought breast and braids of thew:
>   They could téll him for hóurs, dándled the tó and the fró
>   Through the cobbled foam-fleece. (121–28)

The Nun's "tongue told" or professed a resolute faith; the sailor's body "tell[s]" of human selflessness and fragility. "The tortured body," as Moran suggests, "reveals a precious inscape of the soul's beauty" ("Hopkins and Victorian" 3/9). "Dandle" deliberately disturbs the scene: to compare the corpse buffeted by the storm to a child playfully bounced on someone's knee reinforces the relations of force at work in the storm and in the poem. Similarly, God is saluted paradoxically as the "Father and fondler of heart thou hast wrung" (line 71).

The sailor's dedication and the Tall Nun's fierce address ("a líoness aróse" [line 135]) only sharpen the speaker's self-scrutiny. In stanza 18, at the physical center of the poem, the speaker rehearses a lacerating mea culpa, a ritualistic, public humiliation made all the more acute by the second-person stance, a temporary break in the speaker's subject position that implies an even more drastic self-examination:

> Ah! touched in your bower of bone,
>   Are you! turned, for an exquisite smart,
> Have you! make words break from me here all alone,
>   Do you!—móther of béing in me, héart. (137–40)

Accuser and accused, brutalized (the "exquisite smart") and loved by an almighty he has the temerity to imagine, the speaker willingly castigates yet offers up his flesh. Stanza 2 promises nothing less: "I did say yes / O at líghtning and láshed ród" (9–10).

In Caradoc's tour de force, Winefred's body is also absent, its suffering relived by a man almost undone by what he envisages. Caradoc's recreation of the murderous scene is alternately self-assertive and self-tormenting. "What have we seen?" he asks of himself:

> Her head, | sheared from her shoulders, fall,
> And lapped in shining hair, | róll to the bank's edge; then

> Down the beetling banks, | like water in waterfalls,
> It stooped and flashed and fell | and ran like water away.
> Her eyes, oh and her eyes!
> In all her beauty, . . .
> In all her body, I say, | no place was like her eyes[.] (*PW* 178)[109]

His response is complex. First, he reasserts the "daring" of his actions yet almost immediately worries, "But wíll flesh, Ó can flésh / Second this fiery strain?"[110] (*PW* 179). Then he relives the scene of Winefred's beheading as a symbolic enactment of his own divided self:

> I all my being have hacked | in half with hér neck: one part,
> Reason, selfdisposal, | choice of better or worse way,
> Is corpse now, cannot change; | my other self, this soul,
> Life's quick . . .
> Must all day long taste murder. (*PW* 179)

That he "tastes" the murder reiterates the "bitterness" of the flesh motif I have traced in several Hopkins poems. As Isobel Armstrong observes, taste "makes taster and thing tasted inseparable."[111] It is not surprising that the soliloquy was drafted in the same Dublin notebook used to compose "Sibyl's Leaves";[112] both feature speakers "whélm[ed]" with "self ín self stéepèd and páshed—qúite / Disremembering, dísmémbering | áll now" (*PW* 191).

Caradoc's speech and "The Wreck" are in many respects mirror opposites. He adamantly asserts, "I do nót repent" (*PW* 178); both the Nun and the speaker of "The Wreck" are embodiments of confession. Caradoc's defiance makes the Tall Nun's humility all the more vivid, but both are represented by lions; his boast, "What Í have dóne víolent / I have líke a líon dóne, | líonlíke dóne" (*PW* 178), is almost a parody of the ode's praise: "Till a líoness aróse bréasting the bábble" (line 135). Caradoc is "loyal" only "to his ówn soul, láying his | ówn law dówn, nor láw nor / Lord now curb hím for ever" (*PW* 179); Nun and speaker endure the harshness of God's law but embrace the Lawgiver, saluting Christ as the ultimate figure of justice ("Thy unchancelling poising palms were weighing the worth" [line 166]). There is no miraculous recovery for the Nun: she dies, as do so many in the shipwreck. Because of her inspired "witness," however, the speaker recuperates his religious zeal and reaffirms the possibility of England recovering from the Reformation (many critics do not admire the ode's closing stanzas). Caradoc, according to legend, either falls dead when cursed by Beuno or is swallowed up by the earth (*PW* 440), like the antagonist at the end of a medieval morality play. But Winefred is physically restored and raised from the dead, another confirmation of Christ's resurrection. The holy well that allegedly springs from her fallen head is associated with myriad bodies restored to health and "things," as Hopkins's Beuno states, "things with a revival, things with a recovery" (*PW* 180).

To recover the Victorians' complex relations with their "flesh filled" (*PW* 181) lives, the discussion has ranged from early Christian teachings and medieval legend to headlines from the *Times* in 1875. Religious warnings, cultural prohibitions, and medical treatises, all of which contribute to "robust power structures" (*WDTT* 126), have been imbricated with exceptional poetry to tell the flesh's story. How the flesh is embedded in Christian subjectivity—how "one's relationship to one's self is organized" (Bernauer, S.J., and Mahon 146)—and how the latter is implicated in power-knowledge relations has also been examined. As "The Wreck" especially demonstrates, Hopkins uses a rope motif variously to represent control, affiliation, and mortification. Foucault uses the same motif to explain how "the care of the self" functions: "It is especially an institutional, political, and historical problem to know how in a given society the individual binds to his own truth" (*WDTT* 19). In the following chapter, the aesthetic implications of such truths are explored in relation to the Pre-Raphaelite poetry and paintings, and the aesthetic writings of Walter Pater, so crucial to Hopkins.

4

PROFESSING THE FLESH

A style or manner in art or literature can only be explained or reproduced through those special conditions of society and culture out of which it arose, and with which it forms one group of phenomena.
—**WALTER PATER**, "Winckelmann"[1]

FROM THE LATE 1840s UNTIL the fin-de-siècle 1890s, like-minded poets, artists, and aesthetic commentators reacted strongly against the vilification of the flesh that I have been documenting. But their works, in turn, inspired one of the most rancorous attacks imaginable, by a critic who thought they had pledged themselves "to extol fleshliness as the distinct and supreme end of poetic and pictorial art."[2] This chapter presents three final contexts in which to consider Hopkins's writings: the aestheticization of the flesh practiced by male members of the Pre-Raphaelite circle;[3] the sensationalization of the flesh produced by their most histrionic critic, Robert Buchanan; and the centrality of the flesh in the emergence of what became known as "decadent" discourse. A comparison of Hopkins's texts and those of Walter Pater, chief theorist of aestheticism and decadence, constitutes the chapter's second half. Throughout the discussion, the issue of the "strange" and grotesque, and the frisson of the corpse, will resonate.

(As Jerome McGann observes, "The Pre-Raphaelite effect emerges as a translation of the familiar into the strange" ["A Thing" 59].) The basic questions animating the analysis are: What was at stake in the creative works and their negative reception? Why the protestations of outrage? What were the main differences between the arguments *for* art being proffered—art for its own sake—and the arguments for the social and moral responsibilities of art? Which "special conditions of society and culture" mattered the most, and to what effect? And, fundamentally, how is one's understanding of Hopkins's enfleshed texts enriched by comparisons with those of D. G. Rossetti, A. C. Swinburne, and Walter Pater?

The analysis is necessarily intermedial: a concentration on somatic materiality was shared equally among poets, prose writers, and visual artists such as Dante Gabriel Rossetti and Simeon Solomon. Pre-Raphaelite paintings that reimagined the Middle Ages were not typically "fleshly," but Rossetti's evocation of female "stunners" such as *Bocca Baciata* (1859), *Lady Lilith* (1866–68), and *Astarte Syriaca* (1877) certainly were. Interestingly, two paintings of the era that received intense press attention—and censure—concerned the flesh of Jesus Christ, a topic that resonated so deeply with Hopkins. In John Everett Millais's *Christ in the House of His Parents* (1849–50), a young lad holds up, for his mother's loving attention, a wound in his hand that prefigures the crucifixion. Charles Dickens, unsparing in his dislike of the canvas, was only one of its many detractors:

> You behold the interior of a carpenter's shop. In the foreground of that carpenter's shop is a hideous, wry-necked, blubbering, red-headed boy, in a bed-gown, who appears to have received a poke in the hand, from the stick of another boy with whom he has been playing in an adjacent gutter, and to be holding it up for the contemplation of a kneeling woman, so horrible in her ugliness, that (supposing it were possible for any human creature to exist for a moment with that dislocated throat) she would stand out from the rest of the company as a Monster, in the vilest cabaret in France, or the lowest ginshop in England. (13)

Dickens's angry words and snide remarks (*gutter, creature, cabaret, ginshop*) are a stark reminder that intimations of the flesh are never absent class implications. Hopkins countered such criticism of Millais in an 1881 letter to Bridges: "He has, I have always seen, no feeling for beauty in ^abstract^ design and ^he^ never designs; but he has a deep feeling, it is plain, for concrete beauty, wild or natural beauty, much as Keats had. The element of ugliness in him is like the element of ugliness in nature" (*CW* 1:450).[4] In the second painting, William Holman Hunt's *The Shadow of Death* (1870–73), the comely young carpenter, torso bare, stretches up his arms in a pose that anticipates his death on the cross.[5] The image could be read as a tribute to the "muscular" Christian ideals of Charles Kingsley and Thomas Hughes, and a complement to Hopkins's writings about "hardy handsome" bodies (*PW* 165) doing God's work of service. Clearly, the painting made a deep impression on Hopkins. In his 1874 journal, he first mentions *The Shadow of Death* comparatively, citing Hunt's execution and juxtapositioning of "very true and original . . . details" (*CW* 3:576).[6] Then he tries to capture its complex, unsettling impact on the viewer. "First impression," he states:

> great glare and lightsomeness . . . true sunset effect—that is / the sunset light lodged as the natural light and only detected by its heightening the existing reds; esp. in the golden-bronze skin he has given to our Lord's figure, and by contrast in the blue shadows on white drapery and puce-purple ones on pink silk. Also . . . most realistic anatomy of arms and leg. Also type of figure not very pleasing—seems smaller from the waist down, head overlarge, and the feet not inscaped but with a scapeless look they sometimes no doubt have . . . veined too, which further breaks their scaping. On the whole colour somewhat overglaring. The pale withered weathered brick (?) interior throws up the glare of the our Lord's figure. Face beautiful, sweet and human but not quite pleasing. Red and white embroidery of broad flat belt giving a graceful inscape and telling in the picture. Clever addled folds of the white cloth. . . . No inscape of composition whatever—not known and if it had been known it cd. scarcely bear up agst. the such realism[.] (*CW* 3:582)

In the spirit of Rossetti affixing an eponymous poem to a painting's frame, or Swinburne composing "Before the Mirror" for James Whistler's *Symphony in White No. 2: The Little White Girl*, Hopkins's 1879 sermon on "the ^matchless^ beauty of Christ's body" (*CW* 5:225–26), discussed in chapter 3, could serve as a gloss for *The Shadow of Death*. Yet Francis Kilvert

(1840–79), an Anglican clergyman and devout diarist, pronounced the painting "a waste of a good shilling. I thought the picture theatrical and detestable and wished I had never seen it."[7]

DECODING "THE HYSTERIC TONE AND OVERLOADED STYLE"

What Francis Kilvert confided to his diary, Robert Buchanan conveyed to as many readers as possible. According to Buchanan, who tried mightily to succeed as a poet, novelist, critic, and dramatist, Rossetti, Swinburne, and their ilk were professing the flesh in every "erotic direction" possible ("FS" 1329). Buchanan published his denunciations twice: first in an October 1871 essay for the *Contemporary Review* (cloaked in the secrecy of a pseudonym, "Thomas Maitland") and then in the pamphlet version issued several months later. My brief critique of Buchanan's excoriating composition demonstrates how heated the cultural conversation about the flesh became; comments as to how Hopkins was variously indebted to or shares affinities with Buchanan's principal targets, the works of Rossetti[8] and Swinburne, consolidate one's understanding of how complexly intertextuality flourishes. In more general terms, I explore how "sensuousness" emerges as a central problematic in Pre-Raphaelite art and aestheticism, and why some, particularly Hopkins, are quick to aver its "dangerous" properties and predilections. Buchanan's prose is juxtaposed with that of Pater to demonstrate how the "counter-conduct" of the argument unfolded. To borrow Foucault's words about Édouard Manet, this is a chapter about the "audacity" of nineteenth-century avant-garde strategies: how "the place of the viewer in relation to the picture" or the text shifted (*Manet* 32),[9] and how representation "forms an integral part of processes of social differentiation, of exclusion, assimilation, and control."[10]

Buchanan's attack, entitled "The Fleshly School of Poetry: Mr. D. G. Rossetti," is ostensibly a review of the fifth edition of Rossetti's *Poems*. If Rossetti is the text's "overthought," however, Swinburne is the more obsessive "underthought."[11] (Tennyson and Arnold function as the argument's intellectual, aesthetic, and moral "touchstones."[12]) One of the things that offends Buchanan the most, as Isobel Armstrong notes, is knowing that works by Rossetti and Swinburne "sold well"; they were neither "coterie" poets nor "subversive by subterfuge, as [A. H.] Hallam understood the poetry of sensation to be.... They sold because they were shocking" (377). Buchanan's essay is carefully organized, but in some passages shock and outrage threaten lucidity. When comparing Rossetti's paintings and "verses" (Buchanan will not deign to call them "poems"), he expatiates: "There is the same thinness and transparence of design, the same combination of the simple and the grotesque, the same morbid deviation from healthy forms of life, the same sense of weary, wasting, yet exquisite sensuality; nothing virile, nothing tender, nothing completely sane; a superfluity of extreme sensibility" ("FS" 1331). Sentences seem to strain under the burden of verbal fault-finding.

Flesh is everywhere in Buchanan's essay: "fleshly" is used seventeen times, including the title; "fleshliness," which turns a material property of the body into a "state" of mind and then demonizes it (as a code word for immorality), is deployed five times. Sometimes, the terms are crowded into the same sentence, to the point of obliterating meaning: "the fleshly gentlemen have bound themselves by solemn league and covenant to extol fleshliness as the distinct and supreme end of poetic and pictorial art" ("FS" 1330). What begins as a characterization of poetry all too easily becomes the denunciation of an individual. Rossetti is "fleshy all over from the roots of his hair to the tips of his toes"; his like-minded peers are no more than "fleshly persons" (1336, 1339). As the essay unfolds, antonyms for "fleshly" multiply, including *pure, healthy, wholesome*. Only gradually does Buchanan's underlying motive emerge: harnessing the rhetorical power to articulate, reiterate, and police norms. He is asserting, at every turn, the role of the critic in establishing and maintaining public standards (of art, of behavior), the power to synthesize aesthetic values (is this an accomplished poem, or not, and why?) and moral values (does this literary work encourage the ideas, attitudes, and conduct that society deems legitimate?). "Norms" may seem like a safe, even mundane word—what "everyone" or at least most people deem customary and acceptable. But "norms," I have been arguing, are authoritative, even coercive tools used by experts and institutions to define that which is normal and suitable and that which is abnormal. To quote Foucault, the norm "lays claim to power. The norm is not simply and not even a principle of intelligibility; it is an element on the basis of which a certain exercise of power is founded and legitimized.... The norm brings with it a principle of both qualification and correction" (*Ab* 50). Buchanan is claiming the right to discern and impose norms because he, apparently, has an "unprejudiced mind" ("FS" 1329). More accurately, he is a self-appointed judge who needs to impugn the moral worth of Rossetti and Swinburne, and by extension, the value of their artistic work. ("It must not be supposed," Buchanan intones, "that all of Mr. Rossetti's poems are made up of trash" [1332].)

Buchanan clearly assumed that an attack on the "fleshly school" using religious discourse would resonate with his readers. The *Contemporary Review* had been established in January 1866 as "the church-minded counterpart of the resolutely secular *Fortnightly Review*," a forum "for open, erudite inquiry into controversial theological and philosophical issues" (McGann, "Scholarly"). Thus, Swinburne is denounced by Buchanan as someone "more outrageous, more blasphemous" ("FS" 1331–32) than his peers. In the assertion quoted previously, that "the fleshly gentlemen have bound themselves by solemn league and covenant," there is the suspicion planted that they belong to a cult. To the canon of "great" poets—Dante, Milton, Shakespeare, Goethe—Buchanan adds Tennyson, for "poems born and delivered from the soul" (1339).[13] The "fleshly persons," on the other hand, "create form for its own sake" (1339). Furthermore, Buchanan does not shy away from arousing anti-Catholic feelings. Quotations from Rossetti's "The Blessed Damozel" are followed by the suggestion that "the general effect is that of a queer old painting in a missal, very affected and very odd" (1333). A missal is a distinctly Roman Catholic volume, one containing the order of the Mass for an entire year.[14]

Buchanan's faith in the critic's power to anoint those who are "great" poets and smear those who are merely "second-rate" is tremendous; one can only imagine the pleasure derived from insisting, again and again, that the "fleshly school" consists of inconsequential or "small" writers and painters. The essay's controlling conceit: major writers like Dante, Shakespeare, and Tennyson are the protagonists of a play; minor writers are merely the "walking gentlemen" or players like Rosencrantz and Guildenstern who are noticed, if at all, because of "their lesser identities" and "their smaller idiosyncrasies" (1329). (One wonders if "walking gentleman" was also designed to suggest "street walkers" or sex workers, alluding to another kind of prostitution and socially transmitted disease.) By diminishing the poets' reputations, Buchanan clearly hopes to vitiate the impact of their "viciousness of thought and style" (1336). Aesthetic and moral discourses are effortlessly combined—another Victorian hallmark—in order to assert, "A great and good poet, however, is great and good irrespective of manner, and often in spite of manner; he is great because he brings great ideas and new light, because his thought is a revelation; and, although it is true that a great manner generally accompanies great matter, the manner of great matter is almost inimitable" (1338). One more great/matter/manner ploy and the passage could win a place in Lewis Carroll's Wonderland. In hindsight, there is something fantastic, rather than merely ludicrous, about Buchanan's condemnation of the "fleshly school." Fear of the sensuous, the audacious, is palpable. Pater had predicted as much in the opening paragraph of "Coleridge's Writings" (1866): "Then comes the spectacle of the reserve of the elder generation exquisitely refined by the antagonism of the new. That current of new life chastens them as they contend against it. Weaker minds do not perceive the change, clearer minds abandon themselves to it."[15]

With his "tactics of reactionary rage," Buchanan describes "as immoral what is politically complex and unsettling" (Isobel Armstrong 376). His indignation also helps to explain the fraught politics of "professing the flesh" in Hopkins's lifetime. The two authors about whom Buchanan obsesses—Rossetti and Swinburne—will be considered in the following segments, and the Hopkins links noted. As Swinburne queries in "Anactoria," "who hath cursed / Spirit and flesh with longing?," and how (*Poems* 64)?[16]

ROSSETTI: "A THING TO WONDER ON"

Several times, Buchanan faults Rossetti for eschewing publication and not exhibiting his paintings. Yet Rossetti's reluctance to publish—partly, to avoid critical opprobrium such as Buchanan dished out—did not prevent Hopkins from reading the Pre-Raphaelite's poetry in the mid-1860s. His source: a manuscript sheaf of poems lent to him by his Latin tutor Robinson Ellis.[17] As Hopkins discerned, Rossetti uses the word "flesh" infrequently, clinically: in "Eden's Bower," it is "Adam's flesh" that is noted;

in "Dante at Verona," Can Grande mocks the exiled poet by saying, will he feed on flesh; and in "Ruggiero and Angelica," a scene from Ariosto's *Orlando Furioso,* Angelica's flesh is imperiled by a vicious beast. Overall, however, a frankness about sexual desire and pleasure is frequently expressed (typically, within marriage, but also in relation to Mary Magdalene and a contemporary "harlot," Jenny), and a sensuous appreciation of women's bodies is stressed: their breasts, their undulating hair, and that particular Pre-Raphaelite obsession, their mouths.[18]

"The Blessed Damozel" is a type of corpse poem: of the two figures featured, one is the suffering survivor, who bemoans the "gold bar" separating heaven from earth and him from his beloved, and the other, the damozel of such enduring, dynamic beauty that "her bosom must have made / The bar she leaned on warm" (Rossetti, *Poems* 1). Interestingly, it is the spirit of the dead woman that speaks; the man's thoughts are provided in parentheses. Trappings of Christian piety are everywhere in the text: biblical intertextual gestures; white lilies symbolic of the Virgin Mary; dutiful mentions of the holy Trinity (including the Dove or Holy Spirit); and references to the beneficence of eternal life with God. As Pater will also insist, however, knowledge is only possible *through* the physical; transcendence is actually the physical fully incarnated. Rossetti's lovers remain focused on themselves: after their eventual reunion in heaven, they will "find some knowledge at each pause, / Or some new thing to know" (Rossetti, *Poems* 5)—the implication being they will enjoy some new carnal knowledge together. All in all, the poem reiterates the strength of the flesh. Even more subversively, the poem suggests that the erotic and the Christian are wholly compatible—the opposite of Hopkins's conclusion, in "To what serves Mortal Beauty," that the sensuous is "dangerous; does set danc- / Ing blood" (*PW* 182).

A dead woman is also prominent in "A Last Confession," but only at the end of the speaker's narrative does one learn that, consumed with jealousy, the Italian patriot has murdered the young woman who had been his ward since he rescued her from war-enforced poverty. Given that the poem, subtitled "(Regno Lombardo-Veneto, 1848)," is associated with the First Italian War of Independence, the allegorical thrust of the melodramatic text is not difficult to discern: even a seemingly benevolent guardian becomes oppressive, evenly deadly.[19] Most immediately, the dramatic monologue casts the reader in the position of a Roman Catholic confessor.[20] As such, one learns how the patriot's feelings of paternal love and concern were gradually replaced by sexual yearning as he noticed "Beneath [her] growing throat the breasts half globed / Like folded lilies deepset in the stream" (Rossetti, *Poems* 68). What he cannot accept, however, is the fact that she is an independent person rather than his eroticized ideal and private property. So when he notices "some impenetrable restlessness / Growing in her," and hears her laugh in the company of another man, possessiveness takes hold: he assumes her to be faithless, imagines her to be "a brown-shouldered harlot," and stabs her (75, 82). The speaker is not gloating about a murder, like Browning's Duke of Ferrara in "My Last Duchess" or "Porphyria's Lover," but "A Last Confession" is another case in which a controlling man resorts to violence against a woman (who is blamed for enticing and unsettling him).

"A Last Confession" is more than 550 lines long but not once is "she" given a name. Would naming her make her too real, too much of a person rather than a too-familiar virgin/whore, angel/demon stereotype? What "she" does have, among other features, is luxuriant hair, tresses that are all the more alluring when wet. In "Jenny," the eponymous sex worker is distinguished by golden hair, a color somewhat at odds with her tarnished reputation. Her flesh is warmly intimated: "Your silk ungirdled and unlac'd / And warm sweets open to the waist" (Rossetti, *Poems* 111).[21] The speaker may seem to be morally "unlaced," but he too judges Jenny, and cannot appreciate her beauty for its own sake. Shame is the occasion, the catalyst, for contradictory thoughts—Jenny's and the speaker's. He congratulates himself that he is "not drunk or ruffianly" with her, then observes,

> For sometimes, were the truth confess'd,
> You're thankful for a little rest,— . . .
> Yes, from the daily jeer and jar,
> From shame and shame's outbraving too,
> Is rest not sometimes sweet to you? (112)

His need for her flesh intensifies thoughts of shame. "And do not let me think of you," he enjoins, "Lest shame of yours suffice for two" (113). On the one hand, he objects to those who would associate Jenny with the leaves of a "vile text"; on the other hand, he predicts the prostitute's "sure decay":

"And so the life-blood of this rose, / Puddled with shameful knowledge, flows / Through leaves no chaste hand may unclose" (120, 121). Finally, the speaker is as trapped by the same machinations of shame as Jenny is:

> And must I mock you to the last,
> Ashamed of my own shame,—aghast
> Because some thoughts not born amiss
> Rose at a poor fair face like this? (126)[22]

The speaker's confessional impulses return him to the fold of moralization (the "dark paths" to be avoided in the future). Speaker, text, and reader indulge in pleasures that are eventually castigated. Initially, the speaker seems truly bohemian, comfortable with "Lazy laughing languid Jenny, / Fond of a kiss and fond of a guinea" and comfortable with his defiance of middle-class values (109). His socioeconomic status seems to be confirmed by the way in which she is paid—not in shillings and pounds, but guineas, coins of status and professional activity (each worth one pound and one shilling).[23] Worth mentioning, however: the coins were named for the west African region where the gold needed to produce them was mined (each guinea contained approximately one-quarter of an ounce of the precious metal). In other words, sexual transactions between the speaker and Jenny are inextricably connected to transactions in the slave trade, an abuse of the flesh also fiercely debated in the nineteenth century.

Like "Jenny," most of the sonnets in *Poems* eschew historical trappings (or displacements); they are more direct, contemporary in their ambience, and more sensuous. The latter qualities certainly contributed to the shock experienced by readers like Buchanan. When the god of love is invoked, it is an adult and manly Eros, not some "winged, bold boy" (Pater, *Marius* 46).[24] Desire is articulate; pleasure is enjoyed; the soul is expressed through the body, not saved from its clutches (in "Secret Parting," "as she kissed, her mouth became her soul" [Rossetti, *Poems* 208]; in "Love-Lily," body and soul are indistinguishable). Virginal females become sexually satisfied and satisfying brides, "leap[ing]" against their bridegrooms' "side[s]."[25] Similar to "Jenny," several sonnets including "Sleepless Dream" are set in a postcoital moment in which the woman sleeps and the man thinks, a reiteration of gender norms very typical of Pre-Raphaelite poetry. Yet, instead of identifying how and why each sense is ensnared in the flesh (the method of Christina Rossetti's "The Convent Threshold" and Hopkins's "The Habit of Perfection"[26]), poems like "Parted Love" pay tribute to "every sense to which she dealt delight" (209). But always in Rossetti's texts, the quality of life and "riotous longing" in the present are measured against the fact of death, the "dusty bed" that awaits everyone.[27]

A brief discussion of one other sonnet will conclude this assessment of Rossetti's dedication to the flesh. Several texts in *Poems* treat Christian themes seriously ("Mary Magdalene at the Door of Simon the Pharisee," "The Passover in the Holy Family," "On the 'Vita Nuova' of Dante," "Saint Luke the Painter," "Mary's Girlhood"), but one, "Love's Redemption," borrows from Catholic ritual and iconography for amatory purposes. The speaker salutes his lover in terms that are meant to sacralize the erotic (a discursive strategy that always incensed Rossetti's critics):

> O Thou who at Love's hour ecstatically
> Unto my lips dost evermore present
> The body and blood of Love in sacrament;
> Whom I have neared and felt thy breath to be
> The inmost incense of his sanctuary;
> Who without speech hast owned him, and intent
> Upon his will, thy life with mine hast blent,
> And murmured o'er the cup, Remember me!—(190)[28]

One could complain that the poem is blasphemous; there is no record of Hopkins's thoughts on the matter. Typically, for a Rossetti text, even as bonds of love are asserted, protectively—that "sanctuary" of Love shared by the couple—the ephemerality of all experiences, all emotions, is stressed. This is "Love's hour," not Love's eternity. Without doubt, the aim is to redeem desire and pleasure from condemnations of the flesh, and at the same time challenge those who would censor artistic expression. And what Rossetti does in measured ways, Swinburne does in the most deliberately outrageous manner possible.

SWINBURNE: "FLESH AND FLOWERS AND DEMOCRACY AND DAMNATION"

In the middle of the nineteenth century, two auburn-haired young men of relatively short stature "go up" to Oxford only a few years apart. Both have been raised in large, affluent High Anglican families, with fathers associated with maritime interests and culturally refined mothers. Both were deemed fearless by their peers while growing up. Both attend Balliol College, where Benjamin Jowett is their principal tutor (but only one will take his degree).[29] Both admire the Arthurian murals in the Oxford Union created by Dante Gabriel Rossetti, Edward Burne-Jones, William Morris, and several others.[30] Both are intrigued by the works of Edgar Allan Poe.[31] Both become friendly with Walter Pater and discuss aesthetics and philosophy with him. Both are interested in the arts, especially poetry, and can compose adeptly in English, Latin, and Greek. Both will produce poems that are verbally dexterous, metrically innovative,[32] and, in relation to the middle-class Protestant values inculcated by home, public school, and university, thematically shocking. Both will write texts invoking Christ, but one will disparage him as the "pale Galilean" and the other will embrace him fervently as "our Lord." Furthermore, only one will prepare extravagant fantasies of lesbian love, necrophilia, neo-paganism, and revolutionary politics, and use the works of William Blake,[33] Théophile Gautier, and Charles Baudelaire to defend and promote art for art's sake.

Hopkins bristled whenever considering A. C. Swinburne's poems, some of which he knew well, and resented when comparisons were made about their texts. As this brief rather than exhaustive discussion will demonstrate, however, both made the flesh one of the central concerns of their oeuvres. Swinburne announced his fleshly concerns to the public in 1866, when *Poems and Ballads* created a major critical stir—as it was designed to do. Buchanan (whose own 1866 volume, *London Poems*, had been favorably received) informed readers of the *Athenaeum* that *Poems and Ballads* and its author were "unclean for the mere sake of uncleanness."[34] Hopkins judged them with similar distaste, suggesting to Baillie in September 1867 that "it is impossible not personally to form an opinion against the morality of a writer like Swinburne.... [W]hat is innocent in a writer, ~~becom~~ ^if it^ ^must^ cause~~s~~ certain scandal to readers becomes wrong on that ground.

This too is a question of degree ... for perhaps we are not bound to consider those who will take scandal from everything: it is required that the number only shd. be small" (*CW* 1:157–58). A decade later, he told Bridges that Swinburne and Victor Hugo, among the "great names" of contemporary literature, are actually "plagues of mankind"; Swinburne is "often wicked and in general is a great vanity and full of impious brag and a blackguard and unspiritual mind" (*CW* 1:267). In February 1879, Hopkins praised Bridges for *not* writing like Swinburne, that is, "very thinly costuming a strain of conventional passion, kept up by stimulants, and crying always in a ~~highhead~~ headvoice about flesh and flowers and democracy and damnation" (*CW* 1:337–38).[35] Similar critiques were offered to Dixon (July 1886, July 1888), Coventry Patmore (August 1883), and Katharine Tynan (September 1888), demonstrating how Hopkins used his knowledge of Swinburne to seem au courant. Each comparison focused his critical lens more acutely, refining his opinions about archaisms (a "blight"[36]), diction, rhythm ("dactyls and anapests [that] are halting"[37]), and the ways in which art and beauty should "serve" morality.

On four other occasions, while discussing the merits of Bridges's verse, Hopkins used Swinburne as a point of contrast, reluctantly acknowledging that "Swinburne's genius is astonishing, but it will, I think, only do one thing" (*CW* 1:354). And in what proved to be Hopkins's last letter to Bridges, 29 April 1889, the habit of comparison persisted:

> Swinburne has a new volume out, which is reviewed in its own style: "The rush and the rampage, the pause and the pull-up, ~~th~~ of these lustrous and lumpophorous lines." It is all now a "self-drawing web"; a perpetual functioning of genius without truth, feeling, or any adequate matter to be at function on. There is some heavydom, in long waterlogged lines (he has no real understanding of rhythm, and thoughe he sometimes hits brilliantly at other times he misses badly) ... a bottomless ^blethery^ bathos into which Hugo and he from opposite coasts have ~~been~~ long driven ~~e~~Channel-tunnels. I am afraid I am going too ^far^ with the poor fellow. Enough now, but his babies make a Herodian of me. (*CW* 2:990)[38]

The comments are so much fun, and the parody so pitch-perfect (we know, from family, what an excellent mimic Hopkins was[39]), that the seriousness of his critique ("without truth, feeling, or any adequate matter") can seem beside the point. Hopkins's satirical bite is all the fiercer because he castigates poet, verse, and critic.

Swinburne's self-appointed role as agent provocateur for Victorian poetry, poetics, and politics informs all of his texts, even a minor lyric like "Félise" (*Poems and Ballads,* 1866). "Ye must have gods," the speaker admits, "the friends of men, / Merciful gods, compassionate," but they are only part of the happiness and security people desire; if "love or sin, / If shame or fear" could hold love "fast," life would be secure—but they cannot, and it is not. In the physical and thematic centre of the poem the reader finds this stanza:

> For many loves are good to see;
>   Mutable loves, and loves perverse;
> But there is nothing, nor shall be,
>   So sweet, so wicked, but my verse
>   Can dream of worse. (*Poems and Ballads* 195)

"Mutable" links the text to the relativism and philosophy of "flux" that aesthetes, including Pater, are beginning to theorize. Suggesting that wickedness is "sweet" rather than abhorrent is only half of the poem's radical assertion; insisting that this verse is more imaginatively wicked is the other. Courting that which is "perverse" and naming it as such is all part of concerted efforts to *épater le bourgeois*.[40] The choice of end-rhymes embeds "verse" within "perverse" and indelibly promises "dreams of worse." And all of that in four lines of tetrameter and a fifth, foreshortened line that emphasizes the kinds of dangerous dreams being proffered.

Of the four topics mentioned by Hopkins—"flesh and flowers and democracy and damnation" (*CW* 1:338)—flesh and damnation are pursued insistently by Swinburne. Both provide opportunities for his signature outrage and verbal contradictions, and allow him to luxuriate in pleasure/pain dichotomies.[41] "Laus Veneris," for example, begins with the goddess's lips and Tannhäuser's, then introduces Eros "[c]rowned with gilt thorns and clothed with flesh like fire," a singularly "perverse" allusion to Christ's Passion.[42] Sappho, the speaker of "Anactoria," tells her lover that "thy sharp sighs / Divide my flesh and spirit with soft sound" (*Poems and*

Ballads 57), demonstrating how Swinburne challenges heteronormativity *and* gender norms from several different perspectives. And he does so directly: Sappho not only tastes the blood of Anactoria's "sweet small wounds" and wishes that "I could drink thy veins as wine, and eat / Thy breasts like honey" (an erotic subversion of Christian Eucharistic motifs that outdoes Rossetti's "Love's Redemption"), she desires that her lover's "body were abolished and consumed, / And in my flesh thy very flesh entombed!" (*Poems and Ballads* 61). As McGann, Louis, and Saville have thoroughly demonstrated, Swinburne's "criticism of High Church sacramentalism is at once radical and exact" (Louis 3) and his Shelleyan Romanticism is unwavering, "moral, comprehensive, and committed to social transformation" (McGann, "Swinburne's Radical" 206) and emancipation of all kinds (political, religious, social, sexual).[43]

Democratic causes are also all-consuming for Swinburne, as the volume *Songs before Sunrise* (1871) vividly demonstrates.[44] In poems such as "The Eve of Revolution," "The Halt Before Rome," and "Mentana: First Anniversary," his audacious wit and poetics support the Risorgimento specifically and republicanism generally throughout Europe and North America (see, for example, "The Litany of Nations," "Hymn of Man," and "To Walt Whitman in America"[45]). In the best poems, including "Mater Dolorosa" and "A New Year's Message. To Joseph Mazzini," Swinburne transposes Christian tropes to endorse all those struggling to earn a "republican name" and state (*Songs before Sunrise* 167). In the collection, every gesture celebrating the death of God is counterbalanced by a huzzah for the birth of a democracy. According to the speaker of "A New Year's Message," "under twilight stars we wait / By Time's shut gate / Till the slow soundless hinges turn, / And through the depth of years that yearn / The face of the Republic burn" (166).[46]

No doubt Swinburne's sustained and ruthless anti-Catholicism rankled Hopkins; Swinburne treated popes and Jesuits (and kings and emperors) with the same piercing denigration with which he dismissed conventional morality. "A Dead King" in *Songs of Two Nations* (1875), for example, exults in the moment when "the long-tongued slack-lipped litanies / Fail, and the priest has no more prayer to sell— / Now the last Jesuit found about thee is / The beast that made thy fouler flesh his cell" (*Songs* 55).[47] "Before a Crucifix" is contemplative rather than scathing, but its critique of the

"God of this grievous people, wrought / After the likeness of their race" is no less devastating (*Songs before Sunrise* 93). The poem protests "the institutionalized sanctification of suffering and impoverishment" and suggests that both "ecclesiastical and secular tyranny" must be overthrown (Saville, "Cosmopolitan" 707). The penultimate stanza, however, may have offered Hopkins a metaphor he could not refuse:

> Thou bad'st let children come to thee;
>   What children now but curses come?
> What manhood in that God can be
>   Who sees their worship, and is dumb?
> No soul that lived, loved, wrought, and died,
> Is this their carrion crucified. (*Songs before Sunrise* 101)

Only in Dublin would Hopkins repurpose such "carrion comfort" to declare how religious despair could be overcome (*PW* 183). Before the spectacle of Christ's flesh crucified, Swinburne finds spiritual bankruptcy, but Hopkins finds hard-won abundance.

Other comparisons of Swinburne and Hopkins's poetic discourse could feature the dialogue between the choruses in Swinburne's *Atalanta in Calydon* and Hopkins's "*Ad Mariam*"; "Dolores" and "*Rosa Mystica*";[48] "Dolores" and "Easter Communion"; the poets' evocations of springtime; Swinburne's Baudelaire-inspired ennui and languor and Hopkins's poems "charged" with human, natural, and especially divine energy (even sorrow, suffering, and spiritual dryness are dynamic experiences); appreciations of St. Dorothea; and the evocation of sea and land in "Hymn to Proserpine" (1866) and Hopkins's lyric "Moonrise June 19 1876." Swinburne also relies upon repetition and verbal echoes, fashioning "synonym chains" (Isobel Armstrong 394) to assert the primacy of his new order of "spirit and flesh"[49] and to argue that morality impedes desire and sexual difference. One could follow, for example, the kiss / bliss / pain / strange / sin lexical chain throughout Swinburne's canon and understand more fully how his rhetoric of saturation and excess functions. As Isobel Armstrong suggests, Hopkins's "fiercely totalising metaphor[s] offe[r] to inscape and organise relationships, fusing them in a simultaneous moment of systemic identity and difference. Swinburne, on the other hand, disorganises and unfixes relationships of similarity and difference" (394). Like Rossetti, Swinburne uses shame to profess the flesh, but a typical Swinburne speaker relishes shame for its private and public manifestations.⁵⁰ Swinburne might have been the flesh's most devoted advocate among Victorian poets, but his dedication to "going too ^far^" (*CW* 2:990) antagonized readers like Hopkins mightily.

HOPKINS AND PATER: STRANGENESS AND BEAUTY

How is it that Hopkins vehemently denounced Swinburne yet cultivated the friendship of Walter Pater, the most notorious champion of art and experience, fleshly or otherwise, from the late 1860s to the 1890s? How is it that Pater served as Hopkins's academic "coach" during his final sixteen months at Oxford, April 1866 to July 1867 (the tumultuous time of his conversion)? In 1866 it was probably Jowett, Hopkins's principal tutor and Pater's former instructor, who made the coaching arrangements—to help Hopkins prepare for the grueling final exams ("Greats"), in which he hoped to distinguish himself; to offset the burdensome Tractarian influence of Liddon; and to assist Pater, then establishing himself at Brasenose and supporting himself and his sisters.⁵¹ When Hopkins returned to Oxford from October 1878 to November 1879 to be assistant curate at St. Aloysius, Pater was "one of the men [he] saw most of."⁵² Hopkins not only wrote a series of six essays for "W. H. Pater, Esq."⁵³ while preparing for Greats, he subsequently conducted dialogues with Paterian aesthetics and self-fashioning in three significant poems: "Pied Beauty," "To what serves Mortal Beauty," and "Heraclitean Fire."⁵⁴

Comparing their works accords with Pater's "disjunctive"⁵⁵ and contrapuntal method, designed to provide "a new perspective ... which familiar thoughts attain by novel juxtaposition."⁵⁶ I am juxtaposing Pater and Hopkins to suggest that in 1860s Oxford, *avant la lettre,* the intellectual, aesthetic, and eroticizing potential of decadent discourse was being explored—before decadence became both "an appropriate *nom de guerre* for the artist when decay from the vigorous norm of society was itself a paradoxical mark of excellence" (Spivak 233) and a "psycho-medical" diagnosis of "degeneration" before its "valuable subversive agency" (Bernheimer

13, 5) had "congealed" ("CW" 122) or been routed by the Wilde trials. Pater was just the person to effect this discursive alchemy. His polymathic, always historicizing "breadth" of reading, a most "generous eclecticism" (*Marius* 2:126), included classical texts by Heraclitus, the latest by John Stuart Mill and Matthew Arnold, and "modern" and subversively Continental works by Fichte, Hegel, Hugo, and Baudelaire.

In spring 1866, Pater's intellectually daring contributions to the Old Mortality essay society were already well known to Hopkins, because his friend Samuel Brooke had been a member of the group—that is, until Pater's unorthodox ideas about a "diaphanous" subjectivity and "moral sexlessness" scandalized Brooke into quitting.[57] But at the same time that Pater was formulating a new notion of "self-culture" and condemning any faith in the absolute, Hopkins's profound commitment to the Real Presence of Christ in the Eucharist was inspiring a religious conversion. And yet—the minds of both were whetted with "sharp intellectual craving" ("Winck" 81). Both knew the advantages and disadvantages of being tutored by Jowett; both avidly attended Arnold's lectures as Oxford's Professor of Poetry; both enjoyed architectural studies.[58] Both developed a precocious knowledge of ancient sculpture and expressed admiration for the *Belvedere Apollo*. But, while Pater happily contemplated all aspects of the "archer god"[59] Hopkins prudishly observed, "the study of anatomy for wh. marble offers so great a field has become so peculiarly the pursuit of sculpture that it sometimes has, by a convention, banished drapery, representing as naked what shd. be, or shd. more naturally be, clothed" (*CW* 4:178). Both admired the Pre-Raphaelites, as I have demonstrated, and esteemed John Henry Newman (but only Hopkins wanted to emulate Newman, personally and vocationally).[60] Both coach and student had written jejune verses concerning Oxford, faith and doubt, and self-scrutiny, but only Hopkins was translating a devotion to Keats and Christina Rossetti into such distinctive works as "Barnfloor and Winepress" and "The Habit of Perfection." Hopkins was the brilliant "star" of Balliol; Pater was a don at Brasenose (known for its athletes and beer), which had offered him a rare, nonclerical fellowship.[61] From all accounts, Pater's was a gently ironic demeanour—and therefore far removed from the judgmental attitudes of Jowett or Liddon. It is not surprising that Hopkins responded to a mind that "delighted in paradox, and in a kind of whimsical perversity" (Benson

91), a "challenging" temperament that was "crisp, terse, and mentally athletic even in being aesthetic" (Levey 116). As for Pater's status as a neologian (technically, a rationalist; in religion-wracked Oxford, practically an apostate), Hopkins could always look beyond a reputation.

In 1866 Pater was "talking two hours agst. Xtianity," according to Hopkins's diary (*CW* 3:363), and crafting challenging yet wry assertions such as this: "Did Christianity quicken that decline [from 'the Hellenic ideal']? The worship of sorrow, the crucifixion of the senses, the expectation of the end of the world, are not in themselves principles of artistic rejuvenescence. Christianity in the first instance did quicken that decay" ("Winck" 106). For Hopkins, Pater set taxing essay topics including "the origin of our moral ideas,"[62] "Plato's view of the connection of art and education," "the Pagan and Christian virtues" (both Pater and Hopkins were engaging with Arnold's 1863 lecture "Pagan and Medieval Religious Sentiment"), "the relations of Plato's Dialectic to modern logic and metaphysics," "shew cases in wh. acts of apprehension apparently simple are largely influenced by the imagination," and a study of ancient ethics. After 1879, Pater's experiences of Hopkins's priestly self would be translated into the pages of *Marius the Epicurean,* which Pater began writing soon after Hopkins left Oxford. Ten years after that, at "a third remove" in Ireland, Hopkins would summon the lessons of Pater again to counter the "Heraclitean Fire" of natural existence and decay with the "comfort" of his faith.

Little in Pater's academic background—classical studies at the King's School, Canterbury; personal studies in French and German; the *literae humaniores* program at Oxford, where he honed his knowledge of Latin and Greek—obviously prepared him for the exceptional range of essays and creative texts that he produced in almost thirty years of public intellectual work. Yet, the first three (unsigned) essays that he published in the 1860s, which Hopkins undoubtedly read, audaciously indicate the breadth of aesthetic and literary experience he would develop and share: an analysis of Coleridge's prose (1866),[63] a study of the late-eighteenth-century German scholar of ancient sculpture and culture, Johann Winckelmann (1867), and William Morris's poetry (1868). "Coleridge's Writings" prompts a reconsideration of Romanticism and the relationship between absolutism and relativism. "Winckelmann" focuses on "paganism," Hellenism, and sculpture, and presents *sotto voce* a defense of same-sex desire. "Poems by

William Morris" surveys the stories of "rebellious flesh" ("Poems" 301) in which Morris specializes and at the same time presents a radically new kind of historiography in which "pagan," medieval, and modern sensibilities are compared and differentiated. So many ideas crucial to Pater's aesthetic are explored in the review that he repurposed it twice: the final seven paragraphs, in which he theorizes the "moment" of experience and validates art for its own sake, became the infamous "Conclusion" to *The Renaissance* (1873). The essay as a whole was revised substantially and republished as "Aesthetic Poetry" in *Appreciations* (1889).

Pater was friends with Pre-Raphaelite painter Simeon Solomon, and probably introduced Hopkins to Solomon on 29 May 1868.[64] He also took Hopkins to Solomon's studio on 17 June 1868. Pater was friendly with Swinburne—until Swinburne, tremendously upset in a self-serving way when Solomon was arrested, in February 1873, for "buggery" in a public lavatory, urged Pater to shun Solomon. Interestingly, Pater never wrote about Swinburne's poetry, despite their shared intellectual and aesthetic interests (not just classical texts but William Blake, Charles Baudelaire, and James Whistler). Yet Pater greatly admired D. G. Rossetti, and in 1883 published an introduction to his verse in T. Humphry Ward's *The English Poets,* second edition. Morris's poetry, the occasion of Pater's third publication, had the most multifaceted impact on the Brasenose don: it was the impetus for defining the place of the literary grotesque in Pre-Raphaelite art[65] and deciphering how the "two threads of sentiment," paganism and Christianity, could be "interwoven and contrasted" and then "confronted" by the appreciative critic ("Poems" 309). Morris, I hope to demonstrate, was for both Pater and Hopkins a crucial figure in catalyzing decadent discourse. Before doing so, however, what Pater and his readers discerned by studying Coleridge and Winckelmann must be considered.

"CRITICAL" SPIRITS

For his first published essay, Pater is reviewing *Conversations, Letters, and Recollections of S. T. Coleridge* edited by Thomas Allsop. His remit is to consider the Romantic author's prose: *Aids to Reflection* (1825), *Biographia Literaria* (1817), several volumes of *Specimens of the Table Talk of Samuel*

Taylor Coleridge (1830s), and *Confessions of an Inquiring Spirit* (1840). In an antithetical gesture that will shape so much of his writing—working counter to the cultural grain—Pater uses the esteemed critic's writings about religion and philosophy to define the relative or "critical spirit" required for "modern" life ("CW" 108).

Coleridge's great gift to English culture, according to Pater, is promoting German Romanticism and "transcendental philosophy, chiefly as systemized by Schelling" and articulated by Kant (even if it is "an attempt to reclaim the world of art as a world of fixed laws") ("CW" 117, 118). Coleridge's "theological opinions" are organized under "three heads: the general principles of supernaturalism, orthodox dogmas, the interpretation of Scripture. With regard to the first and second, Coleridge ranks as a Conservative thinker," Pater insists, "but his principles of Scriptural interpretation . . . entitle him to be regarded as the founder of the modern liberal school of English theology" (124). Newman is cited several times in the essay, very favorably (for his "original religious genius"), but Pater provocatively suggests that "religious belief, the craving for objects of belief, may be refined out of our hearts, but they must leave their sacred perfume, their spiritual sweetness, behind" (126–27). Moreover, he joins a number of Victorians in intoning the end of Christianity's supremacy:

> Theology is a great house, scored all over with hieroglyphics by perished hands. When we decipher one of those hieroglyphics, we find in it the statement of a mistaken opinion; but knowledge has crept onward since the hand dropped from the wall; we no longer entertain the opinion, and we can trace the origin of the mistake. Dogmas are precious as memorials of a class of sincere and beautiful spirits, who in a past age of humanity struggled with many tears, if not for true knowledge, yet for a noble and elevated happiness. That struggle is the substance, the dogma only its shadowy expression; received traditionally in an altered age, it is the shadow of a shadow, . . . twice removed from substance and reality. (129)[66]

Small wonder that Hopkins, when he began working with Pater, referred to him as "'Bleak-faced Neology'" (*CW* 3:352). When compared with the writings of Newman, Pusey, Liddon, and Faber, Pater's ideas were either a breath of fresh air or another kind of "unwholesome" and "creedless" "trash" ("FS" 1330). Yet, unlike fiery rhetoricians who announce the "death of God" or angrily denounce organized religion, Pater seems, for the purposes of the Coleridge essay, both compassionate toward the self-avowedly faithful ("Dogmas are precious memorials") and convinced that religion has an important cultural role to fulfill.[67]

When Pater suggests, contra Coleridge, "To the modern spirit nothing is or can be rightly known except relatively under conditions," he anticipates Foucault in two respects. First, Pater is arguing that regimes of truth must be acknowledged as such, rather than embraced as absolutes. "A faculty for truth is a power of distinguishing and fixing delicate and fugitive details," he insists, not endorsing fixed, inherited beliefs: "The moral world is ever in contact with the physical; the relative spirit has invaded moral philosophy from the ground of the inductive sciences. There it has started a new analysis of the relations of body and mind, good and evil, freedom and necessity. Hard and abstract moralities are yielding to a more exact estimate of the subtlety and complexity of our life" ("CW" 107). Second, Pater insists that numerous discourses, institutions, and historical circumstances produce the "conditions" of possibility for the constitution of the subject. People are the product of "physical conditions" as well as "vibrations of long past acts reaching" us in the present (107). "The truth of these relations experience gives us," he further suggests: "not the truth of eternal outlines effected once for all, but a world of fine gradations and subtly linked conditions, shifting intricately as we ourselves change" (108). In an essay crowded with intriguing thoughts about history, culture, art, and religious discourse, one other point stands out: Pater's suggestion that "what constitutes an artistic gift is first of all a natural susceptibility to moments of strange excitement, in which the colours freshen upon our threadbare world, and the routine of things about us is broken by a novel and happier synthesis" (123). I will return to Pater's theory of "the moment" of experience, and Hopkins's poetic achievement of "moments" of perceptive ecstasy, in a subsequent section. At this juncture, it is important to note that it is a "strange" excitement to which the critic is most susceptible.

The shift from Coleridge's dogmatic writings to Winckelmann's aesthetic investments encourages Pater to articulate more fully how the body and soul, "the human spirit," should be equally valued. Pater is using Winckelmann, an eighteenth-century art critic and archaeology devotée, to make an argument for "the sensuous side of art" and language—a lesson that not only inspired Pater's commitment to an opulent, mannered prose style, but also encouraged the "kind of intoxication" of wordplay and prosody that Hopkins pursues in his poetry ("CW" 104). Pater begins his article by positioning Winckelmann as "the teacher" of Goethe and Hegel—a "strange pregnancy" through which Winckelmann's writings "opened a new sense for the study of art" ("Winck" 80). Pater and his writings provided a similar "new sense" and new appreciation of sensuousness for Hopkins. One can also use the "Winckelmann" essay to define the particular burdens of "enthusiasm" (a privileged term in Pater's essay) that "stain[ed]" Hopkins's "thoughts with its bloom" even as he was finalizing his decision to convert to Catholicism.[68] Paradoxically, Pater's texts help one to understand why resisting relativism was vital for Hopkins; which artistic practices he deemed too "dangerous" to pursue as a priest;[69] and how an aesthetics of difference and strangeness informs "the achieve of, the mastery" of the vividly experimental poems composed in the 1870s and 1880s.

So taken is Pater with Winckelmann's "handling of the sensuous side of Greek art" ("Winck" 103) that he returns to the notion—and the phrase—several times in his essay, refining and "moulding"[70] his appreciation of the art historian's commitment to Hellenic idealism and a "shameless" appreciation of "whole bodies in exquisite service" to aesthetic refinement (102). Simultaneously, however, Pater discerns what would become the "double and treble lights" of decadent theory and style: the enrichment of rarified sensibilities; a historical fixation on cycles of birth, decay, and rebirth; an appreciation for that which is culturally subversive; an intense focus on somatic sensuality and the demands of the flesh; "a consciousness brooding with delight over itself"; intimations of "sexuality, violence, and esoteric thought" (Constable 3); and a sense of what he terms a "sad fatality" so acute it seems "a rush of home-sickness" ("Winck" 92).

SENSUOUS ELEMENTS

"Coleridge's Writings" is the kind of defiant, anti-orthodox text one publishes immediately *after* tenure is secured. It is a provocation: an act of intellectual disobedience and a reminder that decadent transgression is often catalyzed by bourgeois shibboleths. Hopkins, however, was unpersuaded; an 1867 undergraduate essay, "The Probable Future of Metaphysics," archly begins, "The Positivists foretell and many other people begin to fear, the end of all metaphysics is at hand" (*CW* 4:287). But "these are shortsighted expectations," he proceeds to argue (4:287).

"Poems by William Morris" demonstrates Pater's fledgling critical acumen and assurance when discussing contemporary literature (reviewing French and English poetry and fiction will be a mainstay of his periodical work for twenty-five years). Almost more importantly, the essay provides a blueprint for understanding Pater's historicizing imagination. It is the substantial range of Morris's texts—*The Defense of Guenevere, The Life and Death of Jason, The Earthly Paradise*—that encourages Pater to rethink relations among ancient, medieval, and modern culture. Pater praises Morris's medievalism because, like "some strange second flowering after date, it renews on a more delicate type the poetry of a past age, but must not be confounded with it" ("Poems" 300). Two distinct approaches to "the medieval spirit" and culture emerge from the essay (301). Positively, Pater acknowledges "its mystic religion at its apex in Dante and Saint Louis, and its mystic passion, passing here and there into the great romantic loves of rebellious flesh, of Lancelot and Abelard" (301). He also suggests, in a quietly inflammatory way, that one characteristic of the Arthurian materials is "the strange suggestion of a deliberate choice between Christ and a rival lover" (301). As well, "a wild, convulsed sensuousness in the poetry of the middle age" emerged, "in which the things of nature begin to play a strange delirious part" (303). Thus, even before Pater has developed his avant-garde argument in favor of the Renaissance's cultural significance (including its embrace of classical art, literature, and letters), he is reframing the argument as to why and how medieval culture had to be superseded.[71] And that is the major aspect of his second, negative approach to "the medieval spirit." According to Pater, it was too inflected by "the sad-coloured world of abstract philosophy"; too ready to accept the "loss" of "the life of the senses" (309, 301). When the "mood of the cloister" took a "new direction," that direction was too far away from the world (the religious too successfully learned "the art of directing towards an imaginary object sentiments whose natural direction is towards objects of sense" [302]).

How closely was Hopkins taking note of Pater's apprentice work as a critic? On 2 July 1868, Hopkins informed Fr. Ignatius Ryder that he had hoped to write "an article for a review," perhaps the *North British Review* or the *Dublin Review,* as a means of making money to fund a month-long trip to Switzerland (*CW* 1:183). And the subject? The "subject wd. be Wm. Morris' last poem and the medieval school of poets" (*CW* 1:183). The essay did not materialize, but the trip to Switzerland did.[72] It is fascinating to realize that, as a Jesuit student of theology, Hopkins became immersed in the medieval intellectualism that Pater renounces (Abelard, Aquinas, and Scotus).

The "Winckelmann" project provided Pater with an exceptional example of how someone could escape from anti-sensuous cultural pressures (overdetermined by the critic as "nocturnal" impulses) and in doing so rediscover the "earthly paradise," the "broad daylight," of ancient art. The essay is the first Paterian exercise in transformative historiography and biography: an account of how, away from the library and the high table, immersed in new and sometimes "fervid" experiences, a critic and scholar becomes first a student of the sensuous in art and then a sensuous being. Rome is the space of possibilities for Winckelmann, but only as it provides access to ancient Greek marbles and relics that represent the apotheosis of "pure form." On behalf of any reader who would "handle the antique" even vicariously, Pater's Winckelmann develops what Foucault would term new techniques of the self as a practice of freedom. Or in Pater's words, "And that [pagan] world in which others had moved with so much embarrassment, seems to call out in Winckelmann new senses fitted to deal with it. He is *en rapport* with it; it penetrates him, and becomes part of his temperament" ("Winck." 88). Winckelmann's "handling of the sensuous side of Greek art" (103) in a truly "pagan manner" is possible because he, like the artists who have inspired him, refuses to separate spirit and body, and eschews any notion of a "tyranny of the senses." Just the opposite. The "spiritual motive" of Greek art is "not lightly and loosely attached to the sensuous form, as the meaning to the allegory, but saturates and is identical with it" (95). Furthermore, Pater insists, whereas the spiritualist "is satisfied in seeing the sensuous element escape from his conceptions; his interest grows, as the dyed garment bleaches in the keener air," the artist "steeps his thought again and again in the fire of colour" (103). Such an ethos of saturation, made all the keener by the inflammatory phrasing, are but two of Pater's gifts to decadent discourse.

In "Winckelmann," Pater briefly laments the death of the classical spirit in and after the too-Christian Middle Ages: in his words, it was tantamount to "the crushing of the sensuous, the shutting of the door upon it, the flesh-outstripping interest" (105). In "Poems by William Morris," he reemphasizes this historical "chill," declaring, "The Christianity of the middle age made way among a people whose loss was in the life of the senses" ("Poems" 301). And yet—in the final paragraphs of the essay (later the "Conclusion" to *The Renaissance*), Pater appreciatively notes an alternative, "wild, convulsed sensuousness in the poetry of the middle age" ("Poems" 303). (Had he read the poems of Hopkins, he would have discerned a complementary, "wilder wring" of words [*PW* 182].) In the Morris review, Pater salutes the "extravangan[t]" medieval fusion of erotic and spiritual idolatry that will become a hallmark of late nineteenth-century decadent writing: "to be the servant of love, . . . *to taste* the subtle luxury of chastisement, of reconciliation—the religious spirit, too, knows that" ("Poems" 302; my emphasis). The speaker of Hopkins's 1865 poem "Easter Communion" knows exactly that: "Pure fasted faces draw unto this feast: / God comes all sweetness to your Lenten lips" (*PW* 70). In "The Kind Betrothal," another Oxford-era text inspired by Christina Rossetti, the speaker, a nun about to take the veil, conducts a taxonomic survey of every sense she is renouncing, including:

> Palate, the hutch of Like and Lust,
> Wish now no tasty rinse of wine:
> The flask will be so clear, the crust
> So fresh that come in fasts divine! (*PW* 91)

"The Wreck of the Deutschland" recombines gustatory and punitive tropes with a celebratory, Keatsian zest:

> Oh,
> We lash with the best or worst
> Word last! How a lush-kept plush-capped sloe
> Will, mouthed to flesh-burst,

> Gush!—flush the man, the being with it, sour or sweet
> Brim, in a flásh, fúll!—[.] (*PW* 121)

By the time Hopkins is writing poetry in Dublin, as I have already discussed, the "tasting" of self is no longer a "luxury," as Pater had imagined it; for Hopkins's Ignatian speaker, it is a scourge and a necessity, the oral intimacy of which intensifies the bitterness of a "selfstuff" far removed from the Comforter's "[d]elicious kindness" (*PW* 185). Selving, for Hopkins, is to be flush with divine elements and individual agency. When they are balanced, the "achieve" of the self is stable and sure, "its wellbeing of a self-wise self-will." (The latter phrase, from "The Bugler's First Communion," is a reminder of why the Eucharistic experience, for Hopkins, is both the intaking of Christ's essence, a literal and spiritual ingestion, and the confirmation of a "dauntless" self.) When the "sour" aspects of humanity "whelm" a person, however, the risk of being reduced to the equivalent of "gall" and "heartburn," is acute, both "unbound" and "unselve[d]." One of the hallmarks of Hopkins's decadent poetics is the vehement, flamboyant juxtaposition of sensuousness and *âscesis*. The author of *Marius the Epicurean* would have been aghast for his former pupil, but delighted for the sake of art.

"GIVE ME EXCESS OF IT"

"Coleridge's Writings" is intellectually daring but stylistically spare. In the prose of "Winckelmann," however, one discerns a new commitment to embodying, in words, the sensuousness which the Greek statues and the German scholar exemplify. With the same "utmost attenuation of detail" Pater applauds in creative writing ("Winck" 98), his critical prose demonstrates a flair for the dramatic:

> And now there opened for [Winckelmann] a new way of communion with the Greek life. Hitherto he had handled the words only of Greek poetry, stirred indeed and roused by them, yet divining beyond the words an unexpressed pulsation of sensuous life. Suddenly he is in contact with that life still fervent in the relics of plastic art.... [W]e can hardly

imagine how deeply the human mind was moved when at the Renaissance, in the midst of a frozen world, the buried fire of ancient art rose up from under the soil. . . . On a sudden the imagination feels itself free. ("Winck" 83)

This "fervid" passage marks the turning point in Winckelmann's life *and* Pater's essay. In "Poems by William Morris," the prose is even more intense, syntactically challenging, and lush, and the work of art an occasion for critical expressiveness: "[Morris] has diffused through *King Arthur's Tomb* the maddening white glare of the sun, and tyranny of the moon, not tender and far-off but close down—the sorcerer's moon, large and feverish. The colour is intricate and delirious, as of 'scarlet lilies.' The influence of summer is like a poison in one's blood, with a sudden bewildered sickening of life and all things" ("Poems" 303). Aubrey Beardsley's moons for Oscar Wilde's *Salome,* Wilde's lilies, and Ernest Dowson's poisonous loves have just been adumbrated in their first "wild, convulsed sensuousness" (303).

A congruent intensification of effects is found in Hopkins's canon. Exceeding boundaries and limits[73]—of prosody, genre, religious decorum—inspires ever-more audacious articulations of wonder, grace, disenchantment, and despondency. Sprung rhythm, the more "authentic cadence" (*PW* 84) he developed after Oxford and before launching "The Wreck of the Deutschland," confounds the hegemony of iambic pentameter by stressing syllables—or not—as the poem demands, not as conventions dictate. Consequently, lineation is fractured, or lines are hyperextended; strange enjambments defy the rules of syllabic division. Straining against the limits of the English lexicon, the man who also knew Greek, Latin, French, and Welsh finds a new pitch for words or invents his own compounds, from "leafmeal" and "heart-fleshed" to "lovely-asunder / Starlight" and "king- / dom of daylight's dauphin, dapple-dawn-drawn Falcon." (Pater decried Coleridge's orthodox ideas but appreciated his singular style of utterance: "To note the recondite associations of words, old or new . . . to recover the interest of older writers who had a phraseology of their own—this was a vein of inquiry allied to his undoubted gift of tracing out and analysing curious modes of thought" ["CW" 82].) Hopkins seizes upon the "narrow room" of the sonnet but sometimes adds a coda (or three, in the case of "Heraclitean Fire") to expand its expressive domain spatially and temporally or trims the octave and sestet to produce a new "curtal" version. Pater redefines the possibilities of the critical essay and develops a new creative genre, the imaginary portrait.

Like Pater, Hopkins develops a style of writing that is dense, almost profligate, with allusions. When his speaker declares in "The Sea and Skylark," "Our make and making break, are breaking, down / To man's last dust, drain fast towards man's first slime" (*PW* 143), one realizes that only Hopkins can bring Parmenides, Genesis, Milton, Ruskin, and Tyndall together on the page and make them sing.[74] The dramas of abjection that constitute the sonnets of desolation feature extravagant personifications: the speaker who refuses to "feast" on Despair's "carrion comfort" confronts the tormentor who would "scan / With darksome devouring eyes my bruisèd bones" (*PW* 183). When he tries to rein in such excesses, the results—as in "To what serves Mortal Beauty"—are well-mannered, in all senses of the word, rather than engrossing.

In "To what serves Mortal Beauty," the speaker's Paterian gaze may stray to "Those lovely lads once, wet-fresh" in the octave (*PW* 183), but a Ruskinian purposefulness, schooled by Pope Gregory, soon restores order in the sestet (understood by the speaker as "God's better beauty"). As critics such as Linda Dowling and James Eli Adams have demonstrated, the surcharged eroticism that becomes a received topos of decadent discourse is indebted to the homoerotic textual gaze refined and fully enjoyed in "Winckelmann" yet also strategically managed, encoded so that readers can enjoy the transgressive articulations—or not. Thus, the German scholar's "temperament" is "nurtured and invigorated" by "fervid friendships" with young men that "kept him ever in direct contact with the spirit of youth. The beauty of the Greek statues was a sexless beauty; the statues of the gods had the least traces of sex" ("Winck" 103). "Longing" is articulated, savored to excess—and then almost disavowed, controlled to the point of eroticizing such restraint. Pater constructs "not only a model of homoerotic desire, but a history that authorizes his pleasures" (Adams 169), and Plato is the sanctioning agent. "But the element of affinity which [Plato] presents to Winckelmann," Pater insists, "is that which is wholly Greek and wholly alien from the Christian world, represented by that group of brilliant youths in the Lysis, still uninfected by any spiritual sickness, finding the end of all endeavour in the aspects of the human form, the continual stir and motion of a comely human life" ("Winck" 82). The phrase "wholly alien" works quietly yet effectively to imply an alternative or other sense of belonging and identity—sexual difference and dissidence—without the judgmental frisson that "strange" would evoke. Strategically, Pater "handles" yet endorses "powerful erotic investments in the Greek ideal" (Adams 174) in which he (contra Arnold and Jowett and most Victorian Hellenists) invests the subversive potential of queer desire. Decadent sensibilities are not necessarily hetero- or homoerotic, of course, but "liberation from naturalized gender identities" and sexual preferences is encouraged (Bernheimer 70).

Thus, the male body in Pater's writings becomes at once an aesthetic spectacle, an object of desire, and a "medium of understanding" (Adams 169). Hopkins's texts adamantly refuse anything overtly, sensually "dangerous," but Pater's insistence that the male body epitomizes beauty is avidly taken up in his student's poetry and prose—alienated from its original insinuations, apparently—and made the occasion of textual indulgence. The extent to which Hopkins believed this enthusiasm to be wholly circumspect is best understood in terms of a poem that rejoices in "Churlsgrace." As chapter 3 demonstrated, "Harry Ploughman" fully embodies the complexity of Hopkins's keen textual responsiveness: aesthetic, sensuous, and religious desires intertwine to produce "Each limb's barrowy-brawnèd thew" and feast for the observer's eye (*PW* 193). Winckelmann and Pater were inspired by ancient Greek marbles; Hopkins, by William Hamo Thornycroft's bronze statue of *The Sower* (1886) and Frederick Walker's painting of *The Plough* (1870).[75] However powerful the erotic underthought of the poetic anatomizing, from Harry's "wind-lílylócks-láced" to his "fŕowning féet," the speaker justifies his own labor in remarking the "features, ín flesh" because Harry's "Amansstrength" is devoted to the deeds for which the ploughman is "charged" and responsible: the "sínew-sérvice" that prepares the "shining-shot furls" of the earth for sowing. Harry is thus everyman and an *alter Christi*.

Hopkins's celebration of Christ's body in his November 1879 sermon was analyzed in chapter 3. The religious and the sensuous not only coexist in the homily (as in the poems), they interact: through words and *in* their textual "realty." But the sensationalism also produced by these words is unmistakable. That Hopkins considered this ensarcotic glorification of Christ appropriate material for a Sunday evening sermon in a working-class suburb of Manchester reminds one to pause before assuming how the articulations of desire can or cannot be read or overdetermined. The sermon is not a parody of religious discourse, as in some fin de siècle decadent texts; it *is* rhapsodic religious discourse. Hopkins is not breaching the boundaries between the human and divine in order to shock, to excite with blasphemous pleasure; he is confounding the boundaries in order to express what is for him the actuality of Christ's humanity and thus the utter enormity of his death by crucifixion.

For their very different reasons, both Pater and Hopkins develop styles that are, in comparison with their contemporaries', inordinate, surfeit. They challenge the limits of the sayable and the unsayable to authorize new modes of experience, textual and otherwise.

MAKING "STRANGE"

"Decadence" was a term that both men used sparingly but approvingly. In the first, 1873 edition of *The Renaissance,* Pater insists that the poems of Joachim du Bellay "pu[t] forth in France an aftermath, a wonderful later growth, the products of which have to the full that subtle and delicate sweetness which belongs to a fine and comely decadence" (*Ren* xxiii). In May 1888, two months before composing "That Nature is a Heraclitean Fire," Hopkins warns Bridges that "decadence" is now "a criticism that they sling about between the ~~emphatic~~ ^bursting^ Yes and blustering No, for want of more things to say" (*CW* 2:938). The following February, apparently reiterating his friend's negative comments, Hopkins parries: "'The first touch of decadence destroys all merit whatever': this is a hard saying. What, all technical merit—as chiaroscuro, anatomical knowledge, expression, feeling, colouring, drama? It is plainly not true. And, come to that, the age of Raphael and Michelangelo, was ~~an age of~~ ^in a^ decadence and its excellence is technical. Everything after Giotto is decadent in form, ~~but~~ though advancing in execution" (*CW* 2:981). Paterian Hopkins observes with an expansive, historically refined gaze; he abjures narrow periodization. Bridges, one might suggest, was among those who too easily invoked "decadence" censoriously to express disapproval—of art, attitudes, and behaviors both ancient and contemporary.[76] Hopkins and Pater, on the other hand, typically welcomed the innovative and seemingly strange.

If one accepts, with Bernheimer, that "decadence is a stimulant that causes a restless movement between perspectives" (27), then Pater and Hopkins's shared commitment to that which is "strange" formally, stylistically, and/or thematically should not surprise. Once Pater identifies, in "Coleridge's Writings," that "what constitutes an artistic gift is first of all a natural susceptibility to moments of strange excitement, in which the colours freshen upon our threadbare world, and the routine of things about us is broken by a novel and happier synthesis" ("CW" 123), his critical gaze looks for it everywhere, and exults. Thus the "strange pregnancy" of Goethe's art criticism and Winckelmann's Hellenic experiences, the "strange power" of Morris's transhistorical verse (which inspires *twelve* different meditations on the "strange complex of conditions" ["Poems" 302] that it embodies and articulates[77]). Denying "passion"—in art, in life— "begets a tension in the nerve," Pater suggests, borrowing from medical discourse to intensify his aesthetic appreciation of Morris's poetry: in its "wild, convulsed sensuousness" the "things of nature begin to play a strange delirious part" (303). Human nature is also inflected with strangeness: Morris's poems inspire the first exploration of an always mobile, contingent, and decadent subjectivity, "that vanishing away, that strange perpetual weaving and unweaving of ourselves" (311).

Hopkins vehemently eschewed such a transgressive and "pagan" ontological framework, but, after he studied with Pater, his aesthetic perspective was always committed to difference. An undergraduate essay acknowledges, "In art we strive to realise not only unity, permanence of law, likeness, but also, with it, difference, variety, contrast: it is rhyme we like, not echo, and not unison but harmony" (*CW* 4:221). But it is Hopkins's 1878 poem "Pied Beauty" that "tells" the Paterian lesson more directly, celebrating the "dappled things" of creation:

> Áll things counter, original, spáre, stránge;
>   Whatever is fickle, frecklèd (who knows how?)
>   With swíft, slów; sweet, sóur; adázzle, dím[.]
>   (*PW* 144; emphasis added)

Despite the Christian grace note summoned to complete the poem (the Creator's "beauty is past change"), the tune is wholly Paterian. Hopkins's attempts to orchestrate the oral performance of the poem by marking the syllables to be stressed (featured in bold) is further indication of how his theory and practice of sprung rhythm and counterpointed verse are designed to estrange the reader—and his words—from the overly familiar patterns of iambic pentameter, and in the process refract rhythm, syntax, and meaning. Using one's medium deftly, adventurously, is Pater's basic lesson about "Style": the writer "alone can expose that inward sense of things, the purity of this medium, its laws or tricks of refraction" (*Appreciations* 33). Stylistically, both Pater and Hopkins attend to rhythmic effects to suspend ordinary patterns of reading and comprehension, to create a different kind of textual experience. And this too, I am suggesting, is nascent decadence.

"YOU SIT WITHIN YOUR CORPSES"

Diagnoses of poetic "delirium" and "fever dream" throughout "Poems by William Morris" anticipate yet counter the "biomedical model" of later Victorian culture promoted by positivist sciences (criminology, psychiatry, anthropology, and sexology) to pathologize any outbreak of discursive or artistic difference (Bernheimer 139). "When the actual relics of the antique were restored to the world," Pater wryly observes in "Winckelmann," "it was to Christian eyes as if an ancient plague pit had been opened: all the world took the contagion of the life of nature and the senses" ("Winck" 106). Jowett taught both Pater and Hopkins to be wary of "signs of health and decay in the arts." The essay of that name Hopkins wrote for Jowett confidently chimes in, asserting that "a declining Art . . . degenerates into mere touch, trick and mannerism. . . . How then is it that decline in Art sets in? It need not of course[;] . . . with genius abounding and in a time of national health, there would be no degeneracy" (*CW* 4:111). Pater, however, resists such a too-easy "possession of truths" ("Poems" 309). "He seems to gibe," as Adams suggests, "at contemporary constructions of a moral hygiene that identified sexual discipline with effective sanitation, and hence might find the erotic freedom of Greek art 'unhealthy'" (173). Instead, Pater advocates an intensification of aesthetic experiences that are an integral part of an ethical "condition" of being—yet, "a strange delirious part" ("Poems" 303).

An acute and "sudden bewildered sickening of life and all things" ("Poems" 303) is just as frequently encountered in Pater's essays and prose fiction as it is in Hopkins's poetry. In both canons, disease motifs promote a fascination with dying and death that will become a staple of fin de siècle decadence. Pater's first published sentence—"Forms of intellectual and spiritual culture often exercise their subtlest and most artful charm when life is already passing from them" ("CW" 106)—reminds one that an Oxford mind in the 1860s had to absorb the competing temporal-historiographic shocks and suggestions of Heraclitus, Gibbon, and Darwin, each of whom bequeathed a new fascination with fatal tropes of decline and decay. Pater was inspired to produce "a new analysis of the relations of body and mind, good and evil, freedom and necessity" that he termed "the 'relative' spirit in place of the 'absolute'" ("CW" 107); Hopkins could only "live imaginatively within the domain of death" (Bernheimer 78) by embracing the eschatological certainties and stringencies of Roman Catholicism.[78] In such a faith he found light and heat, and wrote "laced with fire of stress" (*PW* 119) because death, ultimately, had no dominion (save as a conduit to eternal grace or damnation). Pater, in the first phase of his career, found only "a strange winter, a strange suspension of life" in such religious and philosophical steadfastness ("CW" 115). And yet, however antithetical they were in their spiritual commitments, both vividly embraced the textual promise of death.

Absent any reliance upon or dedication to a Christian promise of eternal life, Pater's texts in the 1860s recall a crucial "characteristic of the pagan spirit" that he terms "the continual suggestion, pensive or passionate, of the shortness of life" ("Poems" 309). He finds "the sense of death and the desire of beauty; the desire of beauty quickened by the sense of death" equally in Morris's poetry and Winckelmann's aesthetic writings ("Poems" 309). Reading Winckelmann as he contemplates marble relics of ancient Greece and Morris as he "transfigure[s]" classical, Old Norse, and Arthurian themes encourages Pater to aspire to an expansion of consciousness that acutely grasps how the "elements" of existence, "birth and gesture and death and the springing of violets from the grave are but a few out of the ten thousand resulting combinations" of the "forces" of "the whole physical life" ("Poems" 310). Thereafter, with unsettling frequency and force, death's irruptions and interruptions energize Pater's writings, to the point where life itself is "one of [death's] more exquisite intervals."[79]

Time and again Pater imagines a critic, an artist, a god, or a fictional character "troubled with thoughts of a limit to duration, of inevitable decay, of dispossession," an apprehension that "has already a touch of the corpse in it" ("Winck" 105). Hence the "gem-like flame" of desire or "ecstasy" that provides the "purest energy" for life at the same time guarantees its annihilation ("Poems" 311).

According to Pater, realizing that life "condemns" one to death inspires the "literary sense" and compulsion to write for Jean-Jacques Rousseau, Victor Hugo, and Morris ("Poems" 312). A similar devotion to death—even a "craving" ("Winck" 81)—will inspire key essays in *The Renaissance,* including "Two Early French Stories," "Sandro Botticelli," "Leonardo da Vinci," and "Winckelmann," and motivate imaginary portraits of Marius the Epicurean, Gaston de Latour, Duke Carl of Rosenmold, Emerald Uthwart, and the painter Antoine Watteau. But "commerce with the dead" (Shuter 93)[80] is only part of the Paterian "experience" and its decadent afterlife. It is the "passionate" insistence on the "pleasure" that life variously affords— "exquisite" and brief, and all the more exquisite because of its "awful brevity"—that provokes and provides "so high an experience" that anything less is insufficient ("Winck" 110).

The "awful brevity" of life noticed in "Winckelmann" becomes, in "Poems by William Morris," a more thoroughly articulated and nuanced temporal theory with profound epistemological and ontological implications. The discussion of "exquisite intervals" begins in relation to nature ("the moment, for instance, of delicious recoil from the flood of water in summer heat" ["Poems" 310]) but soon focuses on the human condition: "This at least of flame-like our life has, that it is but the concurrence renewed from moment to moment of forces parting sooner or later on their ways" (310).[81] His "analysis goes a step further still" by suggesting that life is, fundamentally, a series of "moments" that are "gone while we try to apprehend" them; the stream of impressions one receives—of a loved one, a work of art, the natural world in its diversity—constitutes "what is real in our life" (311). How should one conduct one's life given that every "mood of passion or insight or intellectual excitement is irresistibly real and attractive for us for that moment only" (311)? According to Pater, nothing less than a seismic shift in priorities and actions is required: "Not the fruit of experience but experience itself is the end. . . . To burn always with this hard gem-like flame, to maintain this ecstasy, is success in life" (311). Pater's radical rethinking of subjectivity, temporality, and moments of experience generated such a storm when these paragraphs became the "Conclusion" to *The Renaissance* in 1873—Samuel Wilberforce, the bishop of Oxford, offered to burn the book in public—that he removed the "Conclusion" from the second edition of the book.[82]

Hopkins, of course, never wavered from his commitment to the "fruit of experience." Reconsidering his poetry in relation to the Paterian "moment," however, occasions a fresh appreciation of how so many texts begin by capturing arresting experiences: "I awoke in the Midsummer not-to-call night," "The world is charged with the grandeur of God," "Look at the stars, look up at the skies!," "On ear and ear two noises too old to end / Trench," "I caught this morning morning's minion," "I walk, I lift up, I lift up heart, eyes," "My heart, where have we been? | What have we seen, my mind?," "I wake and feel the fell of dark, not day," and stanzas 2 and 28, especially, of "The Wreck." Typically, the poems explore the moment with verbal dexterity before explaining its subjective, ecological, or religious significance. Permanent truths are discovered or heralded by Hopkins's speaker—but the moments' evanescence makes those lessons all the more vivid and keen. To overstate the case somewhat, each moment, whether delightful or harrowing, is both a birth and death. Certainly, that is the Paterian underthought of "To R. B.": "The fine delight that fathers thought; the strong / Spur, live and lancing like the blowpipe flame, / Breathes once and, [is] quenchèd faster than it came" (*PW* 204).

Hopkins's training in the *Spiritual Exercises* infused a Paterian zest for aestheticizing mortality with a keen religious zeal. General meditations on the "end of man" and the "end of creatures" are followed by soul-searching and self-lacerating exercises on sin, hell, and death. For the latter, one begins by contemplating the agony of dying, pausing over one's "inanimate body in the coffin," and the anguish of loved ones during the funeral rites, and then ponders the harrowing mystery of ultimate judgment. The *Exercises*, of course, were designed to save the individual from the excesses of life, flesh, and sinful death. However much the Ignatian prose seems to savor the sensuous evocation of fatality, it does so only to provide the means of reversing an iniquitous doom.

The Petrarchan sonnet, the genre best suited to Hopkins's dialectically trained intelligence and most manageable for someone with his pastoral and professional commitments, is an apt poetic space in which to explore the wealth of natural and human beauty—especially as it "tells" the divine presence within—or to construct a potential drama of defilement or destruction. Death's imminence is a felt pressure in most poems, literally or metaphorically. Yet its purpose, in part, is to sweeten the relief of divine rescue (whether in this life or the next; peril also produces exquisite sensations in Hopkins's texts).

The one poem in which the "hearse-of-all night" is figuratively unrelieved, wholly decadent because produced by excessive and *unmitigated* melancholy and fear, is "Spelt from Sibyl's Leaves" (1884–86), which features a "selfwrung, selfstrung" speaker who "strains" toward a conclusion, would welcome an "end" to all suffering, but instead only knows the "rack" of existence. Speaker and text are tortured: he is a "self ín self stéepèd and páshed—qúite / Disremembering, dísmémbering | áll now" (*PW* 191); the poem is "home-of-all" manner of idiosyncrasies including overly accented syllables, emphatic caesurae intensified by musical markings (|), difficult compound words and phrases, arresting coinages, and deliberately broken terms (earth's "dápple is at énd, as- / Tray or aswarm, all throughther, in throngs" [*PW* 191]).

Death's variety knows no bounds in Hopkins's canon: poplars are hacked down; farriers are "broke[n]" by sickness; adults accomplished in "mould or mind" are "consume[d]" (*PW* 140); children grieve; ships are wrecked and their progeny, "sea-corpse[s] cold" (*PW* 151); devout young women are violently punished for dedicating their virginity to God. For the poet, however, as for Pater, death is more than a sensational experience to be exploited; it is the ground of all perception, "the random grím fórge" (*PW* 165) upon which the human condition is fashioned.[83]

ENOUGH!

Yet: death, for Hopkins, is neither the end nor the answer. It can be the grimmest aspect of the human condition, when "Flesh fade[s], and mortal trash / Fáll[s] to the resíduary worm" (*PW* 198), but Hopkins's faith in a life of the spirit after death—in the resurrection of the body—sustained him, provided the underthought for every utterance. I have already suggested that "Pied Beauty" and "To what serves Mortal Beauty" constitute dialogues with Paterian aesthetics. In this final segment, I would like to discuss the ways in which "That Nature is a Heraclitean Fire and of the comfort of the Resurrection" also answers Pater (similar to the way in which the Golden Echo reacts and replies to the Leaden Echo).

The first five lines of "Heraclitean Fire" are a festival of Ruskinian "elements": a "dazzling" and ebullient cloudscape of "heaven-roysterers" (*PW* 197) that harkens back to the diary entries and drawings of his Oxford years. Natural "puffballs" are "mined with a motion" (*PW* 120), delightfully subjected to a host of verbs: tear, flaunt, chevy, build, throng, glitter, arch, tackle, lace, lance, pair. As air gives way to earth, however, then earth to water and water to fire ("nature's bonfire burns on" [*PW* 198]), Paterian lessons about Heraclitean flux come to the fore.[84] How Pater would have discussed Heraclitus with Hopkins, how he explained the pre-Socratic philosopher's "influence" on Plato—"though himself a Heraclitean in early life, [it] was by way of antagonism or reaction" (*Plato* 7)—can be surmised from the pages of *Plato and Platonism* (1893), in which Pater transforms a series of lectures for Oxford students into a more popular intellectual medium.[85] The first lecture, "Plato and the Doctrine of Motion," begins by asserting the significance of "forethoughts" for any new "intellectual production" (*Plato* 1). In the case of Plato, chief among those forethoughts was Heraclitus's assertion that "Πάντα ῥεῖ All things fleet away" (*Plato* 1). Moreover, Heraclitus is presented as "a writer of philosophy in prose, yet of a philosophy which was half poetic figure, half generalized fact, in style crabbed and obscure, but stimulant, invasive, not to be forgotten" (*Plato* 7). His philosophy "was no matter of formal treatise or system," Pater insists,

> but of harsh protesting cries.... All things give way: nothing remaineth.... Perpetual motion, alike in things and in men's thoughts about them,—the sad, self-conscious, philosophy of Heraclitus ... [rests upon] masterful currents of universal change, stealthily withdrawing the apparently solid earth itself from beneath one's feet. The principle of disintegration, the incoherency of fire or flood (for Heraclitus these are but very lively instances of movements subtler yet more wasteful still) are inherent in the primary elements alike of matter and of the soul. (*Plato* 9–10)

Pater stresses the implications of flux for defining both subjectivity—what in "Poems by William Morris" is defined as "that strange perpetual weaving and unweaving of ourselves" ("Poems" 311)—and religious beliefs. Hopkins, on the other hand, subjects this doctrine of flux and fire to Christological absolutism.

In the central section of "Heraclitean Fire," all seems imperiled. Could this be another "Sibyl's Leaves," in which praise of "Fíre-féaturing héaven" gives way to fears about the earth ("her béing has unbóund; her dápple is at énd") and a desperate denial of release from being "selfwrung, selfstrung, sheathe- and shelterless" (*PW* 191)? (The structural parallels between "Sibyl's Leaves" and "Heraclitean Fire" are striking.) No. The speaker of "Heraclitean Fire" adamantly refuses to succumb to thoughts of "disintegration, the incoherency of fire or flood." An emphatic and dramatic "Enough!" ends the dialogue with relativism and instead offers "the Resurrection, / A héart's-clarion!" And then, the poem stages the verbal alchemy so admired by Hopkins's readers. The lines are worth repeating in the context of this chapter because the final segment begins with the flesh and concludes with a resplendent, recuperative image of avowal, Hopkins's own version of Pater's "hard gem-like flame":

> Flesh fade, and mortal trash
> Fáll to the resíduary worm; | world's wildfire, leave but ash:
> In a flash, at a trumpet crash,
> I am all at once what Christ is, | since he was what I am, and
> Thís Jack, jóke, poor pótsherd, | patch, matchwood, immortal diamond,
> Is immortal diamond. (*PW* 198)

Yet even in the resounding finale of "Heraclitean Fire" there is a Paterian note. As previously mentioned, Hopkins heard about Pater before he met him: Pater's contributions to the Old Mortality essay society scandalized Samuel Brooke (among others). The text of only one of those compositions is extant: "Diaphaneitè." According to Pater, the diaphanous character is "rare, precious above all to the artist," an example of "supreme moral charm" and "moral expressiveness" such as one finds in Dante's Beatrice or an "Imitatio Christi."[86] Pater's description of "this clear crystal nature" may have contributed to Hopkins's choice of climactic image: "It does not take the eye by breadth of colour; rather, it is that fine edge of light, where the elements of our moral nature refine themselves to the burning point. It crosses rather than follows the main current of the world's life. The world has no sense fine enough for those evanescent shades.... But the character we have before us is a kind of prophecy of this repose and simplicity, coming as it were in the order of grace, not of nature" (*Misc* 253, 248, 249). Pater's words, including his suggestion that the diaphanous figure is featured in "poetry and poetical history" as "some human victim... sent down into the grave," are refined to the burning point in Hopkins's deeply retrospective text.

Especially if one agrees with Linda Dowling about the "idea of Decadence as counterpoetics and critique" (*Language* 10), then time spent with Pater and Hopkins provides "an inexhaustible gift of suggestion" on the subject ("Winck" 80). Placing Hopkins's texts in conversation with those of Pater, Rossetti, Swinburne—and even Buchanan—demonstrates how vividly the Victorian aesthetic project of professing the flesh was, for Hopkins, "stimulant, invasive, not to be forgotten" (*Plato* 7). The chapter began with a trenchant quotation from "Winckelmann": "A style or manner in art or literature can only be explained or reproduced through those special conditions of society and culture out of which it arose and with which it forms one group of phenomena" ("Winck" 107). The texts of Pater and Hopkins have much to teach one about the emergence of decadent discourse in the later nineteenth century. The Brasenose don willingly embraced its strange potential; the Jesuit priest no doubt thought he was doing otherwise. And yet, to quote the final, arresting question of "Winckelmann," "Who, if he foresaw all, would fret against circumstances which endow one at the end with so high an experience?" (110).

CONCLUSION

COMFORT?

I call it "consolation" when there is set up in the soul some inward motion, whereby the soul begins to be on fire with the love of her Creator and Lord; and, consequently, when she can love no created thing on the face of the earth in itself, but only in the Creator of them all.
—IGNATIUS, *Spiritual Exercises*, First Week

There is a comfort in the strength of love.
—WILLIAM WORDSWORTH, *Michael*

IN THE DISCUSSION OF "HERACLITEAN FIRE" that concluded chapter 4, one crucial element of the poem (prominently signaled in the title, an overextended heading for an overextended sonnet) was not addressed: the idea of "comfort." The term functions as a noun in the phrase "and of the Comfort of the Resurrection," the bridge between the phenomenal world and the noumenal, the apparent and the promised, yet it also lives as a verb, the kind of multivalency that Hopkins often enjoyed. At the outset of this project, I enumerated some of the costs of conversion and religious life as Hopkins experienced them. To conclude, a brief discussion of the rewards of religious certainty is offered, focusing on comfort as one of the themes explored with substantial urgency in Hopkins's writings. In this way, one can glimpse what an absolutist religious culture feels like *inside* the parameters of shared beliefs.

The more formal term, often used in religious texts (including the *Spiritual Exercises*), is "consolation." Ignatius explains that the desolation experienced while doing the *Exercises* should help "prepare and dispose" the exercitant for the "consolation to come" (*SE* 6): "I call 'consolation' any increase of hope, faith and charity, and any inward joy that calls and attracts to heavenly things and to the salvation of one's own soul, rendering her restful and pacifying her in her Creator and Lord" (*SE* 68–69). As Rickaby, S.J., glosses the Fourth Week of the *Exercises,* "Appearances of Christ," "Consolation is a thing that we can neither procure for ourselves nor merit of God: it is a gratuitous gift, as is also all 'higher prayer.' But we dispose or indispose ourselves for it" (*SE* 205). Faber refers to commuting "consolation into increased strength" (*Growth* 360); Pusey reassures readers of Gaume that absolution is "also a consolation and help against sin and an evil conscience" ("Preface" xxix). But Hopkins preferred the homelier English word, one that can be traced back to the first Book of Common Prayer (1549), in relation to the Eucharist, and even further back to the *Ancrene Riwle* (Guide for anchoresses, ca. 1200), where it is positioned against the flesh: "Of flesliche vondunges . . . and kunfort aȝeines ham" (of fleshly temptations . . . and of comfort against them) (14, 15). Support and succor are the first characteristics of comfort, but so too are notions of strength, sustenance, and solace.[1]

As I have demonstrated, Christians' relations with their God and with the self are structured along an axis of fear/desolation and redemption/consolation;[2] comfort functions as the antidote or answer to the fear regulating a "confessing society" that has learned to demonize the flesh. Confession names several different modes of expression and revelation: witnessing to one's religious truths; acknowledging sin and accepting the penalties required; enjoying the absolution; and also experiencing a kind of self-proclamation. The penitential sacrament, as Pusey explains, is a "source of increased comfort to laden or anxious souls who feel that they need what is more special to themselves" (*Penitence* 10). Complete disclosure is designed to alleviate the acute state of spiritual discomfort one feels and one knows. The confessor's role, as Foucault suggests, is to participate in unlocking "the secrets of your conscience" and the "secrets of your own heart" (*WDTT* 172). This is especially true if one knows that death is imminent: Hopkins's "instructions" to parishioners included the promise of "God's deathbed mercies," the "comforting sacrament[s] of death" (confession, holy communion, the anointing of the sick) (*CW* 5:536).³

Also requiring constant watchfulness: the dangers of false comfort. Job, of course, is the Old Testament's most vivid example of steadfastness in the face of the inadequate comfort offered by humans and the too-grim realities of one's flesh, metaphorically "clothed with worms and clods of dust."⁴ Victorians such as Faber were quick to remind people, in various mini-jeremiads, that the physical comforts and material advantages of the world endanger their souls. Modern "luxury and effeminacy," he warns, are "the reigning vices of the world; and therefore in these days ... the worship of comfort and extravagances of luxury" must be abjured (Faber, *Growth* 317).⁵ When Rickaby, S.J., adumbrates the "renunciation of things lawful in themselves," he includes "comforts, home ties, the haunts of one's youth, sight of friends, honours, independence, affluence, reputation, power."⁶

Genuine spiritual consolation or comfort, on the other hand, is a gift from God—but it too is subject to flux (the "desolation that will come on afterwards" [*SE* 71]). During the First Week of the *Exercises,* in the "Rules for the Discernment of Spirits" (*CW* 5:506 ff), one learns, "Let him who is in desolation *labour to hold on in patience,* such patience as makes against the vexations that harass him; let him consider soon he shall be consoled, using diligent efforts against such desolation" (*SE* 70;⁷ my emphasis). Hopkins tries to accept this temporary loss, and its alleviation, in prose and verse. In his notes on the *Spiritual Exercises,* he observes, "The purport of this body of rules, Fr. Whitty⁸ says, is that consolation shd. be our normal state and that when God recov withdraws it he wishes us to strive to recover it. Cf. 'da nobis in eodem Spiritu recta sapere et de ejus semper consolatione gaudere [grant us in the same Spirit to be truly wise and always to rejoice in his consolation]'" (*CW* 5:515–16). In the Ireland poems of 1886–87, the patience that Ignatius requires for comfort is the subject of yet another allegorical confrontation:

> Patience, hard thing! the hard thing but to pray,
> But bid for, patience is! Patience who asks
> Wants war, wants wounds; weary his times, his tasks;

> To do without, take tosses, and obey.
> Rare patience roots in these, and, these away,
> Nowhere. Natural heart's-ivy Patience masks
> Our ruins of wrecked past purpose. There she basks
> Purple eyes and seas of liquid leaves all day.
> We hear our hearts grate on themselves: it kills
> To bruise them dearer. Yet the rebellious wills
> Of us wé dó bid God bend to him even so.
> And where is he who more and more distills
> Delicious kindness?—He is patient. Patience fills
> His crisp combs, and that comes those ways we know. (*PW* 185)

Unlike the personalized anguish of "To seem the stranger," "I wake and feel," "Carrion comfort," or "My own heart let me more have pity on," the "Patience" poem is impersonal, articulated on behalf of "we who do" and "know," however imperfectly, that God's gift of patience, albeit hard-won, constitutes a "Delicious kindness." Perhaps the "hardest" thing about this kind of patience is that it requires a "dearer" price: not quiescence, but absolute obedience. Once again, "rebellious wills" are at fault and bodies and spirits are consequently bruised. Submission is devoutly to be wished for: "we do bid God bend to him" our wills, the speaker prays. And without said patience, according to the speaker, we are "Nowhere." "Patience, hard thing!" is an accomplished Petrarchan sonnet: the allegorical octave is answered in the sestet by the lesson of "we" who struggle to acquire and maintain this virtue. Structurally, the poem has the circularity Hopkins enjoys:[9] Patience in the abstract comes round to the ineffable patience that is the Almighty's, part of his honeycomb of sweet rewards ("crisp combs") for those with sufficient fortitude.[10] It is also a very intratextual poem: revisiting and revising motifs of shipwrecks, roots, battered hearts, the "taste" of divine grace, and the mantra of "patience, penance, prayer" (*PW* 176).

And yet—the poem hums with the counterpoised energy of consolation/desolation, but "comfort" itself is never mentioned. It proliferates, however, in the Ireland poems that dramatize the poet's worst states of abjection.[11] "And in this darksome world," Caradoc demands, "what comfort can I find? / Down this darksome world | cómfort whére can

I find / When 'ts light I quenched[?]" (*PW* 179). Despair offers "carrion comfort" with ghoulish flair. In "My own heart let me more have pity on," a quieter and more reflective text, the speaker ruefully admits, "I cast for comfort I can no more get / By groping round my comfortless than blind / Eyes in their dark can day" (*PW* 186). (In this poem, the suffering of Milton's Samson Agonistes is evoked rather than that of Job, but both figures hover between the lines of the Ireland texts.) Turning the adjective "comfortless" into a noun only enhances the sense of destitution being portrayed; the spatializing gesture ("groping round my comfortless") prepares the ground for the sestet's major metaphor, "leave comfort root-room" (*PW* 186). In "No worst, there is none," the "wilder" and wildest cry of the speaker is "Comforter, where, where is your comforting," but the only apparent answer comes from within, not from his deliverer: "Here! creep, / Wretch, under a comfort serves in a whirlwind" (*PW* 182). And what comfort would or could that be? The reference to a whirlwind brings the reader back, again, to Job's abjection, when the Lord answers him "out of the whirlwind" and demands, "Where was thou when I laid the foundations of the earth?" (Job 38:4). Only when Job is truly humiliated, wholly humbled—"I abhor myself, and repent in dust and ashes" (Job 42:6)—do his trials end and he begins, again, to enjoy his Lord's blessings.

In book 11 of the *Confessions*, Augustine praises God for "all your exhortations and all your terrors and consolations and directives, by which you brought me to preach your word and dispense your sacrament to your people" (*Confs* 221). So often in Hopkins's poetry and religious writings, comfort is paired with fear, as his 1884 meditation on the parable of the repentant tax collector and his 1885 sermon (*CW* 5:338) on the same topic demonstrate: "This one incident, which lasted perhaps but a few minutes, is all we hear [about the Pharisee and the publican]. In that short time all was done, one man put in to the way of salvation; the other, as wd. seem, of eternal ruin. There is then a suddenness about the story and the suddenness seems rather to terrify than to comfort, as if the way of God were full of incalculable hurricanes and reverses, in an instant building up and in the same casting down" (*CW* 7:162–63). The candor of those comments, however, is outmatched by the enthusiasm of his April 1880 sermon designed to prepare auditors for Pentecost (the post-Easter event when the Holy Ghost appeared as "tongues of fire" before the assembled disciples). His goal is to suggest that Christ is the first paraclete and the Holy Ghost, the second. Thus he begins by defining "Paraclete":

> For God the Holy Ghost is the Paraclete, but what is a Paraclete? Often it is ~~transl called~~ ^translated^ Comforter, but a Paraclete ~~is~~ ^does^ more than comfort. ~~There~~ word is Greek; there is no one English word for it and no one Latin word, Comforter is not enough. A Paraclete is one who comforts, ^who cheers,^ who encourages, ~~who stirs up, who urges on ^forward^, who exhorts who persuades, who exhorts,~~ who stirs up, who urges forward, who calls on; ~~what a trumpet is to brave soldiers,~~ what the spur and word of command is to a horse, what clapping of hands is to a speaker, what a trumpet is to the soldier, that a Paraclete is to the soul: <u>one who calls us on</u>, that is what it means, a Paraclete is one who calls us on to good. One sight is before my mind, it is homely but it comes home: you have seen at cricket how when one of the batsmen at the wicket has made a hit and wants to score # a run, the other doubts, hangs back, or is ready to run in again, how ~~the first~~ eagerly the first will cry / Come on, come on!—a Paraclete is just that, something that cheers the spirit of man, with signals and with cries[.] (*CW* 5:284)

Once again Hopkins tries to convey the most abstract theological or spiritual concepts in the most concrete and energized way possible. (The humor of the cricket analogy delights some but was the kind of fresh thinking that worried his Jesuit superiors—enough to insist that he write his sermons in advance and submit them for approval.[12]) His auditors may or may not have been "The keener to come at the comfort for feeling the combating keen" ("Wreck," line 200).

Whether Anglican or Catholic, John Henry Newman believed in the "comfort vouchsafed to us in being able to contemplate Him whom the Apostle calls 'the man Christ Jesus,' the Son of God in our flesh."[13] He also suggested that faith is "illuminative, not operative; it does not force obedience, though it increases responsibility; it heightens guilt, it does not prevent sin" (*Certain* 286). Analyzing the complex, sometimes contradictory inflections of "confessing the flesh" is illuminative in terms of Hopkins's writings and those of his contemporaries—how they reassessed inherited discourses and showed themselves to be disobedient or obedient to them with vigor and determination.

In an appendix to *Confessions of the Flesh,* Foucault reiterates the "penchant for discourse and the will to know (*volonté de savoir*) that characterize the experience of self and others in our societies" (*HW* 4:294). My project of reading Hopkins in various aesthetic, religious, and cultural contexts has demonstrated, I hope, how the experience of the Victorian self was conditioned by debates about the disposition of the body, the mind, and this life in relation to the next. Hopkins's poetry and prose are distinguished by the will to know *more:* about language, about the natural world, the Creator responsible for such pied beauty, and the reaches of his own astonishing, sacramentary imagination. What he learned from auricular confession, as an Anglican, compelled him to learn more about Roman Catholicism, truths that led to his conversion and ordination—which in turn put him in the position of training others to put their fears, sins, and hopes into discourse, into the confessions that he would hear and judge in order to grant absolution. Confessing the flesh engenders Hopkins's most searing personal, vocational, and textual experiences, but the "exquisite smart" (*PW* 123) portends, at least, "the heaven-háven of the reward" (*PW* 128).

APPENDIX

A CENTURY OF EVENTS AND PUBLICATIONS CONCERNING CATHOLICISM (INCLUDING THE SOCIETY OF JESUS) AND RITUALISM IN ENGLAND

Events in Hopkins's life are noted in *italics*. Titles of novels or autobiographies with anti-Catholic or anti-Jesuit elements appear in ***bold italics***.

1796	Matthew Lewis, ***The Monk.***
1797	Ann Radcliffe, ***The Italian, or the Confessional of the Black Penitents.***
1823	Grace Kennedy, ***Father Clement: A Roman Catholic Story.***
1828	G. Mutter, *On Confession, Absolution and Penance.*
1829	The Catholic Relief Act (also known as the Catholic Emancipation Act) offers freedom from basic discrimination and civil disabilities (previously, Roman Catholics could not purchase land, hold civil or military offices, or practice their religion without civil penalties) and limited rights to Roman Catholics in the UK, including the right to be members of business corporations.[1] Jesuits, however, were "required to register with the justices of the peace" (Peschier 284).
1833	May Martha Sherwood, ***The Nun.***
1835	Rebecca Reed, ***Six Months in a Convent.***
1836	Maria Monk, ***Awful Disclosures: The Confessions of Maria Monk, Shewing the Cruelties, Persecutions, and Insults She Endured during a Five Years' Residence in a Nunnery.*** Nicholas Wiseman, *On the Principal Doctrines and Practices of the Catholic Church.*

1842	Frances Trollope, *A Visit to Italy*.
1844	*28 July: Birth of Gerard Manley Hopkins*.
1845	Jules Michelet, *Du Prêtre, de la femme, de la famille*; published the same year in English as *Priests, Women, and Families*. William Sewell, **Hawkstone, a Tale of and for England in 184-**. Eugene Sue, **The Wandering Jew**. 9 October: John Henry Newman is received into the Roman Catholic faith.
1847	Elizabeth Harris, **From Oxford to Rome**. Elizabeth Sewell, **Margaret Perceval**. Andrew Steinmetz, **The Jesuit in the Family**. George Stephen, **The Jesuit at Cambridge**. Frances Trollope, **Father Eustace: A Tale of the Jesuits**. 30 May: John Henry Newman is ordained a priest.
1848	Elizabeth Harris, **Rest in the Church**.[2] John Henry Newman, **Loss and Gain**.
1849	Newman establishes the Oratory of St. Philip Neri in Birmingham.
1850	Dinah Mulock Craik, **Olive**. John Henry Newman, *Certain Difficulties Felt by Anglicans in Catholic Teaching*. 29 September: Pope Pius IX's papal bull *Universalis Ecclesiae* reestablishes the Roman Catholic hierarchy in Britain (a territorial hierarchy of twelve bishoprics in England; critics referred to this as "Papal Aggression").
1851	Giacinto Achilli, *Dealings with the Inquisition; or, Papal Rome, Her Priests, and Her Jesuits*. George Borrow, **Lavengro; The Scholar—The Gypsy—The Priest**. Richard P. Blakeney, *Manual of Romish Controversy: Being a Complete Refutation of the Creed of Pope Pius IV*. Charles Kingsley, **Yeast**. Newman, *Lectures on the Present Position of Catholics in England*. John Ruskin, *The Stones of Venice*, one appendix of which declares that "Romanism should be deprived of the miserable influence

which its pomp and picturesqueness have given it over the weak sentimentalism of the English people" (*Works* 9:436).

Jemima Thompson, **The Female Jesuit, or a Spy in the Family.**

November: Achilli charges Newman with libel, for statements made in *Lectures on the Present Position of Catholics*.

1852 Richard P. Blakeney, *Popery in Its Social Aspect.*

G. R. Prynne, *Private Confession, Penance and Absolution Authoritatively Taught in the Church of England.*

Catharine Sinclair, **Beatrice; or, The Unknown Relatives.**

M. Hobart Seymour, *Convents or Nunneries: A Lecture in Reply to Cardinal Wiseman.*

William Thackeray, **The Adventures of Henry Esmond.**

L. H. Tonna, *Nuns and Nunneries: Sketches Compiled Entirely from Romish Authorities.*

May: Cardinal Wiseman visits Bath and gives a public lecture to refute recent anti-Catholic protestations; he lectures throughout England in 1852.

21 June: Achilli's libel trial against Newman commences; Newman is found guilty and fined.

22 September: A public inquiry led by Henry Phillpotts, bishop of Exeter, is held at the Royal Hotel, Plymouth, "to examine alleged improprieties in the practice of private confession in the Church of England. Representatives from the laity as well as the press attended, and three young girls read statements of their ordeals in the confessional" (Anne Hartman 535).

1853 Charlotte Brontë, **Villette.**

Charles Kingsley, **Hypatia.**

Charles Seager, **The Female Jesuit Abroad.**

1854 Emma Robinson, **Westminster Abbey.**

Charlotte Yonge, **The Caste-Builders.**

Pope Pius IX declares the doctrine of the "immaculate conception" of Mary, the mother of Christ (feast day: 8 December).

Hopkins begins his studies at Highgate School.

	1855	Helen Dhu [Charles Edwards Lester], **Stanhope Burleigh: The Jesuits in Our Home.** Charles Kingsley, **Westward Ho!**
	1856	John Armstrong, *The Confessional: Its Wickedness. A Lecture.* Willliam Conybeare, **Perversion; or, The Causes and Consequences of Infidelity.**
	1857	George Borrow, **The Romany Rye.**
	1858	F. Baring, *Astounding Revelations of Puseyism in Belgravia, Containing the Most Frightful Disclosures of Diabolical Plots against Female Chastity by the Rev. Mr. Poole and Miss Joy, at the Fashionable Church of St. Barnabas, Pimlico.* F. D., *A Plea for St. Barnabas: The Confessional versus the Social Evil.* Charles Maurice Davies, **Philip Paternoster.**
	1860	Frederick William Robinson, **High Church.**
	1863	George Eliot, **Romola.** *17 April: Hopkins begins his studies at Balliol College, Oxford.*
	1864	Charles Kingsley, **Hereward the Wake.** *2 February: Henry Liddon becomes Hopkins's Anglican confessor.* *8 December: The Vatican issues the Syllabus of Errors, a list of eighty heresies or "errors" of faith.*
	1865	Eliza Smith Richardson, **The Veil Lifted.** Protestant Electoral Union publishes *The Confessional Unmasked.* *Hopkins continues his studies at Oxford but becomes obsessed with recording his "sins" in his diaries. Liddon and Edward Pusey are his Anglican confessors.*
	1866	[John Charles Chambers], *The Priest in Absolution*, part 1, is published by the Society of the Holy Cross for Anglican clergy. Charles Reade, **Griffith Gaunt; or, Jealousy.** *June: Anti-Catholic riots in Plymouth.* *July: Hopkins decides to convert. In October, he meets with Newman; on 21 October he defies his parents' wishes by becoming a Roman Catholic (he is "received" by Newman). On 4 November, he is confirmed by Archbishop Manning.*

11 December 1866: Pusey writes to the *Times* and initiates "a heated exchange of letters."[3]

1867 H. J. Brockman, *Letter to the Women of England: On the Confessional.*
[Church Association], *Church Association Lectures: Delivered at St. James' Hall, Piccadilly, London.*
William Goode [Dean of Ripon], *Rome's Tactics; or, A Lesson for England from the Past... with a Brief Notice of Rome's Allies in the Church of England.*
Orby Shipley, ed., *The Church and the World: Essays on Questions of the Day in 1867.*
February: Anti-Catholic riot in Wolverhampton.
16 June: Anti-Catholic communal fighting in Birmingham.
June: Hopkins completes his studies at Oxford.
10 September: Hopkins begins teaching at the Oratory school for boys in Birmingham.

1868 Benjamin Shaw, "Confession," *Quarterly Review* 124 (1868): 83–116.
Church of England Laymen's Defense Association, *Church Reform: and the Report of the Royal Commission on Ritual, Being the Second Annual Report of the Church of England Laymen's Defense Association; together with a Note on Sacerdotalism.*
Regina v. Hicklin, an obscenity trial (using the Obscene Publications Act, 1857), is brought against the editor and publisher of *The Confessional Unmasked* (religious exposé or pornography?). The decision sets the legal standard for defining obscenity in the UK and the Commonwealth until the 1950s, and in the US as well (Supreme Court, 1896).[4]
April: Hopkins undergoes two private retreats at the Jesuits' Manresa House in Roehampton (near London).
2 May: Hopkins resolves to become a priest; decides to become a Jesuit.
7 September: Hopkins joins the Society of Jesus and begins a two-year novitiate.

1869 T. T. Carter, *The Doctrine of Confession in the Church of England.*
Emma Jane Worboise, **Overdale; or, The Story of a Pervert: A Tale for the Times.**

8 December: The First Vatican Council is convened; deliberations continue until 20 October 1870.

1870   [John Charles Chambers], *The Priest in Absolution,* part 2, is published by the Society of the Holy Cross.
Benjamin Disraeli, **Lothair.**
H. C. Moule, *Confession.*
Newman, *An Essay in Aid of a Grammar of Assent.*
M. Hobart Seymour, *The Confessional: An Appeal to the Primitive and Catholic Forms of Absolution, in the East and the West.*
The First Vatican Council declares the pope infallible in doctrinal matters of morals and faith.
8 September: Hopkins takes his first vows as a Jesuit.
9 September: As a Jesuit Scholastic, Hopkins begins a three-year course of study at Stonyhurst, in Lancashire.

1871   C. F. Lowder, *Sacramental Confession Examined by Pastoral Experience.*
Provisions in the Universities Tests Act open UK universities to Roman Catholics. Previously, students, fellows, and professors had to take religious "tests" proving they were members of the Church of England.

1873   Anon., *Scandalous Revelations. The Confessional: An Exposure of Its Mysteries and Iniquities as Practised in Foreign and English Convents by Priests and Their Victims.*
Edward Pusey et al., *Declaration on Confession and Absolution, as Set Forth by the Church of England.*
The Society of Holy Cross petitions the Church of England's Convocation "to permit confessors to be trained and licensed" (Shuttleworth 629).
June: Hopkins sits his examinations in philosophy.
9 September: Hopkins begins a year of teaching at Roehampton.

1874   N. Greenwell, *Priesthood, Confession, and Absolution.*
C. F. Lowder, *Sacramental Confession Examined by Pastoral Experience. A Letter to the Right Rev. and Right Hon. the Lord Bishop of London.*
S. A. Walker, "Priestcraft," in *Tracts against Treason.*
7 August: Royal assent is given to the Public Worship Regulation Bill, introduced by Archibald Tait, archbishop of Canterbury, and

endorsed by British Prime Minister Benjamin Disraeli. The legislation is designed to curb Ritualist activities, including auricular confession.
28 August: Hopkins begins three-year course of study at the Jesuit Theologate in St. Beuno's, Wales.
November: William Gladstone, *The Vatican Decrees in Their Bearing on Civil Allegiance: A Political Expostulation.*[5]
6 December: Members of the St. Beuno's Debating Club, including Hopkins, discuss the Vatican decrees and Gladstone's pamphlet.

1875 A. B. Wildered, Parishioner, *The Ritualist's Progress; A Sketch of the Reforms and Ministrations of the Rev. Septimius Alban, Member of the E.C.U., Vicar of St. Alicia, Sloperton.*

1877 T. T. Carter, *The Freedom of Confession in the Church of England: A Letter to His Grace the Lord Archbishop of Canterbury.*
Alessandro Gavazzi, *The Priest in Absolution: An Exposure.*
S. A. Walker, *Tracts against Treason, part 2, "Confession"; The Priest in Absolution: A Criticism, a Protest, and a Denunciation.*
3 March: Hopkins successfully completes the moral theology exam and the exam "ad audiendas confessiones" (and is now permitted to hear confessions).
14 June: The Earl of Redesdale, outraged, informs the House of Lords about The Priest in Absolution.[6] *Archibald Tait, archbishop of Canterbury, also denounces it.*
23 September: Hopkins is ordained to the priesthood.

1878 Edward Pusey publishes an edited translation of Abbé Gaume's *Manual for Confessors* (adapted for Anglicans).
July to November, Hopkins is assigned to Jesuit churches in London.
December: Hopkins begins a ten-month assignment in Oxford.

1879 Eliza Lynn Linton, **Under Which Lord?**
Charlotte Yonge, **Heartsease; or, The Brother's Wife.**
12 May: Newman is appointed cardinal by Pope Leo XIII.
October: Hopkins begins a series of parish assignments in industrial areas such as Bedford Leigh, Liverpool, and Glasgow.

1880 Charles Chiniquy, *The Priest, the Woman, and the Confessional.*

1881 Joseph Shorthouse, **John Inglesant.**

	10 October: Hopkins begins his tertianship at Manresa House, Roehampton; until 15 August 1882, when he pronounces his final vows as a Jesuit.
1882	*31 August: Hopkins moves to Stonyhurst to teach Latin and Greek.*
1884	Robert Buchanan, **Foxglove Manor.** *February: Hopkins is named Professor of Latin and Greek, University College, and a Fellow of the Royal University of Ireland; on 18 February, he arrives at 85–86 St. Stephen's Green, Dublin.*
1886	Charles Chiniquy, *Fifty Years in the Church of Rome.*
1889	*8 June: Death of Hopkins.*
1897	W. Walsh, *Secret History of the Oxford Movement.*
1898	Mary Arnold [Mrs. Humphry] Ward, **Helbeck of Bannisdale.**

NOTES

INTRODUCTION

1. Gerard Manley Hopkins, *The Poetical Works of Gerard Manley Hopkins,* ed. Norman H. MacKenzie (Oxford: Clarendon Press, 1990), 144. Hereafter cited as *PW*.
2. See also Martin Dubois, *Gerard Manley Hopkins and the Poetry of Religious Experience* (Cambridge: Cambridge University Press, 2019), 17.
3. "Despise not the *day of small things.* The breathing of faith proves the life of faith as well as the loud voice of faith." Isaac Ambrose, *The Christian Warrior, Wrestling with Sin, Satan, the World and the Flesh,* ed. Thomas Jones (London: R. B. Seeley and W. Burnside, 1837), 81.
4. The "chameleon poet tak[es] the colour of his surroundings" and the poetry "tends to be dramatic rather than autobiographical." Norman H. MacKenzie, *Excursions in Hopkins* (Philadelphia: Saint Joseph's University Press, 2008), 50.
5. Hopkins grew up with the Renaissance English translation of the Protestant Bible (the King James version, or KJV); even in his Jesuit days, quotations from the KJV and the Church of England's Book of Common Prayer sang within his lines. As a convert and a Jesuit, he used the Douay-Rheims (D-R) Latin version of the Roman Catholic Bible (which features several books, including Wisdom, not found in the KJV; the Psalms are numbered differently). For more on Hopkins's Bibles, see Hopkins, *Sermons and Spiritual Writings,* ed. Jude Nixon and Noel Barber, S.J. (Oxford: Oxford University Press, 2018), 96–115. Hereafter cited as *CW* 5.
6. Hopkins's command of Greek and Latin is well known. Beginning in his Jesuit novitiate, he was expected to converse in Latin. His French was passable. He enjoyed learning to read, write, and speak Welsh while living at St. Beuno's, 1873–77, but his efforts were curtailed by his superiors. See Hopkins, *Correspondence,* 2 vols., ed. R. K. R. Thornton and Catherin Phillips (Oxford: Oxford University Press, 2013), 1:206, 598, 601, 602. Hereafter cited as *CW* 1 and *CW* 2.
7. Foucault exposes the historically embedded "grids of intelligibility" whereby order is "at one and the same time, that which is given in things as their inner law, the hidden network which determines the way they confront one another,

and also that which has no existence except by the grid created by a glance, an examination, a language." Michel Foucault, *The Order of Things: An Archaeology of the Human Sciences,* trans. Alan Sheridan (New York: Vintage Books, 1973), xx. Hereafter cited as *Order.*

8. "Sibyl's Leaves" (*PW* 191).
9. At a time when some thought Roman Catholic converts were traitors, Hopkins was an ardent nationalist who supported Britain's "world wide empire" (*CW* 2:928; see also *CW* 2:773, 783, 785, 863).
10. As an undergraduate, he first read about Hinduism and Buddhism in Max Müller's *Chips from a German Workshop;* see Hopkins, *Oxford Essays and Notes,* ed. Lesley Higgins (Oxford: Oxford University Press, 2006), 295-99. Hereafter cited as *CW* 4. For remarks to Baillie about "the history of heathen religions," see *CW* 2:761.
11. Hopkins comments on Spanish "exiled novices" in a letter to his mother 5 Feb. 1869: "To be persecuted in a tolerant age is a high distinction" (*CW* 1:190).
12. The 1829 Catholic Relief (or Catholic Emancipation) Act offered freedom from basic discrimination and civil disabilities; see chap. 2. Jesuits, however, were "required to register with the justices of the peace." Diana Peschier, "Vulnerable Women and the Danger of Gliding Jesuits: England in the Nineteenth Century," *Women's Writing* 11.2 (2004), 284. These were the strictures that required Hopkins and other Jesuits to write out their vows rather than profess them publicly (see *CW* 5:140-43).
13. A term Fr. Hopkins uses in his sermons; see, for example, Nov. 1879 (*CW* 5:233).
14. Blougram may have been based on Nicholas Wiseman, the Roman Catholic cardinal who in 1850 became the first archbishop of Westminster; see F. E. L. Priestly, "Blougram's Apologetics," *University of Toronto Quarterly* 15.2 (January 1946): 139-47, and Robert Laird, "'He Did Not Sit Five Minutes': The Conversion of Gigadibs," *University of Toronto Quarterly* 45.4 (Summer 1976): 295-313.
15. As the painter Edward Burne-Jones observes of Newman: "In an age of materialism he taught me to venture all on the unseen." Qtd. in David Corbett, *Edward Burne-Jones* (London: Tate Publications, 2004), 12-13.
16. Jean-Joseph Gaume (1802-79), a theologian and author, published the *Manuel des confesseurs* in 1843; Pusey translated it into English and edited it to help the Tractarian cause (see chap. 2). Gaume, *Advice for Those Who Exercise the Ministry of Reconciliation through Confession and Absolution, Being the Abbé Gaume's Manual for Confessors or His Extracts from the Works of S. Francis de Sales, Charles Borromeo, S. Philip de Neri, S. Francis Xavier, and Other Spiritual Writers,* abridged, 2nd ed., ed. and trans. Edward Pusey (Oxford: James Parker, 1878), 254. Hereafter cited as Gaume.
17. Pusey, preface to *The Confessions of St. Augustine,* trans. E. B. Pusey (London: Dent and Sons, 1907), xix.

18. In the guide for novices written by Hopkins's Jesuit peer John Morris, S.J., one learns that "your Guardian Angel is going with you to the refectory, where he will be by your side, a witness of how you behave"; when examining one's conscience, "ask yourself... what your Guardian Angel thought." Morris, S.J., *Daily Duties: An Instruction for Novices of the Society* (London: Manresa Press, 1889), 19, 36 (see also 55, 60).
19. The doctrine of the immaculate conception became Roman Catholic dogma in 1854 (Pius IX, *Ineffabilis Deus*). Stanza 30 of "The Wreck" is devoted to Mary; Marian adulation is the focus of seven poems: "*O praedestinata bis*," "*Ad Mariam, Ad Matrem*," "*Rosa Mystica*," "The May Magnificat," "*Angelus*," and "Blessed Virgin compared." See also Hopkins's poem "Duns Scotus' Oxford." For a cultural history, see Marina Warner, *Alone of All Her Sex: The Myth and Cult of the Virgin Mary* (Oxford: Oxford University Press, 1976).
20. Ignatius Loyola, *The Spiritual Exercises*, 2nd ed., ed. and trans. by Joseph Rickaby, S.J. (New York: Benziger Brothers, 1923), 228. Hereafter cited as *SE*. This is "the most famous of all these Rules," according to Rickaby (*SE* 228). Rickaby (1845–1932), one of the "Stonyhurst Philosophers," was one of Hopkins's friends in the Society; they were ordained the same day.
21. In version C of the manuscript, the phrase is "Truth himself speaks truly, or there's nothing true" (*PW* 113).
22. Letter to Henry Liddon, 7 Nov. 1866; *CW* 1:128.
23. Michel Foucault, *The History of Sexuality*, vol. 1: *An Introduction [The Will to Know]*, trans. Robert Hurley (New York: Vintage Books, 1990), 59. Hereafter cited as *HS* 1.
24. For "women's confessional modes" in novels such as *Villette*, *Lady Audley's Secret*, and *Tess of the d'Urbervilles*, see Susan David Bernstein; and Patrick R. O'Malley, *Catholicism, Sexual Deviance, and Victorian Gothic Culture* (Cambridge: Cambridge University Press, 2006).
25. I am also indebted to E. A. Livingstone et al., *Oxford Concise Dictionary of the Christian Church*, 3rd ed. (Oxford: Oxford University Press, 2013).
26. Edward Pusey, *The Minor Prophets, with a Commentary Explanatory and Practical*, 2 vols. (New York: Funk and Wagnalls, 1885), 1:194.
27. Foucault, *Wrong-Doing, Truth-Telling: The Function of Avowal in Justice*, ed. Fabienne Brion and Bernard E. Harcourt, trans. Stephen W. Sawyer (Chicago: University of Chicago Press, 2014). Hereafter cited as *WDTT*.
28. As Dubois cautions, however, too often "we expect the faith of his poems to be somehow perfect, regularizing what may be strange or contingent in their meaning" (16).
29. E. R. Norman, *Anti-Catholicism in Victorian England* (New York: Barnes and Noble, 1968); Susan Budd, *Varieties of Unbelief* (New York: Holmes and Meier, 1977); A. N. Wilson, *God's Funeral* (New York: Ballantine Books, 1999); Susan

M. Griffin, *Anti-Catholicism and Nineteenth-Century Fiction* (Cambridge: Cambridge University Press, 2004); Derek J. Holmes, *More Roman than Rome: English Catholicism in the Nineteenth Century* (London: Burns and Oates, 1978); Patrick Allitt, *Catholic Converts* (Ithaca, NY: Cornell University Press, 2000); Susan David Bernstein, *Confessional Subjects: Revelations of Gender and Power in Victorian Literature and Culture* (Chapel Hill: University of North Carolina Press, 1997); Chloë Taylor, *The Culture of Confession from Augustine to Foucault: A Genealogy of the "Confessing Animal"* (New York: Routledge, 2009); James Eli Adams, *Dandies and Desert Saints: Styles of Victorian Masculinity* (Ithaca, NY: Cornell University Press, 1995); Oliver Buckton, *Secret Selves: Confession and Same-Sex Desire in Victorian Autobiography* (Chapel Hill: University of North Carolina Press, 1998); Herbert Sussman, *Victorian Masculinities: Manhood and Masculine Poetics in Early Victorian Literature and Art* (Cambridge: Cambridge University Press, 1995); Julia Saville, *A Queer Chivalry: The Homoerotic Asceticism of Gerard Manley Hopkins* (Charlottesville: University Press of Virginia, 2000); Eve Kosofsky Sedgwick, *Between Men: English Literature and Male Homosocial Desire* (New York: Columbia University Press, 1985); Maureen Moran, *Catholic Sensationalism and Victorian Literature* (Liverpool: Liverpool University Press, 2007).

30. Foucault insists that ancient Greek society should not serve as a model: "It is a morality for men: a morality thought, written, taught, by men and addressed to men, obviously free men. Virile morality, therefore, in which women appeared only as objects." Foucault, *The History of Sexuality,* vol. 2: *The Use of Pleasure,* trans. Robert Hurley (New York: Vintage Books, 1985), 22. Hereafter cited as *HS* 2. In the more informal context of a *Vanity Fair* interview, he declares, "The Greek ethics of pleasure is linked to a virile society, to nonsymmetry, exclusion of the other, an obsession with penetration, and a kind of threat of being dispossessed of your own energy, and so on. All that is quite disgusting!" Foucault, "How We Behave. Interview with Paul Rabinow and Hubert L. Dreyfus," *Vanity Fair* (Nov. 1983), 63.

31. "Other methods will suggest themselves," he explains to Alexander Baillie, 28–29 Apr. 1886 (*CW* 2:778).

32. Foucault, *Power/Knowledge: Selected Interviews and Other Writings, 1972–1977,* ed. Colin Gordon, trans. Colin Gordon, Leo Marshall, John Mepham, Kate Soper (New York: Harvester Wheatsheaf, 1980), 92, 93. Hereafter cited as *P/K*.

33. The original back cover of *The History of Sexuality,* vol. 1, names the other volumes planned: *The Children's Crusade; The Wife, the Mother, and the Hysteric; The Perverts;* and *Population and Races.*

34. Readers of the English volumes in *The History of Sexuality* are disadvantaged by the translator's choices. Vol. 1, in French, is titled *The Will to Know* (*La Volonté de savoir*); in English, merely *An Introduction.* Vol. 2, in French, acknowledges multiplicity: *L'Usage des plaisirs;* in English, it is only *The Use of Pleasure.* The title

of vol. 3 in English, *The Care of the Self,* seems to endorse liberal-humanist categories; in French, *Le Souci de soi* uses the impersonal, grammatical construct, *soi.*

35. Stuart Elden, "Review: Michel Foucault, *Histoire de la sexualité 4: Les aveux de la chair,*" *Theory, Culture, and Society* 35.7-8 (2018), 293. Elden provides a concise history of the volume's textual development.

36. According to Gros, the published volume is a posthumous editorial construct, based on the manuscript and a corrected typescript. Frédéric Gros, "Foreword," in Michel Foucault, *Confessions of the Flesh,* trans. Robert Hurley (New York: Pantheon Books, 2021), xi.

37. Thus, criticism published prior to 2018 or 2021 is based on brief observations in vol. 1 of the *History of Sexuality;* in *Abnormal: Lectures at the Collège de France, 1974-1975;* and in the 1979 Tanner lecture "Omnes et Singulatim." Huffer considers *Confessions of the Flesh* to be a failure; Harcourt deems it the "completion" of Foucault's intellectual projects. Lynn Huffer, "Foucault's Queer Virgins: An Unfinished History in Fragments," *Foucault Studies* 29.1-5 (Apr. 2021), 22-37; Bernard Harcourt, "Foucault's Keystone: *Confessions of the Flesh,*" *Foucault Studies* 29.1-5 (Apr. 2021), 48-70.

38. Sexuality is "the crucial field of operation" for biopolitics because it involves both "the individual and the social bodies." James Bernauer, S.J., and Michael Mahon, "The Ethics of Michel Foucault," in Gary Gutting, ed., *The Cambridge Companion to Foucault* (Cambridge: Cambridge University Press, 1994), 143-44. They are quoting *HS* 1:143.

39. Foucault, *The History of Sexuality,* vol. 4: *Confessions of the Flesh,* trans. Robert Hurley (New York: Pantheon Books, 2021), 7. Hereafter cited as *HS* 4.

40. Foucault, "Security, Territory, Population," in *Ethics, Subjectivity, Truth,* vol. 1, *The Essential Works of Michel Foucault,* 3 vols., ed. Paul Rabinow (New York: New Press, 1997), 1:68. Hereafter cited as *EWF.*

41. Other dimensions of truth-telling are explored by Foucault in his studies of *parrhēsia* ("fearless speech") and in *Wrong-Doing, Truth-Telling.*

42. Clinton Machann, "The Construction of Masculinity in Victorian Autobiography," *Nineteenth-Century Prose* 26.2 (Fall 1999), 11; James Eli Adams, *Dandies and Desert Saints: Styles of Victorian Masculinity* (Ithaca, NY: Cornell University Press, 1995), 3.

43. For his musical setting of the poem, see *CW* 2:952.

44. Overholser follows Linda Colley in suggesting the "importance of the Protestant providential narrative—that God directs his nation, and protects it from its enemies—in forming England's national identity." Renée Overholser, "'Our King Back, Oh, upon English Souls!': Swinburne, Hopkins, and the Politics of Religion," *Religion and the Arts* 5.1-2 (2001), 81.

45. Newman's nine lectures (and subsequent volume) are a response to the public outcry generated by the 1850 "papal aggression"; see appendix A and chap. 2.

46. *Spectata fides:* Leo XIII to the English bishops, dated 27 Nov. 1885: "We love with a paternal charity that island, which was not undeservedly called the Mother of Saints, and we see in the disposition of mind of which we have spoken [fidelity to "the ancient faith"] the greatest hope and as it were a pledge, of the welfare and prosperity of the British people" (*CW* 2:756, n3).
47. Hopkins was born in 1844; Heinrich Kaan's *Psychopathia Sexualis* (1846) catalyzed the "the opening up of the great medico-psychological domain of the 'perversions,' which was destined to take over form the old moral categories of debauchery and excess" (*HS* 1:118).
48. Jowett once referred to Liddon as an "Anglican perverter." Benjamin Jowett, *Dear Miss Nightingale: A Selection of Benjamin Jowett's Letters to Florence Nightingale,* eds. Vincent Quinn and John Prest (Oxford: Clarendon Press, 1987), 51. See also O'Malley, *Catholicism,* 91.
49. Foucault, "Different Spaces" (*EWF* 2:179).
50. Inscape defines or captures the "individually-distinctive" (*CW* 1:334) or innermost pattern or design of a thing (whether a tree, flower, sonnet, or human form); instress refers to the force emanating from the object that the sensitive viewer can apprehend. Inscape is ontological, what William Blake terms the "inmost form" ("The Crystal Cabinet"); instress, epistemological, the charged relations between perceiver and perceived. See *CW* 4:169, 300, 311 ff. See also Atti Virag, "The Grammar of Instress: Gerard Manley Hopkins and the Victorian Philosophers of Mind," *New Literary History* 51 (2020), 501–22.
51. In his 1977–78 lectures, Foucault puts aside notions of "dissidence" or "resistance" to explore how "counter-conduct" modifies "force relations between individuals." Foucault, *Security, Territory, Population: Lectures at the Collège de France, 1977–1978,* trans. Graham Burchell (London: Palgrave Macmillan, 2007). Hereafter cited as *STP.* See Arnold Davidson, "In Praise of Counter-conduct," *History of the Human Sciences* 24.4 (2011), 25–41.
52. Swinburne, however, is always faulted for his immorality, the "extreme cases" of his subject matter "in their own kind" (*CW* 1:157).

I. HISTORICAL INVESTMENTS

1. Michel Foucault, *Abnormal: Lectures at the Collège de France, 1974–1975,* ed. Valerio Marchetti and Antonella Salomin, trans. Graham Burchill (New York: Picador, 1999), 174. Hereafter cited as *Ab.*
2. William Addis (1844–1917) and Hopkins met at Balliol in April 1863; they were roommates while living out of college in spring 1866. Addis converted to Catholicism two weeks before Hopkins; they were confirmed the same day (Addis's father, a Church of Scotland minister, disowned him). Addis was ordained a priest in 1872 but renounced Catholicism in 1888 (see *CW*

1:lxxxii–lxxxiii). Tom Arnold (1823–1900), an English literature scholar, the son of Thomas Arnold ("of Rugby"), younger brother of Matthew, and father of novelist Mary ("Mrs. Humphry") Ward, was well known for his serial conversion crises; he and Hopkins were colleagues at University College in Dublin from 1884 to 1889.

3. *Confiteor* (Latin for "I confess") is the first word of the prayer typically declaimed as a penitential exercise during the Roman rite of the Mass and recited during the sacrament of penance. The text remained largely unchanged in the Tridentine Roman Missal (written by members of the Council of Trent, 1545–63) from 1570 to 1962: "I confess to God and to blessed Mary ever-Virgin, to blessed Michael the Archangel and blessed John the Baptist and to the holy apostles Peter and Paul and to blessed Leutherius and Cassian and blessed Juvenal along with all the saints and you Father: through my fault (*thrice*) I have sinned by pride in my abundant, evil, iniquitous, and heinous thought, speech, pollution, suggestion, delectation, consent, word and deed, in perjury, adultery, sacrilege, murder, theft, false witness, I have sinned by sight, hearing, taste, smell and touch, and in my behaviour, my evil vices. I beg blessed Mary ever-Virgin and all the saints and these saints and you, Father, to pray and intercede for me a sinner to our Lord Jesus Christ." Adrian Fortescue, "Confiteor," *The Catholic Encyclopedia,* vol. 4 (New York: Robert Appleton, 1908), http://www.newadvent.org/cathen/04222a.htm.

4. See also R. G. Davis, *Catechism for First Confession* (London: R. Washbourne, 1878).

5. For Newman's account of penitents "crowding for admission" at the confessional, treating the experience like an "errand," and the priest who might have "on his face a look almost of impatience … at the voluble and superfluous matter which is the staple of" someone's confession, see *Certain Difficulties* 2:284–85.

6. Brett Beasley, "Acting Christ: The Christocentric Exemplarism of Gerard Manley Hopkins," *Literature and Theology* 34.2 (June 2020): 239 (my emphasis). Beasley's argument is based on that of Linda Zagzebski, *Exemplarist Moral Theory* (New York: Oxford University Press, 2017).

7. *Summa Theologica* 1a, question 79, a. 13; qtd. Robert H. Dailey, S.J., *Introduction to Moral Theology* (New York: Bruce Publishing, 1970), 82.

8. Hopkins admires the "justice and candour and gravity and rightness of mind" in all of Newman's writings, but faults *Grammar* for "a narrow circle of instance and quotation" (Aug. 1873; *CW* 1:226). Nonetheless, in 1883 he asked Newman's permission to write a commentary on the *Grammar,* but Newman declined (see *CW* 2:571, 575).

9. *The Raccolta: or, Collection of Indulged Prayers,* trans. Ambrose St. John (London: Burns and Lambert, 1857), 34, https://en.wikisource.org/wiki/The_Raccolta_(1857).

10. Mary had "neither the guilt nor yet ~~the~~ concupiscence, the worst effect, of original sin," Hopkins declares in his Bedford Leigh sermon, 5 Dec. 1879 (*CW* 5:239).
11. For Hopkins's discussion of guilt in relation to the will (and the Ignatian *De Cogitatione*), see *CW* 5:372-76. The metaphor of "coming home" used in the 1880 meditation echoes "The Candle Indoors" (Oxford, 1879): "Come you indoors, come home."
12. "We are conscious of sin when we knowingly and freely do something which we recognize to be against our conscience (commission), or omit to do something which conscience tells us we ought to do (omission)." Robert H. Dailey, S.J., *Introduction to Moral Theology* (New York: Bruce Publishing Company, 1970), 141.
13. William Addis and Thomas Arnold, *A Catholic Dictionary, Containing Some Account of the Doctrine, Discipline, Rites, Ceremonies, Councils, and Religious Orders of the Catholic Church* (London: Kegan Paul, 1884), 647. Evagrius Ponticus, one of the ultra-ascetic "Desert Fathers" (345-99 CE), suggested that there are seven or eight major sins; his pupil, John Cassian, codified the seven "cardinal" sins (envy, gluttony, greed, lust, pride, sloth, and wrath) in *The Institutes*.
14. For further discussion of these "truth obligations," see James Bernauer, S.J., "Confessions of the soul: Foucault and Theological Culture," *Philosophy and Social Criticism* 31.5-6 (2005), 557-72.
15. In a letter to Baillie, 10-13 July 1863, Hopkins encourages him to "see the force of the metaphor" (*CW* 1:43).
16. The Mass has two parts: the liturgy of the Word, culminating in the homily, and the Eucharistic liturgy, whereby the priest transubstantiates wafer and wine into the body and blood of Christ. To prepare for holy communion, the congregation recites the prayer known as *Agnes Dei* ("Lamb of God"), reaffirming John the Baptist's address to Christ (John 1:29).
17. The catechism approved by the Council of Trent and promulgated in 1566 advises "how diligent priests must be in explaining the sacrament [of penance], and refers to God as the good pastor binding the wounds of his sheep and healing them with the medicine of penance. Later the priest is portrayed as a presiding judge, to whom the case must be shown." John Mahoney, S.J., *The Making of Moral Theology: A Study of the Roman Catholic Tradition* (Oxford: Clarendon Press, 1987), 24.
18. Medical discourse was weaponized by opponents to Anglican auricular confession. An 1867 lecturer declared that the confessional is "'a moral malaria,—a cauldron from which pestiferous clouds daily ascend, which kill the very souls of men.'" [Church Association], *Church Association Lectures: Delivered at St. James' Hall, Piccadilly, London* (London: William MacIntosh, 1867), IV: 12.
19. The speaker of "The beginning of the end," also from May 1865, confesses that "I am so consumèd with my shame" (*PW* 75).

20. For Hopkins's translation of Chrysostom's sermon on the Fall of Eutropius, see *CW* 5:580–83.
21. As I discuss below, what worked for Seneca was also part of Ignatian training: before bedtime, Jesuits adumbrate their prayer notes for the next day. For Hopkins's preparatory notes while living in Dublin, see *CW* 7.
22. In a July 1879 sermon, Hopkins suggests that "anger, shame, fear, interest, suspense ... all tell that something we prize, something important to us is at stake" (*CW* 5:179).
23. For Hopkins's notes on Cassian, see *CW* 5:521.
24. See John Bossy, "The Social History of Confession in the Age of the Reformation," *Transactions of the Royal Historical Society* 25 (1975): 22–23.
25. The Fourth Lateran Council also "affirmed that there was no salvation outside the Church; condemned various heretics; approved the term 'transubstantiation'; founded what was to become the Inquisition; forbade the founding of any further religious orders; [and] appealed for a Crusade against Islam" (Mahoney, S.J. 17).
26. Augustine, *Confessions,* trans. Henry Chadwick (Oxford: Oxford University Press, 1991), 15. Hereafter cited as *Confs*. Keble also believed children need "Early Encouragements" for self-examination and praises the moment "When bosoms with confession heave." See John Keble, *Lyra Innocentium: Thoughts in Verse on Christian Children, Their Ways, and Their Privileges* (Oxford: John Henry and James Parker, 1861), 167. Shame is mentioned sixteen times in the volume.
27. Mahoney, S.J., observes that Ignatius "recommended his followers to have a high regard in their ministry for the hearing of confessions[,] ... and he required all priests of the Society of Jesus to have at least sufficient learning and experience of cases of conscience to make them good confessors, seeing in the popular practice of confession not only one of the greatest pastoral aids to the salvation and perfection of souls but also ... one of the most serious pastoral weaknesses of the Church of his day" (26).
28. See also Catherine Rider, "Lay Religion and Pastoral Care in Thirteenth Century England: The Evidence of a Group of Short Confession Manuals," *Journal of Medieval History* 36 (2010): 327–40.
29. For the Psalms, however, Hopkins's base text would be the Book of Common Prayer, with the translation by Miles Coverdale (following William Tyndall).
30. In D-R 142:9, the phrase is "O Lord, to thee have I fled"; in KJV 143:9, the present tense is featured: "I flee unto thee to hide me."
31. "Let me confess what I know of myself" is Augustine's guiding principle (*Confs* 182).
32. "The sudden increase in translations of the *Confessions* during the nineteenth century is only one indication of the romantics' interest in Augustine. In England, the same translation served from 1670 until 1807; then, seven new

translations appeared in the three years from 1807 to 1810." Susan M. Levin, *The Romantic Art of Confession: DeQuincey, Musset, Sand, Lamb, Hogg, Frémy, Soulié, Janin* (Columbia, SC: Cambden House, 1998), 3.

33. Some translations omit the biblical references; Chadwick embeds them.
34. "You therefore command me to praise you for that [creating "a living being"] and to 'confess to you and to sing your name, Most High' (Ps. 91:2)" (*Confs* 100). See also 10, 72, 248.
35. "And why do I include this episode?," Augustine asks in book 2. "It is that I and any of my readers may reflect on the great depth from which we have to cry to you (Ps. 129:1). Nothing is nearer to your ears than a confessing heart and a life grounded in faith" (*Confs* 26).
36. In Chloë Taylor's succinct phrase, "Having looked in for nine books, Augustine then looks up in the last four" (29). Augustine's conversion is the narrative high point, but not the emotional climax—that is reserved for the death of his mother, Monica (*Confs* 176-78).
37. The conversion scene is an excellent example of narrative flair and sacred tradition. Augustine retreats to a garden in Milan, the better to understand how "in the agony of death I was coming to life. I was aware how ill I was, unaware of how well I was soon to be" (*Confs* 146). The heterotopic location echoes both the garden of Eden (site of Adam and Eve's sinful actions) and the garden of Gethsemane (Christ's redemptive actions). In all three, a struggle of will is enacted (see *Confs* 146, Gen. 3, Matt. 26:31).
38. Hopkins's alternate phrase: "not man's fathoming" (*PW* 182).
39. Augustine recognizes the machinations of Satan, identified as "the Enemy" (see *Confs* 214), but stresses human culpability at every turn.
40. In *Confessions of the Flesh*, Foucault positions Augustine "at the end of a long tradition" of self-examination and investigates his teachings on virginity, chastity, and marriage.
41. St. Patrick's *Confession* is found in the Book of Armagh (Cotton MS Nero E.I.). I am quoting from the Celtic Literature Collective's online edition, which divides the text into paragraphs (denoted by ¶). See https://www.ancienttexts.org/library/celtic/ctexts/p01.html.
42. Hopkins discusses the fame/obscurity antinomy several times, but see especially his letter to Dixon, 13-15 June 1878 (*CW* 1:304-6).
43. "But I have long been Fortune's football," Hopkins informs Bridges 5-6 Aug. 1883; "I shall be sorry to leave Stonyhurst; but go or stay, there is no likelihood of my ever doing anything to last" (*CW* 2:584).
44. *Everyman and Medieval Miracle Plays*, ed. A. C. Cawley (London: J. M. Dent, 1993), 199. Hereafter cited as *Everyman*.
45. My emphasis. I will return to these words in the conclusion.
46. Thomas Pollock Oakley, *English Penitential Discipline and Anglo-Saxon Law in Their Joint Influence* (New York: Columbia University Press, 1923), 43.

47. Public penance, ranging from rigorous fasts, prostration, alms, prayers, and pilgrimages, "was required particularly for publicly known sins of a heinous character: chiefly homicide, rape, usury, fornication, adultery, perjury[,] ... arson, robbery, soothsaying, magic" (Oakley 45).
48. Unlike Augustine and many Renaissance Catholic theologians, Gaume tried to exclude ancient authors from works of religious formation; paganism, he claimed, was dangerous. Fierce opposition ensued; a compromise was reached among French religious leaders, but Gaume insisted that ancient texts should be carefully redacted or expurgated and taught circumspectly. "Jean-Joseph Gaume," *Catholic Encyclopedia,* http://www.newadvent.org/cathen/06398b.htm.
49. For Hopkins's comments on St. Teresa's writings, see *CW* 5:415 and *Diaries, Journals, and Notebooks,* ed. Lesley Higgins (Oxford: Oxford University Press, 2015), 562-63. Hereafter *CW* 3.
50. Rickaby, S.J., discusses Christ in "His office of Consoler" in relation to the Fourth Week of the Exercises, "Resurrection" (*SE* 200).
51. Prov. 28:14.
52. In his forties, Hopkins succumbed to feelings of distress and dread beyond his spiritual experiences: "For indeed it seems a spirit of fear I live by" (*CW* 7:138, 140). He also experienced an advanced state of otherness as an English convert in Ireland. As Griffin suggests, "The 'Otherness' of Catholicism is especially fearful because it awakens something alien within the British themselves" (*Anti-Catholicism* 133).
53. Gaume recommends that children be introduced to the sacrament at age seven (159).
54. All three are crucial in "trying" one's beliefs. In his Dominical or practice sermon while studying at St. Beuno's (11 Mar. 1877), Hopkins discusses the miracle of the loaves and fishes: Christ commissions Philip to find more provisions "to try him—to try his patience, his charity, humility, obedience; to try his faith" (*CW* 5:157).
55. For Foucault's analysis of the role of obedience in monasticism, see *WDTT* 134-37.
56. The "gift" of obedience is also explored in the sermons "Self-Denial the Test of Religious Earnestness" and "Secret Faults." Newman's conversion was the greatest act of disobedience to the Church of England.
57. See Dan Lyons, "Plato's Attempt to Moralize Shame," *Philosophy* 86.337 (July 2011), 353-74.
58. See *HS* 2:168-69; for a discussion of Cassian's use of shame, *HS* 4:106.
59. See also *Confs* 19, 21, 27, 29, 46, 52, 109, 111.
60. Hopkins's friendship with Patmore began in summer 1883; see *CW* 2.
61. For Foucault's complementary comments on shame, see *Ab* 173, *HS* 2:204, and *WDTT* 184 ff. See also Owen Flanagan, *How to Do Things with Emotions: The Moral of Anger and Shame across Cultures* (Princeton, NJ: Princeton University Press, 2021).

62. For Alcuin, see *Ab* 173. Cardinal Wiseman quotes Origen regarding the blushing sinner in "Lecture the Tenth. On the Sacrament of Penance. Part II," *Catholic Standard and Times* 5.33 (24 Aug. 1837), Catholic Research Resources Alliance, http://thecatholicnewsarchive.org.
63. According to Sedgwick, "The entire world [cannot] be divided between (supposedly primitive) 'shame cultures' and (supposedly evolved) 'guilt cultures,' but rather . . . as an affect, shame is a component (and differently a component) of all." Eve Kosofsky Sedgwick, *Touching Feeling: Affect, Pedagogy, Performativity* (Durham, NC: Duke University Press, 2003), 62.
64. In 1878, however, Bridges reported to their mutual friend Lionel Muirhead that he visited Hopkins at the Farm Street church in London: "He is not at all the worse for being a Jesuit; as far as one can judge without knowing what he would have been otherwise" (qtd. *CW* 1:lix–lx).
65. The information is provided by Liddon's diary, not Hopkins's.
66. Hopkins may have kept the lists for Feb. 1864 to Feb. 1865 in a separate "[l]ittle bk. for sins" (*CW* 3:291).
67. Catholics could not enroll at Oxford because all students had to subscribe to the "39 Articles" of the Anglican faith. (These "tests" were withdrawn in 1871.) The life of an Oxford "papist" could be fraught. Hopkins and fellow convert Alexander Wood attended Mass at "the chapel of St. Ignatius in a house in St. Clements" (Alfred Thomas, S.J., *Hopkins the Jesuit: The Years of Training* [London: Oxford University Press, 1969], 14). "There was only one Mass at half-past ten, and so it was an easy matter for the University authorities to ascertain whether any of those *in statu pupillari* were being beguiled by the Scarlet Woman. One morning when [Hopkins and Wood] were leaving the chapel they were accosted by the 'bulldogs' and had their names taken, being given an appointment with the Junior Proctor for 9.15 the next morning. At this they were fined for their breach of University discipline" (Joseph Crehan, S.J., "More Light on Gerard Hopkins," *The Month*, n.s., 10.4 [Oct. 1953]: 210).
68. Liddon's diaries, now housed in Pusey House, Oxford, demonstrate that he practiced self-examination faithfully. They also show how carefully he targeted Balliol students because he was suspicious about Jowett's liberal-mindedness. Pusey, in his introduction to Gaume's manual, quotes John Keble on the subject of writing down one's sins (Preface, cxlvi); see chap. 2, note 6.
69. For ease of reading and quoting, I have removed the thin, dark cancellation lines in these diary entries. See *CW* 3 for their full visual impact, and fig. 1 (chap. 1, p. 71).
70. Letter to Baillie, 24 Apr.–17 May 1885; *CW* 2:729.
71. Gaume advises confessors to "ask children, 1) if they have nourished hatred towards their parents . . . ; 2) if they have disobeyed them in serious and just matters" (131).

72. The anonymous pamphlet is reproduced in *EPM*, 204-6. Hereafter cited as *Questions*.
73. Faber warns against "morbid" and "perpetual hankering after our past confessions, a wish to rake them up and overhaul them, and see if we cannot find matter for some choice scruple in them.... a delightful misery, a wretchedness in which a scrupulous spirit revels." Frederick Faber, *Growth in Holiness; or, The Progress of the Spiritual Life* (Baltimore, MD: John Murphy, 1855), 248.
74. The diaries and other papers passed through several Jesuit hands from 1889 until the 1950s (poetic manuscripts and related papers were sent to Bridges, who destroyed materials he thought irrelevant). By 1906, most of the personal journals were in the safekeeping of Joseph Keating, S.J., assistant editor of the Jesuit journal *Month*, who organized publication of the nature-related entries and assisted the group of peers preparing, for the *Dublin Review*, a biographical essay and brief journal selections (1920). The first major publication of journal entries occurred in Oct. 1935, when the *Criterion*, edited by T. S. Eliot, featured seventeen pages of extracts. Two years later, Humphry House published, with Keating's support, *The Note-Books and Papers of Gerard Manley Hopkins*, and subsequently the *Journals and Papers* (1959). Not once, in any of these publications, were the entries related to his "sins" included. The rationale that was repeated, until the 2010s, was that the lists were covered by the "seal" of the confessional—but Hopkins was an Anglican when he made them, so his penitential activities were not sacramental. Anthony Bischoff, S.J., admitted the reason for some people's hesitancy to print or discuss the 1865-66 diaries: "Quoted out of context such passages might indicate that at this time Hopkins was homosexual; in context, however, they prove quite the contrary." Actually, they do not. Bischoff, "The Manuscripts of Gerard Manley Hopkins," *Thought* 26.102 (Sept. 1951): 567.
75. Thomas Carter, *The Freedom of Confession in the Church of England: A Letter to His Grace the Lord Archbishop of Canterbury* (Oxford: Rivingtons, 1877), n.p. http://anglicanhistory.org/england/ttcarter/freedom.html.
76. In a letter to Rev. Edward Urquhart, 31 Dec. 1867, he observes, "I am glad you go to confession although there is nothing of a Sacrament in the ordinance as you use it, but still it has its value ex opere operantis [from the work of the agent] and in some cases the shadow of Peter may cure where the touch of Peter is not to be had" (*CW* 1:169).
77. In the nineteenth century, "mission" work was local as well as international; Protestant and Catholic preachers drew large crowds. For Hopkins's Maryport mission, see *CW* 5:23.

2. VICTORIAN CONFESSIONAL CRISES

1. See the chronology in the appendix.
2. See also Robert Klaus, *The Pope, the Protestants, and the Irish* (New York: Garland, 1987), 216–17.
3. To read the entire act, see *The Statutes at Large, from Magna Carta to the End of the Eleventh Parliament of Great Britain, Anno 1761, Continued*, vol. 37 (Cambridge: John Archdeacon, 1790); Google Books. Titles of previous legislation were even more disparaging: the 1698 Popery Act and the Papists Act of 1778.
4. An Act for the Relief of His Majesty's Roman Catholic Subjects. See https://books.google.ca/books?id=wZY3AAAAMAAJ&pg=PA49&redir_esc=y#v=onepage&q&f=false.
5. In all, nine sections of the Act (sec. 28–36) refer directly or indirectly to Jesuits.
6. The *Times* of London responded, "If this appointment be not intended as a clumsy joke, we confess we can only regard it as one of the grossest acts of folly and impertinence which the court of Rome has ventured to commit since the crown and people of England threw off its yoke" (qtd. Griffin, *Anti-Catholicism*, 116–17).
7. In terms of aesthetic appreciation and cultural awareness, consult the comprehensive study by Mrs. [Anna] Jameson, *Legends of the Madonna as Represented in the Fine Arts* (1852), beautifully illustrated with etchings and woodcuts. Hopkins was familiar with Jameson's art criticism and her Shakespeare studies (see *CW* 1:46).
8. "Julia Kristeva has suggested in 'Stabat Mater' that Pius IX declared the Immaculate Conception in order to counter contemporary gender disequilibrium. Yet, this strategic elevation of a woman by a priest was not perceived at the time as a conservative attempt to keep women and men in their places" (Griffin, *Anti-Catholicism* 117).
9. The *Syllabus* was published the same year as Newman's *Apologia pro Vita Sua*. For Newman's response to the document, see "The Syllabus" in *Certain Difficulties Felt by Anglicans*, vol. 2 (1874); reprinted in *The Newman Reader*: https://www.newmanreader.org/works/.
10. St. Patrick's College, Maynooth, the national seminary for Ireland and a pontifical university, was established in 1795. At one time, it was the world's largest seminary.
11. The author is one of several British writers railing against Flemish Catholic theologian Pieter Dens (1690–1775) and the 1836 publication of *Dens' Theology: Extracts from Peter Dens on the Nature of Confession and the Obligation of the Seal* (Dublin: O'Neill, 1836). See chap. 2, p. 94.
12. See John Wolffe, "Stowell, Hugh," *Oxford Dictionary of National Biography*, online.
13. See Denis G. Paz, *Popular Anti-Catholicism in Mid-Victorian England* (Stanford, CA: Stanford University Press, 1992), 33.

14. *The Oxford and Roman Railway* suggests that Jesuits' "infamous treachery" includes entering the homes of wealthy families, under the pretext of being tutors, and corrupting their charges (92). See Peschier 283.
15. William Ullathorne (1806–89), a recusant Catholic, was appointed bishop in 1850. Together with Newman, Manning, and Wiseman, he was one of the major figures in Victorian Catholicism. Hopkins mentions the bishop's "good" answer to Gladstone's "*Expostulation* with Catholics upon the Vatican decrees and syllabus" in his journal, 1875 (*CW* 3:610).
16. According to Zaniello, Jesuits and Oratorians were the "two groups that rankled anti-Catholics the most, the former because of their supposed stealth methods of recruitment . . . [and] the latter because of Cardinal Newman's leadership." Tom Zaniello, *Saints and Sinners in Queen Victoria's Courts: Ten Scandalous Trials* (Jefferson, NC: McFarland, 2021), 11.
17. Familiarity with Taylor's *Golden Grove; or, A Manuall of Daily Prayers and Litanies* (1655) may have contributed to the opening lines of Hopkins's "Spring and Fall": "Márgarét, áre you gríeving / Over Goldengrove unleaving" (*PW* 166).
18. *A Peep behind the Curtain; or, An Exposure of the Popish Confessional, Furnished by Popish Writers* (London: Partridge, 1859).
19. Wai Chee Dimock, *Through Other Continents: American Literature across Deep Time* (Princeton, NJ: Princeton University Press, 2006).
20. Chiniquy, already cited for his conspiracy theory about Jesuits and Lincoln's assassination, pays homage to Michelet in the title of his study. Chiniquy states that he left the priesthood because the confessional, "really the cornerstone" of priests' "stupendous power; it is the secret of their almost irresistible influence," is also "one of the most stupendous impostures which Satan has invented." Charles Chiniquy, *The Priest, the Woman, and the Confessional* (New York: Fleming H. Revell Company, 1880), 77.
21. *The Confessional, and the Conventual System: Extracted from Michelet's "Priests, Women, and Families"* (London: Seeleys, 1850). The original book was enjoying its eighth edition in 1870.
22. For similar indignation, see H. J. Brockman, *Letter to the Women of England: On the Confessional* (London: Protestant Electoral Union, 1867), in which Brockman declares, "I know not another reptile in all animal nature so filthy, so much to be shunned and loathed, and *dreaded by females,* both married and single, as a Roman Catholic Priest . . . who practices the degrading and demoralizing office of Auricular Confession" (2).
23. Page 175; qtd. in Paz 55.
24. See Eleanor McNees, "*Punch* and the Pope: Three Decades of Anti-Catholic Caricature," *Victorian Periodicals Review* 37.1 (Spring 2004): 18–45.
25. "Expectations from Rome," *Punch,* 9 Nov. 1850, 193.

26. See also "The Kidnapper.—A Case for the Police," *Punch*, 29 March 1851, 129. A bare-footed, tonsured, and overfed monk stands in a doorway trying to entice a young woman with a veil. ("*Kidnapper.* 'There's a be-autiful veil!!! Give me your parcel, my dear, while you put it on.'") The girl is carrying a large sack of money, her "dowry" for the convent.
27. The reference to "Jack Priest" (a nod to John Bull, an archetypal figure from the 1700s to WWI, and the "Union Jack" or British flag) recalls Hopkins's use of popular slang: the everyday figures of "Jessy or Jack" in "The Candle Indoors" and "This Jack, joke" who undergoes a religious transformation (to "immortal diamond") in "Heraclitean Fire" (*PW* 158, 198).
28. On 9 Dec. 1865, one of Hopkins's "sins" is "Scrupulosity abt. *Punch*," but no specifics are provided (*CW* 3:338).
29. See *CW* 1:210, 330, 379; *CW* 2:914.
30. Arthur Hopkins (1847–1930), a professional artist, contributed to the *Illustrated London News*, *Graphic* (he was a member of its staff for twenty-five years), *Belgravia*, and *Punch* (*CW* 1:xci). Everard Hopkins (1860–1928), the youngest sibling, also an illustrator, worked regularly for *Illustrated London News*, *Woman's World*, *Life*, and contributed frequently to *Punch* in the 1890s and early twentieth century (*CW* 1:xcii).
31. The journal was established in 1836 by Michael Quinn, Daniel O'Connell, and Cardinal Wiseman. Hopkins describes it to Bridges as "the first of the Catholic periodicals" in Dec. 1885 (*CW* 2:753).
32. Francis Cowley Burnand (1836–1917) wrote more than two hundred plays and pantomimes and collaborated with Arthur Sullivan on *Box and Cox* (1866). He was knighted in 1902.
33. Draft letter to Hopkins, 18 Oct. 1866 (*CW* 1:120).
34. "In the pervasive late Victorian discourse of anti-Catholicism, Jesuit priests are associated with insinuation, deception, persuasion, and seduction (whether literal or figurative)." Kirstie Blair, "Priest and Nun? *Daniel Deronda*, Anti-Catholicism and The Confessional," *George Eliot Review* 400 (2001): 45.
35. The fifth title would be Walter Walsh, *The Jesuits in Great Britain: An Historical Inquiry into Their Political Influence* (London: George Routledge and Sons, 1905). Jesuits, he concludes, should be expelled "from the British dominions—not only from the mother country, but from all our Colonies and Dependencies" (328).
36. The 1843 book was first translated into English in 1846. Two years later, it was enjoying its fourth edition.
37. In the same letter Newman, an Oratorian, bluntly states that Hopkins, who lived and taught at the Birmingham Oratory from Sept. 1867 to Apr. 1868, did not have "a vocation for us. This I clearly saw you had *not*, from the moment you came to us" (*CW* 1:178).

38. For a discussion of Brontë's "caricatures drawn from the antipapist arsenal," see Bernstein 61–62. The scene of Lucy Snowe's confession is "only one example of how the traditional Protestant abhorrence of the confessional is enlisted at different historical moments" (Griffin, *Anti-Catholicism* 154).
39. The novel features a Jesuit subplot in which an infirm senior is pressured to deed everything to the Society. As Griffin suggests, the "contemporary horror of Thuggee and the more traditional revulsion at property turn out to be complementary aspects of a sort of imperial panic" (*Anti-Catholicism* 135).
40. Arthur Hopkins illustrated Collins's *Haunted Hotel* (1878).
41. Collins is caricatured in a *Punch* "Fancy Portrait" in 1882: "WILKIE COLLINS, as the Man in White Doing Ink-and-Penance for having written the *Black Robe.*"
42. Major Hynd laments his "disagreeable" wife; Stella Eyrecourt's manipulations are second only to the Jesuits'; her mother is a garrulous Dickensian figure who tries too hard to look half her age. In chap. 3, during the ill-fated card game in France, racist undertones prevail.
43. Mrs. Eyrecourt comments, "The audacity of these Papists is really beyond belief. You remember how they made Bishops and Archbishops here, in flat defiance of our laws?" (Wilkie Collins 2:208).
44. The topic was a Jesuit staple: compare the meditation on hell in the *Exercises*; Hopkins's sermons and retreat notes (especially *CW* 5:527-31); and James Joyce's *A Portrait of the Artist as a Young Man,* chap. 3, in which one of Hopkins's University College colleagues is fictionalized.
45. Hopkins burned his manuscripts voluntarily before joining the Society and decided himself to give up poetry. Gaume's manual suggests why artistic endeavors would be frowned upon: "The Priest, being consecrated to God by ordination, should employ himself solely in things which are holy . . . ; in a word, he ought to follow a rule of life, and not be desultory" (113).
46. The Irish poet Katharine Tynan, who met Hopkins several times in Dublin, recalls that he was "small and childish-looking, yet a child-sage, nervous too and very sensitive, with a small ivory-pale face." Qtd. in R. K. R. Thornton, ed., *All My Eyes See: The Visual World of Gerard Manley Hopkins* (Sunderland Arts Centre: Ceolfrith Press, 1975), 11.
47. See also Joanna Shaw Myers, "Hopkins and Mrs. Humphry Ward's *Helbeck of Bannisdale,*" in *Rereading Hopkins: Selected New Essays,* edited by Francis Fennell, 63–83 (Victoria, BC: University of Victoria Press, 1996).
48. Mary Arnold Ward (1851–1920) was born in Van Diemen's Land (Tasmania) but moved to England with her family in 1856. In 1872 she married T. Humphry Ward, a Brasenose don; their neighbors and friends included Walter Pater and his sisters, Clara and Hester (Pater and Ward were Brasenose colleagues), and Charlotte and Thomas Hill Green. The Wards moved to London in Nov. 1881, when Humphry became art critic for the *Times.*

49. When Tom Arnold returned to Catholicism, his wife, Julia, wrote to Newman to condemn him for encouraging Tom to "'ignore every social duty and become a pervert.... From the bottom of my heart I curse you for it'" (qtd. in Moran, *Catholic Sensationalism* 211).
50. See *CW* 7.
51. After the suicide of Beata Rosmer, her husband, Johannes, and her friend Rebecca West, both of whom live at Rosmersholm, become close. Burgeoning romance, however, is overshadowed by guilt about Beata's death; they carry out a suicide pact by jumping into the same mill-race where Beata took her life. Ibsen's play debuted in London in 1891.
52. For at least one reviewer, Fountain's death is an "ignorable catastrophe" and the novel, overall, a "wicked and cruel libel on the teachings of the Catholic Church." R. F. Clarke, S.J., "A Catholic's View of 'Helbeck of Bannisdale,'" *Nineteenth Century* 44 (Sept. 1898): 463, 461. See also Griffin, *Anti-Catholicism* 211–16, and "The Yellow Mask, the Black Robe, and the Woman in White: Wilkie Collins, Anti-Catholic Discourse, and the Sensation Novel," *Narrative* 12.1 (Jan. 2004): 55–73; and Judith Wilt, "Three Women Writers and the 'Jesuit Sublime': Or, Jesuits in Love," *Religion and the Arts* 13 (2009): 9–11.
53. Matthew Arnold, "Stanzas from the Grand Chartreuse," in Thomas J. Collins and Vivienne J. Rundle, eds., *The Broadview Anthology of Victorian Poetry and Poetic Theory* (Peterborough, Ont.: Broadview Press, 1999), 725.
54. In 1854 Charles Westerton, a churchwarden, protested the use of Ritualist ornaments (candlesticks, altar cloths, crosses) and practices in his church, St. Paul's in Knightsbridge; the complaint was adjudicated by the bishop of London.
55. "Contemporaries used the adjectives Puseyite and even Newmanite to describe the adherents of the [Oxford] Movement, but nobody ever thought of calling them Kebelians. It is, however, this very quality of 'reserve', this tendency to stay in the background, which constitutes ... Keble's chief intellectual legacy." Joe Phelan, "The Eye of the World," *Times Literary Supplement*, 18 Feb. 2005, 26.
56. Hopkins hoped to purchase and/or read "*Tracts for the Times*" in Winter 1865 (*CW* 3:277).
57. Hopkins to Ernest Coleridge (the poet's grandson), 1 June 1864; *CW* 1:62. See also his letter to his father, Manley Hopkins, 16–17 Oct. 1866 (*CW* 1:115).
58. "By 1837 there had been sixteen editions and by Keble's death [in 1866] there were ninety-five. When copyright expired in 1873 there were 158 editions and copyright sales stood at 379,000" (Percy Butler, "Keble, John," *Oxford Dictionary of National Biography*, online ed.). Newman praised it as "the most soothing, tranquilizing, subduing work of the day" ("John Keble," *Essays Critical* 1:441). See Stephen Prickett, "Tractarian Poetry," in Alison Chapman et al., eds., *The Blackwell Companion to Victorian Poetry* (Oxford: Blackwell, 2002), 279–89.

59. Both Blair and Paxton cogently discuss Hopkins's poetic indebtedness to Keble. Lines from Keble's "Fourth Sunday in Advent," for example—"But patience! There may come a time / When these dull ears shall scan aright / Strains, that outring Earth's drowsy chime"—echo in the Dublin poem that begins "Patience, hard thing! the hard thing but to pray, / But bid for, patience is!" (*PW* 185). John Keble, *The Christian Year: Thoughts in Verse for the Sundays and Holydays throughout the Year*, 1827 (London: Elliot Stock, 1897), 23.

60. Shame catalyzes such exposure: although "shame makes the sinner shrink and draw back, and not endure to have his thoughts and doings watched or seen by any eye whatever," it is possible to let "natural shame to work a good" and inspire both "strict and aweful self-examination" and confession to a clergyman (Keble, *Sermons* 3:140, 144, 148).

61. Although Keble, an Oxford graduate (hons. BA 1811), was elected to an Oriel fellowship, and was Oxford's Professor of Poetry (1832–41), he preferred parish commitments and served in Hursley from 1825 until his death. In Hopkins's vocational poem "The Lantern out of doors," the speaker worries that "Death or distance soon consumes" people but affirms that Christ is "Their ransom, their rescue, and first, fast, last friend" (*PW* 140).

62. For Hopkins's comments about Tractarianism, see his letter of 16–17 Oct. 1866 (*CW* 1:115–17). Telling a story about the "Bishops' Memorial" was a sin committed 25 Nov. 1865 (*CW* 3:337).

63. Keble advised, "On the whole matter you will find good directions in Bishop Taylor's 'Holy Dying' and 'Golden Grove'; and also in Kettleworth's 'Companion to the Penitent.'" John Keble, *Letters of Spiritual Counsel and Guidance*, 3rd ed., ed. R. F. Wilson (Oxford and London: James Parker, 1875), 100. See John Kettlewell's *A Companion to the Penitent, and for persons troubled in mind consisting of an office for the penitent, to carry on their reconciliation with God* (London: Robert Kettleworth and Benjamin Bragg, 1694).

64. The first part of Pusey's *Eirenicon* (an attempt to reconcile Anglican and Roman doctrine and practices), an open *Letter to Keble*, was published in 1865. Two additional parts were published in 1869 and 1870. Hopkins recommends *Eirenicon* to his mother Kate in Oct. 1866 (*CW* 1:125).

65. Keble, typically, gave qualified assent to the idea of keeping a written list of sins. "I will only just say," he informed a correspondent, "be not too scrupulous in setting down things, nor yet too general, but take some one or more as specimens in any kind which may have become habitual, and describe the frequency of the habit . . . by the number of sins in a given time, and the degree. . . . What you write is best written in some kind of cypher or abbreviation, lest it be lost, and do harm" (*Letters* 99–100).

66. Carefully revised by Hopkins and given a new title, "The Kind Betrothal" (*PW* 90).

67. Hopkins is aware that other friends (and fellow Balliol students) are relying on Pusey and Liddon as spiritual directors. See, for example, *CW* 1:92.
68. In winter 1865 Liddon was encouraging Hopkins to miss class: "Walk with Liddon on Tuesday at 1.30. But how about Jowett's lecture?" (*CW* 3:274).
69. In 1854 Liddon was appointed vice principal of the Anglican theological college at Cuddeson, near Oxford. He "caused a scandal by urging confession on the ordinands, and he had to be pressured into resigning" (MacKenzie, *Excursions* 54). Liddon was then transferred to Christ Church College, Oxford.
70. Elisha saves people from poisonous gourds when he reveals "there is death in the pot" (2 Kings 4:38-41).
71. See his letter to Kate Hopkins, 23 Jan. 1864 (*CW* 1:55).
72. For the full reports, see https://hansard.parliament.uk/Lords/1867-08-19/debates/c72c0dce-c5ec-4462-8c2c-ab9235c33fe5/Ritualism%E2%80%94TheRoyalCommission%E2%80%94ReportOfTheCommissioners.
73. The Public Worship Regulation Act 1874. HL Deb 20 April 1874 vol 218 cc786-808. http://hansard.millbanksystems.com/lords/1874/apr/20/presented-first-reading, ¶ 786, 790.
74. Ibid., ¶ 790, 786.
75. Ibid., ¶ 791.
76. Ibid., ¶ 789.
77. Ibid., ¶ 802, 799.
78. See also Rene Kollar, "Power and Control Over Women in Victorian England: Male Opposition to Sacramental Confession in the Anglican Church," *Journal of Anglican Studies* 3.1 (2005): 11-32.
79. *Hansard Parliamentary Debates,* 3rd ser., vol. 234 (1877), cols. 1741-45.
80. Ibid., ¶ 1751, 1753.
81. Rev. Charles Dodgson [Lewis Carroll], who was Pusey and Liddon's colleague at Oxford's Christ Church College, submitted a letter to the *Pall Mall Gazette* in July 1877 that equates the "Roman theory of confession" with a "morbid imagination" and suggests that "every question" posed in *The Priest in Absolution,* and in the confessional, is "an injury," one that could very well lead to "cases of melancholia with suicidal tendencies" ([Carroll], "The Priest in Absolution," *Pall Mall Gazette,* 14 July 1877, 4-5).
82. As mentioned earlier, however, Hopkins was familiar with Ritualism, denouncing these men for being "imperious, uncommissioned, without common sense, and without knowledge of moral theology" (*CW* 1:257).
83. A letter to Bridges, 22-24 Sept. 1866, summarizes Hopkins's first meeting with Newman, who "spoke with interest and kindness and appreciation of all that Tractarians reverence" (*CW* 1:98).

3. LIVING "IN FLESH"

1. The reference is to KJV Ps. 78:79 / D-R Ps. 77:39.
2. Foundational texts for these analyses: Maurice Merleau-Ponty, *Phenomenology of Perception*, trans. Colin Smith (London: Routledge and Kegan Paul, 1962); Mary Douglas, *Purity and Danger: An Analysis of Concepts of Pollution and Taboo* (London: Routledge and Kegan Paul, 1966); Bryan Turner, *The Body and Society* (Oxford: Basil Blackwell, 1984); Elaine Scarry, *The Body in Pain: The Making and Unmaking of the World* (Oxford: Oxford University Press, 1985); Thomas Laqueur, *Making Sex: Body and Gender from the Greeks to Freud* (Cambridge, MA: Harvard University Press, 1990); and Judith Butler, *Gender Trouble: Feminism and the Subject of Identity* (London: Routledge, 1990). See also Roy Porter, "History of the Body," in Peter Burke, ed., *New Perspectives on Historical Writing* (Cambridge: Polity Press, 1991), 206–32.
3. Mahoney, S.J., cites the general "predilection for the Pauline 'works of the flesh' of Galatians chapter five and First Corinthians chapter six" (7). According to Brown, "Paul crammed into the notion of the flesh a superabundance of overlapping notions. The charged opacity of his language faced all later ages like a Rorschach test: it is possible to measure, in the repeated exegesis of a mere hundred words of Paul's letters, the future course of Christian thought." Peter Brown, *The Body and Society: Men, Women, and Sexual Renunciation in Early Christianity* (New York: Columbia University Press, 1988), 48.
4. Michel Foucault, *Discipline and Punish: The Birth of the Prison*, trans. Alan Sheridan (New York: Vintage, 1979), 25–26. Hereafter cited as *DP*. As Foucault states, "We are often reminded of the countless procedures which Christianity once employed to make us detest the body; but let us ponder all the ruses that were employed for centuries to make us love sex, to make the knowledge of it desirable and everything said about it precious" (*HS* 1:159). Insisting that sexuality is learned, not innate, the effect of competing cultural norms, social discourses, and institutions, Foucault argues that it is, in Diprose's summation, "the naturalized product of a moral code which, through techniques of discipline, surveillance, self-knowledge and confession, organizes social control by stimulation rather than repression" (25).
5. "Since the inception of philosophy as a separate" discipline, Grosz states, it has "established itself on the foundations of a profound somatophobia.... In the *Cratylus*, Plato claims that the word *body* (*soma*) was introduced by Orphic priests, who believed that man was a spiritual or noncorporeal being trapped in the body as in a dungeon (*sēma*). In his doctrine of the Forms, Plato sees matter itself as a denigrated and imperfect version of the Idea. The body is a betrayal of and a prison for the soul, reason, or mind" (5).

6. For a comparison of the social and physical body, see Mary Douglas, "The Two Bodies," 'in Mariam Fraser and Monica Greco, eds, *The Body: A Reader* (London: Routledge, 2005), 78–81.
7. See Linda Dowling, *Hellenism and Homosexuality in Victorian Oxford* (Ithaca, NY: Cornell University Press, 1994); and Lesley Higgins, "Jowett and Pater: Trafficking in Platonic Wares," *Victorian Studies* 37.1 (Autumn 1993): 43–72.
8. For the "illicit homoerotic pleasures of spectatorship" in Hopkins's writings, see Maureen Moran, "The Art of Looking Dangerously: Victorian Images of Martyrdom," *Victorian Literature and Culture* 32.2 (2004): 475–93, and Saville, *Queer Chivalry*.
9. See Hopkins's letter to Baillie, 12 Feb. 1868, for his acknowledgment that aesthetic discourse necessarily involves and articulates eroticized positions (*CW* 1:176); see also "To what serves Mortal Beauty?" (*PW* 182–83).
10. Hopkins, *The Later Poetic Manuscripts of Gerard Manley Hopkins in Facsimile,* ed. Norman H. MacKenzie (New York: Garland, 1991), 412 (plate 488); hereafter cited as *LPM*.
11. "There may be no other poet in English who founds a style as fundamentally ... on the apprehension of an analogy between intellectual and bodily experience." Susan Chambers, "Gerard Manley Hopkins and the Kinesthetics of Conviction," *Victorian Studies* 51.1 (Autumn 2008): 19.
12. As Hartman suggests, "Rhythm, sound, and sight involve for Hopkins a sense of the body, the total and individual body, and his poems and notes are full of pride and despair at the inseparable sensuous character of his vision." Geoffrey Hartman, *The Unmediated Vision: An Interpretation of Wordsworth, Hopkins, Rilke, and Valery* (New York: Harcourt, Brace, and World, 1966), 17. See also Marylou Motto, *"Mined with a Motion": The Poetry of Gerard Manley Hopkins* (New Brunswick, NJ: Rutgers University Press, 1984).
13. See *CW* 3:294.
14. Kingsley's virulent anti-Catholicism was displayed in the 1860s during his public disputes with Newman. Yet perhaps "more than any other middle-class writer, Kingsley placed the male body into widespread circulation as an object of celebration and desire—a project recognized in the contemporary tag, 'Apostle of the Flesh'" (Adams, *Dandies* 150).
15. One's goal, Newman informed Oxford undergraduates, should be to join "the company of mature, manly Christians" ("Christian Manhood," *Parochial* 1:345).
16. The "perimeters and properties of Victorian masculinities were imperfectly secured through ongoing processes of differentiation, denigration, and appropriation" and were "as fretted and fractured as the class and gender ideologies of the era, ones that only appear seamless to us when we mistake bombast for self-assurance." Donald Hall, "Muscular Christianity: Reading and Writing

the Male Social Body," in Donald Hall, ed., *Muscular Christianity: Embodying the Victorian Age* (Cambridge: Cambridge University Press, 1994), 3–4.
17. Hopkins mentions Carlyle familiarly in his letters but with some exasperation. In 1864 he declares Carlyle an extremist (*CW* 1:71); in 1868 Carlyle is "with 'the true men'" (*CW* 1:175).
18. Hopkins suggests to Bridges, 3–8 Apr. 1877, that "what acts is masculine, what receives action feminine" (*CW* 1:265). For Hopkins's "undeniable antifeminist tendencies" see Simon Humphries, "Hopkins's Silent Men," *ELH* 77.2 (Summer 2010): 463.
19. Sedgwick analyzes the social and textual implications of Victorian sphere ideologies, the "increasingly stressed nineteenth-century bourgeois dichotomy between domestic female space and extrafamilial, political and economic male space" (*Between Men* 189).
20. Hopkins's life coincided with (and was marked by) a paradigmatic shift from the demonization of mental life to the pathologization of mental life. "Sexuality played a key role in the territorial war between priests and physicians. Psychiatry had taken the soul and turned it into a mind, an eminently treatable and physical entity." Sally Shuttleworth, "Spiritual Pathology: Priests, Physicians, and *The Way of All Flesh*," *Victorian Studies* 54.4 (Summer 2012): 643.
21. *Questions for Self-Examination,* 10; *EPM* 206.
22. Ibid., 7; *EPM* 205.
23. For a discussion of Aretaeus (a renowned Greek physician, first century CE, known as "the Cappadocian") and his treatise *On the Causes and Signs of Chronic Diseases,* see *HS* 2:15–16 and *HS* 3:115.
24. Clough, *The Oxford Diaries of Arthur Hugh Clough,* edited by Anthony Kenny (Oxford: Clarendon Press, 1990), 105, 106, 112, 55, 57, 59. Clough (1819–61), also a Balliol student, also a poet, also died in his early forties.
25. St. Augustine "describes his relationship to his concubine as a mere indulgence in physical satisfaction and 'habit.' (In Latin, 'habit,' *consuetudo,* is an attested euphemism for marital intercourse.)" (Chadwick xvii).
26. MacKenzie believes otherwise; see "Introduction. Part II: Notes on the Daily Examination of Conscience," in *EPM,* 22.
27. "In describing his sins and emotional crises, Clough adopts some disguises, so that the meaning would not be obvious to, say, a prying Balliol scout; but it is commonly easy to disambiguate. . . . There is something comic about the contrast between Clough's daily denunciations of his folly and wickedness, and the uniform praise for his diligence and exemplary character in his tutors' reports and his contemporaries' reminiscences" (Kenny lxii).
28. Foucault, qtd. in Carrette, "Prologue to a Confession of the Flesh," in *Michel Foucault, Religion and Culture,* ed. Jeremy Carrette (New York: Routledge, 1999), 45.

29. Foucault's term is "autopathologization" (*Ab* 242).
30. Thomas Laqueur, *Making Sex* and *Solitary Sex: A Cultural History of Masturbation* (New York: Zone Books, 2003); Roy Porter; Lesley Hall, "Forbidden by God, Despised by Men: Masturbation, Medical Warnings, Moral Panic, and Manhood in Great Britain, 1850–1950," in John C. Fout, ed., *Forbidden History: The State, Society, and the Regulation of Sexuality in Modern Europe* (Chicago: University of Chicago Press, 1992), 293–315.
31. Foucault is quoting from and summarizing Hippocrates, *The Seed;* see *HS* 2:131. "'Sperm is the purest extract of the blood, and according to the expression of Feruel, *totus homo semen est* [the whole man is the seed].' This was the ancient belief that blood was life, and that life's transmission fluid, semen, was the sum and representation of its bearer" (Barker-Benfield 49). See also Sedgwick, "Jane Austen and the Masturbating Girl," *Critical Inquiry* 17.4 (Summer 1991): 819.
32. See also Daniele Lorenzini, "The Emergence of Desire: Notes Toward a Political History of the Will," *Critical Inquiry* 45 (Winter 2019): 460.
33. "There are the famous nightshirts," Foucault reports, "with low drawstring hems and corsets and bindings. There is the famous Jalade-Laffont belt... comprised [of] a sort of metal corselet that was attached to the pelvic area with, for boys, a little metal tube lined with velvet and with a number of holes pierced at the end through which he could urinate. The device was closed, padlocked, and opened only once a week in the presence of the parents so the child could be cleaned" (*Ab* 252). Ritualist members of the Society of the Holy Cross debated, in 1876, "'remedies and penances for sins of impurity,'" which included chewing bitter aloes, or changing position, or "'rough gloves or fastened hands at night.'" Nigel Yates, "'Jesuits in Disguise'?: Ritualist Confessors and their Critics in the 1870s," *Journal of Ecclesiastical History* 39.2 (Apr. 1988): 212.
34. Qtd. in Ed Cohen, *Talk on the Wilde Side* (London: Routledge, 1993), 35.
35. See Hare 5.
36. See also Robert MacDonald.
37. John Law Milton, *On Spermatorrhea: Its Pathology, Results, and Complications* (London: Henry Renshaw, 1881), 30–31; qtd. in Ed Cohen 47.
38. "It was believed that every youth who masturbated endangered the vitality of his future children; and for 200 years the horrid phantom of racial decay terrified the physicians and educators of the western world." E. H. Hare, "Masturbatory Insanity: The History of an Idea," *Journal of Mental Science* 108.452 (Jan. 1962): 16.
39. See Ed Cohen 57.
40. See also Lesley Hall, "Forbidden," 302. These fears persisted into the twentieth century: in Lord Baden-Powell's 1908 handbook *Scouting for Boys* and the 1922 *Rovering to Success,* instructors are advised to tell the boys that

"self-abuse . . . brings with it weakness of head and heart, and, if persisted in, idiocy and lunacy" (qtd. in Lesley Hall, "Forbidden," 301).

41. Gaume's *Manual* stresses the need for specificity when tallying sexual sins; masturbation is implied: "If you cannot be at all clear as to the probable number, then explain the duration and frequency of the sin. E.g. 'When I was fifteen, a bad companion taught me such a sin, and I committed it two or three times a week, until I was thirty, and since then at intervals once a week, or sometimes I may have been free for a week'" (387).

42. The influence of Ruskin is felt throughout Hopkins's diaries, sketchbooks, and undergraduate essays, from comments on Gothic and Pre-Raphaelite art, and architectural drawings (see *CW* 3:129), to his reverential approach to nature. As a sketch artist, Hopkins adhered to Ruskin's *Elements of Drawing* (1857). As an aesthetic critic, Hopkins admired *Pre-Raphaelitism* (1851) and *Modern Painters* (5 vols., 1856), but also felt compelled to disagree with Ruskin. In July 1863 Hopkins explained to Baillie that he was "sketching (in pencil chiefly) a good deal . . . in a Ruskinese point of view" (*CW* 1:43), but two months later suggested that, as a critic, "Ruskin often goes astray" (*CW* 1:46). In Sept. 1883, Hopkins informed Patmore that Ruskin "has the insight of a dozen critics, but intemperance and *wrongness* undoes. . . . ^his^ good again" (*CW* 2:611). Ruskin was the model for the Professor in Hopkins's 1865 "Platonic Dialogue" (*CW* 4:136–73). Hopkins's sketches during his tour of Switzerland, July 1868 (see *CW* 4:436–58; *CW* 6-pt2), should be compared to Ruskin's; see John Hayman, *John Ruskin and Switzerland* (Waterloo: Wilfrid Laurier University Press, 1990).

43. See also Amelia Bonea et al., *Anxious Times: Medicine and Modernity in Nineteenth-Century Britain* (Pittsburgh, PA: University of Pittsburgh Press, 2019) and the project's website and database, https://diseasesofmodernlife.web.ox.ac.uk/home#.

44. Fiegel suggests it was "probably an infected phimosis"; Kenneth Fiegel, "My Winter World: The Illness of Gerard Manley Hopkins," *Lancet* 9057, vol. 347 (1997): 1017.

45. Curtis had been a scholar at Trinity College, Dublin; at University College, he was professor of natural science. See Martin, *Gerard Manley Hopkins* 377–79.

46. The "Monita" or community rules for St. Mary's Hall, Stonyhurst, include "The walk on Sunday evening and once on Thursday is to be taken for at least an hour and a half"; "Those who fish are to keep out of the water"; "Bathing is only allowed at Hodder Roughs, with special leave: bathing drawers are always to be used" (*CW* 3:652).

47. For a discussion of nineteenth-century emphases on the "pleasurable and hygienic care of the body," see Pamela K. Gilbert, "Popular Beliefs and the Body," in Michael Sappol and Stephen P. Rice, eds., *A Cultural History of the*

Human Body in the Age of Empire (Oxford: Berg, 2010), 140–41. See Mauss's "descriptive ethnology" to consider how, depending on class, gender, and biological elements, a Victorian body was educated, including "this notion of the prestige of the person who performed the ordered, authorized, tested action," and the historically inflected "techniques of the body" that, for a priest, would include how he used his body, especially his hands, while saying Mass. Marcel Mauss, "Techniques of the Body (1935)," *Economy and Society* 21 (Feb. 1973): 70, 73, 83.

48. Victorians' "celebratory visions of male bodily strength were heavily racialized … it was not only vitality that was on display, or even male vitality, but white male vitality." Stephen P. Rice, "Picturing Bodies in the Nineteenth Century," in Michael Sappol and Stephen P. Rice, eds, *A Cultural History of the Human Body in the Age of Empire* (Oxford: Berg, 2010), 230.

49. For comments linking poverty and "the degradation even of our race," see *CW* 1:505. For a discussion of how Malthus's *Essays on the Principles of Population* (1798) constituted a "revaluation of the social meaning of the healthy body, a revaluation fundamental to nineteenth-century social discourses and practices," see Catherine Gallagher, "The Body versus the Social Body in the Works of Thomas Malthus and Henry Mayhew," *Representations* 14 (Spring 1986): 83.

50. The 1830s and 1840s were memorable for the "frequency of concurrent epidemics" and contagions that swept through Britain: cholera, influenza, typhoid, measles, whooping cough, and tuberculosis. Government commissions and sanitary reform reports of 1838 and 1845 culminated in the Public Health Bill 1848 (Haley 5).

51. "Binsey Poplars" is occasioned by the "corpses" of trees that have been cut down.

52. Of the many references to σάρξ, Romans 8 is particularly instructive: "For what the law could not do, in that it was weak through the flesh, God sending his own Son in the likeness of sinful flesh, and for sin, condemned sin in the flesh. … So then they that are in the flesh cannot please God. But ye are not in the flesh, but in the Spirit, if so be that the Spirit of God dwell in you" (Rom. 8:3, 8–9).

53. "In seeking for you," Augustine tells God, "I followed not the intelligence of the mind, by which you willed that I surpass the beasts, but the mind of the flesh" (*Confs* 43).

54. *Hamlet* 3.2.62–63. Hopkins quotes the lines in his Liverpool sermon 25 Oct. 1880 (*CW* 5:318).

55. To quote Hopkins's notes on the *Contemplatio* ["Contemplation to Obtain Love"], Christ "has suffered in the flesh as man, the Word but really made flesh" (*CW* 5:474).

56. In his *SE* notes, Hopkins considers that "[i]f Adam had not fallen it seems that Xt and his mother wd. not have been born among his descendants. But

as the Bd. Virgin, who bore Xt as in the flesh without birthpangs, is with great birthpangs the mother of all men in the spirit, so she wd. then have been their mother in the spirit but without sorrow" (*CW* 5:433).
57. See Trent Pomplun, "The Theology of Gerard Manley Hopkins: From John Duns Scotus to the Baroque," *Journal of Religion* 95.1 (Jan. 2015): 1-34.
58. Is. 53:2.
59. The metaphor is reiterated in 1 Pet. 1:24.
60. Stanza 8 of "The Wreck" suggests "How a lush-kept plush-capped sloe / Will, mouthed to flesh-burst, / Gush!" (*PW* 121).
61. In a fragment for *Floris in Italy* (1864), Floris declares, "Madam! That I love you desperately you know well"; that the love is not reciprocated is the cause of his "diet of gall and ~~bitterness~~ the mortifying of tears" (*CW* 3:230).
62. Typologically, the statement answers the Psalmist's lament "They gave me also gall for my meat, and in my thirst they gave me vinegar to drink" (Ps. 69:21). In the Old Testament, turning away from God is akin to "a root that beareth gall and wormwood" (Deut. 29:18).
63. Shakespeare, *Twelfth Night* 3.2.48.
64. See Lesley Higgins and Julianna Will, "'Quelled or quenched in leaves': The Poplar Experiments of Pater, Monet, and Hopkins," *Journal of Pre-Raphaelite Studies* 29 (Fall 2020) 1-19.
65. See *CW* 7:2-3, 86-89, 112-13. The poem had a long gestation: it was begun before the "terrible sonnets" but only completed afterward. It should be read in relation to "Carrion Comfort" and "I wake and feel" especially.
66. The phrase and discursive strategy are borrowed from Simon Richter's study of the ancient statue and its importance for eighteenth-century German aesthetics.
67. Saville comments on "the strange coexistence of psychic anguish and theatrical self-display in the 'terrible' sonnets" (*Queer* 15).
68. See especially the exercises on dying and death, *SE* 96-99, 320-23, and Hopkins's comments, *CW* 5:334, 359-61, 536.
69. Grigson notes that Hopkins "was interested in the gash, the bloody flow, the bloody hour of the martyrs. Self-humiliation, and pain in others[,] . . . were always important to him." Geoffrey Grigson, "Blood or Bran," in Walford Davies, ed., *Gerard Manley Hopkins* (London: Dent, 1979), 203-4.
70. For an excellent discussion of "Hopkins' investment in gendered suffering," see Paxton, *Willful Submission.*
71. See also David Morris, *The Culture of Pain* (Berkeley: University of California Press, 1992); Lucy Bending, *The Representation of Bodily Pain in Late Nineteenth-Century English Culture* (Oxford: Oxford University Press, 2000); Susannah B. Mintz, *Hurt and Pain: Literature and the Suffering Body* (London: Bloomsbury, 2013); and Rachel Ablow, *Victorian Pain* (Princeton, NJ: Princeton University Press, 2017).

72. The First Exercise on Hell stresses the eternal "torment" that awaits the "condemned": "The society of his body, which, to the infectious corruption of a corpse, will unite all the sensibility of a living frame, and every member of which will have its torment and its pain" (*SE* 80).
73. See "The Victorian Sermon: Pulpit and Preachers" in the introduction to *CW* 5:34-46.
74. It is also the subject of a 22 July 1883 sermon at Clitheroe and at Sydenham in summer 1885 (for the notes, see *CW* 7:162-63).
75. A note at the end of the sermon, "Jan. 11 1882," suggests that he preached a similar homily two years later (*CW* 5:280).
76. Hopkins argues that Christ is the first Paraclete and the Holy Ghost, the second (*CW* 5:286).
77. Qtd. in "Mortification of the Flesh," Tract 21 (Newman, *Mortification* 2).
78. During his novitiate, in Jan. 1869, Hopkins notes the new primroses yet states, "[A] penance which I was doing fr. Jan 25 to July 25 prevented my seeing much that half-year" (*CW* 3:47). According to Thomas, S.J., Hopkins "would be allowed to practise only such penances as his Superior judged fit. This in itself was an act of obedience. In the matter of penance Fr. Gallwey, far from stifling spontaneity, upheld the view that it is what you do 'of your own initiative, extra prayer or mortification or work of any kind which really counts'" (*Hopkins* 39).
79. Tertullian "touched on this theme of virginity many times," Foucault observes, but "much more markedly than Tertullian, Cyprian singles out the state of virginity, showers it with singular praises, and gives it a fitting role" (*HS* 4:120; see also 118-20).
80. See also *HS* 4:154-55. "Virginity exemplifies early Christian forms of *askesis*: ethical practices of an 'exercise of oneself upon oneself'. These practices organize themselves under a different sexual code than the regulatory system for marriage and procreation" (Huffer 24).
81. Other noteworthy Pre-Raphaelite representations of St. Dorothea: Christina Rossetti, "'Rivals': A Shadow of Saint Dorothea" (1858), Swinburne, "St. Dorothy" (1866), and Edward Burne-Jones's watercolor *Theophilus and the Angel* (1863-67).
82. Foucault, *Religion and Culture* 143.
83. See also his sermons "Secret Faults" and "Self-Denial" in *Parochial and Plain Sermons*. In the homily "Dangers to the Penitent," however, he modifies his stance, and advises, "Be on your guard, not only against becoming committed to some certain mode of life or object of exertion, but guard against excess in such penitential observances as have an immediate claim upon you, and are private in their exercise" (Newman, *Sermons* 44).
84. "My mother does not let me fast at all," Hopkins informed Baillie in Mar. 1864, "and says I in particular must never do it again, and in fact I believe I must not.

I feel like the Hindoos when the Suttee was abolished; but that is to me almost greater mortification of the spirit than the fasting of the flesh" (*CW* 1:58). Among the sins for Easter 1865: "Foolish and proud thoughts abt. fasting" (*CW* 3:292). As a public school student, Hopkins went without water for three weeks, to prove a point about sailors' deprivations; his tongue reportedly went black (see Martin, *Gerard Manley Hopkins* 17). For his fascination with "fasting girl" Sarah Jacob, a Welsh young girl who died 17 Dec. 1869, see *CW* 3:496.

85. For a discussion of the "immense literature of flagellation produced during the Victorian period," see Marcus 260 and Saville, *Queer* 153.

86. Bridges assigned the title "Carrion Comfort." See *PW* 455.

87. The manuscript has both "wring-world" and "wring-earth" (*PW* 183).

88. Despair figures prominently in another Ireland poem, "Tom's Garland" (1877): the unemployed are "by Despair, bred Hangdog dull; by Rage, / Manwolf, worse" and "their packs infest the age" (*PW* 195). See also Hopkins's journal entry, Aug. 1873: "darkness and despair. In fact being unwell I was quite downcast: nature in all her parcels and faculties gaped and fell apart, *fatiscebat*, like a clod . . . holding only by strings of root" (*CW* 3:557).

89. See also Dennis Meadows, *Obedient Men* (New York: Appleton-Century-Crofts, 1954), 44–45.

90. The phrase "Time's eunuch" appears again in "Thou art indeed just, Lord" (17 Mar. 1889).

91. The *Exercises* stress the "three great truths which are the foundation of all the Exercises: *I come from God; I belong to God; I am destined for God*" (*SE* 22).

92. The passage from the Vulgate (Luke 2:52) states, "*et Iesus proficiebat sapientia aetate et gratia apud Deum et homines*" [And Jesus advanced in wisdom and age and grace with God and men] (*CW* 5:229 n. 9).

93. Hopkins is echoing Duns Scotus's argument in *Reportatio* III, dist. 7, qu. 4: "I say that glory is granted to Christ's soul, and to His body insofar as it is capable of being gloried. And since glory was granted to Christ's soul when it was assumed, so it would have been granted to His body, had such glory not been delayed on account of a greater good, namely, that people could be redeemed from the power of the devil through a mediator who was both possible and fitting because the glory of the blessed redeemed by the passion of His flesh is a greater good than the glory of Christ's body alone" (trans. in Pomplun 28).

94. I am distinguishing between the writings that concentrate on the human body of Christ and those devoted to the miraculated flesh within the Eucharist, the "Real Presence" made possible by sacramental transubstantiation. As Charles Coupe, S.J., suggests, "The Holy Eucharist is the Incarnation perpetually present" (*Lectures on the Holy Eucharist* [London: R. and T. Washbourne, 1906], 227).

95. For Hopkins's 1884 notes on the Feast of the Lance and the Nails, see *CW* 7:74, 190. A commonly used seal of the Society of Jesus features an image of the

"Holy Name" under which are three nails, the whole surrounded by emanating rays representing the light of the resurrection.

96. Both Scotus and Aquinas agree "that the Incarnation is a free act of an infinitely free God" (Pomplun 44).

97. Although unable to complete *St. Winefred's Well,* Hopkins composed the lines for St. Beuno (cited above), a chorus, and Caradoc's soliloquy. Beuno's speech is supposed to confirm Christ's healing powers. "The Leaden Echo and the Golden Echo" relies upon conventions of feminine vanity and body-consciousness to reaffirm the *vanitas* of human existence yet extend the promise of heavenly "everlastingness" (*PW* 170). As the gender ideology of Hopkins's day would have it, the self-absorbed "girlgrace" of the "Leaden Echo" (*PW* 170) contrasts markedly with the productive "churlsgrace" of Harry Ploughman (*PW* 194).

98. For the Lucifer comparison, see Howard W. Fulweiler, *Letters from the Darkling Plain: Language and the Grounds of Knowledge in the Poetry of Arnold and Hopkins* (Columbia: University of Missouri Press, 1972), 154; for the Stevenson, see Max Sutton, "Selving as Individuation in Hopkins: A Jungian Reading," *Hopkins Quarterly* 2.3 (Oct. 1975): 124.

99. Typically, I provide only page numbers for Hopkins's poems, most of which are fourteen-line sonnets. For the 280-line ode (*PW* 119–28), line references are given.

100. The nuns, affiliated with the Franciscan order, were expelled because of the 1873 Falk Laws (named for Bismarck's education minister, Adalbert Falk) enacted in the newly unified Germany to support the government's *Kulturkampf* conflict with the papacy (which vehemently opposed the separation of church and state in Europe). Each English-language account of the shipwreck, off the coast of Kent, provided a different interpretation (almost, a different nun). The 11 Dec. 1875 London *Times* report refers to "the chief sister, a gaunt woman 6 ft. high, calling out loudly and often 'O Christ, come quickly!' till the end came"; two days later, the newspaper cites one nun, "noted for extreme tallness, [as] the lady who, at midnight . . . kept exclaiming, in a voice heard by those in the rigging above the roar of the storm, 'My God, my God, make haste, make haste.'" Survivor William Leick's account for the *New York Herald* was even more melodramatic: "The Stewardess at last induced the Sisters to come up to the entrance of the [ship's] companion, but she was herself struck by a [wave] and washed across the deck and back again. The nuns fled back terrified into the saloon. . . . One of them, a very large woman, with a voice like a man's, got halfway up through the skylight, and kept shrieking in a dreadful way, 'Mein Gott! Mach es schnell mit uns! Give us our death quickly!'" (qtd. Martin, *Gerard Manley Hopkins* 25). Cardinal Manning ventured from the truth in his funeral oration in order to foster an image of Victorian Catholic femininity at its most passive: "'And these holy souls were so resigned in the tranquility of their

confidence in God, that they showed not the slightest sign of agitation or fear. They remained quietly in their cabins'" (*Franciscan Monthly*, 1897; qtd. Martin, *Gerard Manley Hopkins* 25).

101. For a thorough analysis of stanza 28, see Higgins, "Reckoning up the Ellipses in Hopkins's Poetry," *Hopkins Quarterly* 40.3-4 (Summer-Fall 2013), 69-94.
102. In 1878 Hopkins urged Bridges to read "The Wreck" again: "When a new thing, such as my ventures in the Deutschland are, is presented us our first criticisms are not our truest, best, most homefelt, or most lasting but what come easiest on the instant. They are barbarous and like what the ignorant and the ruck say. This was so with you. The Deutschland on her first run worked very much and *unsettled* you, thickening and clouding your mind" (*CW* 1:295; my emphasis).
103. Vendler coined the term in *The Breaking of Style: Hopkins, Heaney, Graham* (Cambridge, MA: Harvard University Press, 1995); its psychological nuances are explored by Chambers.
104. "Havoc" enters Hopkins's canon with "Binsey Poplars" (1879): the "Strókes of havoc únsélve / The sweet especial scene" (*PW* 157). After Caradoc's speech, "havoc" shapes the disturbing prolepsis of "On the Portrait" ("What worm was here, we cry, / To have havoc-pocked so" [*PW* 192]) and marks "The Shepherd's Brow" ("The shepherd's brow, fronting forked lightning, owns / The horror and havoc and the glory / Of it" [*PW* 201]).
105. Hopkins is recycling tropes from an 1865 lyric, the first stanza of which begins, "My prayers must meet a brazen heaven / And fail and scatter all away," and concludes, "[I] feel the long success of sin" (*PW* 83).
106. The *Spiritual Exercises* frequently cite Christ's "heroism" and recommend, "[D]o not be afraid of the sacrifices [God] may ask of you" (*SE* 20, 18-19).
107. Five nuns from Salzkotten (now in Nordrhein-Westfalen, western Germany) died: Srs. Barbara Hultenschmidt (Hopkins's "Tall Nun"), Norbeta Reinkobe, Aurea Badziura, Brigitta Damhorst, and Henrika Fassbender (whose body was never found).
108. For a discussion of the rope/lash/strand motif in the poem that intensifies the mortification theme, see Robert B. Martin, "The Poet, the Nun, and the Daring Young Man," in Lyall H. Powers, ed., *Leon Edel and Literary Art* (Ann Arbor: UMI Research Press), 29-41.
109. The text implies, however, that a severed head is preferable to a ruptured maidenhead; Winefred loses her life to preserve her virginity and thus honor family and God. The miraculous resurrection that follows echoes the promise of Christ's resurrection: her body and spirit are "come-back-again things, | things with a revival, things with a recovery" (*PW* 180).
110. The speaker of "The Wreck" notes "the midriff astrain with leaning of, laced with fire of stress" (line 16).

111. Isobel Armstrong, *Victorian Poetry: Poetry, Poetics and Politics* (London: Routledge, 1996), 422.
112. Hopkins, *The Dublin Notebook*, ed. Lesley Higgins and Michael F. Suarez, S.J. (Oxford: Oxford University Press, 2014), 90-91. Hereafter cited as *CW 7*.

4. PROFESSING THE FLESH

1. I will be quoting from the first version of Pater's "Winckelmann" essay, which Hopkins would have read. Walter Pater, "Winckelmann," *Westminster Review*, n.s., 87 (Jan. 1867): 80-110, at 107. See also Pater, "Winckelmann," *The Renaissance: Studies in Art and Poetry*, the 1893 text, ed. Donald L. Hill (Berkeley: University of California Press, 1980), 141-85.
2. Robert Buchanan [Thomas Maitland], "The Fleshly School of Poetry: Mr. D. G. Rossetti," in *The Broadview Anthology of Victorian Poetry and Poetic Theory*, ed. Thomas J. Collins and Vivienne J. Rundle, 1329-40 (Peterborough, Ont.: Broadview Press, 1999), 1330. Hereafter cited as "FS." Rossetti responded with his own essay, "The Stealthy School of Criticism," *Athenaeum*, 16 Dec. 1871; see http://www.rossettiarchive.org/docs/34p-1870.raw.html. Swinburne responded in *Under the Microscope* (London: D. White, 1872).
3. For excellent studies of female Pre-Raphaelite writers and artists, see Jan Marsh, *The Pre-Raphaelite Sisterhood* (London: Quartet Books, 1985); Jan Marsh and Pamela Gerrish Nunn, *Pre-Raphaelite Women Artists* (New York: Thames and Hudson, 1999); and Amanda Paxton, "Love, Dismemberment, and Elizabeth Siddal's *Corpus*," *Journal of Pre-Raphaelite Studies* 22.2 (2013): 4-23.
4. In 1863 Hopkins declared Millais a "genius": "he is the greatest English painter, one of the greatest in the world" and in his works are "at last arriving at Nature's self" (*CW* 1:43).
5. Hunt's immensely popular *Light of the World* (1853-54) features a fully clothed Christ, his crown of thorns haloed in gold, a lantern in his left hand. Some people, including Thomas Carlyle, declared the ecclesiastical robes "papist," yet the painting became so popular that Hunt was asked to paint a second version, only larger, and he complied.
6. Hopkins, who met Hunt in summer 1864 (*CW* 1:506), consistently praised his work as part of the "modern medieval school" (*CW* 1:506).
7. Kilvert, diary entry for 27 June 1874. Francis Kilvert, *Selections from the Diary of the Rev. Francis Kilvert, 1870-79*, ed. by William Plomer, Elizabeth Divine, and Edward Ardizzone (London: Cape, 1976), 241.
8. Hopkins was equally indebted to Christina Rossetti's poetry, especially her command of the Petrarchan sonnet; he thought her work surpassed that of her brother in its "pathos and pure beauty" (*CW* 1:216). He had the pleasure

of meeting her at a friend's home in July 1864. Rossetti's "The Iniquity of the Fathers upon the Children" focuses on shame. "The Three Enemies" explores "the world, flesh, and the devil" motif. "The Convent Threshold," which Hopkins greatly admired (and "answered" in "A Voice from the World"), is a purgatorial poem in which each sense is chastised and martyrs are admired. See Margaret Johnson, *Gerard Manley Hopkins and Tractarian Poetry* (Aldershot, UK: Ashgate, 1997), 2; Blair, *Form and Faith;* and Paxton, *Willful Submission* 120-36.

9. Foucault delivered his Manet lectures in Milan, 1967; Tokyo and Florence, 1970; Tunis, 1971. The book *Le peinture de Manet* is a transcription of the Tunis version.
10. Nicholas Bourriaud, "Michel Foucault: Manet and the Birth of the Viewer," in Michel Foucaut, *Manet and the Object of Painting,* trans. Matthew Barr (London: Tate Publishing, 2011), 15, 13. For Bourriaud's suggestion that a painting is a heterotopia, an "anti-location" or space of "separation," see 17-19.
11. Hopkins distinguishes between "two strains of thought running together and like counterpointed": the "overthought that which everybody, editors, see" and the "underthought, ˆconveyedˆ chiefly in the choice of metaphors etc used and often only half realised by the poet himself" (*CW* 2:564).
12. Arnold introduced the "touchstone" concept in the preface to *Poems* (1853). See also "The Study of Poetry," first published as the introduction to T. Humphry Ward's 1880 anthology, *The English Poets,* and reprinted in the posthumous 1888 volume, *Essays in Criticism,* second series.
13. Buchanan does not mention Tennyson's "St. Simeon Stylites" (1833; first published in 1842), a dramatic monologue that exposes the Christian ascetic's zealous confidence in his own holiness. To the crowd that has gathered he urges, "Mortify / Your flesh, like me, with scourges and with thorns; / Smite, shrink not, spare not" (lines 176-78) (Tennyson 183-86).
14. In 1884 Buchanan published his own anti-Ritualist, anti-Catholic novel, *Foxglove Manor.* In chap. 12 the new Puseyite vicar, Charles Santley, declares, "The fathers of the desert had subdued the lusts of the flesh by hunger and stripes and physical suffering, and if mortification could exorcise the evil spirit within him, he would have no mercy on himself," but the narrator condemns such affectations.
15. Pater, "Coleridge's Writings," *Westminster Review,* n.s., 29.1 (Jan. 1866): 106-32, at 106. Hereafter cited as "CW."
16. See also *Algernon Charles Swinburne: Major Poems and Selected Prose,* ed. Jerome McGann and Charles L. Sligh (New Haven, CT: Yale University Press, 2004), 97.
17. The holograph manuscript, a "commonplace" collection of poems by everyone from Christina and D. G. Rossetti to Ralph Waldo Emerson, is now housed in the Bodleian Library (Eng. poet e. 90). The D. G. Rossetti poems copied out were "Lost Days," "Sudden Light," "Sibylla Palmifera," "Venus Verticordia," and "The Blessed Damozel." For Ellis, see *CW* 3:66.

18. Each figure is a new "thing to wonder on." From "The Portrait," in D. G. Rossetti, *Poems* (London: F. S. Ellis, 1870), 127.
19. After the Napoleonic Wars and the Congress of Vienna (1814-15), Italy was substantially controlled by the Austrian empire and the papacy. The difficult, multifaceted process of *Risorgimento* ("resurgence") or unification began with local insurrections in the 1830s and continued with the First War of Independence, Mar. 1848-Aug. 1849; the Second War of Independence, Apr. 1859-Sept. 1860, followed by the first consolidation of some city-states and territories into the kingdom of Italy, 1861; the Third War, 1866; the capture of Rome in 1871; and the Treaty of Rapallo, 1920. Two major leaders of the *Risorgimento*, Giuseppe Mazzini (1805-72) and Giuseppe Garibaldi (1807-82), were lionized by many in England. Rossetti's father, Gabriele, an ardent nationalist, moved from Italy to London in 1824. See Maura O'Connor, *The Romance of Italy and the English Political Imagination* (London: St. Martin's, 1998).
20. The speaker feels compelled to confess but doubts that he deserves absolution. "But you *must* hear me," he demands: "If you mistake my words / And so absolve me, Father, the great sin / Is yours, not mine: mark this: your soul shall burn / With mine for it" (Rossetti, *Poems* 77).
21. Similarly, the Blessed Damozel, although beyond life, continues to inflame: "her bosom must have made / The bar she leaned on warm," the speaker imagines.
22. See also sonnet 44, "The Sun's Shame," in which "The blushing morn and blushing eve confess / The shame that loads the intolerable day" (Rossetti, *Poems* 232). The two lovers referenced in "Known in Vain" are "amazed with shame" (Rossetti, *Poems* 218).
23. The guinea, minted between 1663 and 1814, remained notional after 1816, representing twenty-one shillings. Pounds replaced guineas as the major currency units after the 1816 "Great Recoinage." Virginia Woolf calls into question the coin's status and its many connections to slavery and imperialism in her feminist, anti-fascism polemic *Three Guineas* (1938).
24. In the retelling of "the story of Cupid and Psyche," chap. 5 of *Marius*, Cupid morphs from boy to man and sexual partner: "smooth he was, and touched with light" (Pater, *Marius the Epicurean* [London: Macmillan, 1924], 55). In the drawings and paintings of Simeon Solomon, Eros is a tall, muscular figure (*Love in Autumn*, 1866; *Sacramentum Amoris*, 1868; *Love at the Waters of Oblivion*, 1891).
25. "Plighted Promise" (Rossetti, *Poems* 243).
26. Hopkins revised the poem and renamed it "The Kind Betrothal" (*PW* 89-91).
27. "Love-Lily" and "The Morrow's Message" (Rossetti, *Poems*, 240, 206).
28. "The Hill Summit" also borrows religious motifs emphatically; see Rossetti, *Poems* 222.
29. Swinburne (1837-1909) matriculated at Oxford in Jan. 1856; his studies were not his main priority, however, and he was "rusticated" or suspended for a

term in early 1860. He left Oxford in June 1860 without sitting his final exams or taking his degree. For Swinburne's appreciation of Jowett, see his memorial essay "Recollections of Professor Jowett" (1893). Both Swinburne and Pater were members of the Old Mortality essay society. See Rikky Rooksby, "Swinburne, Algernon Charles," *Oxford Dictionary of National Biography,* online ed.; and the Algernon Charles Swinburne Project, http://webapp1.dlib.indiana.edu/swinburne/.

30. The murals were executed in the Debating Society chamber, now the library, of the Oxford Union; begun in 1857, they presented scenes from Thomas Malory's *Morte d'Arthur.* The project was technically disastrous: the walls were improperly prepared (the painters merely whitewashed the new brick). See the Rossetti Archive: http://www.rossettiarchive.org/docs/. In Hopkins's "Platonic Dialogue," a Ruskinian professor of aesthetics questions Hanbury, an artist associated with the project (see *CW* 4:136–72).

31. Swinburne first read about Poe (1809–49) in the works of Charles Baudelaire, who greatly admired the American writer and borrowed from his works the figure of the *flâneur,* the disinterested middle-class male who walks the city streets and records his impressions. When Hopkins's friend Marcus Clarke left Highgate school for Australia, he "gave Hopkins a volume of Poe's poetry, which Gerard passed on to Cyril when he joined the Jesuits." Norman White, *Hopkins: A Literary Life* (Oxford: Oxford University Press, 1992), 29. Among Hopkins's "sins" for May 1865: "Wasting time in looking at Poe's poems" (*CW* 3:304).

32. Schneider was the first to argue that "one of the mainsprings" for sprung rhythm is Swinburne's metrically challenging verse. See Elisabeth Schneider, *The Dragon in the Gate: Studies in the Poetry of G. M. Hopkins* (Berkeley: University of California Press, 1968). For other comparisons of Hopkins and Swinburne, see Isobel Armstrong and Renée Overholser.

33. For the resurgence of interest in Blake in Victorian aesthetic circles, see Higgins, "Mounting the 'Kindled Stairs,' Aesthetically," *Journal of Pre-Raphaelite Studies* 30 (Spring 2020): 21–40.

34. Robert Buchanan, "*Poems and Ballads.* By Algernon Charles Swinburne," *Athenaeum* 2023 (4 Aug. 1866): 137–38. Buchanan presents Swinburne as a poet who began "with considerable brilliance" but has proven himself to be "imitative" and "impure," and "imagines that rank blasphemy will be esteemed very clever" (138, 137, 138).

35. Swinburne's second series of *Poems and Ballads* was published in 1878.

36. Hopkins to Patmore, 16 Aug. 1883; *CW* 2:595.

37. Hopkins to Bridges, 21 Aug. 1877; *CW* 1:280.

38. Swinburne's *Poems and Ballads,* third series, was published in April 1889. The story of how Herod, king of Judea, ordered all Jewish children under two years of age slaughtered is recounted in Matt. 2:16.

39. See Higgins and Amanda Paxton, "'A Memoir of "Uncle Gerard"': by Beatrice Handley-Derry," *Hopkins Quarterly* 41.3-4 (Summer-Fall 2014): 57-68.
40. Morley's antagonistic review of *Poems and Ballads* demonstrates Swinburne's success: "He is either the vindictive and scornful apostle of a crushing ironshod despair, or else he is the libidinous laureate of a pack of satyrs." John Morley, "Review of Swinburne, *Poems and Ballads*," *Saturday Review*, 22 Aug. 1866, 147.
41. Isobel Armstrong compares the two men's interest in flagellation and uses Roland Barthes's *Sade Fourier Loyola* (1971) to juxtapose the Sadean Societé des Amis du Crime and the Society of Jesus (391, 393).
42. Swinburne, *Poems and Ballads* 11, 12; McGann and Sligh, eds., *Algernon Charles Swinburne: Major Poems and Selected Prose* 71.
43. For in-depth studies of Swinburne's conjoined political and poetic interests, see Jerome McGann, *Swinburne: An Experiment in Criticism* (Chicago: University of Chicago Press, 1972) and "Swinburne's Radical Artifice; or, The Comedian as A.C.," *Modernism/modernity*, 11.2 (Apr. 2004): 205-18; Margot K. Louis, *Swinburne and His Gods: The Roots and Growth of an Agnostic Poetry* (Montreal and Kingston: McGill-Queen's Press, 1990); Julia Saville, "Cosmopolitan Republican Swinburne, the Immersive Poet as Public Moralist," *Victorian Poetry* 47.45 (Winter 2009): 691-713; and Yisrael Levin, ed., *A. C. Swinburne and the Singing Word: New Perspectives on the Mature Work* (Farnham: Ashgate, 2010).
44. Swinburne's poems about Italy should be compared to Elizabeth Barrett Browning's *Casa Guidi Windows* (1851).
45. Whitman was anathema to Hopkins, who bristled at the suggestion that his poetic experiments were similar to the American poet's "marked and original manner" because, apparently, Whitman was "a very great scoundrel" (*CW* 1:542). The entire letter of 18-19 Oct. 1882 is instructive; see also *CW* 2:672, 895. For the importance of Whitman to an emerging late nineteenth-century queer sensibility and poetics, see the "Coda" to Sedgwick, *Between Men*. As Saville admits, Swinburne could "engage imaginatively with certain varieties of sexual difference and thereby prompt the kind of public controversy that followed the appearance of *Poems and Ballads* in 1866; yet, privately, he himself remained unable to restrain his visceral intolerance of male homosexuality—an intolerance which became increasingly public later in his life coloring even his admiration for Whitman" ("Cosmopolitan" 696).
46. Hopkins's loyalty to England was wholly antithetical—yet he did suggest, in Aug. 1871, that he was "a Communist" (*CW* 1:120) and eventually changed his mind about Irish "Home Rule." For his comments about "Socialists," see the letter to Bridges, 10 Feb. 1888 (*CW* 2:919).
47. For Swinburne's familiarity with Ignatius of Loyola's writings, see "*Perinde Ac Cadaver*" [as if he were a dead body] in *Songs before Sunrise*.
48. See Bump, 108-9, and Saville, *Queer* 41.

49. See especially "Anactoria," lines 175–81.
50. See for example "The Leper," a historical poem with Poe/Baudelaire-like flair: the speaker is a clerk who once served Yolande de Sallières, an aristocrat who suffered from the disease. He keeps her corpse hidden for six months, kissing it repeatedly to undo the social power of shaming.
51. Jowett's attitude changed from helpful to punitive in 1874 when W. H. Mallock, the future author of *The New Republic* (1877), a satire of Oxford, showed him suggestive letters exchanged between Pater and a Balliol undergraduate, William Money Hardinge. Jowett proceeded to block Pater's professional life at Oxford for almost two decades. See Billie Andrew Inman, "Estrangement and Connection: Walter Pater, Benjamin Jowett, and William M. Hardinge," in *Pater in the 1990s*, ed. by Laurel Brake and Ian Small (Greensboro, NC: ELT Press, 1991), 1–20.
52. Hopkins to Baillie, 22 May–18 June 1880 (*CW* 1:396). See also the letter to Bridges, 2–3 Apr. 1878 (*CW* 1:291).
53. The essays are included in *Oxford Essays and Notes* (*CW* 4).
54. A fourth poem, unfinished and untitled ("Who shaped these walls"), was composed on the back of letter from Pater dated 20 May [1879]: "My dear Hopkins, It will give me great pleasure to accept your kind invitation to dinner on Thursday at 5.30" (*PW* 409). The subject is architecture, but the dominant leitmotif is music: "Who shaped these walls has shewn/ The music of his mind,/ Made known, though thick through stone/ What beauty beat behind" (*PW* 159). In 1877 Pater published one of his most original essays, "The School of Giorgione," which declares: *"All art constantly aspires towards the condition of music"* (*Renaissance* 106).
55. "Pater is a master of the disjunctive and the discursive, of the sudden shift in tone or subject, of the abrupt right angle in the direction of his argument." J. B. Bullen, "The Sentient Body and Pater's 'Conclusion' to *The Renaissance*," in *Walter Pater: Le Forme della Modernità*, ed. by Elisa Bizzotto and Franco Marucci (Bologna: Cisalpino, 1996), 33.
56. Walter Pater, *Plato and Platonism* (London: Macmillan, 1893), 8. Hereafter cited as *PP*. Pater's historical reassessments are often staged dialogically, comparing, for example, Coleridge and Wordsworth, Winckelmann and Goethe, and Dante and Giotto.
57. Walter Pater, "Diaphaneitè," *Miscellaneous Studies*, ed. Charles Shadwell (London: Macmillan, 1895), 253. See Higgins, introduction to *CW* 4:10, 18; Monsman.
58. William Shuter quotes Thomas Wright on the subject (*Re-Reading Walter Pater* [Cambridge: Cambridge University Press, 1997], 34–35). For Hopkins's architectural notes and sketches, see *CW* 3, especially for 1864–65.
59. Walter Pater, "Poems by William Morris," *Westminster Review* 34 (Oct. 1868): 302. Hereafter cited as "Poems."

60. As Linda Dowling suggests, Pater "composed in the intellectual and stylistic penumbra" of Newman (*Language and Decadence in the Victorian Fin de Siècle* [Princeton, NJ: Princeton University Press, 1987], 168). The manuscript of Pater's major essay on Newman, unfinished in 1894, is housed in the Houghton Library, Harvard.
61. Pater was elected to a probationary fellowship at Brasenose 5 Feb. 1864; the position became permanent exactly one year later.
62. In this first essay, Hopkins observes, "Beauty lies in the relation of the parts of a sensuous thing to each other, that is in a certain relation, it being absolute at one point and comparative in those nearing it or falling fr[om] it" (*CW* 4:219).
63. In his short biography of Richard Watson Dixon, Hopkins suggests that his friend's poetry displays "the very rare gift of pure imagination, such as Coleridge had" (*CW* 2:699). As a student at Highgate school, Hopkins was close friends with the poet's grandson, Ernest Hartley Coleridge (see *CW* 1:lxxxvi). When Hopkins joined the Society, he became a colleague of Henry James Coleridge, S.J., one of Ernest's cousins (as editor of the *Month,* the Jesuit journal, Henry Coleridge rejected "The Wreck").
64. The diary entry reads: "Took my degree.—Saw Swinburne. Met Mr. Solomon" (*CW* 3:426).
65. See especially David Latham, "A 'World of Its Own Creation': Pre-Raphaelite Poetry and the New Paradigm for Art," *Journal of Pre-Raphaelite Studies,* n.s., 25 (Spring 2016), 5-27.
66. Pater pointedly connects Roman Catholicism with the "present day" phenomenon of "Pius IX, the true descendant of the fisherman, issuing the Encyclical, pleading the old promise against the world with a special kind of justice; and on the other side, the irresistible modern culture, which, as religious men often remind us, is only Christian accidentally" ("CW" 115). He must be alluding to *Quanta cura* [Condemning Current Errors], published in Dec. 1864; attached to the encyclical was the *Syllabus of Errors* (discussed above).
67. See Pater's novel *Marius the Epicurean* (1885), set in the era of Marcus Aurelius.
68. See Higgins, introduction to *CW* 4:68-72, and "Essaying 'W. H. Pater Esq.': New Perspectives on the Tutor/ Student Relationship Between Pater and Hopkins," in *Pater in the 1990s,* ed. Laurel Brake and Ian Small (Greensboro, NC: ELT Press, 1991): 77-94.
69. Drawing the human form, Hopkins decided, was inappropriate. As he explained to Bridges in late Oct./early Nov. 1879 (after his Oxford posting), "[T]hink then no one can admire beauty of the body more than I do.... But this kind of beauty is dangerous. Then comes the beauty of the mind, such as genius, and this is greater than the beauty of the body and not to call dangerous" (*CW* 1:374). The passage echoes throughout "To what serves Mortal Beauty?" (1885).
70. For Hopkins's use of "mould," see chap. 3, pp. 122-23.

71. Pater credits Morris with effecting this "transition which, under many forms, is the one law of the life of the human spirit, and of which what we call the Renaissance is only a supreme instance" ("Poems" 305).
72. For Hopkins's sketches and notes during his Switzerland tour, see *CW* 3 and 6 pt. 2.
73. "It is that flawless temperament in Wordsworth," Pater suggests, "which keeps his conviction of a latent intelligence in nature within the limits of sentiment or instinct, and confines it to those delicate and subdued shades of expression which perfect art allows" ("CW" 109).
74. The connection between Parmenides and primordial ooze is forged in an 1868 notebook kept by Hopkins while teaching at Newman's Oratory school in Birmingham: "Men, [Parmenides] thought, had sprung from slime" (*CW* 4:317). The first entry in the notebook begins, "Great feature of the old Gk. philosophy, Pater said, its holding certain truths, chiefly logical, out of proportion to the rest of its knowledge" (*CW* 4:304).
75. See *PW* 481; Thornton, ed., *All My Eyes See*, 105.
76. Plampin explains that the critique of Renaissance art shared by Ruskin, Lord Lindsay, and Anna Jameson was influenced by Alexis-François Rio's *De la poésie Chrétienne* (*Poetry of Christian Art*, 1836), which identifies the subservience of Renaissance artists to "profane tendencies" and naturalism as their "great element of decadence." Matthew Plampin, "A Stern and Just Respect for Truth: John Ruskin, Giotto, and the Arundel Society," *Visual Culture in Britain* 6.1 (Summer 2005): 61–62.
77. "Strange" emerges as a privileged term in all three Morris volumes that Pater reviews.
78. For Hopkins's attempt to distinguish between *"objective and subjective* morality," see the first essay he wrote for Pater, "The origin of our moral ideas" (*CW* 4:218–22).
79. Ibid.
80. Shuter also suggests that the "phenomenon of relic worship" in Pater's texts represents "an extreme form of one of the most complex of Pater's motifs, that of the grave visit.... [For] Pater it functions not only as a motif but also as a motive, a stimulus for the generation of art, of religion, of philosophy, indeed of culture itself" (93).
81. Pater also argues that one's subjectivity and understanding of the world rely upon "impressions unstable, flickering, inconsistent" ("Poems" 310).
82. It was deleted in the 1877, second edition (for which the book's title was changed from *Studies in the History of the Renaissance* to *The Renaissance: Studies in Art and Poetry*) and restored, with an amended text, in the third edition of 1888.
83. Thus he stressed in his "Meditation on Death," "This is the one certain thing of your place of death; you are there now, you sit within your corpses; look no farther: there where you are you will die" (*CW* 5:532).

84. For a reading of the poem in terms of "synthesis rather than dualism," see Joel Cuthbertson, "Gerard Manley Hopkins' Essentialising Fire," *Literature and Theology* 31.1 (Mar. 2017): 33-35.
85. The ten lectures were delivered in Oxford in 1891; four were published as individual essays in the *Contemporary Review*, 1892; all were brought together and revised for a volume in 1893.
86. Walter Pater, *Miscellaneous Studies*, ed. Charles Shadwell (London: Macmillan, 1895), 247, 249, 248. Pater also recommends "the mind of Savonarola [as] has been subtly traced by the author of Romola" (ibid., 249). Eliot's novel was a particular success in Oxford; see Hopkins's letters to Baillie, 5 Jan. 1865 (*CW* 1:75) and to Edward Urquhart, 6-10 Jan. 1865 (*CW* 1:78).

CONCLUSION

1. For representations of comfort, "the soul's sweet guest," in Hopkins's undergraduate poems, see "Why should their foolish bands" (*PW* 30), "A Voice from the World" (*PW* 49), and *"Ecquis binas"* (*PW* 97).
2. "[C]onsolation is contrary to desolation, in the same way the thoughts that spring from consolation are contrary to the thoughts that spring from desolation" (First Week, Rules [*SE* 69]). See *CW* 5:506-9.
3. Pusey quotes the Anglican theologian John Pearson: "'The unfeigned exercise of religion is undoubtedly, as never more necessary, so never so comfortable, as upon the bed of our sickness, especially upon the approach of death; wherefore the Church hath taken great care that the minister shall attend, and how he shall behave himself in the visitation of the sick for their comfort and advantage'" (Pusey, "Preface" cxxvi). For the solace a priest provides to a dying parishioner, see Hopkins's "Felix Randal": "My tongue had taught thee comfort" (*PW* 165).
4. Job 7:5. See James Finn Cotter, "Hopkins and Job," *Victorian Poetry* 33.2 (Summer 1995), 283-93.
5. See also Pusey, *Penitence* 23. Rickaby, S.J., decries "the natural desire of life and comfort, wealth, and honour" ("Modes of Humility," *SE* 139).
6. Rickaby, S.J., Second Week (*SE* 82). During years spent in industrial cities and then enduring the inhospitable conditions of St. Stephen's Green, Dublin, Hopkins appreciated physical comfort. In "Valley of the Elwy," the speaker notes that "Cómforting smell breáthed at very entering,/ Fetched fresh, as I suppose, off some sweet wood" (*PW* 143).
7. See also *CW* 5:508.
8. Robert Whitty, S.J. (1817-95), entered the Society in 1857. From 1881 to 1886, he was an instructor of Tertians.

9. See, for example, "God's Grandeur," "Pied Beauty," "In the Valley of the Elwy," and the first stanza of "The Wreck."
10. Abbé Gaume suggests that one should expect to be tested by God: "God withdraws His Sweetnesses only in order to prove our courage; and if we are brave and triumph over these temptations and discouragements, He restores favour and consolations to us" (57).
11. Yost argues that the Dublin sonnets "appear to have been written by a poet who, because he lacks spiritual comfort, fails to discern spiritual dignity in his suffering." Julia Yost, "'And What Does Anything At All Matter': Asceticism and the Hermeneutics of Comfort in Hopkins's Terrible Sonnets," *Religion and the Arts* 18 (2014): 332.
12. See Martin, *Gerard Manley Hopkins* 282.
13. Newman, "Sermon 9: Christian Sympathy" (*Parochial* vol. 5), 1.

APPENDIX

1. "Catholic Emancipation," *Britannica*, https://www.britannica.com/event/Catholic-Emancipation#ref174216.
2. Harris's novel "sparked a three-way debate in fictional form among John Henry Newman (*Loss and Gain*, 1848), Charles Kingsley (*Hypatia*, 1853), and Nicholas Wiseman (*Fabiola*, 1854), with Newman replying to both in *Calista* (1855). These historic novels battled over the issues of apostolic authority, patristic infallibility, and the continuity of Classical Christianity with the Roman Catholic Church" (Paz 64).
3. Pusey, "Dr. Pusey on Confession," *Times*, 11 Dec. 1866, 4 (Shuttleworth 635).
4. *The Confessional Unmasked: Showing the Depravity of the Priesthood, the Immorality of the Confessional, and the Questions Put to Females in Confession*, published by the Protestant Electoral Union (PEU) in 1865, featured excerpts from theological and confessional manuals. The PEU distributed copies to all members of Parliament in 1865 (Shuttleworth 628).
5. Although claiming "to eschew not only religious bigotry, but likewise religious controversy" (9), Gladstone laments the many conversions among "the highest classes of this country in the last thirty years" (61) and labels all such activities "domestic treason" (112). He attacks papal supporters, papal "aggression," and the "domination" of organizations such as the Jesuits, "the deadliest foes that mental and moral liberty have ever known" (58).
6. *Hansard Parliamentary Debates*, 3rd ser., vol. 234 (1877), cols. 1741–45.

BIBLIOGRAPHY

Adams, James Eli. *Dandies and Desert Saints: Styles of Victorian Masculinity.* Ithaca, NY: Cornell University Press, 1995.

Addis, William E., and Thomas Arnold. *A Catholic Dictionary, Containing Some Account of the Doctrine, Discipline, Rites, Ceremonies, Councils, and Religious Orders of the Catholic Church.* London: Kegan Paul, 1884.

Aldis, John. *Priestly Confession: The Bane of Priests and People.* London: Elliot Stock, 1874.

The Algernon Charles Swinburne Project. University of Indiana. http://webapp1.dlib.indiana.edu/swinburne/view#docId=swinburne/acs0000508-01.xml.

Ambrose, Isaac. *The Christian Warrior, Wrestling with Sin, Satan, the World and the Flesh.* Edited by Thomas Jones. London: R. B. Seeley and W. Burnside, 1837.

The Ancren Riwle; A Treatise on the Rules and Duties of Monastic Life. Edited and translated by James Morton. London: Camden Society, 1853.

Anderson, Benedict. *Imagined Communities: Reflections on the Origin and Spread of Nationalism.* London: Verso, 1991.

Anon. *The Confessional Unmasked: Showing the Depravity of the Priesthood, the Immorality of the Confessional, and the Questions Put to Females in Confession, Etc., Etc., Being Extracts from the Theological Works Used in Maynooth College and Sanctioned by the "Sacred Congregation of Rites"; With Notes.* London: Protestant Evangelical Mission and Electoral Union, 1873.

Anon. *The Oxford and Roman Railway: The Chief Ministers in Church and State and Their Ladies Are Directors and Managers.* 3rd ed. London: Protestant Evangelical Mission and Electoral Union, 1871.

Armstrong, Isobel. *Victorian Poetry: Poetry, Poetics and Politics.* London: Routledge, 1996.

Armstrong, John E. *The Confessional: Its Wickedness. A Lecture.* Brighton: Edward Verrall, 1856.

Arnold, Matthew. *Lectures and Essays in Criticism. The Complete Works of Matthew Arnold.* Edited by R. H. Super, vol. 3. Ann Arbor: University of Michigan Press, 1962.

Augustine. *The City of God.* Translated and edited by Marcus Dods. 2 vols. Edinburgh: T. and T. Clark, 1871.

———. *Confessions.* Translated by Henry Chadwick. Oxford: Oxford University Press, 1991.

Avery-Quash, Susanna, and Silvia Davoli. "The National Gallery Searching for Leonardo: Acquisitions and Contributions to Knowledge about the Lombard School." In *Leonardo in Britain: Collections and Historical Reception,* edited by Juliana Barone and Susanna Avery-Quash, 141–67. Florence: Leo S. Olschki, 2019.

Aviram, Amittai. *Telling Rhythm: Body and Meaning in Poetry.* Ann Arbor: University of Michigan Press, 1994.

Barker-Benfield, Ben. "The Spermatic Economy: A Nineteenth Century View of Sexuality." *Feminist Studies* 1.1 (Summer 1972): 45–74.

Barringer, Tim, Jason Rosenfeld, and Alison Smith, eds. *Pre-Raphaelites: Victorian Avant-Garde.* London: Tate Publishing, 2012.

Beasley, Brett. "Acting Christ: The Christocentric Exemplarism of Gerard Manley Hopkins." *Literature and Theology* 34.2 (June 2020): 228–44.

Becker, Joseph, S.J. *The Re-Formed Jesuits.* San Francisco: Ignatius Press, 1992.

Bell, Alan. "Stephen, Sir Leslie." *Oxford Dictionary of National Biography.* Online ed. https://doi-org.ezproxy.library.yorku.ca/10.1093/ref:odnb/36271.

Bending, Lucy. *The Representation of Bodily Pain in Late Nineteenth-Century English Culture.* Oxford: Oxford University Press, 2000.

Benson, A. C. *Walter Pater.* London: Macmillan, 1906.

Bentley, James. *Ritualism and Politics in Victorian Britain: The Attempt to Legislate for Belief.* Oxford: Oxford University Press, 1978.

Bergonzi, Bernard. *Gerard Manley Hopkins.* New York: Collier Books, 1977.

Bernauer, James, S.J. "Confessions of the Soul: Foucault and Theological Culture." *Philosophy and Social Criticism* 31.5–6 (2005): 557–72.

———. "Fascinating Flesh: Revealing the Catholic Foucault." In *Confessions of the Flesh,* special issue, *Foucault Studies* 29.1–5 (April 2021): 38–47.

———. "Foreword: Cry of Spirit." In Michel Foucault, *Religion and Culture,* edited by Jeremy Carrette, xi–xvii. New York: Routledge, 1999.

Bernauer, James, S.J., and Michael Mahon. "The Ethics of Michel Foucault." In *The Cambridge Companion to Foucault,* edited by Gary Gutting, 141–58. Cambridge: Cambridge University Press, 1994.

Bernheimer, Charles. *Decadent Subjects: The Idea of Decadence in Art, Literature, Philosophy, and Culture of the* Fin de Siècle *in Europe.* Edited by T. Jefferson Kline and Naomi Shor. Baltimore, MD: Johns Hopkins University Press, 2002.

Bernstein, Susan David. *Confessional Subjects: Revelations of Gender and Power in Victorian Literature and Culture.* Chapel Hill: University of North Carolina Press, 1997.

Bischoff, D. Anthony, S.J. "The Manuscripts of Gerard Manley Hopkins." *Thought* 26.102 (September 1951): 551–80.

Bizup, Joseph. "'The Wreck of the Deutschland' and Hopkins' Theology of 'News.'" *Victorian Poetry* 30.2 (Summer 1992): 135–49.

Blair, Kirstie. *Form and Faith in Victorian Poetry and Religion.* Oxford: Oxford University Press, 2012.

———. "Priest and Nun? *Daniel Deronda,* Anti-Catholicism and the Confessional." *George Eliot Review* 400 (2001): 45–50.

Blau, Herbert. "Rhetorics of the Body: Do You Smell a Fault?" In *Cultural Artifacts and the Production of Meaning: The Page, the Image, and the Body,* edited by Margaret Ezell and Katherine O'Brien O'Keefe, 223–39. Ann Arbor: University of Michigan Press, 1994.

Bonea, Amelia, et al. *Anxious Times: Medicine and Modernity in Nineteenth-Century Britain.* Pittsburgh: University of Pittsburgh Press, 2019. https://diseasesofmodernlife.web.ox.ac.uk/home#.

Bossy, John. "The Social History of Confession in the Age of the Reformation." *Transactions of the Royal Historical Society* 25 (1975): 21–38.

Bourriaud, Nicolas. "Michel Foucault: Manet and the Birth of the Viewer." In Michel Foucaut, *Manet and the Object of Painting,* translated by Matthew Barr, 9–19. London: Tate Publishing, 2011.

Brake, Laurel, and Ian Small, eds. *Pater in the 1990s.* British Authors Series. Greensboro, NC: ELT Press, 1991.

Bridges, Robert. *The Testament of Beauty: A Poem in Four Books.* Oxford: Clarendon Press, 1929.

Brockman, H. J. *Letter to the Women of England: On the Confessional.* London: Protestant Electoral Union, 1867.

Brooks, Peter. *Troubling Confessions: Speaking Guilt in Law and Literature.* Chicago: University of Chicago Press, 2000.

Brown, Peter. *The Body and Society: Men, Women, and Sexual Renunciation in Early Christianity.* New York: Columbia University Press, 1988.

Browning, Elizabeth Barrett. *Aurora Leigh and Other Poems.* Edited by Cora Kaplan. London: The Women's Press, 1978.

Browning, Robert. *The Complete Poetic and Dramatic Works.* Edited by Horace E. Scudder. Boston: Houghton, Mifflin, 1895.

Buchanan, Robert. *Foxglove Manor.* 1884. https://www.gutenberg.org/files/48471/48471-h/48471-h.htm.

———. "*Poems and Ballads.* By Algernon Charles Swinburne." *Athenaeum* 2023 (4 August 1866): 137–38.

———. [Pseud.: Thomas Maitland]. "The Fleshly School of Art: Mr. D. G. Rossetti." In *The Broadview Anthology of Victorian Poetry and Poetic Theory,* edited by Thomas J. Collins and Vivienne J. Rundle, 1329–40. Peterborough: Broadview Press, 1999.

Buckton, Oliver S. *Secret Selves: Confession and Same-Sex Desire in Victorian Autobiography.* Chapel Hill: University of North Carolina Press, 1998.

Budd, Susan. *Varieties of Unbelief.* New York: Holmes and Meier, 1977.

Bullen, J. B. "The Sentient Body and Pater's 'Conclusion' to *The Renaissance.*" In *Walter Pater: Le Forme della Modernità,* edited by Elisa Bizzotto and Franco Marucci, 33–44. Bologna: Cisalpino, 1996.

Bump, Jerome. "Hopkins' Imagery and Medievalist Poetics." *Victorian Poetry* 15 (1977): 99–119.

Burgwinkle, Bill. "Medieval Somatics." In *The Cambridge Companion to the Body in Literature,* edited by David Hillman and Ulrika Maude, 10–23. Cambridge: Cambridge University Press, 2015.

Burnand, F. C. "'PUNCH' and Pontiffs." *Dublin Review* 147.294/295 (1901): 306–21.

Butler, Percy. "Keble, John." *Oxford Dictionary of National Biography.* Online ed. https://doi-org.ezproxy.library.yorku.ca/10.1093/ref:odnb/15231.

Büttgen, Philippe. "Foucault's Concept of Confession." In *Confessions of the Flesh,* special issue, *Foucault Studies* 29.1–5 (April 2021): 6–21.

"Catholic Relief Acts." UK Parliament. https://www.parliament.uk/about/living-heritage/transformingsociety/private-lives/religion/overview/emancipation.

Carrette, Jeremy. *Foucault and Religion.* London: Routledge, 2000.

———. "Prologue to a Confession of the Flesh." In Michel Foucault, *Religion and Culture,* edited by Jeremy Carrette, 1–47. New York: Routledge, 1999.

[Carroll, Lewis]. "The Priest in Absolution." *Pall Mall Gazette,* 14 July 1877, 4–5.

Carter, Thomas T. *The Freedom of Confession in the Church of England: A Letter to His Grace the Lord Archbishop of Canterbury.* Oxford: Rivingtons, 1877. http://anglicanhistory.org/england/ttcarter/freedom.html.

Castelli, Elizabeth. "'I Will Make Mary Male': Pieties of the Body and Gender Transformation of Christian Women in Late Antiquity." In *Body Guards: The Cultural Politics of Gender Ambiguity,* edited by Julia Epstein and Kristina Straub, 29–49. New York: Routledge, 1991.

Casteras, Susan P. "Virgin Vows: The Early Victorians Artists' Portrayal of Nuns and Novices." *Victorian Studies* 24.2 (Winter 1981): 157–84.

Caughie, Pamela L. "'Passing' and Identity: A Literary Perspective on Gender and Sexual Diversity." In *God, Science, Sex, Gender: An Interdisciplinary Approach to Christian Ethics,* edited by Patricia Jung and Aana Vigen, 195–215. Chicago: University of Illinois Press, 2010.

Chadwick, Henry. Introduction to Augustine, *Confessions,* ix–xxvi. Oxford: Oxford University Press, 1991.

[Chambers, John Charles]. *The Priest in Absolution: A Manual for Such as Are Called unto the Higher Ministries in the English Church.* London: Joseph Masters, 1866.

———. *The Priest in Absolution: A Manual for Such as Are Called unto the Higher Ministries in the English Church, Part II.* London: Joseph Masters, 1870.

Chambers, Susan. "Gerard Manley Hopkins and the Kinesthetics of Conviction." *Victorian Studies* 51.1 (Autumn 2008): 7–35.

Chaucer, Geoffrey. *The Works of Geoffrey Chaucer.* 2nd ed. Edited by F. N. Robinson. Boston: Houghton Mifflin, 1957.

Chiniquy, Charles, *Fifty Years in the Church of Rome.* Revised ed. London: Protestant Truth Society, 1885.

———. *The Priest, the Woman, and the Confessional.* New York: Fleming H. Revell, 1880.

Chitty, Susan. *The Beast and the Monk: A Life of Charles Kingsley.* Toronto: Hodder and Stoughton, 1974.

[Church Association]. *Church Association Lectures: Delivered at St. James' Hall, Piccadilly, London.* London: William MacIntosh, 1867.

Clarke, R. F., S.J. "A Catholic's View of 'Helbeck of Bannisdale.'" *Nineteenth Century* 44 (September 1898): 455–67.

Clements, Elicia, and Lesley Higgins, eds. *Victorian Aesthetic Conditions: Pater across the Arts.* Basingstoke: Palgrave Macmillan, 2010.

Clough, Arthur Hugh. *The Oxford Diaries of Arthur Hugh Clough.* Edited by Anthony Kenny. Oxford: Clarendon Press, 1990.

Cobb, Peter G. "Pusey, Edward Bouverie." *Oxford Dictionary of National Biography.* Online ed. https://doi-org.ezproxy.library.yorku.ca/10.1093/ref:odnb/22910.

Cobbe, Frances Power. *Darwinism in Morals, and Other Essays.* London: Williams and Norgate, 1872.

Cohen, Ed. *Talk on the Wilde Side.* London: Routledge, 1993.

Cohen, Richard. "Merleau-Ponty, the Flesh, and Foucault." *Philosophy Today* 28.4 (Winter 1984): 329–38.

Coleridge, John Taylor. *A Memoir of the Rev. John Keble.* Oxford: James Parker, 1870.

Colley, Linda. *Britons: Forging the Nation, 1707–1837.* New Haven, CT: Yale University Press, 1992.

Collins, Thomas J., and Vivienne J. Rundle, eds. *The Broadview Anthology of Victorian Poetry and Poetic Theory.* Peterborough: Broadview Press, 1999.

Collins, Wilkie. *The Black Robe.* 2 vols. Leipzig: Bernhard Tauchnitz, 1881.

Confession, a Help to Heaven. London: Church Press, 1869.

Constable, Liz, Dennis Denisoff, and Matthew Potolsky. Introduction to *Perennial Decay: On the Aesthetics and Politics of Decadence,* 1–32. Philadelphia: University of Pennsylvania Press, 1999.

Corbett, David. *Edward Burne-Jones.* London: Tate Publications, 2004.

Cotter, James Finn. "Hopkins and Job." *Victorian Poetry* 33.2 (Summer 1995): 283–93.

Coupe, Charles, S.J. *Lectures on the Holy Eucharist.* London: R. and T. Washbourne, 1906.

Crehan, Joseph, S.J. "More Light on Gerard Hopkins." *Month,* n.s., 10.4 (October 1953): 205–14.

Crossley, Nick. *The Social Body: Habit, Identity, Desire.* London: Sage Publications, 2001.

Cruise, Colin, ed. *Love Revealed: Simeon Solomon and the Pre-Raphaelites*. London: Merrell, 2005.

Cumming, John. *Ritualism, The Highway to Rome: Twelve Lectures*. London: J. Bislet, 1867.

Cuthbertson, Joel. "Gerard Manley Hopkins' Essentialising Fire." *Literature and Theology* 31.1 (March 2017): 33–46.

Dailey, Robert H., S.J. *Introduction to Moral Theology*. New York: Bruce Publishing, 1970.

Davidson, Arnold I. "Ethics as Ascetics: Foucault, the History of Ethics, and Ancient Thought." In *The Cambridge Companion to Foucault,* edited by Gary Gutting, 115–40. Cambridge: Cambridge University Press, 1994.

———. "In Praise of Counter-Conduct." *History of the Human Sciences* 24.4 (2011): 25–41.

Davis, Lloyd. "The Virgin Body as Victorian Text: An Introduction." In *Virginal Sexuality and Textuality in Victorian Literature*. Edited by Lloyd Davis, 3–24. Albany: State University of New York Press, 1993.

———, ed. *Virginal Sexuality and Textuality in Victorian Literature*. Albany: State University of New York Press, 1993.

Dhu, Helen. *Stanhope Burleigh: The Jesuits in Our Homes*. London: Stringer and Townsend, 1855.

Dickens, Charles. "Old Lamps for New Ones." *Household Words* 12 (15 June 1850): 12–14.

Dimock, Wai Chee. *Through Other Continents: American Literature across Deep Time*. Princeton, NJ: Princeton University Press, 2006.

Diprose, Rosalyn. *The Bodies of Women: Ethics, Embodiment, and Sexual Difference*. London: Routledge, 1994.

Dollimore, Jonathan. "The Cultural Practice of Perversion: Augustine, Shakespeare, Freud, and Foucault." *Textual Practice* 4.2 (1990): 179–96.

Douay-Rheims Bible. Summa-Theologiae.org. http://www.drbo.org/index.htm.

Douglas, Mary. *Purity and Danger: An Analysis of Concepts of Pollution and Taboo*. London: Routledge and Kegan Paul, 1966.

———. "The Two Bodies." In *The Body: A Reader,* edited by Mariam Fraser and Monica Greco, 78–81. London: Routledge, 2005.

Dowling, Linda. *Hellenism and Homosexuality in Victorian Oxford*. Ithaca, NY: Cornell University Press, 1994.

———. *Language and Decadence in the Victorian Fin de Siècle*. Princeton, NJ: Princeton University Press, 1987.

Dubois, Martin. *Gerard Manley Hopkins and the Poetry of Religious Experience*. Cambridge: Cambridge University Press, 2019.

Durbach, Nadja. "Smallpox, Vaccination, and the Marked Body." In *A Cultural History of the Human Body in the Age of Empire,* edited by Michael Sappol and Stephen P. Rice, 191–212. Oxford: Berg, 2010.

Elden, Stuart. "Review: Michel Foucault, *Histoire de la sexualité 4: Les aveux de la chair.*" *Theory, Culture, and Society* 35.7-8 (2018): 293-311.

Everyman and Medieval Miracle Plays. Edited by A. C. Cawley. London: J. M. Dent, 1993.

Faber, Frederick. *The Foot of the Cross; or, The Sorrows of Mary.* London: Thomas Richardson and Son, 1858.

———. *Growth in Holiness; or, The Progress of the Spiritual Life.* Baltimore: John Murphy, 1855.

Faber, Geoffrey. *Oxford Apostles: A Character Study of the Oxford Movement.* London: Faber, 1974.

Falk, Pasi. "Written in the Flesh." *Body and Society* 1.1 (1995): 95-105.

Feeney, Joseph, S.J. *The Playfulness of Gerard Manley Hopkins.* Farnham: Ashgate, 2008.

Fiegel, Kenneth M. "My Winter World: The Illness of Gerard Manley Hopkins." *Lancet* 347.9057 (1997): 1017-19.

Fifield, Peter. "The Body, Pain and Violence." In *The Cambridge Companion to the Body in Literature,* edited by David Hillman and Ulrika Maude, 116-31. Cambridge: Cambridge University Press, 2015.

FitzGerald, Edward. *The Rubáiyát of Omar Khayyam.* In *The Broadview Anthology of Victorian Poetry and Poetic Theory,* edited by Thomas J. Collins and Vivienne J. Rundle, 147-55. Peterborough: Broadview Press, 1999.

"The Flare Up in the Confessional. The Pussey Cats are Coming." 1850. https://digital.nls.uk/english-ballads/archive/74892397?mode=fullsize.

Flynn, Thomas. "Foucault's Mapping of History." In *The Cambridge Companion to Foucault,* edited by Gary Gutting, 28-46. Cambridge: Cambridge University Press, 1994.

Fortescue, Adrian. "Confiteor." In *The Catholic Encyclopedia,* vol. 4. New York: Robert Appleton, 1908. http://www.newadvent.org/cathen/04222a.htm.

Foucault, Michel. *Abnormal: Lectures at the Collège de France, 1974-1975.* Edited by Valerio Marchetti and Antonella Salomin, translated by Graham Burchill. New York: Picador, 1999.

———. *Discipline and Punish: The Birth of the Prison.* Translated by Alan Sheridan. New York: Vintage, 1979.

———. *The Essential Works of Michel Foucault.* Edited by Paul Rabinow. 3 vols. New York: New Press, 1997.

———. *Foucault Live: Collected Interviews, 1961-1984.* Edited by Sylvère Lotringer. Paris: Semiotext(e), 1989.

———. *The History of Sexuality.* Vol. 1: *An Introduction* [*The Will to Know*]. Translated by Robert Hurley. New York: Vintage Books, 1990.

———. *The History of Sexuality.* Vol. 2: *The Use of Pleasure.* Translated by Robert Hurley. New York: Vintage Books, 1985.

———. *The History of Sexuality.* Vol. 4: *Confessions of the Flesh.* Translated by Robert Hurley. New York: Pantheon Books, 2021.

———. "How We Behave: Interview with Paul Rabinow and Hubert L. Dreyfus." *Vanity Fair,* November 1983, 61-69.

———. *The Order of Things: An Archaeology of the Human Sciences.* Translated by Alan Sheridan. New York: Vintage Books, 1973.

———. *Power/Knowledge: Selected Interviews and Other Writings, 1972-1977.* Edited by Colin Gordon, translated by Colin Gordon, Leo Marshall, John Mepham, and Kate Soper. New York: Harvester Wheatsheaf, 1980.

———. *Religion and Culture.* Edited by Jeremy Carrette. New York: Routledge, 1999.

———. *Security, Territory, Population: Lectures at the Collège de France, 1977-1978.* Translated by Graham Burchell. London: Palgrave Macmillan, 2007.

———. *Wrong-Doing, Truth-Telling: The Function of Avowal in Justice.* Edited by Fabienne Brion and Bernard E. Harcourt, translated by Stephen W. Sawyer. Chicago: University of Chicago Press, 2014.

Fraser, Nancy. "Foucault's Body-Language: A Post-Humanist Political Rhetoric?" *Salmagundi* 61 (Fall 1983): 55-70.

Fulweiler, Howard W. *Letters from the Darkling Plain: Language and the Grounds of Knowledge in the Poetry of Arnold and Hopkins.* Columbia: University of Missouri Press, 1972.

Fuss, Diana. "Corpse Poem." *Critical Inquiry* 30.1 (Autumn 2003): 1-30.

Gallagher, Catherine. "The Body versus the Social Body in the Works of Thomas Malthus and Henry Mayhew." *Representations* 14 (Spring 1986): 83-106.

Gallwey, Peter, S.J. *How Some of the Poor Are Wisely Oppressed in Workhouses: A Sermon.* London: Burns and Lambert, 1861.

Gaume, Jean-Joseph. *Advice for Those Who Exercise the Ministry of Reconciliation through Confession and Absolution* [*Manuel des confesseurs,* 1843]. Abridged, 2nd ed. Edited by Edward Pusey. Oxford: James Parker, 1878.

Gilbert, Pamela K. "Popular Beliefs and the Body." In *A Cultural History of the Human Body in the Age of Empire,* edited by Michael Sappol and Stephen P. Rice, 125-48. Oxford: Berg, 2010.

Gilley, Sheridan. "Faber, Frederick William." *Oxford Dictionary of National Biography.* Online ed. https://doi-org.ezproxy.library.yorku.ca/10.1093/ref:odnb/9050.

———. "Keble, Froude, Newman, and Pusey." In *The Oxford Handbook of the Oxford Movement,* edited by Stewart J. Brown et al., 97-110. Oxford: Oxford University Press, 2017.

Goldstein, Laurence. *The Male Body: Features, Destinies, Exposures.* Ann Arbor: University of Michigan Press, 1994.

Goodwin, Sarah Webster, and Elisabeth Bronfen. Introduction to *Death and Representation,* edited by Sarah Webster Goodwin and Elisabeth Bronfen, 3-25. Baltimore, MD: Johns Hopkins University Press, 1993.

Griffin, Susan M. *Anti-Catholicism and Nineteenth-Century Fiction.* Cambridge: Cambridge University Press, 2004.

———. "The Yellow Mask, the Black Robe, and the Woman in White: Wilkie Collins, Anti-Catholic Discourse, and the Sensation Novel." *Narrative* 12.1 (January 2004): 55-73.

Grigson, Geoffrey. "Blood or Bran." In *Gerard Manley Hopkins,* edited by Walford Davies, 203-06. London: Dent, 1979.

Gros, Frédéric. Foreword to Michel Foucault, *Confessions of the Flesh,* translated by Robert Hurley, vii-xiii. New York: Pantheon Books, 2021.

Grosz, Elizabeth. *Volatile Bodies: Toward a Corporeal Feminism.* Bloomington: Indiana University Press, 1994.

Hahn, Alois. "Narrative Identity and Auricular Confession as Biography-Generators." In *Self, Soul, and Body in Religious Experience,* edited by A. I. Baumgarten, J. Assmann, and G. G. Strousma, 26-52. Leiden: Brill, 1998.

Haley, Bruce. *The Healthy Body and Victorian Culture.* Cambridge, MA: Harvard University Press, 1978.

Hall, Donald. *Fixing Patriarchy: Feminism and Mid-Victorian Male Novelists.* New York: New York University Press, 1996.

Hall, Lesley A. "Forbidden by God, Despised by Men: Masturbation, Medical Warnings, Moral Panic, and Manhood in Great Britain, 1850-1950." In *Forbidden History: The State, Society, and the Regulation of Sexuality in Modern Europe,* edited by John C. Fout, 293-315. Chicago: University of Chicago Press, 1992.

Hansard Parliamentary Debates. 3rd ser., vol. 234 (1877), cols. 1741-45, 1751-53.

Harcourt, Bernard. "Foucault's Keystone: *Confessions of the Flesh.*" In *Confessions of the Flesh,* special issue, *Foucault Studies* 29.1-5 (April 2021): 48-70.

Hare, E. H. "Masturbatory Insanity: The History of an Idea." *Journal of Mental Science* 108.452 (January 1962): 1-25.

Harris, Daniel. *Inspirations Unbidden: The "Terrible Sonnets" of Gerard Manley Hopkins.* Berkeley: University of California Press, 1982.

[Harris, Elizabeth]. *From Oxford to Rome: and How It Fared with Some Who Lately Made the Journey.* London: Longman, Brown, Green, and Longmans, 1847.

Hartman, Anne. "Confession as Cultural Form: The Plymouth Inquiry." *Victorian Studies* 47.4 (Summer 2005): 535-56.

Hartman, Geoffrey. *The Unmediated Vision: An Interpretation of Wordsworth, Hopkins, Rilke, and Valery.* New York: Harcourt, Brace, and World, 1966.

Hayman, John. *John Ruskin and Switzerland.* Waterloo: Wilfrid Laurier University Press, 1990.

Higgins, Lesley. "Essaying 'W. H. Pater Esq.': New Perspectives on the Tutor/Student Relationship between Pater and Hopkins." In *Pater in the 1990s,* edited by Laurel Brake and Ian Small, 77-94. Greensboro, NC: ELT Press, 1991.

———. "'Heraclitean Fire' and Eucharistic Flame: The Poetry of Transformation in Hopkins." *Month* 250.1463 (November 1989): 423-28.

———. "Jowett and Pater: Trafficking in Platonic Wares." *Victorian Studies* 37.1 (Autumn 1993): 43-72.

———. *The Modernist Cult of Ugliness: Aesthetic and Gender Politics.* New York: Palgrave Macmillan, 2002.

———. "Mounting the 'Kindled Stairs,' Aesthetically." *Journal of Pre-Raphaelite Studies* 30 (Spring 2020): 21–40.

———. "The 'Necessity' of Corot and Whistler in Pater's 'Network' of Painters." In *Victorian Aesthetic Conditions: Pater across the Arts,* edited by Elicia Clements and Lesley Higgins, 47–67. Basingstoke: Palgrave Macmillan, 2010,

———. "Reckoning up the Ellipses in Hopkins' Poetry." *Hopkins Quarterly* 40.3–4 (Summer-Fall 2013): 69–94.

———. "'She Rears Herself': Feminist Possibilities in Hopkins's Poetry." *Studies* 84.334 (Summer 1995): 130–40.

Higgins, Lesley, and Amanda Paxton. "A Memoir of 'Uncle Gerard': by Beatrice Handley-Derry." *Hopkins Quarterly* 41.3–4 (Summer-Fall 2014): 57–68.

Higgins, Lesley, and Julianna Will. "'Quelled or Quenched in Leaves': The Poplar Experiments of Pater, Monet, and Hopkins." *Journal of Pre-Raphaelite Studies* 29 (Fall 2020): 1–19.

Hollywood, Amy. "Spiritual but Not Religious: The Vital Interplay between Submission and Freedom." *Harvard Divinity Bulletin,* Winter/Spring 2010. https://bulletin.hds.harvard.edu/spiritual-but-not-religious/.

Hopkins, Gerard Manley. *The Collected Works of Gerard Manley Hopkins.* 9 vols. Oxford: Oxford University Press, 2006–25.

———. *Correspondence.* Edited by R. K. R. Thornton and Catherine Phillips. Vols. 1 and 2 of *Collected Works.* Oxford: Oxford University Press, 2013.

———. *Diaries, Journals, and Notebooks.* Edited by Lesley Higgins. Vol. 3 of *Collected Works.* Oxford: Oxford University Press, 2015.

———. *The Dublin Notebook.* Edited by Lesley Higgins and Michael Suarez, S.J. Vol. 7 of *Collected Works.* Oxford: Oxford University Press, 2014.

———. *The Later Poetic Manuscripts of Gerard Manley Hopkins in Facsimile.* Edited by Norman H. MacKenzie. New York: Garland, 1991.

———. *Oxford Essays and Notes.* Edited by Lesley Higgins. Vol. 4 of *Collected Works.* Oxford: Oxford University Press, 2006.

———. *The Poetical Works of Gerard Manley Hopkins.* Edited by Norman H. MacKenzie. Oxford: Clarendon Press, 1990.

———. *Sermons and Spiritual Writings.* Edited by Jude Nixon and Noel Barber, S.J. Vol. 5 of *Collected Works.* Oxford: Oxford University Press, 2018.

House of Lords. "Confessional—'The Priest in Absolution'—Observations," 14 June 1877. https://hansard.parliament.uk/lords/1877-06-14/debates/94c863ff-b5ce-4f55-bad5-ca0ddefcbbe6/TheConfessional%E2%80%94ThePriestInAbsolution%E2%80%94Observations.

Huffer, Lynn. "Foucault's Queer Virgins: An Unfinished History in Fragments." In *Confessions of the Flesh,* special issue, *Foucault Studies* 29.1–5 (April 2021): 22–37.

Humphries, Simon. "Hopkins' Silent Men." *ELH* 77.2 (Summer 2010): 447-75.

Hurley, Michael D. "Wrestling with Gerard Manley Hopkins." *Textual Practice* 35.6 (2021): 921-40.

Hyder, C. K., ed. *Swinburne: The Critical Heritage.* London: Routledge and Kegan Paul, 1970.

Ignatius Loyola. *The Spiritual Exercises.* 2nd ed. Edited and translated by Joseph Rickaby, S.J. New York: Benziger Brothers, 1923.

Inman, Billie Andrew. "Estrangement and Connection: Walter Pater, Benjamin Jowett, and William M. Hardinge." In *Pater in the 1990s,* edited by Laurel Brake and Ian Small, 1-20. Greensboro, NC: ELT Press, 1991.

Jacobs, Joseph. "The Dying of Death." *Fortnightly Review* 72 (July-December 1899): 264-69.

"Jean-Joseph Gaume." *Catholic Encyclopedia.* 1913. *New Advent.* http://www.newadvent.org/cathen/06398b.htm.

Johnson, Margaret. *Gerard Manley Hopkins and Tractarian Poetry.* Aldershot, UK: Ashgate, 1997.

Johnston, J. O. *Life and Letters of Henry Parry Liddon.* London: Longmans, Green, 1904.

Jowett, Benjamin. *College Sermons.* 3rd ed. Edited by W. H. Fremantle. London: John Murray, 1896.

———. *Dear Miss Nightingale: A Selection of Benjamin Jowett's Letters to Florence Nightingale.* Edited by Vincent Quinn and John Prest. Oxford: Clarendon Press, 1987.

Keble, John. *The Christian Year: Thoughts in Verse for the Sundays and Holydays throughout the Year.* 1827. Facsimile ed. London: Elliot Stock, 1897.

———. *Letters of Spiritual Counsel and Guidance.* 3rd ed. Edited by R. F. Wilson. Oxford and London: James Parker, 1875.

———. *Sermons for the Christian Year.* 10 vols. Oxford: James Parker, 1875.

Kenny, Anthony. "Biographical Introduction." In Clough, *The Oxford Diaries of Arthur Hugh Clough,* edited by Anthony Kenny, i-lxxv. Oxford: Clarendon Press, 1990.

Kilvert, Francis. *Selections from the Diary of the Rev. Francis Kilvert, 1870-79.* Edited by William Plomer, Elizabeth Divine, and Edward Ardizzone. London: Cape, 1976.

Klaus, Robert. *The Pope, the Protestants, and the Irish.* New York: Garland, 1987.

Kollar, Rene. "Power and Control over Women in Victorian England: Male Opposition to Sacramental Confession in the Anglican Church." *Journal of Anglican Studies* 3.1 (2005): 11-32.

Kristeva, Julia. "*Stabat Mater.*" In *The Female Body in Western Culture: Contemporary Perspectives,* edited by Susan Rubin Suleiman, 99-118. Cambridge, MA: Harvard University Press, 1986.

Laidlaw, John. *God's Way of Pardon.* Stirling: Drummond's Tract Depot, n.d.

Laird, Robert G. "'He Did Not Sit Five Minutes': The Conversion of Gigadibs." *University of Toronto Quarterly* 45.4 (Summer 1976): 295-313.

Laqueur, Thomas W. *Making Sex: Body and Gender from the Greeks to Freud.* Cambridge, MA: Harvard University Press, 1990.

———. *Solitary Sex: A Cultural History of Masturbation.* New York: Zone Books, 2003.

Larsen, Timothy. "While You've a Lucifer: How the Victorians Thought about—and Laughed at—the Devil." *Times Literary Supplement,* 14 May 2021, 13.

Latham, David. "A 'World of Its Own Creation': Pre-Raphaelite Poetry and the New Paradigm for Art." *Journal of Pre-Raphaelite Studies,* n.s., 25 (Spring 2016): 5-27.

Latour, Bruno. "How to Talk about the Body? The Normative Dimension of Science Studies." *Body and Society* 10.2-3 (2004): 205-29.

Lea, Henry Charles. *A History of Auricular Confession and Indulgences in the Latin Church.* Vol. 1: *Confession and Absolution.* Philadelphia: Lea Brothers, 1896.

Le Goff, Jacques. *The Birth of Purgatory.* Chicago: University of Chicago Press, 1984.

Lessing, Gotthold. *The Laocoon.* Translated by Robert Phillimore. London: Routledge, 1905.

Levey, Michael. *The Case of Walter Pater.* London: Thames and Hudson, 1978.

Levin, Susan M. *The Romantic Art of Confession: DeQuincey, Musset, Sand, Lamb, Hogg, Frémy, Soulié, Janin.* Columbia, SC: Cambden House, 1998.

Lewes, George Henry. "Michelet on Auricular Confession and Direction." *Foreign Quarterly Review* 35 (1845): 188-98.

[Lewes, George Henry]. "Training in Relation to Health." *Cornhill Magazine* 9 (1864): 219-31.

Linton, E. Lynn. *Under Which Lord?* 3 vols. London: Chatto and Windus, 1879.

Livingstone, E. A., et al. *Oxford Concise Dictionary of the Christian Church.* 3rd ed. Oxford: Oxford University Press, 2013.

Lorenzini, Daniele. "The Emergence of Desire: Notes toward a Political History of the Will." *Critical Inquiry* 45 (Winter 2019): 448-70.

Louis, Margot R. *Swinburne and His Gods: The Roots and Growth of an Agnostic Poetry.* Montreal and Kingston: McGill-Queen's Press, 1990.

Lyons, Dan. "Plato's Attempt to Moralize Shame." *Philosophy* 86.337 (July 2011): 353-74.

MacDonald, Robert. "The Frightful Consequences of Onanism: Notes on the History of a Delusion." *Journal of the History of Ideas* 28 (July-Sept. 1967): 423-31.

Machann, Clinton. "The Construction of Masculinity in Victorian Autobiography." *Nineteenth-Century Prose* 26.2 (Fall 1999): 9-23.

MacKendrick, Karmen. "Impossible Confessions." In *Material Spirit: Religion and Literature Intranscendent,* edited by Gregory Stallings, Manuel Asensi, and Carl Good, 35-48. New York: Fordham University Press, 2014.

MacKenzie, Norman H. *Excursions in Hopkins.* Philadelphia: Saint Joseph's University Press, 2008.

Mahoney, John, S.J. *The Making of Moral Theology: A Study of the Roman Catholic Tradition.* Oxford: Clarendon Press, 1987.

Marsh, Jan. *The Pre-Raphaelite Sisterhood*. London: Quartet Books, 1985.

Marsh, P. T. *The Victorian Church in Decline*. London: Routledge, 1969.

Marcus, Steven. *The Other Victorians: A Study of Sexuality and Pornography in Mid-Nineteenth-Century England*. London: Routledge, 1964.

Martin, Robert B. *Gerard Manley Hopkins: A Very Private Life*. New York: G. P. Putnam's Sons, 1991.

———. "The Poet, the Nun, and the Daring Young Man." In *Leon Edel and Literary Art*, edited by Lyall H. Powers, 29-41. Ann Arbor: UMI Research Press, 1988.

Mauss, Marcel. "Techniques of the Body." *Economy and Society* 21 (February 1973): 70-88.

Maynard, John. "Like a Virgin: Coventry Patmore's Still *Unknown Eros*." In *Virginal Sexuality and Textuality in Victorian Literature*, edited by Lloyd Davis, 129-40. Albany: State University of New York Press, 1993.

Mazurek, Monika. "Perverts to Rome: Protestant Gender Roles and the Abjection of Catholicism." *Victorian Literature and Culture* 44 (2016): 687-723.

McClintock, Anne. "Soft-Soaping Empire: Commodity Racism and Imperial Advertising." In *The Body: A Reader*, edited by Mariam Fraser and Monica Greco, 271-76. London: Routledge, 2005.

McFarland, Ian A., et al. *The Cambridge Dictionary of Christian Theology*. Cambridge: Cambridge University Press, 2014.

McGann, Jerome. "Scholarly Commentary: *The Contemporary Review*." *The Rossetti Archive*. http://www.rossettiarchive.org/docs/ap4.c7.raw.html.

———. *Swinburne: An Experiment in Criticism*. Chicago: University of Chicago Press, 1972.

———. "Swinburne's Radical Artifice; or, The Comedian as A.C.," *Modernism/modernity* 11.2 (April 2004): 205-18.

———. "'A Thing to Mind': The Materialist Aesthetic of William Morris." *Huntington Library Quarterly* 55.1 (Winter 1992): 55-74.

McGrath, R. "Looking Hard: The Male Body under Patriarchy." In *Beyond the Man: The Male Nude in Photography*, edited by A. Foster, 50-62. Edinburgh: Stills Gallery, 1988.

McNees, Eleanor. "*Punch* and the Pope: Three Decades of Anti-Catholic Caricature." *Victorian Periodicals Review* 37.1 (Spring 2004): 18-45.

Meadows, Dennis. *Obedient Men*. New York: Appleton-Century-Crofts, 1954.

Merleau-Ponty, Maurice. *Phenomenology of Perception*. Translated by Colin Smith. London: Routledge and Kegan Paul, 1962.

Michelet, Jules. *Priests, Women, and Families* [*Du Prêtre, de la femme, de la famille*, 1845]. London: Protestant Evangelical Mission, 1874.

Michelet, Jules, and Edgar Quinet. *Jesuits and Jesuitism*. Translated by G. H. Smith. London: Whitaker, 1846.

Mill, John Stuart. *On Liberty*. In *The Collected Works of John Stuart Mill*, edited by J. M. Robson, vol. 18. Toronto: University of Toronto Press, 1977.

Milton, John Law. *On Spermatorrhea: Its Pathology, Results, and Complications.* London: Henry Renshaw, 1881.

Mintz, Susannah B. *Hurt and Pain: Literature and the Suffering Body.* London: Bloomsbury, 2013.

Monsman, Gerald. "Old Mortality at Oxford." *Studies in Philology* 67 (July 1970): 359-89.

Moran, Maureen. "The Art of Looking Dangerously: Victorian Images of Martyrdom." *Victorian Literature and Culture* 32.2 (2004): 475-93.

———. *Catholic Sensationalism and Victorian Literature.* Liverpool: Liverpool University Press, 2007.

———. "Hopkins and Victorian Responses to Suffering." *Revue LISA* 8.3 (2009). https://journals.openedition.org/lisa/145.

———. "'Lovely Manly Mould': Hopkins and the Christian Body." *Journal of Victorian Culture* 6.1 (2001): 61-88.

Morgan, Thaïs. "The Poetry of Victorian Masculinities." In *The Cambridge Companion to Victorian Poetry,* edited by Joseph Bristow, 203-27. Cambridge: Cambridge University Press, 2005.

Morley, John. "Review of Swinburne, *Poems and Ballads.*" *Saturday Review,* 22 August 1866, 145-47.

Morris, John, S.J. *Daily Duties: An Instruction for Novices of the Society.* London: Manresa Press, 1889.

Morris, William. *The Earthly Paradise: A Poem.* London: F. S. Ellis, 1868.

———. *The Life and Death of Jason, A Poem.* London: Bell and Daldy, 1867.

Motto, Marylou. *"Mined with a Motion": The Poetry of Gerard Manley Hopkins.* New Brunswick, NJ: Rutgers University Press, 1984.

Muller, Jill. *Gerard Manley Hopkins and Victorian Catholicism: A Heart in Hiding.* Florence, KY: Routledge, 2003.

Myrc, John. *Instructions for Parish Priests.* Edited by Edward Peacock. London: Early English Text Society, 1868.

Nelson, James G. "The Rejected Harlot: A Reading of Rossetti's 'A Last Confession' and 'Jenny.'" *Victorian Poetry* 10.2 (Summer 1972): 123-29.

Newman, John Henry. *Certain Difficulties Felt by Anglicans in Catholic Teaching.* 2 vols. London: Longmans, Green, 1901. https://www.newmanreader.org/works.

———. *An Essay in Aid of a Grammar of Assent.* 7th ed. London: Longmans, Green, 1888.

———. *Essays Critical and Historical.* 2 vols. London: Basil Montagu Pickering, 1871.

———. *Lectures on the Present Position of Catholics in England: Addressed to the Brothers of the Oratory in the Summer of 1851.* London: Burns and Lambert, 1851.

———. *Mortification of the Flesh a Scripture Duty.* In *Tracts for the Times,* vol. 1, 1833-34, edited by Members of the University of Oxford, 1-4. 1833. New York: AMS Press, 1969.

———. *Parochial and Plain Sermons.* 8 vols. London: Longmans, Green, 1907. https://www.newmanreader.org/works.

———. *Sermons on Subjects of the Day.* 1869. London: Longmans, Green, 1902. https://www.newmanreader.org/works.

———. *Tracts for the Times.* https://www.newmanreader.org/works.

Nicolini, Giovanni B. *History of the Jesuits: Their Origin, Progress, Doctrines and Designs.* London: Henry G. Bohn, 1854.

Oakley, Thomas Pollock. *English Penitential Discipline and Anglo-Saxon Law in Their Joint Influence.* New York: Columbia University Press, 1923.

O'Connor, Maura. *The Romance of Italy and the English Political Imagination.* London: St. Martin's, 1998.

O'Malley, Patrick R. *Catholicism, Sexual Deviance, and Victorian Gothic Culture.* Cambridge: Cambridge University Press, 2006.

Overbury, Richard W. *The Jesuits.* London: Houlston and Stoneman, 1846.

Overholser, Renée. "'Our King Back, Oh, upon English Souls!': Swinburne, Hopkins, and the Politics of Religion." *Religion and the Arts* 5.1-2 (2001): 81–107.

Pater, Walter. *Appreciations, with an Essay on Style.* London: Macmillan, 1897.

———. "Coleridge's Writings." *Westminster Review,* n.s., 29.1 (January 1866): 106–32.

———. *Marius the Epicurean.* 1885. London: Macmillan, 1924.

———. *Miscellaneous Studies.* Edited by Charles Shadwell. London: Macmillan, 1895.

———. *Plato and Platonism.* London: Macmillan, 1893.

———. "Poems by William Morris." *Westminster Review* 34 (October 1868): 300–12.

———. *The Renaissance: Studies in Art and Poetry.* 1893 text. Edited by Donald L. Hill. Berkeley: University of California Press, 1980.

———. "Winckelmann." *Westminster Review,* n.s., 87 (January and April 1867): 80–110.

Patmore, Coventry. *Tamerton Church-Tower and Other Poems.* London: William Pickering, 1853.

Patrick, St. *The Confession of Saint Patrick.* Book of Armagh; TCD MS 52; Cotton MS Nero E.I. https://www.ancienttexts.org/library/celtic/ctexts/p01.html.

Paxton, Amanda. "Love, Dismemberment, and Elizabeth Siddal's *Corpus.*" *Journal of Pre-Raphaelite Studies* 22.2 (2013): 4–23.

———. *Willful Submission: Sado-Erotics and Heavenly Marriage in Victorian Religious Poetry.* Charlottesville: University of Virginia Press, 2017.

Paz, Denis G. *Popular Anti-Catholicism in Mid-Victorian England.* Stanford, CA: Stanford University Press, 1992.

A Peep behind the Curtain; or, An Exposure of the Popish Confessional, Furnished by Popish Writers. London: Partridge, 1859.

Peschier, Diana. "Vulnerable Women and the Danger of Gliding Jesuits: England in the Nineteenth Century." *Women's Writing* 11.2 (2004): 281–302.

Phelan, Joe. "The Eye of the World." *Times Literary Supplement,* 18 February 2005, 26.

Phelan, J. P. "Buchanan, Robert Williams." *Oxford Dictionary of National Biography.* Online ed. https://doi-org.ezproxy.library.yorku.ca/10.1093/ref:odnb/32153.

Plampin, Matthew. "A Stern and Just Respect for Truth: John Ruskin, Giotto, and the Arundel Society." *Visual Culture in Britain* 6.1 (Summer 2005): 59-78.

Pomplun, Trent. "The Theology of Gerard Manley Hopkins: From John Duns Scotus to the Baroque." *Journal of Religion* 95.1 (January 2015): 1-34.

Porter, Roy. "History of the Body." In *New Perspectives on Historical Writing,* edited by Peter Burke, 206-32. Cambridge: Polity Press, 1991.

Potolsky, Matthew. "Critical Introduction." In Walter Pater, *Classical Studies,* 1-43. Oxford: Oxford University Press, 2021.

Powell, Susan. "Mirk, John." *Oxford Dictionary of National Biography.* Online ed. https://doi-org.ezproxy.library.yorku.ca/10.1093/ref:odnb/18818.

Priestley, F. E. L. "Blougram's Apologetics." *University of Toronto Quarterly* 15.2 (January 1946): 139-47.

The Public Worship Regulation Act 1874. H.L. Deb 20 April 1874 vol 218 cc786-808. http://hansard.millbanksystems.com/lords/1874/apr/20/presented-first-reading.

Pusey, Edward. *The Church of England a Portion of Christ's One Holy Catholic Church, and a Means of Restoring Visible Unity. An Eirenicon, In a Letter to the Author of "The Christian Year."* Oxford: Parker, 1865.

———. *Habitual Confession Not Discouraged by the Resolution Accepted by the Lambeth Conference.* Oxford: James Parker, 1878.

———. *Hints for a First Confession.* London: A. R. Mowbray, 1912.

———. *The Minor Prophets, with a Commentary Explanatory and Practical.* 2 vols. New York: Funk and Wagnalls, 1885.

———. *Penitence, with Rules for Guidance.* London: A. D. Innes, 1899.

———. "Preface of the Editor." In *Advice for Those Who Exercise the Ministry of Reconciliation through Confession and Absolution, Being the Abbé Gaume's Manual for Confessors or His Extracts from the Works of S. Francis de Sales, Charles Borromeo, S. Philip de Neri, S. Francis Xavier, and Other Spiritual Writers,* abridged, 2nd ed., edited by Edward Pusey, iii-clxxiv. Oxford: James Parker, 1878.

———. Preface to *The Confessions of St. Augustine,* translated by E. B. Pusey, v-xxx. London: Dent and Sons, 1907.

———. *Sermons for the Church's Seasons, from Advent to Trinity.* London: K. Paul, Trench, 1883.

———. *Thoughts on the Benefits of the System of Fasting, Enjoined by Our Church,* in *Tracts for the Times.* Vol. 1, 1833-34, edited by Members of the University of Oxford, 1833, 1-28. New York: AMS Press, 1969.

———, ed. *Advice for Those Who Exercise the Ministry of Reconciliation through Confession and Absolution, Being the Abbé Gaume's Manual for Confessors or His Extracts from the Works of S. Francis de Sales, Charles Borromeo, S. Philip de Neri, S. Francis Xavier, and Other Spiritual Writers.* Abridged, 2nd ed. Oxford: James Parker, 1878.

The Raccolta: or, Collection of Indulged Prayers. Edited and translated by Ambrose St. John. London: Burns and Lambert, 1857. https://en.wikisource.org/wiki/The_Raccolta_(1857).

Rahner, Karl, and Herbert Vorgrimler. *Dictionary of Theology*. 2nd ed. New York: Crossroad, 1981.

Reed, John Shelton. "'A Female Movement': The Feminization of Nineteenth-Century Anglo-Catholicism." *Anglican and Episcopal History* 57.2 (June 1988): 199–238.

Rice, Stephen. "Picturing Bodies in the Nineteenth Century." In *A Cultural History of the Human Body in the Age of Empire*, edited by Michael Sappol and Stephen P. Rice, 213–35. Oxford: Berg, 2010.

Richter, Simon. *Laocoon's Body and the Aesthetics of Pain: Winckelmann, Lessing, Herder, Moritz, Goethe*. Detroit: Wayne State University Press, 1992.

Rickaby, Joseph, S.J. Annotations and Notes. *The Spiritual Exercises of Ignatius Loyola*, 2nd ed. Edited and translated by Joseph Rickaby, S.J. New York: Benziger Brothers, 1923.

Rider, Catherine. "Lay Religion and Pastoral Care in Thirteenth Century England: The Evidence of a Group of Short Confession Manuals." *Journal of Medieval History* 36 (2010): 327–40.

Roman Catholic Relief Act 1829. 1829 CHAPTER 7 10 Geo 4 An Act for the Relief of His Majesty's Roman Catholic Subjects [13 April 1829]. https://www.legislation.gov.uk/ukpga/Geo4/10/7/data.pdf.

"Rome's Recruits": *A List of Protestants Who Have Become Catholics since the Tractarian Movement*. London: Whitehall Review, 1878.

Rooksby, Rikky. "Swinburne, Algernon Charles." *Oxford Dictionary of National Biography*. Online ed. https://doi-org.ezproxy.library.yorku.ca/10.1093/ref:odnb/36389.

Ross, John. *On Penance and the Confessional, as Unscriptural and Immoral*. London: Religious Tract Society, 1851.

Rossetti, Christina. *Selected Poems*. Edited by Jan Marsh. London: Phoenix/Orion Publishing Group, 2002.

Rossetti, Dante Gabriel. *Poems*. London: F. S. Ellis, 1870. *Rossetti Archive Textual Transcription*. http://www.rossettiarchive.org/docs/1-1870.1stedn.rad.html#p[vii].

Rouse, Joseph. "Power/Knowledge." In *The Cambridge Companion to Foucault*, edited by Gary Gutting, 92–114. Cambridge: Cambridge University Press, 1994.

Ruskin, John. *The Works of John Ruskin*. Edited by E. T. Cook and Alexander Wedderburn. 39 vols. London: George W. Allen, 1903–12.

Sales, François de. *Introduction to the Devout Life* [*Introduction à la vie dévote*, 1609]. https://ccel.org/ccel/desales/devout_life/devout_life.toc.html.

Saville, Julia. "Cosmopolitan Republican Swinburne, the Immersive Poet as Public Moralist." *Victorian Poetry* 47.45 (Winter 2009): 691–713.

———. *A Queer Chivalry: The Homoerotic Asceticism of Gerard Manley Hopkins*. Charlottesville: University Press of Virginia, 2000.

Sawicki, Jana. "Foucault, Feminism and Questions of Identity." In *The Cambridge Companion to Foucault,* edited by Gary Gutting, 286–313. Cambridge: Cambridge University Press, 1994.

Scarry, Elaine. *The Body in Pain: The Making and Unmaking of the World.* Oxford: Oxford University Press, 1985.

Schneider, Elisabeth. *The Dragon in the Gate: Studies in the Poetry of G. M. Hopkins.* Berkeley: University of California Press, 1968.

Sedgwick, Eve Kosofsky. *Between Men: English Literature and Male Homosocial Desire.* New York: Columbia University Press, 1985.

———. *Epistemology of the Closet.* Berkeley: University of California Press, 1990.

———. "Jane Austen and the Masturbating Girl." *Critical Inquiry* 17.4 (Summer 1991): 818–37.

———. "Queer Performativity: Henry James' *The Art of the Novel.*" *GLQ* 1 (1993): 1–16.

———. *Touching Feeling: Affect, Pedagogy, Performativity.* Durham, NC: Duke University Press, 2003.

Seymour, M. Hobart. *Mornings among the Jesuits at Rome.* 5th ed. London: Seeleys, 1852.

Sha, Richard C. "Othering Sexual Perversity: England, Empire, Race, and Sexual Science." In *A Cultural History of the Human Body in the Age of Empire,* edited by Michael Sappol and Stephen P. Rice, 87–105. Oxford: Berg, 2010.

Shaw, David. "Arthurian Ghosts: The Phantom Art of 'The Defence of Guenevere.'" *Victorian Poetry* 34.3 (Autumn 1996): 299–312.

Shaw, Marion. "'To Tell the Truth of Sex': Confession and Abjection in Late Victorian Writing." In *Rewriting the Victorians: Theory, History, and the Politics of Gender,* edited by Linda M. Shires, 87–100. New York: Routledge, 1992.

Shilling, Chris. *The Body and Social Theory.* 2nd ed. London: Sage Publications, 2003.

Shuter, William. *Re-Reading Walter Pater.* Cambridge: Cambridge University Press, 1997.

Shuttleworth, Sally. "Spiritual Pathology: Priests, Physicians, and *The Way of All Flesh.*" *Victorian Studies* 54.4 (Summer 2012): 625–53.

Silver, Brenda R. *Virginia Woolf Icon.* Chicago: University of Chicago Press, 1999.

Sinclair, Catherine. *Beatrice; or, The Unknown Relatives.* 4th ed. New York: De Witt and Davenport, 1852.

Sinfield, Alan. *The Wilde Century: Effeminacy, Oscar Wilde and the Queer Moment.* London: Cassell, 1994.

Smith, Alison. "Medium and Method in Pre-Raphaelite Painting." In *Pre-Raphaelites: Victorian Avant-Garde,* edited by Tim Barringer, Jason Rosenfeld, and Alison Smith, 18–23. London: Tate Publishing, 2012.

Smith, Barbara Herrnstein. "Contingencies of Value." *Critical Inquiry* 10 (September 1983): 1–35.

Spivak, Gayatri Chakravorty. "Decadent Style." *Language and Style* 7.4 (Fall 1974): 227–34.

The Statutes at Large, from Magna Carta to the End of the Eleventh Parliament of Great Britain, Anno 1761, Continued. Vol. 37. Cambridge: John Archdeacon, 1790. https://books.google.co.uk/books?id=1lTe3ogCholC&pg=PA310#v=onepage&q&f=false.

Steinmetz, Andrew. *The Jesuit in the Family*. London: Smith, Elder, 1847.

Sturrock, June. "Catholic Anti-heroines: Craik, Sewell and Yonge." *Women's Writing* 11.1 (2004): 89-98.

Sussman, Herbert. *Victorian Masculinities: Manhood and Masculine Poetics in Early Victorian Literature and Art*. Cambridge: Cambridge University Press, 1995.

Sutton, Max. "Selving as Individuation in Hopkins: A Jungian Reading." *Hopkins Quarterly* 2.3 (October 1975): 119-29.

Swinburne, Algernon Charles. *Complete Poetical Works*. Delphi Poets Series, 2013. www.delphiclassics.com.

——. *Poems and Ballads*. 1866. London: William Heinmann, 1917.

——. *Songs before Sunrise*. New ed. London: Chatto and Windus, 1883.

——. *Songs of Two Nations*. London: Chatto and Windus, 1875.

Taylor, Charles. *A Secular Age*. Cambridge, MA: Belknap Press, 2007.

Taylor, Chloë. *The Culture of Confession from Augustine to Foucault: A Genealogy of the "Confessing Animal."* New York: Routledge, 2009.

Taylor, Isaac. *Loyola: and Jesuitism in Its Rudiments*. New York: Robert Carter and Brothers, 1857.

Tennyson, Alfred Lord. "St. Simeon Stylites." In *The Broadview Anthology of Victorian Poetry and Poetic Theory*, edited by Thomas J. Collins and Vivienne J. Rundle, 183-86. Peterborough: Broadview Press, 1999.

Thomas, Alfred, S.J. "Hopkins' 'Felix Randal': The Man and the Poem." *Times Literary Supplement*, 19 March 1971, 331-32.

——. *Hopkins the Jesuit: The Years of Training*. London: Oxford University Press, 1969.

Thornton, R. K. R., ed. *All My Eyes See: The Visual World of Gerard Manley Hopkins*. Sunderland Arts Centre: Ceolfrith Press, 1975.

Tosh, John. *Manliness and Masculinities in Nineteenth-Century Britain: Essays on Gender, Family and Empire*. Harlow, UK: Pearson Education, 2005.

Traver, Teresa Huffman. "Losing a Family, Gaining a Church: Catholic Conversion and English Domesticity." *Victorian Review* 37.1 (Spring 2011): 127-43.

Trollope, Mrs. [Frances Milton]. *Father Eustace: A Tale of the Jesuits*. 3 vols. London: Henry Colburn, 1847.

——. *A Visit to Italy*. 2 vols. London: Richard Bentley, 1842.

Tucker, Herbert F. "Representation and Reprisitnation: Virginity in *The Ring and the Book*." In *Virginal Sexuality and Textuality in Victorian Literature*, edited by Lloyd Davis, 67-86. Albany: State University of New York Press, 1993.

Tupper, Martin F. *Three Hundred Sonnets*. London: Arthur Hall, Virtue, 1860.

Turner, Bryan. *The Body and Society.* Oxford: Basil Blackwell, 1984.

———. *Regulating Bodies: Essays in Medical Sociology.* London: Routledge, 1992.

Turner, Frank. "The Victorian Crisis of Faith and the Faith That Was Lost." In *Victorian Faith in Crisis: Essays on Continuity and Change in Nineteenth-Century Religious Belief,* edited by Richard Helmstadter and Bernard Lightman, 9-38. Stanford, CA: Stanford University Press, 1990.

Vendler, Helen. *The Breaking of Style: Hopkins, Heaney, Graham.* Cambridge, MA: Harvard University Press, 1995.

Viladesau, Richard. *The Beauty of the Cross: The Passion of Christ in Theology and the Arts from the Catacombs to the Eve of the Renaissance.* Oxford: Oxford University Press, 2005.

Virag, Atti. "The Grammar of Instress: Gerard Manley Hopkins and the Victorian Philosophers of *Mind.*" *New Literary History* 51 (2020): 501-22.

von Balthasar, Hans Urs. *The Glory of the Lord: A Theological Aesthetics.* Vol. 1. Edited by Joseph Fession and John Riches. Translated by E. Levia-Merikakis. San Francisco: Ignatius Press, 1982.

Walsh, Walter. *The Jesuits in Great Britain: An Historical Inquiry into Their Political Influence.* London: George Routledge and Sons, 1905.

Ward, Mary [Mrs. Humphry]. *Helbeck of Bannisdale.* Edited by Brian Worthington. Harmondsworth: Penguin, 1983.

———. *A Writer's Recollections.* 2 vols. London: Collins, 1918.

Warner, Marina. *Alone of All Her Sex: The Myth and Cult of the Virgin Mary.* Oxford: Oxford University Press, 1976.

Waterhouse, Ruth. "The Inverted Gaze." In *Body Matters: Essays on the Sociology of the Body,* edited by Sue Scott and David Morgan, 105-21. London: Falmer Press, 1993.

White, Norman. *Hopkins: A Literary Life.* Oxford: Oxford University Press, 1992.

Wildered, A. B., Parishioner. *The Ritualist's Progress; A Sketch of the Reforms and Ministrations of the Rev. Septimius Alban, Member of the E.C.U., Vicar of St. Alicia, Sloperton.* London: Samuel Tinsley, 1875.

William Morris Archive. http://morrisarchive.lib.uiowa.edu/exhibits/show/poetry.

Wilson, A. N. *God's Funeral.* New York: Ballantine Books, 1999.

Wilt, Judith. "Three Women Writers and the 'Jesuit Sublime': Or, Jesuits in Love." *Religion and the Arts* 13 (2009): 1-13.

Wiseman, Nicholas. *Fabiola; or, The Church of the Catacombs.* New York: Benziger Brothers, 1886.

———. "Lecture the Tenth. On the Sacrament of Penance. Part I." *Catholic Standard and Times* 5.33 (17 August 1837). *Catholic Research Resources Alliance.* http://thecatholicnewsarchive.org.

———. "Lecture the Tenth. On the Sacrament of Penance. Part II." *Catholic Standard and Times* 5.33 (24 August 1837). *Catholic Research Resources Alliance.* http://thecatholicnewsarchive.org.

———. *On the Principal Doctrines and Practices of the Catholic Church, Delivered at St. Mary's, Moorfields, during the Lent of 1836*. 2 vols. London: Joseph Booker, 1836.

Wolffe, John. "Stowell, Hugh." *Oxford Dictionary of National Biography*. Online ed. https://doi-org.ezproxy.library.yorku.ca/10.1093/ref:odnb/26614.

Woods, Walter J. *Walking with Faith: New Perspectives on the Sources and Shaping of Catholic Moral Life*. Eugene, OR: Wipf and Stock Publishers, 1998.

Worboise, Emma [Mrs. Guyton]. *Overdale; or, The Story of a Pervert*. London: James Clarke, 1869.

Worthington, Brian. Introduction to Mrs. Humphry Ward, *Helbeck of Bannisdale*, edited by Brian Worthington, 13-25. Harmondsworth: Penguin, 1983.

Yates, Nigel. *Anglican Ritualism in Victorian Britain, 1830-1910*. Oxford: Oxford University Press, 1999.

———. "'Jesuits in Disguise'?: Ritualist Confessors and their Critics in the 1870s." *Journal of Ecclesiastical History* 39.2 (April 1988): 202-16.

Yost, Julia Dorothy. "'And What Does Anything at All Matter': Asceticism and the Hermeneutics of Comfort in Hopkins' Terrible Sonnets." *Religion and the Arts* 18 (2014): 325-48.

Zagzebski, Linda. *Exemplarist Moral Theory*. New York: Oxford University Press, 2017.

Zaniello, Tom. *Saints and Sinners in Queen Victoria's Courts: Ten Scandalous Trials*. Jefferson, NC: McFarland, 2021.

Žižek, Slavoj. *The Ticklish Subject: The Absent Centre of Political Ontology*. London: Verso, 1999.

INDEX

Abelard, Peter, 4, 34, 43, 195, 196; *Expositiones*, 138
absolution, 9, 20, 27, 28, 40, 44, 57, 58, 61, 64, 78, 94, 111, 119, 120, 214, 219, 221, 223, 226, 227, 230n16, 262n20
Achilli, Giacinto, 223; *Dealings with the Inquisition*, 222
Acton, William, 132
Adam (Old Testament), 5, 14, 66, 139, 148, 149, 161, 178, 238n37, 254n56. *See also* Eve
Adams, James Eli, 12, 23, 200, 201, 204, 232n29, 233n42, 250n14
Addis, William, 18
Advice... Through Confession, 5, 6, 28, 29, 35, 36, 37, 38, 39, 57, 60–64, 67, 78, 115, 230n16
aesthetic discourse, 134, 250n9
Alcuin of York, 68, 240n62
Ambrose, Isaac, 229n3
Ambrose of Milan, 14, 41
Ancrene Riwle, 214
Andrewes, Lancelot, 111
angels, 5, 53, 56, 110, 149, 152, 180, 235n3; guardian angels, 5, 6, 231n18
Anglicanism, 2, 9, 21, 29, 81, 82, 83, 100, 106, 107, 111, 116, 117, 119, 123, 155, 183, 219, 222, 224, 234n48, 236n18, 240n67, 247n64, 268n3. *See also* Church of England
Annunciation, 107

anti-Catholicism, 11, 18, 19, 21, 58, 81, 82, 83, 84, 85, 86, 87, 88, 89, 90, 91, 92, 94, 95, 97, 99, 102, 103, 105, 108, 158, 177, 186, 221–28; anti-Jesuit, 21, 81, 83, 97, 99, 101, 102, 221; anti-Romanism, 92, 95; "Popery," 83, 88, 89, 98, 108, 223, 242n3
Antichrist, 98
Aquinas, Thomas, 4, 7, 31, 36, 61, 196, 258n96; *Summa*, 43
Aretaeus, 130, 251n23
Ariosto, Ludovico, *Orlando Furioso*, 179
Aristotle: *Nicomachean Ethics*, 74; *Rhetoric*, 66
Armstrong, Isobel, 170, 175, 178, 187, 260n111, 264n41
Armstrong, John E., 91, 224; *The Confessional: Its Wickedness*, 91, 224
Arnold, Julia, 246n49
Arnold, Matthew, 105, 175, 189, 190, 201, 246n53, 261n12
Arnold, Thomas, 107, 235n2
Arnold, Tom, 18, 28, 43, 104, 235n2, 236n13, 246n49
Arthurian literature and art, 183, 195, 199, 205, 263n30
asceticism (*áscesis*), 4, 14, 31, 106, 115, 198; monastic, 41, 43, 122, 239n55
atonement (of Christ), 5, 11
Augustine of Hippo, 14, 36, 47, 54, 55, 78, 122, 124, 130, 138, 152, 237n32,

Augustine of Hippo (*continued*) 251n25; *Confessions,* 20, 29, 41, 43, 46, 47, 48–51, 52, 66, 121, 164, 217, 237n31, 238nn35–40, 254n53

auricular confession. *See* confession

Baden-Powell, Robert, 252n40

Baillie, Alexander, 2, 25, 47, 76, 79, 97, 113, 117, 136, 183, 230n10, 232n31, 236n15, 240n70, 250n9, 253n42, 256n84, 265n52, 268n86

Balliol College (Oxford), 18, 69, 74, 111, 183, 189, 224, 234n2, 240n68, 248n67, 251n24, 265n51

baptism, 6, 27, 42, 53, 56, 108

Barber, Noel, S.J., ix, 31, 163, 229n5

Barthes, Roland, *Sade Fourier Loyola,* 264n41

Basil of Caesarea, 43, 59

Baudelaire, Charles, 183, 187, 189, 191, 263n31, 265n50

Beardsley, Aubrey, illustrations for Wilde's *Salome,* 199

Bede, Venerable, 59

Belvedere Apollo, 189

Benedict XIV (pope), 61

Benedictines, 101, 102

Berkeley, Bishop George, 111

Bernauer, James, S.J., 65, 124, 171, 233n38, 236n14

Bernheimer, Charles, 188, 201, 203, 204, 205

Bernstein, Susan, 12, 88, 89, 231n24, 232n29, 245n38

Beuno of Wales, 128, 152, 167, 171, 258n97

Bible, 2, 22, 66, 70, 86, 138; Douay-Rheims, 47, 229n5; Hopkins's, 22, 138, 229n5; KJV, 46, 229n5

Birmingham Oratory, 33, 89, 104, 128, 222, 225, 244n37, 267n74

Bismark, Otto von, 3

Blake, William, 183, 191, 234n50, 263n33

bodies, 2, 10, 11, 13, 23, 25, 39, 42, 43, 47, 51, 52, 53, 54, 55, 65, 69, 73, 76, 78, 113, 121–25, 126, 127, 130, 133, 134, 135, 136, 137, 141, 142, 143, 144, 145, 146, 150, 151, 152, 153, 155, 168, 169, 170, 176, 181, 182, 186, 193, 201, 205, 207, 219, 249nn2–5, 250n14, 253n47, 254nn48–49, 266n69; of Christ, 108, 140, 148, 153, 154, 160–63, 164, 168, 174, 201, 236n16, 257n93; Christian, 11, 123, 134; as corpses, 122, 137, 139, 141; disciplined, 12, 22, 122, 124, 139, 150, 152, 153, 155, 157, 249n4; mortification of, 55, 66, 154, 157, 158; resurrection of, 6, 42, 208; and soul, 15, 16, 49, 56, 99, 147, 156, 193, 196, 259n109. *See also* flesh

body studies, 11

Bonaventure of Albano, 43

Book of Common Prayer, 2, 109, 119, 214, 229n5, 237n29

Borromeo, Charles, 43, 57–58, 61

Boswell, James, 47

Bridges, Robert, 51, 71, 79, 136, 142, 159, 174, 184, 202, 238n43, 240n64, 241n74, 244n31, 248n83, 251n18, 257n86, 259n102, 264n46, 266n69; *Testament of Beauty,* 70

Brockman, H. J., 21, 225, 243n22

Brompton Oratory, 18

Brontë, Charlotte, 102, 245n38; *Villette,* 102, 223

Brooke, Samuel, 117, 189, 210

Brotherhood of the Holy Trinity, 117

Brown, Ford Madox, *Work,* 127

Browning, Elizabeth Barrett, 96, 264n44

Browning, Robert: "Bishop Blougram," 4; "My Last Duchess," 180; "Porphyria's Lover," 180
Buchanan, Robert (pseud. Thomas Maitland), 172, 175–78, 181, 183, 211, 260n2, 263n34; "The Fleshly School," 23, 175–78; *Foxglove Manor*, 228, 261n14
Buckton, Oliver, 2, 20, 45, 131, 232n29
Burnand, Francis, 94–95, 244n32
Burne-Jones, Edward, 183, 230n15; *Theophilus and the Angel*, 256n81

Canones Hibernenses, 59
Carlyle, Thomas, 101, 127, 251n17, 260n5
Carroll, Lewis (Rev. Charles Dodgson), 178, 248n81
Cassian, John, 3, 42, 43, 140, 152, 235n3, 236n13, 237n23, 239n58
Caswall, Edward, 18
Catholicism. *See* anti-Catholicism; Roman Catholicism
Catholic Relief Act (1829), 21, 84, 92, 221
Caughie, Pamela, 11
Chadwick, Henry, 48, 238n33
Chambers, J. C., 119, 224, 226
Chambers, Susan, 250n11, 259n103
Chaucer, Geoffrey, 10, 56, 122; *Canterbury Tales*, 54
Chiniquy, Charles, 243n20; *Fifty Years in the Church of Rome*, 228; *The Priest, the Woman, and the Confessional*, 227, 243n20
Christ. *See* Jesus Christ
Christianity, 2, 8, 11, 14, 15, 30, 41, 43, 82, 162, 190, 191, 192, 197, 249n4, 269n2
Chrysostom, John, 4, 41, 237n20
Church, R. W., 107
Church of England, 4, 9, 16, 19, 75, 87, 96, 106, 107, 109, 110, 111, 117, 118, 119, 223, 225, 226, 227, 229n5, 239n56, 241n75. *See also* Anglicanism
Cicero, Marcus Tullius, 41, 69
Clement of Rome, 51
Clough, Arthur, 131, 251n24
Coleridge, Samuel Taylor, 190, 191, 192, 193, 199, 265n56, 266n63; *Aids to Reflection*, 191; *Biographia Literaria*, 82, 191; *Confessions of an Inquiring Spirit*, 192; *Specimens of the Table Talk*, 191
Collins, Wilkie, 102, 245nn40–41, 246n52; *The Black Robe*, 102, 103–5
Collins, William, "Ode to Evening," 145
comfort, 20, 23, 29, 36, 55, 70, 101, 141, 146, 147, 166, 190, 209, 213–19, 268n1, 268n3, 268nn5–6, 269n11; and desolation, 23, 54, 140, 156, 167, 200; of Holy Ghost, 5, 198. *See also* consolation
communion. *See* Eucharist; holy communion
concupiscence, 10, 15, 20, 30, 35, 50, 122, 148, 236n10
confession, 1, 2, 8, 10, 13, 14, 20, 27, 28, 30, 34, 35, 36–39, 40–45, 49, 51, 52, 53, 55, 56, 57, 60, 62, 64, 67, 69, 77, 81, 83, 84, 98, 108, 110, 111, 115, 134, 141, 154, 170, 214, 221, 227, 232n29, 241n76, 243n20, 248n81; auricular, 21, 29, 43, 46, 59, 68, 82, 87, 91, 106, 108, 109, 110, 130; for children, 64, 235n4; *confessio fidei*, 30, 48, 165; *confessio laudis*, 30, 48, 165; *confessio peccatorum*, 30, 48, 165; Foucault's critique of, 65–66, 83, 214, 219, 233nn36–39, 236n14; and gender, 1, 3, 58, 64, 125, 231n24, 243n22; Hopkins's confessional notes, 1865–66, 70, 73–77; Ignatius on, 237n27; "instrument of discipline," 44; Keble recommends, 110, 247n60;

confession (continued)
  Pusey recommends, 111–12, 113, 269n3; rite of, 8, 9, 15, 28; and Ritualists, 115–20, 223; "seal" of, 43, 61, 241n74; and "spiritual sickness," 77. See also self-examination
Confession, a Help to Heaven, 86
confessional, 9, 19, 20, 21, 28, 29, 57–58, 59, 63, 78, 83, 84, 86–87, 89, 90–93, 100, 105, 107, 114, 115, 118, 226, 236n18
Confessional Unmasked, The, 224, 225, 269n4
confessors, 5, 28, 38, 59–65, 77, 78, 80, 89, 109, 115, 214; Hopkins as, 58, 79–80
Confiteor ("I confess"), 28, 235n3
conscience, 20, 28, 30, 31–32, 38, 44, 58, 65, 69, 86, 93, 109, 114, 214, 236n12, 237n27; examination of, 9, 27, 78, 231n18, 251n26; "worm of," 143
consolation, 29, 39, 51, 111, 146, 213, 215, 216, 217, 269n10; and Ignatius, 214, 215, 268n2. See also comfort
conversion, 17, 18, 19, 50, 72, 86, 91, 98, 100, 101, 103, 104, 105, 107, 116, 189, 213, 234n2, 269n5; of Hopkins, 17, 18, 21, 24, 65, 73, 74, 81, 97, 113, 117, 120, 188, 194, 224, 230n9, 239n52; of Newman, 107, 239n56; of St. Augustine, 49, 238nn36–37; of St. Patrick, 53; of St. Paul, 47
converts as "perverts," 19, 87, 96, 104, 225, 246n49
Copland, James, 132
Corpus Christi (body of Christ). See Jesus Christ
Council of Châlons (813), 43
Council of Trent (1545–63), 38, 43, 44, 47, 57, 235n3, 236n17
"counter-conduct," 24, 65, 152, 175, 234n51

Counter-Reformation, 43, 56, 57
Coupe, Charles, S.J., *Lectures on the Holy Eucharist*, 160, 257n94
Craik, Dinah Mulock, *Olive*, 222
Cranmer, Thomas, 111
Cupid and Psyche, story of, 262n24
Cyprian of Carthage, 256n79; *De habitu virginum*, 152

Dante Alighieri, 177, 179, 182, 195, 210, 265n56; *Divine Comedy*, 54
Darwin, Charles, 205
Darwinism, 136, 145
Davis, R. G., *Catechism for First Confession*, 235n4
decadence, 23, 172, 188, 191, 194, 195, 197, 198, 200, 201, 202–4, 205, 206, 208, 211, 267n76
Dens, Pieter, 94, 242n11
De Quincey, Thomas, 8, 238n32
devil, 5, 27, 36, 62, 69, 100, 138, 148, 149, 257n93, 261n8. See also Lucifer; Satan
Dhu, Helen, *Stanhope Burleigh*, 98, 224
Dickens, Charles, 173
Dickinson, Emily, 12
Dimock, Wai Chee, 89, 243n19
discipline, 12, 22, 24, 42, 44, 50, 91, 102, 103, 122, 124, 127, 139, 151, 153, 204; and Foucault, 150, 249n4; and Newman, 150–51; and Pusey, 155; and self-discipline, 41, 63, 150
"discipline, the." See mortification of the flesh
Diseases of Modern Life, 253n43
disobedience, 2, 5, 10, 40, 50, 195. See also obedience
Disraeli, Benjamin, 118, 227; *Lothair*, 226
Dixon, Richard Watson, 40, 79, 104, 149, 184, 238n42, 266n63

Dodgson, Charles (Lewis Carroll), 178, 248n81
Dolben, Digby, 71, 77
Dollimore, Jonathan, 8, 19
Dominicans, 44, 101
Dowling, Linda, 200, 211, 250n7, 266n60
Dowson, Ernest, 199
Dr. Pusey's Insane Project Considered, 115
Dubois, Martin, 6, 229n2, 231n28
duty, 9, 30, 33, 37, 38, 63, 69, 79, 86, 109, 110, 137, 148, 151, 154, 155

Eliot, George, 3; *Romola,* 224, 268n86
Eliot, T. S., 241n74
Ellis, Robinson, 178
empires, 12, 254n48; British, 24, 86, 230n9; Christian, 15; Jesuit, 98
Epicureans, 41, 190, 198, 206
eschatology, 6, 123, 147, 205
Eucharist, 5, 117, 154, 160, 186, 189, 198, 214, 236n16, 257n94; Christ's "Eucharistic sacrifice," 140. *See also* holy communion; "Real Presence"
eunuchs, 48, 158, 257n90
Evagrius Ponticus, 236n13
Eve (Old Testament), 5, 14, 66, 148, 149, 161
Everyman, 20, 46, 54–56
exagoreusis, 41
exomologesis, 41
extreme unction, 36, 56

Faber, Frederick, 18, 109, 192; *Growth in Holiness,* 18, 69, 214, 215, 241n73
Faber, Geoffrey, 155
fin-de-siècle culture, 172
flagellation. *See* mortification of the flesh
"Flare Up in the Confessional," 106–7

flesh, 1, 2, 3, 5, 8, 10, 13, 20, 21, 22, 25, 29, 43, 45, 46, 47, 53, 55, 74, 107, 120, 126, 127, 130, 131, 134, 137, 138, 140, 142, 143, 144, 148, 152, 154, 157, 167, 168, 170, 172, 191, 197, 201, 210, 214, 218, 261n8; aesthetics of, 20, 22; and Augustine, 121, 124, 138, 238n40; of Christ, 139, 141, 147, 160, 162, 163, 164, 173, 187, 254n55, 257n93; Christian, 129, 146, 171; and Foucault, 11, 13–16, 22, 122, 124–25, 132, 141, 146, 152, 219, 233nn36–39, 251n28; and Ignatius, 139; insinuations of, 22; medicalized, 135; Pauline, 11, 39, 123, 124, 138, 249n3, 254n52; and Rossetti, 178–79, 181, 182; "self-tormenting," 143; and Swinburne, 183–88; and Tertullian, 10
"Fleshly School of Poetry," 23, 175–78, 260n2
Fortnightly Review, 177
Foucault, Michel, 3, 11, 12, 16, 23, 193, 196, 232n30; and confession, 8, 15, 65; and counter-conduct, 234n51; and discipline, 63, 150; and flesh, 22, 124, 129, 146–47; and heterotopia, 20, 58. Works: *Abnormal,* 44, 131, 176–77, 239n61, 252n33; *Confessions of the Flesh,* 13, 219, 238n40; *Discipline and Punish,* 150, 249n4; *Ethics, Subjectivity, Truth,* 233n40; *History of Sexuality,* 12, 13, 14–15, 30, 39, 42, 66, 113, 122, 124, 129, 152, 153, 155, 252n31, 256n79; "How We Behave," 232n30; *Manet and the Object of Painting,* 175, 261n9; *Order of Things,* 29, 229n7; *Power/Knowledge,* 232n32; *Religion and Culture,* 147, 256n82; *Security, Territory, Population,* 66; *Wrong-Doing, Truth-Telling,* 30, 40, 56, 111, 171, 215, 233n41, 239n55

Fourth Lateran Council (1215), 3, 43, 54, 78, 237n25
Franciscans, 101, 152, 258n100
Francis of Assisi, 61, 100, 168
Francis Xavier, 61
Froude, Hurrell, 107

Gaume, Abbé Jean-Joseph, 5, 6, 29, 38, 57, 61, 64, 69, 79, 157, 230n16, 239n48; *Manual for Confessors*, 35, 36, 37, 38, 39, 60, 61, 62, 63, 65, 67, 78, 80, 111, 115, 119, 158, 227, 239n53, 240n71, 245n45, 253n41, 269n10
Gautier, Théophile, 183
Gavin, Anthony, 89
Geldart, Martin, 74
gender, 1, 3, 16, 37, 58, 85, 102, 125, 128, 146, 153, 201, 242n8, 249n2, 250n16, 258n97; and morality, 127; norms and "scripts," 6, 12, 65, 127, 181, 186; and power, 125, 232n29; and suffering, 255n70; women and confession, 64
Gibbon, Edward, 205
Giotto di Bondone, 202, 265n56, 267n76
Gladstone, William, 18, 86, 95, 118, 243n15; *The Vatican Decrees*, 86, 227, 269n5
God, 3, 4, 5, 6, 8, 9, 10, 17, 28, 31, 32, 33, 35, 36, 38, 40, 41, 43, 46, 48, 49, 50, 52, 53, 54, 55, 56, 62, 63, 69, 78, 80, 109, 118, 121, 122, 125, 128, 137, 139, 140, 143, 144, 146, 147, 148, 149, 154, 156, 160, 162, 164, 165, 166, 168, 170, 179, 187, 197, 207, 208, 214, 216, 217, 235n3, 245n45, 258n96, 269n10; the Father, 169; glory of, 30, 163; grace of, 77, 200; "I belong to God," 257n91; mercy of, 51, 129, 167, 215; presence of, 4, 64, 155; three "persons" of, 4, 7, 124, 161, 163, 218, 254n52; voice of, 32; will of, 151; wrath of, 42, 49; wrestling with, 140. *See also* Holy Ghost; Jesus Christ; Trinity
Goethe, Johann Wolfgang von, 177, 194, 203, 265n56
grace, 9, 31, 32, 36, 55, 56, 58, 77, 96, 199, 201, 203, 205, 211, 216; sanctifying, 36, 149; state of, 78; of Virgin Mary, 33
Greek art, 196, 204; "sensuous side of," 194
Green, T. H., 245n48
Gregory of Nyssa, 59, 152
grids of intelligibility, 229n7
Griffin, Susan, 11, 18, 85, 86, 91, 92, 98, 99, 115, 119, 232n29, 239n52, 242n8, 245n39, 246n52
Gros, Frédéric, 15, 233n36
Grosz, Elizabeth, 16, 125, 138, 249n5
grotesque, 23, 172, 176, 191
guilt, 10, 11, 20, 27, 28, 30, 32, 33–34, 45, 64, 67, 68, 76, 140, 141, 157, 218; "guilt cultures," 240n63; "guiltless" Mary, 236n10
Gunpowder Plot, 88, 89, 98

haecceitas, 24, 126
Hall, Lesley, 131, 133, 134, 252n30
Hardy, Thomas, 3
Harris, Elizabeth, 222, 269n2; *Rest in the Church*, 222
health, 28, 39, 47, 115, 121, 123, 127, 128, 130, 134, 135, 136, 137, 157, 171, 176, 204, 254n49; of Christ, 161; of soul, 65, 121, 137; "total" health, 134
heaven, 5, 6, 7, 35, 46, 47, 102, 124, 137, 138, 142, 156, 161, 167, 179, 209, 210, 258n97, 259n105; "heaven-haven," 167, 219; kingdom of, 48; light of, 162; and mercy, 72

Hegel, Georg Wilhelm, 189, 194
hell, 5, 6, 35, 46, 103, 112, 141, 157, 207, 256n72; Ignatian "Meditation on Hell," 33, 143, 245n44
Hellenism, 125, 190, 194, 203, 250n7
Heraclitus, 189, 205, 209
Herodotus, 74
heterotopia, 20, 29, 58, 261n10
Higgins, Lesley, 230n10, 239n49, 250n7, 255n64, 259n101, 260n112, 263n33, 265n57, 266n68
Hippocrates, 252n31
holy communion (sacrament of), 28, 36, 215, 236n16; "blessed sacrament," 56. *See also* Eucharist
Holy Ghost, 4, 10, 28, 149, 161, 217, 218, 256n76
Holy Spirit, 179. *See also* Holy Ghost
Homer, 11
"Home Rule" for Ireland, 264n46
Hopkins, Arthur (brother), 2, 94, 244n30, 245n40
Hopkins, Everard (brother), 2, 18, 244n30
Hopkins, Gerard Manley: aesthetics, 12; athletics, 136; at Birmingham Oratory, 33, 89, 225; birth, 222; confessional notes, 20, 29, 35, 44, 60, 64, 68, 70-75, 112, 130; conversion, 17, 18, 21, 24, 65, 73, 74, 81, 97, 113, 117, 120, 188, 194, 224, 230n9, 239n52; death, 228; and decadence, 202-4, 211; destroys poetry manuscripts, 158; diaries, 72-75, 77-78, 80, 113, 131, 190, 192; and Digby Dolben, 71, 77; in Dublin, 228; early schooling, 223; health of, 79, 135-36; homo- eroticism, 71, 76, 162; in Ireland, 53; Jesuit training, 33, 35, 47, 70, 75, 88, 104, 119, 139, 141, 151, 157, 164, 225, 226, 227, 228; joins Society of Jesus, 225; masturbation, 131-34; national- ist, 17, 84, 99; and Newman, 10, 18, 30, 31-31; ordination, 227; and Pater, 188-93, 196, 201, 204-5, 210-11; as priest, 11, 28, 58, 78, 80, 88; religious beliefs, 4-6; returns to Oxford (1878), 188; as sketch artist, 72, 253n42, 265n58; at St. Beuno's, 86, 229n6; in Switzerland, 267n72; university student, 24, 69, 71-72, 74, 111, 115, 188, 224, 225
—, correspondence, 2, 25, 40, 47, 51, 73, 77, 79, 86, 97, 100, 108, 113, 123, 131, 142, 149, 158, 159, 174, 183, 184, 185, 188, 202
—, essays, 46, 190, 195, 204
—, poetry: "Ad Mariam," 99, 187; "Alche- mist in the City," 39, 66, 128; "*Angelus ad Virginem,*" 38, 124, 163; "Barnfloor and Winepress," 37, 112, 154, 189; "Blessed Virgin," 80, 85, 99; "Bugler's First Communion," 198; "Caged Skylark," 142, 147; "Candle Indoors," 31; "Caradoc's Soliloquy," 163, 165, 167, 169-71, 207, 216-17; "Carrion Comfort," 50, 54, 156, 187, 200, 216; "Easter Communion," 128, 154, 155, 187, 197; "Epithalamion," 135; "Esco- rial," 123; "Felix Randal," 123, 137, 208; "God's Grandeur," 125, 207; "Habit of Perfection," 112, 182, 189; "Harry Ploughman," 125-26, 127, 201; "Her- aclitean Fire," 49, 122, 135, 147, 188, 190, 199, 202, 208, 209-10; "[Hope holds to Christ]," 160; "Hurrahing in Harvest," 142; "In honour of St. Alphonsus Rodriquez," 127, 163; "In the Valley," 38; "I wake and feel," 48, 143, 216; "Kingfishers catch fire," 78, 114, 160; "Lantern out of doors," 123; "Leaden Echo," 32, 209;

Hopkins, Gerard Manley: poetry (*continued*)
"Loss of the Eurydice," 123; "Margaret Clitheroe," 30, 152; "Moonrise June 19 1876," 187; "My own heart," 49, 216; "My prayers," 35, 155; "Myself unholy," 112, 131; "New Readings," 163; "*Nondum*," 35, 154; "No worst," 35, 197, 217; "*O Deus, ego amo te*," 164; "On the Portrait," 128; "Patience," 39, 215–16; "Pied Beauty," 188, 203; "Ribblesdale," 39; "Richard," 145; "*Rosa Mystica*," 187; "Sea and the Skylark," 200; "Shepherd's brow," 122, 147; "Soldier," 124; "Spelt from Sibyl's Leaves," 48, 170, 208, 210; "Spring," 143; "St. Thecla," 152; "St. Winefred's Well," 128; "*Summa*," 38; "Thou art indeed just, Lord," 48; "Tom's Garland," 136; "To R.B.," 27, 51, 207; "To seem the stranger," 153, 216; "To what serves Mortal Beauty?," 126, 179, 188, 200; "Windhover," 126, 199, 207; "Wreck," 38, 47, 49, 54, 119, 138, 152, 153, 154, 160, 163, 164–69, 171, 207, 218, 219
—, sermons, 33, 41, 122, 147–49, 162–63, 174, 201, 215, 217, 239n54
—, spiritual writings, 20, 22, 33, 36, 47, 48, 67, 112, 140, 141, 143, 144, 157, 161–62, 217–18
Hopkins, Kate (mother), 2, 18, 97, 102, 103, 135, 183, 230n11, 247n64, 248n71
Hopkins, Manley (father), 74, 102, 183, 246n57
Hopkins, Milicent (sister), 117
Hughes, Thomas, 174
Hugo, Victor, 184, 189, 206
Hunt, William Holman, 260n6; *Light of the World*, 162, 260n5; *The Shadow of Death*, 174

Ibsen, Henrik, *Rosmersholm*, 105, 246n51
Ignation spirituality, 2, 4, 6, 29, 61, 112, 134, 138, 139, 140, 144, 158, 214, 231n20, 237n21
Ignatius of Loyola, 22, 47, 67, 101, 126, 139, 140, 143, 153, 157, 158, 215, 237n27, 264n47. See also *Spiritual Exercises*
Iliad, 11
imitatio Christi, 33, 51, 61, 210
Immaculate Conception. See Mary, mother of Christ
imperialism (British), 3, 150, 262n23
Incarnation (of Christ), 5, 22, 65, 141, 145, 152, 160, 257n94, 258n96
infallibility of pope. See papal infallibility
Ingelow, Jean, 3
Innocent III (pope), 43
Innocent XI (pope), 61
inscape, 24, 72, 74, 160, 169, 174, 187, 234n50
instress, 5, 15, 24, 74, 123, 234n50
Instructions for Parish Priests, 60

Jameson, Mrs. (Anna), 267n76; *Legends of the Madonna*, 242n7
Jesuits (and Society of Jesus), 3, 4, 6, 11, 22, 23, 25, 30, 31, 33, 35, 53, 65, 75, 85, 97, 102, 104, 136, 141, 151, 163, 164, 196, 211, 257n95; anti-Jesuit sentiments, 3, 21, 65, 81, 83, 88, 97–101, 102–3, 105, 108, 120, 186, 221–28
Jesus Christ, 5, 7, 8, 11, 24, 27, 32, 34, 37, 42, 49, 53, 67, 109, 113, 114, 124, 128, 138, 145, 149, 152, 156, 157, 159, 163, 164, 165, 167, 183, 195, 198, 202, 210, 218, 235n3, 239n50, 247n61, 257n92; body of, 38, 108, 140, 147,

148, 154, 160–63, 165, 173, 174, 201; *Corpus Christi,* 159; crucifixion of, 141, 144, 153, 168, 187; as Good Shepherd, 5, 37, 63; heroism, 5, 156, 163, 165, 168, 259n106; *imitatio Christi,* 33, 51, 61, 210; Incarnation of, 5, 22, 65, 141, 145, 152, 160; Lamb of God, 37, 49, 168, 236n16; Messiah, 7; miracles of, 239n54; "Real Presence" of, 5, 189, 236n16; resurrection of, 5, 147, 171, 209, 210, 213, 239n50, 258n95, 259n109; "sacred heart" of, 163; Saviour, 38, 55, 57, 139, 153; second coming of, 5; Son of God, 4, 218; Word made flesh, 7, 139, 162, 164, 168, 236n16
Job, biblical book of, 121, 147, 156, 215, 217, 268n4
John the Baptist, 42, 235n3, 236n16
Jowett, Benjamin, 69, 71, 74, 114, 115, 183, 188, 189, 201, 204, 234n48, 240n68, 248n68, 263n29, 265n51
Joyce, James, 245n44
Judgment Day, 5

Kaan, Heinrich, *Psychopathia Sexualis,* 234n47
Kant, Immanuel, 192
Keble, John, 107, 108, 109, 110, 111, 112, 237n26, 240n68, 246n55, 246n58, 247n61; "The Annunciation," 107; *Christian Year,* 109, 247n59; *Letters,* 110, 247n63, 247n65; "National Apostasy," 107; *Sermons,* 109, 247n60
Kempis, Thomas à, *Imitation of Christ,* 33, 61
kenosis, 5, 148
Kilvert, Francis, 174, 175, 260n7
Kingsley, Charles, 82, 127, 154, 174, 224; "Apostle of the Flesh," 250n14; *Hypatia,* 223, 269n2; *Westward Ho!,* 224; *Yeast,* 222

Landells, Ebenezer, 92
Laqueur, Thomas, 131; *Making Sex,* 125, 145, 249n2; *Solitary Sex,* 132, 133, 134
Lateran Council, Fourth (1215), 3, 43, 54, 78, 237n25
Latham, David, 266n65
Latimer, Hugh, 111
Latour, Bruno, 123, 125
Leo XIII (pope), 227, 234n46
Lessing, Gotthold Ephraim, *Laocoon,* 146
Letter to the Women of England, 21, 225, 243n22
Lewes, George Henry, 91, 135
Lewis, Monk, 221
Liberty of Britain Imperilled, The, 8, 21, 86
Liddon, Henry, 7, 10, 22, 33, 44, 70–71, 72, 73, 74–75, 77, 82, 83, 114, 115, 117, 130, 138, 155, 188, 189, 192, 224, 234n48, 240n68, 248nn67–69
Liguori, Alphonsus de, 4; *Theologica Moralis,* 61
Lincoln, Abraham, 243n20
Linton, E. Lynn, *Under Which Lord?,* 91, 227
Lombard, Peter, 3; *Sentences,* 4
Lucifer, 5, 140, 164, 258n98. *See also* devil; Satan
Luther, Martin, 38

MacKenzie, Norman, 86, 112, 229n4, 248n89, 251n26
Mahoney, John, S.J., 31, 34, 36, 37, 38, 43, 44, 45, 59, 124, 153, 236n17, 237n25, 237n27, 249n3
Maitland, Thomas. *See* Buchanan, Robert

Malory, Thomas, *Morte d'Arthur*, 263n30
Malthus, Thomas, 136, 254n49
Manning, Henry, 10, 18, 72, 224, 243n15, 258n100
Manuele sacredotis, 60
Mariolatry, 85
Martin, Robert B., 253n45, 257n84, 258n100, 259n108
Martineau, Harriet, *Autobiography*, 9
Mary, mother of Christ, 6, 38, 80, 99, 107, 118, 139, 142, 167, 179, 182, 231n19, 236n10; "Blessed Virgin," 6, 33, 85, 107, 162, 231n19, 235n3, 255n56; immaculate conception of, 6, 85, 223
Mary Magdalene, 179, 182
Mass, 5, 11, 84, 85, 177, 235n3, 236n16, 240n67, 254n47
masturbation, 22, 122, 132, 134, 252n30, 253n41; and Hopkins, 22, 76, 131; medical consequences, 133, 252n38; *Onania; or The Heinous Sin of Self Pollution*, 132; *L'Onanimse*, 132
Mauss, Marcel, 254n47
Mayhew, Henry, 92. See also *Punch, or The London Charivari*
McGann, Jerome, 173, 177, 186, 264n43
medievalism, 195
"Meditation on Hell," 33, 143, 245n44. See also *Spiritual Exercises*
mens sana in corpore sano, 39, 134
metaphysics, 190, 195
Michelet, Jules, 89, 91, 100, 101, 222, 243n20
Mill, John Stuart, 82, 189; *Autobiography*, 9; *On Liberty*, 24
Millais, John Everett, 23, 173, 260n4; *Christ in the House of His Parents*, 173
Milton, John, 142, 177, 200; *Paradise Lost*, 148, 164; *Samson Agonistes*, 217

Milton, John Law, 133, 252n37
Monica (mother of St. Augustine), 49, 238n36
Monk, Maria, *Awful Disclosures*, 221
Month, 240n67, 241n74, 266n63
"moral hygiene," 204
Moran, Maureen, 2, 12, 17, 19, 30, 65, 98, 99, 127, 146, 162, 169, 232n29, 250n8
Morley, John, 264n40
Morris, John, S.J., 35, 70; *Daily Duties*, 75, 139, 151, 164, 231n18
Morris, William, 183, 190, 191, 195, 196, 197, 199, 203, 204, 205, 206, 209, 267n71; medievalism, 195; *Defense of Guenevere*, 195; *Earthly Paradise*, 195; *King Arthur's Tomb*, 199; *Life and Death of Jason*, 195
mortification of the flesh, 34, 57, 64, 66, 74, 79, 93, 107, 150, 153, 154, 156, 157, 158, 159, 168, 171, 256n77, 259n108; Hopkins's "ethos of mortification," 22, 122, 155, 256n78
Müller, Max, 74; *Chips from a German Workshop*, 230n10
Murphy, William, 88, 89
Myrc, John, 60; *Festial*, 60; *Instructions for Parish Priests*, 60

nation and nationalism, 16, 17, 18, 108
Neri, St. Philip, 35, 61, 69, 115, 122
Newman, John Henry, 1, 10, 18, 22, 25, 30, 32, 35, 72, 73, 74, 90, 97, 102, 104, 109, 127, 151, 160, 189, 192, 218, 223, 224, 227, 230n14, 235n5, 243n16, 244n37, 246n58; conversion to Roman Catholicism, 107, 222, 239n56; and Oxford (Tractarian) Movement, 107–8; "religious genius," 192. Works: *Apologia pro Vita Sua*, 9,

242n9; *Certain Difficulties*, 222; *Grammar of Assent*, 31, 32, 226, 235n8; *Idea of a University*, 121; *Lectures*, 17, 222, 233n45; *Loss and Gain*, 222; "Mortification of the Flesh," 154–55; *Parochial and Plain Sermons*, 40, 66, 158; *Sermons*, 150
Newman, William, 74
New Woman novels, 105
Nicolini, Giovanni, 100, 101
Nightingale, Florence, 234n48

obedience, 2, 6, 15, 30, 41, 44, 64, 66, 69, 75, 91, 98, 99, 154, 216, 218, 219, 239nn54–55; Abraham's, 149; for Jesuits, 65, 256n78. *See also* disobedience
Old Mortality essay society, 189, 210, 263n29
ordination, 6, 245n45
ordo, 36
Origen of Alexandria, 68, 240n62
Overbury, Richard, 98, 101, 108; *The Jesuits*, 100
"overthought." *See* "underthought"
Oxford and Roman Railway, The, 90, 97, 115, 116, 158, 243n14
Oxford Martyrs, 111
Oxford Movement. *See* Tractarian (or Oxford) Movement
Oxford poets, 109
Oxford Union, 263n30; Pre-Raphaelite murals, 183

"pagan" or ancient art, 196
"pagan" or ancient religion, 46, 90, 190, 191, 205, 239n48
pain, 33, 51, 67, 68, 70, 96, 133, 135, 139, 140, 145, 146, 155, 157, 158, 185, 187, 249n2, 255n71, 256n72; aesthetics of, 145; of dying, 141
"Papal Aggression." *See* restoration of Catholic hierarchy
papal infallibility, 86, 269n2
Paraclete, 149, 218, 256n76. *See also* Holy Ghost
Parmenides, 145, 200, 267n74
parrhēsia ("fearless speech"), 233n41
Pascal, Blaise, 56, 102
pastoral power. *See* power
Pater, Walter, 3, 23, 46, 171, 172, 173, 175, 178, 179, 183, 185, 188–91, 192–99, 200, 201, 202–7, 208, 211; "commerce with the dead," 206; critiques Middle Ages, 197; historicizing imagination, 189; the "moment," 3, 191, 193, 203, 206, 207; and relativism, 185, 190, 194, 210. Works: "Coleridge's Writings," 178, 190, 194, 198, 203; "Diaphaneitè," 189, 210, 211; *Marius the Epicurean*, 181, 189, 190, 198, 206, 262n24, 266n67; *Miscellaneous Studies*, 211; *Plato and Platonism*, 209, 211; "Poems by William Morris," 190, 195, 197, 199, 204, 206, 209; *The Renaissance*, 191, 197, 202, 206, 207; "Style," 204; "Winckelmann," 172, 189, 190, 193, 194, 196, 197, 198, 199, 200, 201, 203, 204, 205, 206, 211
Patmore, Coventry, 123, 158, 184, 239n60, 253n42
Patrick of Ireland, 51–54; *Confessions*, 20, 46, 51–54
Paul the Apostle, 11, 22, 29, 31, 38, 47, 51, 123, 124, 151, 152, 249n3
Paxton, Amanda, 247n59, 255n70, 260n3, 264n39
Paz, Dennis, 85, 88, 92, 96, 242n13, 269n2

INDEX

Peep behind the Curtain, A, 89, 98, 243n18

penitential manuals, 5, 20, 21, 29, 35, 45, 46, 53, 59, 60, 61, 65, 67, 79, 94, 112, 119, 130

penitential "practices." *See* mortification of the flesh

Peschier, Diana, 83, 99, 221, 230n12, 243n14

Peter the disciple, 149, 235n3, 241n76

pitch, 33, 67, 143, 166, 199

Pius IX (pope), 6, 85, 222, 223, 231n19, 242n8, 266n66

Plato, 41, 49, 190, 200, 209, 239n57; *Cratylus*, 249n5; *Gorgias*, 66; *Phaedrus*, 66; *Republic*, 74

Plotinus, 41, 49

Poe, Edgar Allan, 3, 183

power, 3, 8, 11, 33, 84, 98, 125, 127, 129, 146, 158, 193, 215; of confession, 37, 117, 120; Foucault theorizes, 12-13, 14, 16, 22, 29, 30, 65, 108, 118, 124-25, 130, 171, 176-77; of God, 38, 49, 161, 164, 258n97; pastoral, 14-15, 44, 65, 109; of priests, 44, 62; of Roman Catholic Church, 6; of Satan, 27, 257n93

"Pre-Raphaelite effect," 173

Pre-Raphaelites, 22, 104, 171, 172, 173, 175, 178, 179, 181, 189, 191, 256n81, 260n3, 266n65; and Ruskin, 253n42. *See also* Dixon, Richard Watson; Hunt, William Holman; Millais, John Everett; Rossetti, Christina; Rossetti, Dante Gabriel; Solomon, Simeon

priesthood, 6, 56, 87, 99, 109, 226

Priest in Absolution, The, 94, 119, 120, 224, 226, 227, 248n81

Psalms, 46, 47, 52, 66, 121, 153, 229n5, 237n29, 255n62; "penitential Psalms," 20, 29, 46, 47, 138

Public Health Bill (1848), 254n50

Public Worship Regulation Act (1874), 21, 118, 119, 226, 248n73

Punch, or The London Charivari, 21, 24, 82, 92, 93-96, 243n24, 244n26, 244n30, 245n41

Purgatory, 33, 35

purity, 14, 27, 43, 64, 87, 113, 204, 249n2; and impurity, 64, 75, 252n33

Pusey, Edward, 5, 10, 21, 29, 36, 70, 74, 77, 83, 93, 106, 108, 109, 112, 113, 115, 117, 138, 192, 225, 230n17, 246n55; asceticism of, 111-12, 155; as Hopkins's confessor, 61, 71, 83, 113, 248n67; satirized, 106-7. Works: *Eirenicon*, 113, 114, 164, 247n64; *Hints for a First Confession*, 113-14; *Penitence*, 4, 67, 113, 114, 214, 268n5; "Preface" to *Advice*, 82, 108, 111, 214, 268n3; *Thoughts on... Fasting*, 107, 155

Pythagoras, 41, 78

Questions for Self-Examination, 74-75

Quinet, Edgar, 89, 100, 101; *Génie des religions*, 89

Radcliffe, Ann, *The Italian*, 221

Rahner, Karl, 27, 42, 43

Raphael (Raffaello Sanzio da Urbino), 202

Raymond of Penyafort, 3, 44, 62

"Real Presence," 5, 108, 159, 189, 257n94. *See also* Eucharist; holy communion

relativism, 23, 185, 190, 192, 193, 194, 205, 210

religion, 2, 3, 14, 15, 16, 18, 19, 31, 57, 70, 82, 84, 89, 98, 101, 108, 109, 136, 151, 192, 193, 195, 221, 267n80, 268n3; dangers of, 105; heathen, 230n10

remorse, 41, 51

resistance, 24, 123; defined by Foucault, 234n51
restoration of Catholic hierarchy (1850), 85, 88, 222
resurrection. See Jesus Christ
Rickaby, Joseph, S.J., 78, 139, 158, 214, 215, 231n20, 239n50, 268n5
Ridley, Nicholas, 111
Rio, Alexis-François, *De la poésie Chrétienne*, 267n76
Rituale Romanum, 58
Ritualism, 21, 23, 69, 115, 117, 118, 221, 248n72, 248n82; satirized, 116–17
Ritualist's Progress, The, 21, 116, 227
Rodriguez, Alphonsus, S.J., 127, 144, 146, 163; *Practice and Perfection of Christian Virtues*, 33
Roman Catholicism, 4, 17, 19, 23, 58, 67, 69, 72, 77, 83, 85–91, 93, 102, 103, 105, 107, 115, 120, 194, 205, 219, 221–28, 266n66; as "perversion," 20, 231n24
Roman Catholic Relief Act (1829), 21, 84, 92, 221
Roman Catholics, 6, 9, 18, 28, 86, 96, 105; legal standing in England, 21, 83–86, 88, 221; suspicions of, 17
Romanticism, 186, 190, 191, 237n32; German, 192
Rome's Recruits, 18, 19
Roothaan, Jan, S.J., 30, 31
Ross, Rev. John, 67; *On Penance and the Confessional*, 84, 99, 108
Rossetti, Christina, 96, 189, 197, 256n81, 260n8, 261n17; "Convent Threshold," 142, 182, 261n8; "Iniquity of the Fathers," 261n8; "Three Enemies," 261n8
Rossetti, Dante Gabriel, 23, 173, 174, 175, 176, 177, 178, 182, 183, 188, 191, 211; essays, 260n2

—, paintings: *Astarte Syriaca*, 173; *Bocca Baciata*, 173; *Lady Lilith*, 173
—, poetry: "Blessed Damozel," 177, 179; "Eden's Bower," 178; "Jenny," 181; "Love-Lily," 181; "Love's Redemption," 186; *Poems*, 175, 179, 180, 182; "Secret Parting," 181; "Sleepless Dream," 181
Rousseau, Jean-Jacques, 8, 49, 206
Ruskin, John, 126, 134, 200, 209, 253n42, 263n30, 267n76; *Elements of Drawing*, 253n42; *Modern Painters*, 253n42; *Praeterita*, 9; *Stones of Venice*, 222
Russell, Lord John, 107
Ryder, Ignatius, S.J., 196

sacraments, 3, 5, 6, 8, 9, 15, 20, 27, 29, 31, 38, 40, 42, 44, 55, 56, 57, 59, 60, 80, 116, 148, 160, 182, 217, 257n94; grace of, 36; "last" sacraments, 36, 141, 215. See also baptism; confession; holy communion; ordination
Sales, Francis de, 56–57, 61, 62, 64, 69, 230n16; *Introduction to the Devout Life*, 57
salvation, 14, 15, 27, 38, 39, 42, 44, 47, 55, 62, 78, 142, 214, 217, 237n25, 237n27
Sand, George (Amantine Dupin), 90, 238n32; *Mademoiselle la Quintinie*, 90
Satan, 36, 42, 53, 90, 96, 99, 100, 138, 140, 238n39, 243n20. See also devil; Lucifer
Saville, Julia, 12, 35, 154, 186, 187, 232n29, 250n8, 255n67, 257n85, 264n43
Scarry, Elaine, 146, 164, 249n2
scientia sexualis, 129
scientific controversies, 1
scientific discourses, 16, 29, 37, 60, 61, 123, 125, 137

Scott, George Gilbert, 111
Scott, Robert, 74
Scotus, Duns, 2, 4, 5, 24, 43, 196, 231n19, 255n57, 258n96; and *haecceitas*, 24; *Reportatio*, 257n93
Scouting for Boys, 252n40
scruples and scrupulosity, 20, 30, 65, 69, 70, 241n73; morbid aspects, 69, 70, 129
sectarianism, 82, 89, 105
Sedgwick, Eve Kosofsky, 12, 20, 68, 71, 76, 232n29, 240n63, 251n19, 264n45
self and "selving" (Hopkins), 3, 9, 11, 13, 14, 16, 21, 27, 31, 32, 33, 41, 42, 49, 52, 65, 76, 78, 80, 91, 114, 124, 125, 131, 139, 143, 144, 145, 157, 170, 188, 190, 198, 208, 210; Christian self, 30, 50, 214; and "pitch," 33; self-abuse, 133; "selfbeing," 33, 143; self-loathing, 50, 76, 166; "selftaste," 33; "selftormenter," 74, 143, 169
self-culture, 189
self-examination, 14, 41, 43, 74, 75, 78, 108, 169, 237n26, 238n40, 247n60
self-formation (Foucault), 40–41, 45, 122, 171, 196, 219; hermeneutics of, 40
self-mortification. *See* mortification of the flesh
Seneca, Lucius Annaeus, 41, 78, 237n21; *De ira*, 41
sensationalism, 12, 92, 102, 201, 232n29
Sewell, Elizabeth, 222
Sewell, William, 222
sex and sexuality, 1, 9, 10, 13, 14, 15, 16, 50, 56, 64, 66, 71, 76, 99, 108, 124, 125, 129–32, 137, 153, 179, 180, 181, 186, 194, 200; "apparatus for producing truth," 14; same-sex desire, 133, 190, 232n29; "sociosexual codes," 152
sexual difference, 12, 20, 187, 201

Seymour, M. Hobart, 102, 226; *Mornings among the Jesuits*, 102, 223
Shakespeare, William, 96, 144, 156, 177, 242n7; *Hamlet*, 156; sonnets, 67; *Twelfth Night*, 144
shame, 20, 30, 33, 39, 50, 65, 66–68, 80, 136, 140, 180, 181, 185, 188, 236n19, 237n22, 237n26, 239n61, 247n60, 261n8, 262n22
"shame culture," 20, 68, 240n63
Shuter, William, 206, 265n58, 267n80
Silver, Brenda, 3
sin and sinning, 1, 2, 4, 5, 6, 8, 9, 10, 11, 15, 20, 21, 27, 28, 30, 32, 33, 34–36, 37–38, 40, 41–45, 47, 48, 50, 51, 52, 53, 54, 55, 57, 58, 59, 60, 61, 62–65, 66, 67, 69, 70, 71, 72, 73, 74, 75, 76, 78, 80, 83, 91, 101, 102, 107, 109, 112, 113, 114, 121, 122, 130–31, 134, 138, 139, 140, 143, 148, 155, 156, 167, 185, 207, 214, 218, 219, 235n3, 236n13, 239n47; "economy" of, 56; "long success of," 142, 155; "mortal" and "venial," 35, 62, 69, 78, 80; "original" sin, 5, 10, 11, 139; as pollution, 39, 43, 132, 133, 235n3, 249n2; "sexual" sins, 39, 44, 45, 64, 90. *See also* confession
Sinclair, Catherine, *Beatrice*, 102, 223
Sinfield, Alan, 16, 133
society, 12, 28, 51, 132, 171, 172, 173, 176, 188, 211; carceral society, 150; "confessing society," 214; disciplinary society, 22, 151
Society of Jesus, 3, 6, 25, 47, 65, 97, 98, 99, 100, 101, 102, 103, 151, 231n18, 237n27, 245n45. *See also* Ignatius of Loyola; Jesuits; *Spiritual Exercises*
Society of the Holy Cross, 94, 114, 119, 224, 226, 252n33
Solomon, Simeon, 23, 173, 191, 266n64; *Love at the Waters of Oblivion*, 262n24;

Love in Autumn, 262n24; *Sacramentum Amoris,* 262n24
Spiritual Exercises (Ignatius of Loyola), 2, 4, 22, 29, 31, 61, 67, 99, 100, 102, 103, 112, 122, 134, 138, 142, 145, 153, 207, 213, 214, 215, 231n20, 259n106; *Contemplatio,* 254n55; First Exercise on Hell, 256n72; First Exercise on the Incarnation, 152; First Week, 67, 139, 143, 157, 213, 215, 268n2; Fourth Week, 214, 239n50; Second Week, 268n6
"sprung rhythm," 126, 166, 199, 204, 263n31
Steinmetz, Andrew, *The Jesuit in the Family,* 98, 222
Stevenson, Robert Louis, *Dr. Jekyll and Mr. Hyde,* 164
St. John, Ambrose, 32
Stonyhurst Philosophers, 231n20
Stowell, Hugh, 87, 88
"St. Patrick's Breastplate," 51
Suárez, Francisco, 4
subjectivity. *See* self and "selving"
Sue, Eugene, 222
Swinburne, Algernon Charles, 23, 84, 173, 174, 175, 177, 178, 182, 183-88. Works: "Anactoria," 178, 185, 186; *Atalanta in Calydon,* 187; "Before the Mirror," 174; "A Dead King," 186; "Dolores," 187; "Félise," 185; "Hymn to Proserpine," 187; "Laus Veneris," 185; "Leper," 265n50; *Poems and Ballads,* 185, 186, 263n34; *Songs of Two Nations,* 186
Syllabus of Errors, 86, 224, 242n9, 266n66
syneidesis, 31

Tait, Archibald, 118, 226, 227
Taylor, Charles, 4, 7
Taylor, Chloë, 12, 29, 41, 43, 53, 58, 232n29
Taylor, Isaac, *Loyola: and Jesuitism,* 101
Taylor, Jeremy, 67, 130, 247n63; *A Dissuasive from Popery,* 89; *Golden Grove,* 243n17; *Holy Living,* 89
Tennyson, Alfred, Lord, 17, 175, 177; "St. Simeon Stylites," 261n13
Teresa of Àvila, 61, 157, 239n49
Tertullian, 10, 41, 42, 152, 256n79; *De anima,* 10; *De paenitentia,* 41, 42; *De resurrectione carnis,* 42
Thackeray, William, 19, 95; *The Adventures of Henry Esmond,* 223
Thomas, Alfred, S.J., 86, 240n67
Thornycroft, William Hamo, *The Sower,* 210
Thucydides, 74
Tissot, Samuel, 132, 134
Tomkins, Silvan, 68
torture. *See* mortification of the flesh
Tractarian (or Oxford) Movement, 4, 33, 61, 74, 82, 90, 93, 106, 107, 108, 112, 114, 115, 118, 119, 120, 123, 155, 188, 230n16, 247n62, 248n83. *See also* Keble, John; Pusey, Edward
Tracts for the Times, 107, 154, 246n56
Trinity (of God, Christ, and Holy Spirit), 4, 42, 60, 117, 138, 179
Trollope, Anthony, *An Autobiography,* 9
Trollope, Frances ("Mrs."), *Father Eustace,* 99; *A Visit to Italy,* 222
truth and truth claims, 1, 7, 11, 13, 15, 19, 24, 25, 29, 30, 32, 40, 41, 42, 46, 52, 78, 96, 104, 108, 122, 124-25, 129, 144, 153, 160, 165, 180, 184, 185, 193, 204, 207, 219, 231n21; Christian, 7, 20, 31, 164, 214; divine, 7; obligations of, 15; production of (Foucault), 14, 171, 233n41; religious, 19

Tupper, Martin, 19, 21, 92, 95–96, 97; *Three Hundred Sonnets*, 96
Turner, Frank, 16, 109
Twain, Mark, 3
Tynan, Katharine, 184, 245n46
Tyndall, John, 200

Ullathorne, William, 88, 243n15
"underthought" (and "overthought"), 100, 142, 175, 201, 207, 208, 261n11
Universities Tests Act (1871), 226
Urquhart, Edward, 117, 241n76

Vatican Council (First), 86, 226
Vendler, Helen, 166, 259n103
Victoria, Queen, 100, 107
Victorians: "cult of suffering," 146; culture, 1, 2, 11, 12, 14, 21, 22, 87, 136, 171, 204; gender norms, 16, 65, 85, 127, 128, 232n29; health and hygiene, 38, 39, 123, 132, 133, 134, 135, 136–37, 153, 204; literature, 9, 185; morality, 11, 127, 178; nationalism, 18; religion, 16, 30, 42, 81, 106, 192
Virgil (Publius Vergilius Maro), 49
virginity, 53, 59, 122, 123, 146, 150, 151, 152, 153, 159, 165, 180, 181, 208, 231n19, 238n40; mystique of, 152
Virgin Mary. *See* Mary, mother of Christ

Walker, Frederick, *The Plough*, 201
Walsh, Walter, 228, 244n35
Ward, Mary Arnold ("Mrs. Humphry"), 71, 245n48; *Helbeck of Bannisdale*, 102, 105–6, 228

Ward, T. Humphry, *The English Poets*, 191, 261n12
Whistler, James McNeill, 191; *Symphony in White No. 2: The Little White Girl*, 174
Whitehall Review, The, 18
Whitman, Walt, 186, 264n45
Whitty, Robert, S.J., 215, 268n8
wickedness, 35, 46, 50, 91, 130, 139, 140; and Swinburne's poetry, 184–85
Wilberforce, Samuel, 207
Wilde, Oscar, 16, 189, 199; *Salome*, 199
Wildered, A. B., *The Ritualist's Progress*, 21, 116–17
Winckelmann, Johann, 172, 190, 191, 193, 194, 196, 198, 199, 201, 203, 205
Winefred, Saint (also Winifred, Gwenffrewi), 152, 167, 169, 170, 171, 259n109. *See also* Hopkins, Gerard Manley, poetry: "St. Winefred's Well"
Wiseman, Nicholas, 85, 95, 221, 223, 230n14, 240n62, 243n15, 244n31; *Fabiola*, 269n2
women, 12, 14, 18, 24, 51, 93, 123, 129, 132, 153, 179, 208; and confessional practices, 21, 58, 64–65, 90, 91, 222, 230n12. *See also* gender; virginity
Woolf, Virginia, 262n23
Wordsworth, William, 32, 213, 265n56, 267n73

"Ye Great Anglican Revival," 21, 116
Yonge, Charlotte, 223, 227

Zaniello, Tom, 243n16

Recent books in the
VICTORIAN LITERATURE AND CULTURE SERIES

Victorian Nightshades: How the Solanaceae Shaped the Modern World
ELIZABETH A. CAMPBELL

Haunting Ecologies: Victorian Conceptions of Water
URSULA KLUWICK

The Turn of Rhythm: How Victorian Poetry Shaped a New Concept
EWAN JONES

Narrative and Its Nonevents: The Unwritten Plots That Shaped Victorian Realism
CARRA GLATT

Victorian Metafiction
TABITHA SPARKS

Strangers in the Archive: Literary Evidence and London's East End
HEIDI KAUFMAN

Evangelical Gothic: The English Novel and the Religious War on Virtue from Wesley to "Dracula"
CHRISTOPHER HERBERT

Reading with the Senses in Victorian Literature and Science
DAVID SWEENEY COOMBS

Parting Words: Victorian Poetry and Public Address
JUSTIN A. SIDER

The Physics of Possibility: Victorian Fiction, Science, and Gender
MICHAEL TONDRE

Willful Submission: Sado-Erotics and Heavenly Marriage in Victorian Religious Poetry
AMANDA PAXTON

Pirating Fictions: Ownership and Creativity in Nineteenth-Century Popular Culture
MONICA F. COHEN

Mathilde Blind: Late-Victorian Culture and the Woman of Letters
JAMES DIEDRICK

Poetry and the Thought of Song in Nineteenth-Century Britain
ELIZABETH K. HELSINGER

The Antagonist Principle: John Henry Newman and the Paradox of Personality
LAWRENCE POSTON

Personal Business: Character and Commerce in Victorian Literature and Culture
AERON HUNT

Second Person Singular: Late Victorian Women Poets and the Bonds of Verse
EMILY HARRINGTON

The Ghost behind the Masks: The Victorian Poets and Shakespeare
W. DAVID SHAW

Victorian Poets and the Changing Bible
CHARLES LAPORTE

Liberal Epic: The Victorian Practice of History from Gibbon to Churchill
EDWARD ADAMS